THE SEPARATION OF POWERS IN THE CONTEMPORARY CONSTITUTION

The Separation of Powers in the Contemporary Constitution examines the dividing lines between the powers of the judicial branch of government and those of the executive and legislative branches in the light of two of the most significant constitutional reforms of recent years: the Human Rights Act (1998) and Constitutional Reform Act (2005). Both statutes have implications for the separation of powers within the United Kingdom constitution. The Human Rights Act brings the judges into much closer proximity with the decisions of political actors than previously permitted by the *Wednesbury* standard of review and the doctrine of parliamentary sovereignty, while the Constitutional Reform Act marks the emergence of an institutionally independent judicial branch. Taken together, the two legislative schemes form the backbone of a more comprehensive system of constitutional checks and balances policed by a judicial branch under-pinned by the legitimacy of institutional independence.

ROGER MASTERMAN is Senior Lecturer in Law at Durham Law School, where his teaching and research interests lie in the area of constitutional law and reform.

THE SEPARATION OF POWERS IN THE CONTEMPORARY CONSTITUTION

JUDICIAL COMPETENCE AND INDEPENDENCE IN THE UNITED KINGDOM

ROGER MASTERMAN

CAMBRIDGE UNIVERSITY PRESS

CAMBRIDGE UNIVERSITY PRESS
Cambridge, New York, Melbourne, Madrid, Cape Town, Singapore,
São Paulo, Delhi, Dubai, Tokyo, Mexico City

Cambridge University Press
The Edinburgh Building, Cambridge CB2 8RU, UK

Published in the United States of America by Cambridge University Press, New York

www.cambridge.org
Information on this title: www.cambridge.org/9780521493376

First published 2011

Printed in the United Kingdom at the University Press, Cambridge

A catalogue record for this publication is available from the British Library

Library of Congress Cataloguing in Publication data
Masterman, Roger.
The separation of powers in the contemporary constitution : judicial competence
and independence in the United Kingdom / Roger Masterman.
p. cm.
Includes bibliographical references and index.
ISBN 978-0-521-49337-6 (hardback)
1. Judicial power–Great Britain. 2. Separation of powers–Great Britain. I. Title.
KD4645.M37 2010
342.41′044–dc22
2010039003

ISBN 978-0-521-49337-6 Hardback

For my parents

'in a government in which they are separated from each other, the judiciary, from the nature of its functions, will always be the least dangerous to the political rights of the Constitution; because it will be least in a capacity to annoy or injure them. The executive not only dispenses the honors but holds the sword of the community. The legislature not only commands the purse but prescribes the rules by which the duties and rights of every citizen are to be regulated. The judiciary, on the contrary, has no influence over either the sword or the purse; no direction either of the strength or of the wealth of the society, and can take no active resolution whatever. It may truly be said to have neither force nor will but merely judgment; and must ultimately depend upon the aid of the executive arm for the efficacy of its judgments.'

J. Madison, A. Hamilton and J. Jay, *The Federalist Papers*
(London: Penguin Classics, 1987), No.LXXVIII

CONTENTS

vii

ACKNOWLEDGEMENTS

The final touches to this manuscript were being applied as the United Kingdom Supreme Court began to hand down its first decisions, in late 2009 and early 2010. Much of the substantive work on bringing this project to fruition was carried out with the assistance of an earlier Arts and Humanities Research Council Research Leave award. During part of this period of leave, I was fortunate enough to be a visiting researcher at the Centre for Comparative Constitutional Studies, University of Melbourne. I am grateful to Carolyn Evans, Simon Evans, Madeline Grey and Cheryl Saunders for accommodating me at the Centre, and to the British Academy Small Grants Scheme for funding that visit.

Of my friends and colleagues in Durham I would in particular like to thank Helen Fenwick, Ian Leigh and Gavin Phillipson for the support and encouragement they have shown me since I joined the Law School. Beyond Durham Law School a number of people have proved an enduring influence and also deserve thanks. Richard Cornes, Conor Gearty, Robert Hazell and Andrew Le Sueur have all at various stages provided me with opportunities, and taught me valuable lessons about being a legal academic, for which I remain immensely grateful.

More specifically, a number of people are due my gratitude for reading chapters in draft or for discussions on some of the ideas that are explored in this book. Lorna Fox-O'Mahony, Aileen Kavanagh, Colin Murray, Jo Murkens, Gavin Phillipson, Erika Rackley and Adam Tomkins all made a contribution to clarifying my thoughts and arguments.

At Cambridge University Press I would like to thank Finola O'Sullivan, Richard Woodham and Helen Francis for their assistance, support, and – perhaps most importantly – forbearance.

However, most of all, I would like to thank Laura.

RMWM

TABLE OF CASES

United Kingdom

European Court and Commission of Human Rights

European Court of Justice

Cases from other jurisdictions

implemented – rather, it has developed, or emerged, over time. And one

~

Introduction

The contemporary separation of powers

Upon the opening of the United Kingdom Supreme Court in October 2009, that court's first president – Lord Phillips of Worth Matravers – noted the symbolic significance of establishing the independence of the country's highest court from Parliament:

> For the first time, we have a clear separation of powers between the legislature, the judiciary and the executive in the United Kingdom. This is important. It emphasises the independence of the judiciary, clearly separating those who make the law, from those who administer it.[1]

This severing of institutional links was certainly decisive, and may come to have a significance that can only be speculated upon in the early stages of the new court's life. But this institutional independence is merely one aspect of the contemporary separation of powers. Understandings of the United Kingdom's unique separation of powers have tended to hold more currency in their emphasis of the 'pragmatic' realities of constitutional practice, rather than the assertion of a 'formal' doctrinal adherence to a version of separation of powers theory.[2] The bright line distinctions hinted at in Lord Phillips' welcome to the new judicial body have rarely been evident across the spectrum of governmental functions visible in the United Kingdom, nor in its institutional divisions.

In part, at least, these institutional overlaps and lack of functional clarity can be attributed to the fact that our constitution has never been implemented – rather, it has developed, or emerged, over time. And one thing that unites commentators' views of the constitution is that its development – for the most part, and at least since the Civil War – has been

---

[1] Press Notice 01/09, 'Supreme Court of the United Kingdom comes into existence' (1 October 2009), available at: www.supremecourt.gov.uk/docs/pr_0109__2_.pdf.

[2] See: K. E. Malleson, 'Modernizing the constitution: completing the unfinished business' in G. Canivet, M. Andenas and D. Fairgrieve, *Independence, Accountability and the Judiciary* (London: British Institute of International and Comparative Law, 2006), p.151.

organic, with change coming incrementally as opposed to in seismic shifts. There are, of course, notable exceptions to this general trend: the passage of the Parliament Acts 1911 and 1949 and the entry into the European Union among them.[3] But recent years have seen an increase in the number and frequency of significant constitutional changes – such that a number of commentators have suggested that the constitution has been formed anew.[4]

The first Blair administration of 1997 began a process of constitutional renovation which has seen the devolution of power to Northern Ireland, Scotland and Wales,[5] the removal of the right of hereditary peers to sit as of right in the House of Lords,[6] the implementation of freedom of information legislation,[7] the independence of the Bank of England, elected mayors in London and elsewhere,[8] and so on. As of 2007, the premiership of Gordon Brown brought with it the promise of further constitutional reform; welcome steps have been taken towards subjecting the prerogative to the control of Parliament, and discussions have begun on the possibility of codifying a Bill of Rights and Responsibilities with the possibility raised – more speculatively, maybe – of writing down the constitution itself.[9]

While the constitutional reforms which have been given effect to since 1997 have been criticised for their lack of coherent guiding principle, they have prompted debate over the nature of this reformed constitution,[10] and of its underlying principles.[11] The purpose of this book is to continue this

---

[3] For a recent survey of some of these 'seismic' events, see: E. Wicks, *The Evolution of a Constitution: Eight Key Moments in British Constitutional History* (Oxford: Hart Publishing, 2006).

[4] A. King, *Does the United Kingdom Still Have a Constitution?* (London: Sweet and Maxwell, 2001); V. Bogdanor, 'Our new constitution' (2004) 120 LQR 242; V. Bogdanor, *The New British Constitution* (Oxford: Hart Publishing, 2009).

[5] Northern Ireland Act 1998; Scotland Act 1998; and Government of Wales Act 1998. See also the Government of Wales Act 2006.

[6] House of Lords Act 1999.

[7] Freedom of Information Act 2000.

[8] Greater London Authority Act 1999; Local Government Act 2000.

[9] Ministry of Justice, *The Governance of Britain* (July 2007), Cm.7170; Ministry of Justice, *Rights and Responsibilities: Developing our Constitutional Framework* (March 2009), Cm.7577.

[10] See, among others, the various perspectives advanced by: King, *Does the United Kingdom Still Have a Constitution?*, above n. 4; M. Bevir, 'The Westminster model, governance and judicial reform' (2008) 61 *Parliamentary Affairs* 559; Bogdanor, *The New British Constitution*, above n. 4.

[11] See the debate on separation of powers instigated by Lord Lester of Herne Hill QC in the House of Lords: HL Debs, 17 February 1999, cols.710–39. See also the various perspectives

trend by examining the separation of powers implications of perhaps two of the most significant of the constitutional reforms of recent years: the Human Rights Act 1998, and the Constitutional Reform Act 2005. The first, *inter alia*, provided for judicially enforceable remedies for violations of the rights found in the European Convention on Human Rights for the first time in domestic law;[12] the latter established a Supreme Court, reformed the Office of Lord Chancellor and reduced the control of the executive over judicial appointments through the creation of an independent Judicial Appointments Committee.[13] Both statutes allocate specific functions to the three branches of government, and both alter the balance of powers among Parliament, the executive and the judiciary as it has been traditionally understood. Both statutes appear to pull in differing directions: the Human Rights Act is argued to have furthered the politicisation of the judicial decision-making process, while the Constitutional Reform Act seeks to insulate the judges from exposure to the political controversy of the legislative branch. As a result of these two, related, legislative projects, a reassessment of the separation of powers in the United Kingdom constitution is perhaps timely.[14]

Yet ideas associated with separation of powers have enjoyed an uneasy relationship with constitutional thought in the United Kingdom. How, it is rightly asked, can the powers of government be truly separated, and concentrations of power avoided, in a system under which ultimate legal authority is said to be placed in but one institution: namely, Parliament? Further, as will be seen in Chapter 1, the constitutional principle of separation of powers is argued to be notoriously difficult to define with any

on parliamentary sovereignty advanced in the House of Lords decision in *Jackson and others* v. *Her Majesty's Attorney-General* [2005] UKHL 56; [2006] 1 AC 262 (discussed at pp.105–10).

[12] For a survey of the Act in this regard, see: I. Leigh and R. Masterman, *Making Rights Real: The Human Rights Act in its First Decade* (Oxford: Hart Publishing, 2008).

[13] For a valuable analysis, see: Lord Windlesham, 'The Constitutional Reform Act 2005: ministers, judges and constitutional change, part I' [2005] PL 806; Lord Windlesham, 'The Constitutional Reform Act 2005: the politics of constitutional reform, part II' [2006] PL 35.

[14] Given that the Human Rights Act 1998 and Constitutional Reform Act 2005 are both of UK-wide application, and that this volume primarily considers overarching principles concerning division of power among the Westminster Parliament, UK executive and senior judiciary, the phrase 'United Kingdom (UK) Constitution' will generally be used in preference to 'British' or 'English Constitution' throughout. It is accepted, however, that a degree of imprecision is also inherent in the use of this phrase, as a result of differences between the three jurisdictions that combine to make up the United Kingdom, and as a result of the devolution of power from Westminster to administrations in Northern Ireland, Scotland and Wales.

precision, and worse, to be of no relevance at all in the United Kingdom due to the fact that two key institutions of government – the executive and legislative branches – display a considerable overlapping membership. It is for these reasons, and others, that ideas associated with separation of powers in the United Kingdom constitution are claimed to be more pragmatic than formal.

As a result, the contemporary relevance of separation of powers to the United Kingdom is not now (if it ever was) to be found entirely in its utility as a template of *institutional* design requiring a clear and inviolable separation of executive, legislative and judicial personnel. Nor should separation of powers in the United Kingdom constitution be thought to compel that all governmental *functions* be exercised by individual and specific branches of government in perpetuity – such a reading would be entirely irreconcilable with the cornerstone of that constitution: the doctrine of parliamentary sovereignty. Instead, the contemporary relevance of separation of powers, it will be argued, lies in a broader reading of the concept, as a dynamic and fluid explanation of how the judiciary interact with the executive and legislative branches. Separation of powers is, from that perspective at least, a multi-dimensional concept. It fulfils a descriptive function, allowing us to explain the divisions between governmental functions, including the institutional separateness of the judicial branch. It is also a variable idea, as it allows us to chart the degree to which circumstances permit the judiciary to exercise a checking and balancing role within the constitution.[15] This reading of separation of powers is, perhaps, in the first instance at least, 'more concerned with territorial boundaries than with providing a constitutional basis for the role of judges'.[16] Yet it is also suggested that this separation of powers is more than simply a descriptive device: just as the unwritten constitution is a construct of the statutes, judicial precedents, conventions and institutions that give life to the system of government, so too are the constitutional principles that inform the relationships between those institutions and determine the hierarchy of norms within the constitution. The separation of powers in the United Kingdom constitution is therefore a product of the legislative, judicial and political decisions that regulate and describe the relationships among the three core branches of government within

---

[15] For a discussion, see: E. Barendt, 'Separation of powers and constitutional government' [1995] PL 599.
[16] D. Woodhouse, 'The English judges, politics and the balance of power' (2003) 66 MLR 920, 924.

the state. It is entirely in keeping with the nature of our constitutional law and constitutional development to say that the cumulative effects of these dynamic relationships and interactions has been to generate principles and standards of normative status – that prescribe how things *should* be done, rather than simply describe how they *are* done. The contemporary separation of judicial power from that of the executive and legislature may well be regarded as a constitutional fundamental displaying normative characteristics, rather than a description of a temporary state caused by a fortuitous collision of legislative and other factors.

The aim of this book, therefore – through an examination of a number of crucial points of interaction between the judicial and the political branches of government – is to highlight the dynamics of the contemporary separation of judicial power from the powers of the legislature and executive. The book is divided into four parts. In Part I, Chapter 1 examines the doctrine(s) of separation of powers in theory and their applicability to the United Kingdom constitution, noting the central objections to the application of separation of powers theory rooted in the doctrine of parliamentary sovereignty. Chapters 2 and 3 assess the driving forces behind the contemporary separation of power: the Human Rights Act 1998 and European Convention on Human Rights. Though seeking to preserve the idea of sovereignty, the Human Rights Act clearly envisages distinct roles for each of the three branches of government while also extending the range and depth of the courts' powers of judicial review of both executive and legislative activity. Chapter 2 therefore charts the allocation of power made by the Human Rights Act itself while Chapter 3 introduces the influence of the European Convention on Human Rights as interpreted by the European Court of Human Rights and analyses whether, and in what circumstances, the Strasbourg jurisprudence requires either a separation of governmental functions or of institutions.

Part II concerns the interface between the legal and the political in judicial decision making and the tools of institutional restraint that underpin the courts' engagement with questions of policy. Chapter 4 explores the withering of justiciability doctrines and the expansion of judicial supervision into areas of the constitution previously thought to fall outside the sphere of judicial influence. Chapter 5 goes on to examine how the 'ubiquitous'[17] language of deference, together with the doctrine of proportionality, hold the potential to regulate the courts' examination

---

[17] B. Goold, L. Lazarus and G. Swiney, *Public Protection, Proportionality and the Search for Balance* (Ministry of Justice Research Series 10/07), September 2007, p.9.

of 'political' matters – providing a principled basis on which to base the potential judicial intervention in matters which frequently engage genuine political choice. While the Human Rights Act 1998 has brought the judicial and the political into much closer relief than traditionally evident in the United Kingdom constitution, the judicial branch is also now possessed of the tools to ensure that its potential intervention in matters which might previously have been regarded as being non-justiciable is based on legal principle, rather than chance or judicial whim. The notion of deference and the doctrine of proportionality provide the structure which guides this separation of powers and ensures that – in the application of this function as a constitutional check – restraint and respect for the views of political actors is inherent in the process of judicial review.

Part III concerns the creative powers of courts. Chapter 6 considers the effect of the Human Rights Act on the law-making abilities of the courts through the lens of section (s.) 3(1) of the Human Rights Act and the courts' powers of statutory interpretation. Chapter 7 goes on to examine the development of the common law and the creative potential available to courts in determining the meaning and application of 'the Convention rights' in domestic law.

Part IV concludes by analysing the institutional independence of the courts and the normative potential of the contemporary separation of powers. The institutional separation of the judiciary from the executive and legislature following the Constitutional Reform Act is examined in Chapter 8. The reform of the office of Lord Chancellor, establishment of a Judicial Appointments Commission and creation of a United Kingdom Supreme Court all contribute to an increased separation of personnel among the three branches of government. As it is the independence of the judiciary that underpins the authority of the judicial role in the constitution, the consequences of this increased separation will be argued to further legitimate the robust review sanctioned by the realigned judicial role, and may cement the constitutional independence of the judicial branch. Finally, Chapter 9 examines the extent to which the contemporary separation of powers can be said to possess enduring qualities that might survive the potential repeal of the legislative provisions that are at the heart of this division of governmental power. This final chapter will assess the cumulative effect of these significant constitutional developments on the status of separation of powers in the United Kingdom, and ask whether the complete functional and institutional separation of the judicial branch can now rightly be regarded a constitutional fundamental immune from legislative interference.

PART I

Separation of powers, the Human Rights Act and
the European Convention on Human Rights

1

A doctrine of uncertain scope and application

The meaning(s) and aim(s) of separation of powers

The meanings and requirements of the separation of powers doctrine have been debated perhaps more than those of any comparable constitutional principle or theory; indeed, 'few doctrines have been subject to more damning and repeated criticism than that to which the separation of powers has been subject'.[1] In his book, *Constitutional Theory*, Geoffrey Marshall's famous dissection of the separation of powers concluded that so many were the potential interpretations and requirements of the doctrine, that 'it may be counted little more than a jumbled portmanteau of arguments for policies which ought to be supported or rejected on other grounds'.[2]

Nowhere, perhaps, has the debate over the meaning, or indeed relevance, of the separation of powers been more heated than in Britain, and more recently, the United Kingdom (UK). At the very best, assessments of the relevance of the separation of powers doctrine have been Janus-like; at worst, they have provoked bouts of academic mud-slinging. In the third edition of his text, *Constitutional and Administrative Law*, Professor De Smith wrote that 'no writer of repute would claim that [the separation of powers] is a central feature of the modern British constitution',[3] presumably condemning M. J. C. Vile to that dubious accolade after he had written ten years earlier that, 'an approach to the study of British government that rules out reference to the "separation of powers" is an inadequate one'.[4] The separation of powers debate has also been seen to

---

[1] J. W. F. Allison, *The English Historical Constitution: Continuity, Change and European Effects* (Cambridge University Press, 2007), p.83.

[2] G. Marshall, *Constitutional Theory* (Oxford: Clarendon Press, 1971), p.124.

[3] S. A. De Smith, *Constitutional and Administrative Law* (3rd edn) (Harmondsworth: Penguin Books, 1977), p.36.

[4] M. J. C. Vile, *Constitutionalism and the Separation of Powers* (Oxford: Clarendon Press, 1967), p.8 (and see also (2nd edn) (Indianapolis: Liberty Fund, 1998)).

polarise academic and judicial perspectives.[5] On the one hand Professor Hood Phillips denounced the doctrine as a 'constitutional myth',[6] while on the other, Lord Diplock was able to confidently assert in the *Duport Steel* case that, 'it cannot be too strongly emphasised that the British constitution, though largely unwritten, is firmly based on the separation of powers'.[7] Further, Robert Stevens has argued – with what Sir Stephen Sedley described as a 'hint of transatlantic self-satisfaction'[8] – that 'nothing underlines the atheoretical nature of the British constitution more than the casualness with which it approaches the separation of powers'.[9] Yet in spite of the contested relevance of separation of powers, commentators have been unable to completely sever examination of the doctrine from studies of the constitution.[10] Even Professor De Smith did not reject the influence of the doctrine outright, and was forced to concede that 'a brief survey of the doctrine brings out more clearly some features of the British system of government'.[11]

Part of the difficulty here lies in the fact that in Britain, as with elsewhere, the debate has been unable to escape the myriad difficulties of attempting to define what separation of powers actually requires in practice. Beyond specifying that there should be three branches of government – the legislature, executive and judiciary – even a 'pure' theory of the doctrine, uncomplicated by local constitutional practices or quirks, proves troublesome. M. C. J. Vile, in his study, *Constitutionalism and the Separation of Powers*, wrote that:

---

[5] See: C. Munro, *Studies in Constitutional Law* (2nd edn) (London: Butterworths, 1999), pp.302–7.

[6] O. Hood Phillips, 'A constitutional myth: separation of powers' (1977) 93 LQR 11. See also S. A. De Smith, who (elsewhere) referred to the separation of powers as a 'tiresome talking point' and an 'irrelevant distraction for the English law student and his teachers', S. A. De Smith, 'The separation of powers in new dress' (1966) 12 *McGill Law Journal* 491, 491.

[7] *Duport Steel* v. *Sirs* [1980] 1 WLR 142, 157. See also: *M* v. *Home Office* [1994] 1 AC 377, 395 (Lord Templeman): 'Parliament makes the law, the executive carry the law into effect and the judiciary enforce the law.'

[8] S. Sedley, 'Above it all' 16 *London Review of Books* 7 (7 April 1994) (quoted in Sir J. Laws, 'Law and democracy' [1995] PL 72, 90).

[9] R. Stevens, *The Independence of the Judiciary: The View from the Lord Chancellor's Office* (Oxford: Clarendon Press, 1993), p.2.

[10] For examination of the doctrine in three of the leading texts on the subject, see: A. W. Bradley and K. D. Ewing, *Constitutional and Administrative Law* (14th edn) (Harlow: Pearson Longman, 2007), ch.5; I. Loveland, *Constitutional Law, Administrative Law and Human Rights: A Critical Introduction* (4th edn) (Oxford University Press, 2006), ch.3; C. Turpin and A. Tomkins, *British Government and the Constitution* (6th edn) (Cambridge University Press, 2007), ch.2.

[11] De Smith, *Constitutional and Administrative Law*, above n. 3, p.36.

> A 'pure doctrine' of the separation of powers might be formulated in the following way: It is essential for the establishment and maintenance of political liberty that the government be divided into three branches or departments, the legislature, the executive, and the judiciary. To each of these branches there is a corresponding feature of government, legislative, executive or judicial. Each branch of government must be confined to the exercise of its own function and not allowed to encroach upon the functions of the other branches. Furthermore, the persons who compose these three agencies of government must be kept separate and distinct, no individual being allowed to be at the same time a member of more than one branch. In this way each of the branches will be a check on the others and no single group of people will be able to control the machinery of the State.[12]

In very basic terms, therefore, a strict separation of powers holds that the legislative, executive and judicial arms should be separate of each other, in respect of both their functions and their personnel. Both senses of governmental separation are, however, problematic. In a functional sense, such a theory presupposes that *all* governmental actions can be neatly placed in either the legislative, executive, or judicial category,[13] and that each branch of government may not exercise power which falls outside those corresponding with its own function. As such, the 'pure' theory makes no allowances for governmental activities which are not easily categorised, or over which there is debate about which of the three branches is most apt to exercise them. Institutionally, the 'pure' theory demands a *complete* separation of each of the three branches; no person or group of persons may be a member of more than one branch. Parliamentary systems on the Westminster model – in which the executive branch forms a part of the legislature – would therefore immediately fall foul of this key requirement of the pure theory of separation.

Additionally, the pure theory version of separation of powers also seems to dismiss the notion that the three branches might actively check the actions of each other – appearing to suggest that the very fact of separation is sufficient to 'establish and maintain liberty'.[14] On this reading, any 'interference' by one branch of government with the functions or activities of another would infringe the separation of powers. As a result, it has been

---

[12] Vile, *Constitutionalism and the Separation of Powers* (2nd edn), above n. 4, p.14. See also E. Barendt, 'Separation of powers and constitutional government' [1995] PL 599, 601.

[13] Cf. G. Marshall, *Constitutional Theory* (Oxford: Clarendon Press, 1971), pp.99–100; I. Jennings, *The Law and the Constitution* (5th edn) (University of London Press, 1967), p.241.

[14] Vile, *Constitutionalism and the Separation of Powers* (2nd edn), above n. 4, p.18.

argued that – for example – judicial review of primary legislation violates the separation of powers for the reason that it involves the judiciary disturbing the functional autonomy of the legislative branch. Yet two of the constitutional states which are commonly held up as archetypes of separate government in the institutional sense – the United States and France – can both be seen to accommodate forms of legislative review.[15] Perhaps the most important difficulty in the 'pure' form separation of powers is that it does not appear to have been adopted, completely unmodified, by any working common law system. As Cheryl Saunders has bluntly put it: '[c]omplete separation is impossible'.[16]

But looking beyond the rigidity of the 'pure' theory of separation, it is clear that various different systems of governance embrace – to a greater or lesser degree – both the division of governmental power among three institutionally distinct branches of state *and* the ability of those branches to exercise a degree of coercive power over each other. Separation of powers is as commonly invoked as a mechanism for restraining and limiting governmental power as it is relied upon as a mechanism for dividing and allocating such power. As Marshall has observed, this is particularly the case in Anglo-American conceptions of the doctrine which hold that, 'the branches of government, when "separated", may legitimately check or act upon each other and indeed are separated precisely so that they may exercise such checks'.[17] Taking the United States as an example; first, the legislative power of Congress is subject to both presidential veto[18] and to judicial review by the Supreme Court.[19] Second, exercise of the executive power of the president may require Congressional endorsement. Further, judgments of the Supreme Court may be reversed by a process of constitutional amendment under Article V of the constitution.[20] In such a system, the judicial review of primary legislation is central, rather than antithetical, to the effective separation of powers.

---

[15] In the United States, the Supreme Court may review the constitutionality of primary legislation: *Marbury* v. *Madison* 5 US 137 (1803). For discussion, see: J. Madison, A. Hamilton and J. Jay, *The Federalist Papers* (London: Penguin Classics, 1987), No.LXXVIII. In France *pre*-legislative review can be undertaken by the *Conseil Constitutionnel*. See Articles 61–2 of the 1958 constitution.

[16] C. Saunders, 'Separation of powers and the judicial branch' [2006] JR 337, 338.

[17] Marshall, *Constitutional Theory*, above n. 13, p.99.

[18] Article I, s. 7, US constitution.

[19] See above n.15.

[20] E.g., the Fourteenth Amendment to the US constitution – which extended provision for the due process and equal protection of laws to all citizens of the United States – overruled the Supreme Court's infamous decision in *Dred Scott* v. *Sandford* 60 US 393 (1857).

Seen in this light, separation of powers emphasises that the powers of the three branches of government should be limited, and that each branch should be allowed a role in holding the others to account. Of course, the avoidance of concentrations of power remains vital to this modified view[21] – commonly known as the partial separation, or partial agency, theory – but this reading of separation of powers is perhaps better understood as a mechanism for restraining governmental power rather than achieving clear institutional and functional separation. Indeed, as Barendt has suggested, it is for this reason that 'separation of powers in some form is arguably the essence of constitutionalism'.[22]

The continuing relevance of separation of powers can perhaps therefore be found in the aspirations which lie behind the doctrine as a constitutional and/or political theory, rather than a template of institutional design. Yet here, too, no uniform conception of the aims of the doctrine – or doctrines – can be found. For example, in Montesquieu's famous espousal of the doctrine, separation of powers was a safeguard for individual liberty:

> When the legislative and executive powers are vested in the same person, or in the same body of magistrates, there can be no liberty; because apprehensions may arise, lest the same monarch or senates should enact tyrannical laws to execute them in a tyrannical manner ... Again, there is no liberty if the power of judging is not separated from the legislative and executive. If it were joined with the legislative, the life and liberty of the subject would be exposed to arbitrary control; for the judge would then be the legislator. If it were joined to the executive power, the judge might behave with violence and oppression. There would be an end to everything, if the same man, or the same body, whether of the nobles or of the people, were to exercise those three powers, that of enacting laws, that of executing public affairs, and that of trying crimes or individual causes.[23]

While Montesquieu has been widely perceived as having misrepresented the British constitution on which he claimed to have based his view of

---

[21] As Madison argued in *The Federalist Papers*, above n. 15, No.XLVII: 'The accumulation of all powers, legislative, executive, and judiciary, in the same hands, whether of one, a few, or many, and whether hereditary, self-appointed, or elective, may justly be pronounced the very definition of tyranny.'

[22] E. Barendt, 'Is there a United Kingdom constitution?' (1997) 17 *Oxford Journal of Legal Studies* 138, 141. See further Vile, *Constitutionalism and the Separation of Powers* (2nd edn), above n. 4; V. Bogdanor, *The New British Constitution* (2009), p.287.

[23] *The Spirit of the Laws*, Book XI, s.6.

separation,[24] and has been criticised on the grounds of his 'credulity, inconsistency and lack of judgment',[25] it is undeniable that his view of separation of powers was, and remains, influential. In a similar vein, James Madison – one of the authors of what Barendt has termed 'the best analysis of the fundamental principles of a liberal constitution ever written in the English language'[26] – wrote in *The Federalist Papers* that the separation of executive, legislative and judicial power is an 'essential precaution in favor of liberty'.[27]

While the avoidance of concentrations of governmental power might therefore serve to protect the individual from suffering under an oppressive regime, it might also serve the aims of good governance more generally. By contrast, therefore, other writers have placed greater emphasis on the ability of separated powers not only to protect freedom, but *primarily* to act as a tool of institutional efficiency. In his discussion of Locke's *Second Treatise on Government*, Barber has written that:

> Locke was advocating a form of separation of powers not in order to slow down the running of the state but in order to ensure that it ran well. Powers were divided in order to facilitate the purposes for which the state existed.[28]

Such debates have persisted; a modern-day parallel can be found in 'red light' and 'green light' theories of administrative law, the former emphasising the checking of governmental power, the latter emphasising law's role as a mechanism for social change.[29] Yet, if governmental efficiency is the key aim of separating powers, then discussion must necessarily return to the allocation of power to the branch most appropriate to exercise it. As noted above, the

---

[24] By, for example, 'ignoring the growth of Cabinet Government to protect the integrity of the three separate powers'. M. Foley, *The Politics of the British Constitution* (Manchester University Press, 1999), p.16.

[25] C. Munro, *Studies in Constitutional Law* (2nd edn) (London: Butterworths, 1999), p.299. Also as Ivor Jennings observed, in *The Law and the Constitution*:

> [Montesquieu] was not concerned to make a precise analysis of the functions of government. He was, rather, trying to find the means by which tyranny could be avoided, and, naturally, he turned to the country where the battle against despotism had been fought and won and where liberty existed in a far greater measure than in his own country (Jennings, above n. 13, p.23).

[26] Barendt, 'Separation of powers', above n. 12, 599.

[27] Madison, Hamilton and Jay, *The Federalist Papers*, above n. 15, No.XLVII.

[28] N. W. Barber, 'Prelude to the separation of powers' (2001) 60 CLJ 59, 64. See also Barendt, 'Separation of powers', above n. 12, 602.

[29] See: C. Harlow and R. Rawlings, *Law and Administration* (3rd edn) (Cambridge University Press, 2009), ch.1.

categorisation of what might amount to an 'executive', 'legislative' or 'judicial' function has also proved problematic. As Jennings observed:

> It is quite impossible to draw a distinction between 'judicial' and 'administrative' functions in terms of the nature or substance of the functions actually exercised by the courts and the administrative authorities in this country. The most that can be said is that the courts are more concerned with questions of law, and the administrative authorities with questions of discretion. Nor is it possible to draw a precise distinction between the functions of Parliament and of the administrative authorities, subject always to the rule that Parliament can by legislation do what it pleases, and that most of the powers of administrative authorities (like the powers of the courts) derive from legislation.[30]

Nevertheless, some general characteristics of governmental decision making can be tentatively extracted.[31] The legislative function includes the making of rules of general application for the governance and order of society. The executive function includes the administration of the state as well as the conduct of foreign affairs, and the design of domestic policy (which may be subject to parliamentary approval prior to implementation). The judicial function includes the independent determination of criminal and civil cases and the interpretation and application of statutory and common law. However, it is immediately apparent that even such basic generalisations may be open to challenge.[32] Parliament may, and does, make legal rules which are designed for individual and quite specific purposes.[33] So, too, may the courts design rules of general application in their development of the common law and interpretation of statutory provisions.[34] As Barendt has argued, a lack of precision in the allocation of functions to the three branches may not condemn separation of powers to constitutional irrelevance; in cases of uncertainty or of contested authority to make a particular decision, '[w]hat is crucial is that the distribution is enforceable by the courts'. In cases of dispute or doubt over the constitutional allocation of functions, '[the courts] are entitled to take the final decision whether in practice a function is to be regarded as

---

[30] Jennings, *The Law and the Constitution*, above n. 13, App. I, pp.293–4.

[31] See: Munro, *Studies in Constitutional Law*, above n. 25, p.294; Jennings, *The Law and the Constitution*, above n. 13, App. I; H. W. R. Wade and C. F. Forsyth, *Administrative Law* (9th edn) (Oxford University Press, 2004), pp.40–2.

[32] See generally: G. Ganz, 'Allocation of decision-making functions (part I) [1972] PL 215; 'Allocation of decision-making functions' (part II) [1972] PL 299.

[33] For a recent example, see: ss.32–8 of the Serious and Organised Crime and Police Act 2005.

[34] E.g., much of the law of negligence and of judicial review.

legislative, executive or judicial'.[35] At first glance from a UK perspective, such a position is hard to reconcile with the Diceyan reading of parliamentary sovereignty.

Far, then, from being Janus-like, perhaps it is more realistic to refer to the idea of separation of powers as being more like the many-headed hydra. And the malleability which has been the result of the multifaceted nature of separation of powers – although clearly responsible for continued doctrinal uncertainty – has also been central to the longevity of the theory. As a result, separation of powers has:

> been combined with other political ideas, the theory of mixed government, the idea of balance, the concept of checks and balances, to form the complex constitutional theories that provided the basis of modern Western political systems. Nevertheless, when all the necessary qualifications have been made, the essential ideas behind the doctrine remain as vital ingredients of Western political thought and practice today.[36]

That separation of powers has endured as a key principle of liberal constitutional thought – in spite of the many attacks to which it has been subjected – clearly indicates that its symbolic significance and ultimate aims and objectives outweigh the debates over the multiple forms in which it may take effect. The answer is arguably to be found in the fact that many of the more definite aims and characteristics of the doctrine – the avoidance of concentrations of power, the preservation of individual liberty, the independence of the judiciary, and so on – reflect values and aspirations that, to varying degrees, are to be found in our contemporary constitution and, of course, in many others.[37]

Separation of powers in the United Kingdom constitution

The disputed relevance of separation of powers to the UK constitution has already been alluded to, and has led to many alternative labels

---

[35] Barendt, Separation of powers', above n. 12, 605. For a US perspective, see *Youngstown Sheet and Tube Co v. Sawyer* 369 US 186, 211 (1962):
> Deciding whether a matter has in any measure been committed by the Constitution to another branch of government, or whether the action of that branch exceeds whatever authority has been committed, is itself a delicate exercise in constitutional interpretation, and is a responsibility of the Court as ultimate interpreter of the Constitution.

The difficulty of reconciling this interpretation of separation of powers with the principle of parliamentary sovereignty is returned to below; see pp.20–6.

[36] Vile, *Constitutionalism and the Separation of Powers*, (2nd edn) above n. 4, pp.2–3.

[37] See e.g.: Articles I, II and III of the US constitution; Chapters 1, 2 and 3 of the Australian constitution; Articles 38–53, 62–9 and 92–104 of the German Basic Law (*Grundgesetz*).

being adopted by those wishing to describe the reality of the division of governmental power: the 'concentration of powers',[38] the 'balance of powers',[39] 'separated institutions sharing powers'[40] among them.

Functionally, the boundaries between executive, legislative and judicial activities have traditionally displayed the flexibility that is characteristic of the UK constitution. Even the dominant characteristic of the constitution – the legislative supremacy of Parliament – has shown itself to be sufficiently fluid to accommodate the delegation of legislative power to the executive branch.[41] This dilution of Parliament's legislative monopoly has been compounded by the general dominance of the House of Commons by the executive; while legal principle may hold that Parliament remains sovereign, the suggestion that the 'executive commands both the principle and the detail of the statute' is perhaps closer to the truth.[42] Equally, acting judges may be seen to exercise 'legislative' functions; both overtly, as a result of the Law Lords' ability to contribute to the legislative process as members of the House of Lords,[43] and also as an indirect result of the adjudicative process.[44] Historically, Parliament has been seen to usurp the judicial function of trying criminal cases by passing Acts of Attainder, judicial and executive functions are blurred in the activities of administrative tribunals,[45] members of the executive have exercised the 'classic

---

[38] Marshall, *Constitutional Theory*, above n. 2, p.97.

[39] R. Stevens, *The English Judges: Their Role in the Changing Constitution* (Oxford: Hart Publishing, 2005), ch.1, esp. pp.8–9; Barendt, 'Separation of powers', above n. 12, 600.

[40] A. King, *The British Constitution* (Oxford University Press, 2007), p.12.

[41] See: G. Ganz, 'Delegated legislation: a necessary evil or a constitutional outrage?' in P. Leyland and T. Woods, *Administrative Law Facing the Future: Old Constraints and New Horizons* (London: Blackstone Press, 1997).

[42] Lord Devlin, 'Judges and lawmakers' (1976) 39 MLR 1, 15.

[43] Prior to the establishment of the Supreme Court, though the Law Lords were entitled to participate in the legislative and debating work of the House of Lords, their contributions had become more infrequent in recent years. See e.g.: Lord Hope, 'Voices from the past – the Law Lords' contribution to the legislative process' (2007) 123 LQR 547; Lord Cooke, 'The Law Lords: an endangered heritage' (2003) 119 LQR 49; and pp.216–18.

[44] See Ch.6. See also: Lord Reid, 'The judge as law maker' (1972–3) 12 *Journal of the Society of the Public Teachers of Law* 22; Lord Devlin, 'Judges and law-makers', above n. 42; Lord Lester, 'English judges as law makers' [1993] PL 269.

[45] T. R. S. Allan, *Constitutional Justice: A Liberal Theory of the Rule of Law* (Oxford University Press, 2001), pp.133–4:

> The existence of tribunals and agencies exercising 'quasi-judicial' powers – where questions of legal right are closely intertwined with those of administrative policy – need not undermine the rule of law. The rigour of the necessary procedural constraints is inevitably a matter of degree; but the closer the jurisdiction to a judicial one, involving the determination of rights independently of public policy, the more strongly the analogy with judicial procedure applies.

judicial function[46] of determining the length of sentence to be served by convicted offenders,[47] and so on. Functional overlap among the three branches has been, in many respects, endemic.

Nor does the UK constitution display a clear separation of powers in institutional terms: as has already been noted, the fact that the members of the government – the executive branch – are also members of the legislature is obviously in contravention of the idea that the three branches be institutionally distinct. While the fact that the executive branch is drawn from the legislative is possibly the most obvious violation of institutional separation, it is by no means the only overlap of personnel. Until the coming into force of Part 3 of the Constitutional Reform Act (CRA) 2005, members of the judiciary – the Lords of Appeal in Ordinary –continued to exercise their judicial functions from within the Upper House of the legislature. The Law Lords possessed the same rights to sit and vote in the legislative business of the House as other members,[48] and exercised their judicial role sitting as a committee of the House of Lords. Similarly, until the coming into force of the CRA 2005, the holder of the office of Lord Chancellor was technically a member of all three branches of government, as a senior member of the Cabinet, Speaker of the House of Lords, and Head of the Judiciary in England and Wales and occasional (though increasingly infrenquent) judge.[49]

As a result of these multiple 'infringements', it has been argued that the separation of powers has either little or no relevance to the effective functioning of the UK constitution,[50] or that, at best, our constitution only displays a selective adherence to the requirements of separation of powers based more on chance than on design. This piecemeal adherence to separation of powers has seen Allison recently describe it as only a 'customary historical constitutional practice' of the constitution, that is:

> a course of conduct relating to government that is followed in variable degrees of consistency, not because it conforms to a standard that has been declared authoritatively, but because it had long been commonly

---

[46] *R v. Secretary of State for the Home Department, ex parte Venables* [1998] AC 407, 526 (Lord Steyn).

[47] For discussion, see: A. Tomkins, 'The struggle to delimit executive power in Britain' in P. Craig and A. Tomkins (eds), *The Executive and Public Law* (Oxford University Press, 2006).

[48] See Ch.8, pp.216–18.

[49] See: D. Woodhouse, *The Office of Lord Chancellor* (Oxford: Hart Publishing, 2001), ch.5, esp. at pp.115–20.

[50] See: Hood Phillips, 'A constitutional myth', above n. 6; De Smith, 'The separation of powers in new dress', above n. 6.

followed, presumably for good reason, and, in being followed, is adapted and continues to evolve.[51]

As Allison suggests, some key features of the constitution can be seen to adhere to, or demand, a separation of governmental power. For example, under s.1(1)(b) of the House of Commons Disqualification Act 1975, those holding judicial office are prevented from sitting as members of the lower House of Parliament. Similarly, s.137(3) of the CRA 2005 now prevents members of the House of Lords (who are also judges) from participating in the business of the House while they hold judicial office.[52] In addition, separation of powers can be seen to exert an influence over constitutional reform and design. Recent reforms to the devolution settlement as it affects Wales established a 'Welsh Assembly Government'[53] to effect a clearer separation between executive functions and the legislative competence of the National Assembly for Wales.[54] Debates over reforms to the office of Attorney-General have not been able to escape the suggestion that the 'political' and 'legal' functions associated with the post should be kept distinct.[55] And deliberations over the notorious proposals that eventually became the Legislative and Regulatory Reform Act 2006 took place within a separation of powers framework under which it was argued to be the responsibility of Parliament, and not of the executive acting alone, to engineer and implement wide-ranging legislative developments.[56]

Aspects of the UK constitution do, therefore, reflect a separation of powers among the three branches of government; both in a functional and in an institutional sense. Not only can we point to the existence of three branches of government, but we can begin to draw tentative conclusions over which particular governmental functions each does exercise. It is when we begin to ask *why* each branch should fulfil a particular constitutional function that we begin to encounter difficulty. Adam Tomkins has argued:

> While we can as a matter of practice identify a distinct legislature, executive and judiciary, that is to say, we can say descriptively that there exist

---

[51] Allison, *The English Historical Constitution*, above n. 1, p.76.
[52] The House of Commons Disqualification Act 1975 has been amended so that the prohibition extends to Justices of the Supreme Court (see: CRA 2005, s.137(1)).
[53] Government of Wales Act 2006, Part 2.
[54] *Ibid.*, Parts 3 and 4. For commentary, see: A. Trench, 'The Government of Wales Act 2006: the next steps on devolution for Wales' [2006] PL 687; A. Sherlock, 'A new devolution settlement for Wales' (2008) 14 EPL 297.
[55] See: House of Commons Constitutional Affairs Committee, *Constitutional Role of the Attorney General* (HC 306), 19 July 2007.
[56] See generally: House of Lords Select Committee on the Constitution, *Legislative and Regulatory Reform Bill* (HL 194), 8 June 2006.

in England a Parliament, a government and a court structure, we cannot argue that the constitution prescribes that such a division should exist. To the limited extent that there is some separation along these lines, it is merely descriptive and not normative.[57]

Tomkins highlights the fact that if the sovereignty of Parliament is to be taken seriously as a legal doctrine, then separation of powers – at least that interpretation of the doctrine that *requires* both a degree of institutional and functional separation – can never fully be realised in the UK constitution. The logical consequence of parliamentary sovereignty is, of course, that power – far from being divided coherently between institutions of government – can ultimately be traced back to Parliament. On such a reading, any final say over where power should reside lies with Parliament and not, as Barendt suggests, with the courts. If it is to be suggested that the principle of separation of powers amounts to anything more than a descriptive device, then the doctrine of parliamentary sovereignty must be analysed in more detail.

The supremacy of Parliament

The role and powers of Parliament are key to any understanding of the UK constitution, and therefore, to any understanding of the separation of powers within that constitution. It is perhaps the defining characteristic of the UK system of government that Parliament, and not the constitution, is supreme.[58] For the most famous proponent of the doctrine, Albert Venn Dicey, the supremacy of Parliament meant that the legislature possesses 'the right to make or unmake any law whatever, and, further, that no person or body is recognised … as having a right to override or set aside the legislation of Parliament'.[59] A number of points flow from this monolithic view of sovereignty. First, whatever separation of power can be said to exist cannot be said to derive from the 'constitution' – no entrenched or higher law determines that political and legal power should be vested in, for example, the executive or courts in perpetuity. Second, by vesting unlimited legal power in one of the three branches of government, the ability of the other two branches effectively to check the power of that branch is reduced: '[t]here is no person or body of persons who can …

---

[57] A. Tomkins, *Public Law* (Oxford: Clarendon Press, 2003), p.38.
[58] A. V. Dicey, *Introduction to the Study of the Law of the Constitution* (Indianapolis: Liberty Fund, 1982).
[59] *Ibid.*, pp.3–4.

make rules which override or derogate from an Act of Parliament'.[60] And finally, as a result of bestowing ultimate legislative authority on Parliament – including for any legislative determination of where governmental functions should from time to time reside – any separation of powers which could be said to exist in the constitution could not be said to possess normative value.

'Theory, as usual, followed upon fact...'[61]

Any attempt to place separation of powers within a distinctly UK context must confront the difficulties of attempting to reconcile the organic development of the constitution with a theory of government which post- rather than pre-dates the establishment of its fundamental features. Adam Tomkins has argued that the historical division of executive, legislative and judicial power that has taken shape in the constitution owes much more to political fact than to political thought. Tomkins suggests that whatever separation of power has come to exist has done so in spite of, rather than as a result of, the demands of 'the constitution'. As Ivor Jennings before him noted, '[i]t was ... not political theory but political experience, the logic or accident of events, which caused England to develop this threefold division'.[62]

Tomkins' historical approach focuses on the British conception of the separation of powers as having stemmed from the division of power between Parliament and the Crown; he argues:

> Civil war; regicide; interregnum, commonwealth and protectorate; restoration; and the so-called 'glorious' revolution of 1689 were the core components of English constitution-making ... an eighteenth century political philosophy cannot explain the English constitution.[63]

As a result, it is hard to disagree with his assertion that it is a nonsense to suggest that the constitutional principle of separation of powers as formulated by eighteenth-century theorists from America and France helped design our constitution.[64] Of course, Tomkins is right also to emphasise the significance of the dominant dynamic in the UK constitution as being the sovereignty of Parliament. Yet to further suggest – as Tomkins does – that the 'separation of power English-style ... is *and remains* a

---

[60] *Ibid.*, p.4.   [61] Jennings, *The Law and the Constitution*, above n. 13, p.20.
[62] *Ibid.*, p.9.   [63] Tomkins, *Public Law*, above n. 57, p.45.
[64] See also: T. C Hartley and J. A. G. Griffith, *Government and Law* (2nd edn) (London: Weidenfeld and Nicolson, 1981), p.2.

confrontational, bi-partisan, bi-polar separation, between the only two powers the constitution has ever recognised as enjoying any degree of sovereignty, namely the Crown, and Parliament',[65] while ultimately accurate at a high level of abstraction does not address the practical deployment of governmental power in the contemporary constitution.

While it might be fair to say that the UK constitution was not *designed* to adhere to any specific conception of the separation of powers doctrine (or not even designed at all), that is not the same as saying that the *development* of the constitution has not been influenced by the perceived demands of separation of powers.[66] Colin Munro has argued, for example, that in spite of the various exceptions to the pure version of the doctrine that exist in the constitution, this should not mean that separation of powers can simply be dismissed as a shaping force of our constitutional arrangements: '[t]he separation in the British constitution, although not absolute, ought not to be lightly dismissed'.[67] If Jennings was correct to suggest that the constitution has been 'constantly added to, patched and partially reconstructed',[68] could it not be argued that the separation of powers has influenced the growth of the constitution over time?[69] To suggest, as Tomkins does, that our version of the separation of powers remains *solely* a question of the division of power between the Crown and Parliament does not give a complete account of the realities of the contemporary constitution.[70]

A relationship of equal branches?

Second, on the traditional Diceyan analysis, the relationship between legislature, executive and judiciary in the British constitution is therefore not one of coexistent and equal branches. As a result, any separation of powers between branches of government is effectively a hierarchical relationship, with Parliament the dominant legal and political force in the

---

[65] Tomkins, *Public Law*, above n. 57, p.46.

[66] Sir Stephen Sedley has argued that 'it is a mistake to imagine that pragmatism cannot be an efficient vehicle for legal and political theory' ('Governments, constitutions and judges' in G. Richardson and H. Genn, *Administrative Law and Government Action: The Courts and Alternative Mechanisms of Review* (Oxford: Clarendon Press, 1994), p.35).

[67] Munro, *Studies in Constitutional Law*, above n. 5, p.332.

[68] Jennings, *The Law and the Constitution*, above n. 13, p.8.

[69] See e.g.: House of Lords Select Committee on the Constitution, *Relations between the Executive, the Judiciary and Parliament* (HL 151), 26 July 2007, para.160; *R v. Secretary of State for the Home Department, ex parte Anderson* [2002] UKHL 46; [2003] 1 AC 837, paras.29 (Lord Bingham), 40 (Lord Steyn) and 76 (Lord Hutton).

[70] For a more recent contribution by Professor Tomkins, see: A. Tomkins, 'The rule of law in Blair's Britain' (2007) 26 *University of Queensland Law Journal* 255, esp. at 258–66.

constitution. So it is entirely arguable that the separation of powers in the UK owes far more to the fact of where Parliament from time to time determines where governmental power shall reside than to any considered and permanent division of competence among the three arms of government. The separation of powers in the UK is both defined and delimited by the doctrine of parliamentary sovereignty and the decisions it takes over where governmental competence may lie at a given time. Hence, Parliament, being omnicompetent, *could* choose to delegate its functions to the executive in the form of delegated legislation. Parliament *could* legislate to provide members of the executive with sentencing powers. Parliament *could* legislate to remove the Law Lords from Parliament and establish a Supreme Court. It could also legislate to undo all of those things. On the traditional, Diceyan, account therefore, it may be enough to say – to paraphrase J. A. G. Griffith – that the separation of powers is simply no more and no less than what Parliament directs should happen.[71]

Obviously, however, there is a difference between asking whether Parliament *could* do something, and whether it actually *would* do that thing. While Parliament may possess the theoretical legal power to enact outrageous, unpopular or draconian legislation, should it in practice do so, 'Parliament must squarely confront what it is doing and accept the political cost.'[72] As Dicey himself admitted, while the sovereignty of Parliament might well be an 'undoubted legal fact',[73] there were nevertheless 'many enactments … which Parliament never would and (to speak plainly) never could pass'.[74] If, though, it is accepted that there are things that Parliament would not legislate to do – such as, for example, abolish the entire court system and allow all legal disputes to be resolved by members of the executive – then it is not so different to imagine that Parliament would not in fact legislate on such issues not simply because of the adverse public reaction which it would suffer, but because it was actually prevented from so doing by the requirements of the rule of law

---

[71] J. A. G. Griffith, 'The political constitution' (1979) 42 MLR 1, 19.

[72] *R* v. *Secretary of State for the Home Department, ex parte Simms* [2000] 2 AC 115, 131.

[73] Dicey, *Introduction to the Study of the Law of the Constitution*, above n. 58, p.24.

[74] *Ibid.*, p.26. See also: Jennings, *The Law and the Constitution*, above n. 13, p.170:
De Lolme's remark that Parliament can do anything except make a man into a woman and a woman into a man is often quoted. But, like many of the remarks which de Lolme made, it is wrong … Though it is true that Parliament cannot change the course of nature, it is equally true that it cannot in fact do all sorts of things. The supremacy of Parliament is a legal fiction, and legal fiction can assume anything.

and separation of powers. As Lord Hope noted in *Jackson* v. *Attorney-General*: 'Parliamentary sovereignty is an empty principle if legislation is passed which is so absurd or so unacceptable that the populace at large refuses to recognise it as law.'[75] It is an inadequate analysis of parliamentary sovereignty to assert without qualification that the legislative power of Parliament is, as a matter of both law and fact, unlimited.

A descriptive, or normative, device?

While describing the existence of three branches of government and charting their respective powers is analysing separation of powers in a sense, advocates of the doctrine as it is traditionally understood would suggest that separation of powers must *require* specific divisions to exist among those three branches, and specific powers to be allocated to those branches. In other words, separation of powers, if it is to be a meaningful principle of constitutionalism, must be normative rather than descriptive.[76] In the UK context, if Parliament does indeed possess unlimited legal power in the constitution, then any separation of powers between governmental institutions can at best be only a descriptive account of the constitutional settlement at a given point in time. However, a number of commentators have sought to argue that separation of powers not only occupies a central place in UK constitutional thought, but also that its influence extends to imposing restraints on the power of Parliament. Eric Barendt, for one, has argued that the 'reciprocal checks and balances between the three branches of government' advocated by Madison in *The Federalist Papers*, bear much in common with the 'fundamental principles of the contemporary British constitution'.[77] Barendt acknowledges the difficulty of reconciling the doctrine of parliamentary sovereignty with an application of separation of powers in the UK context which is of normative value. However, this difficulty, he argues, provides 'an argument for discarding parliamentary sovereignty, rather than treating the separation of powers principle with undue scepticism'.[78]

---

[75] *Jackson and others* v. *Her Majesty's Attorney-General* [2005] UKHL 56; [2006] 1 AC 262, para.120.

[76] W. B. Gwyn, *The Meaning of the Separation of Powers* (The Hague: Martinus Nijhoff, 1965), p.5.

[77] Barendt, Separation of powers', above n. 12; E. Barendt, *An Introduction to Constitutional Law* (Oxford: Clarendon Press, 1998).

[78] *Ibid.*, p.17.

The influence of the sovereignty doctrine in the UK constitution is inescapable. In spite of the fact that membership of the European Union,[79] devolution to Scotland, Wales and Northern Ireland[80] and the enactment and implementation of the Human Rights Act 1998 (HRA)[81] each pose distinct and genuine difficulties for Dicey's monolithic conception of the doctrine, the sovereignty doctrine remains the 'bedrock of the ... constitution'.[82] To suggest that separation of powers possesses normative content is to suggest that parliamentary sovereignty is limited yet further, and that certain functions of government are so apt to be carried out by one distinct branch of government as to be entrenched characteristics of the constitution. T. R. S. Allan has sought to show exactly this by arguing for a separation of judicial power based on the requirements of the rule of law. He suggests that separation of judicial power from that of the executive and legislature is an essential requirement of the rule of law. At first glance, this seems entirely uncontroversial; the independence of judicial process must be regarded as a minimum requirement of a fair trial. Allan, however, goes on to suggest that such is the importance of judicial independence for the legitimate exercise of the judicial role within the constitution, that:

> [t]he separation and independence of judicial power would lose its point, as an essential safeguard against arbitrary power, if courts failed to observe the principles of natural justice: there would be no guarantee that people's rights would be upheld in practice. The integrity of appropriate standards of judicial procedure must therefore be regarded as constitutionally fundamental – substantially immune to legislative abrogation or abridgement, except perhaps in special cases where the courts may acknowledge the justification for departures from ordinary procedure.[83]

Such is the importance of the procedural guarantee of fair process to the rule of law – Allan argues – that the requirements of an independent judiciary amount to a substantive constraint on the legislative ability of Parliament. The aims of separation of powers as a safeguard against arbitrary government are clearly evident in Allan's defence of judicial

---

[79] European Communities Act 1972; R v. *Secretary of State for Transport, ex parte Factortame (No: 2)* [1991] 1 AC 603.

[80] Government of Wales Act 1998; Government of Wales Act 2006; Northern Ireland Act 1998; Scotland Act 1998. On which, see: V. Bogdanor, 'Devolution: decentralisation or disintegration?' (1999) 70(2) *Political Quarterly* 185, 186–9.

[81] See esp. Chs.2 and 6.

[82] *Jackson* v. *Her Majesty's Attorney-General* [2005] UKHL 56, para.9 (Lord Bingham).

[83] Allan, *Constitutional Justice*, above n. 45, p.133.

independence as a virtually entrenched characteristic of the UK constitution. Even in the context of the unwritten constitution – underpinned,
if not dominated, by the sovereignty of Parliament – it is difficult to displace the suggestion that judicial independence is a constitutional fundamental, in the sense suggested by Allan, on positivistic grounds alone.
There is evidently more to be found in the substance of the constitution
than can be clearly traced to Acts of Parliament and decisions under the
common law. To give only a brief example, though the effectiveness of certain individual constitutional conventions may be doubted in practice,[84]
their role in the regulation of political and legal actors within the constitution remains broadly undisputed. Although they may be codified or
declared in written documents,[85] the existence of many conventions owes
little in the first instance to the written word. Moreover, it is also generally agreed that conventions, although not enforceable by the courts,[86]
should possess a degree of coercive authority, for otherwise their value
would be significantly reduced.[87] A positivist analysis of the constitution – which would emphasise the sovereign power of Parliament to the
exclusion of other sources of constitutional authority – would therefore
be an inadequate one.

At this stage, however, it is sufficient to note that Allan's position regarding the nature of judicial independence emphasises two crucial points.
First, that judicial independence is reflective of separation of powers' aim
to avoid arbitrary government. Second, that the constitutional principle of
judicial independence occupies a central position in the UK constitution.

The centrality of judicial independence

While the Westminster model of government embraces the overlap
of executive and legislative actors within the institution of Parliament,

---

[84] Barendt, 'Is there a United Kingdom constitution?', above n. 22, 144.

[85] See e.g.: Parliament Act 1911 (codifying the convention that the House of Lords would
not reject money bills); Ministerial Code (articulating the core principles of individual ministerial responsibility to Parliament); Memorandum of Understanding between
the UK government and the Scottish government (outlining the convention that
Westminster will not legislate in a devolved area without the agreement of the devolved
administration in question (the Sewel convention)).

[86] *Madzimbamuto* v. *Lardner-Burke* [1969] 1 AC 645 (PC); *Attorney-General* v. *Jonathan
Cape* [1976] QB 752.

[87] As Geoffrey Marshall has argued, 'in so far as a convention defines duties or obligations
they remain morally and politically, but not legally, binding' (G. Marshall, *Constitutional
Conventions* (Oxford: Clarendon Press, 1984), p.17, and ch.1 generally). See further:
J. Jaconelli, 'Do constitutional conventions bind?' (2005) 64 CLJ 149.

the judiciary have long been at one step removed from this institutional fusion. As Lord Bingham noted in the Privy Council case of *DPP of Jamaica* v. *Mollison*:

> Whatever overlap there may be under constitutions on the Westminster model between the exercise of executive and legislative powers, the separation between the exercise of judicial powers on the one hand and legislative and executive powers on the other is total or effectively so.[88]

Measures designed to protect the independent judicial process have a lengthy heritage in the development of the constitution. The Magna Carta of 1215, for instance, endorses the independence of a trial process from the influence of prosecuting authority.[89] More saliently, the independence of the judiciary is acknowledged to have been cemented in the British constitution following the Act of Settlement 1701.[90] The Act of Settlement famously provides that 'judges' commissions be made *quamdiu se bene gesserint* and their salaries ascertained and established; but upon an address of both houses of Parliament it may be lawful to remove them'.[91] Through this security of tenure, the judiciary is able to administer the law of the land 'without fear or favour, affection or ill will'. While the Act of Settlement may well provide the basis of judicial independence, the autonomy of the judicial branch is further protected as a result of subsequent law and as a result of convention. For example, the common law has long held that justice should objectively appear to have been fairly administered; this value being perhaps most famously evident in Lord Hewart CJ's statement that 'it is of fundamental importance that justice should not only be done, but should manifestly and undoubtedly be seen to be done'.[92] As has already been mentioned, the House of Commons Disqualification Act 1975 prevents those holding a range of judicial offices

---

[88] *Director of Public Prosecutions for Jamaica* v. *Mollison* [2003] UKPC 6; [2003] 2 AC 411, para.13 (Lord Bingham).

[89] For an outline, see: E. Wicks, *The Evolution of a Constitution: Eight Key Moments in British Constitutional History* (Oxford: Hart Publishing, 2006), pp.3–6.

[90] For an overview, see R. Stevens, *The English Judges: Their Role in the Changing Constitution* (Oxford: Hart Publishing, 2005), ch.1. Although as Stevens recognises, the fact that the British constitution embraced a 'balance of powers' rather than a clear separation, makes the Act of Settlement a less than resounding endorsement of the *complete* separation of the judicial branch (at p.9). See also: R. Stevens, 'The Act of Settlement and the questionable history of judicial independence' (2001) 1(2) *Oxford University Commonwealth Law Journal* 253.

[91] See also: Supreme Court Act 1981, s.11(3); Appellate Jurisdiction Act 1876, s.6; CRA 2005, s.33.

[92] *R* v. *Sussex Justices, ex parte McCarthy* [1924] 1 KB 256, 259.

from standing for election to the lower House of Parliament.[93] Association with party political matters is prevented through the convention that judges should withdraw their membership of any political party to which they belong on appointment to the bench. The independence of specific proceedings is protected by the *sub judice* rule which – as described by the Joint Committee on Parliamentary Privilege – determines that the 'proper relationship between Parliament and the courts requires that the courts should be left to get on with their work' without parliamentary interference.[94] In addition, direct exposure to the matters of political controversy is further guaranteed by the convention that individual judges should not be criticised personally by members of the executive branch.[95]

Hartley and Griffith have argued that the independence of the judicial branch is therefore 'the one aspect of the separation of powers that is accepted in the British constitution'.[96] While Lord Steyn has written that:

> our system is undoubtedly based on a constitutional principle of the separation of powers. In insulating the judicial function from the legislative and executive functions separation of powers in turn rests on the constitutional principles of judicial independence and the rule of law.[97]

Other commentators agree.[98] Yet the complete institutional independence of the judiciary should not also be stated without qualification. Each of the legal and conventional safeguards of judicial independence has a specific purpose – promoting the independence of individual judges rather than of the judiciary as an institution, or as a branch of government. Further, two specific features of the historical constitution in particular had hampered the emergence of a constitutional notion of judicial independence in an institutional sense: the position of Lord Chancellor and those of the Lords of Appeal in Ordinary.

First, the office of Lord Chancellor had – until the reforms first announced in 2003 and enacted (in part, at least) in the CRA 2005 – bestrode all three

---

[93] House of Commons Disqualification Act 1975, s.1(1)(a), and Part I of Sch. 1.

[94] Joint Committee on Parliamentary Privilege, *First Report of 1998–1999* (HL 43-I; HC 214-I), para.192.

[95] Although there is arguably a long history of infringements of this particular convention: A. Le Sueur, 'The judicial review debate: from partnership to friction' (1996) 31 *Government and Opposition* 8; I. Loveland, 'The war against the judges' (1997) 68 *Political Quarterly* 162; A. Bradley, 'Judicial independence under attack' [2003] PL 397.

[96] Hartley and Griffith, *Government and Law*, above n. 64, p.175.

[97] Lord Steyn, 'The case for a Supreme Court' (2002) 188 LQR 382, 383.

[98] See e.g.: Stevens, *The English Judges*, above n. 90, p.79; Lord Hewart, *The New Despotism* (London: Ernest Benn Ltd, 1929), pp.37–45.

branches of government.[99] The holder of the office had been head of the judiciary in England and Wales – and as a result, able to sit as a judge – a member of the Cabinet, and Speaker of the House of Lords.[100] The office of Lord Chancellor therefore arguably contravened separation of powers in both an institutional and a functional sense. Similarly, again until the coming into force of the relevant provisions of the CRA 2005, not only did the Lords of Appeal in Ordinary discharge their judicial functions from within the boundaries of the legislature, but they were able to participate in the legislative business of the Upper House while they were so doing.[101]

It is perhaps unsurprising, given the indeterminate meaning of separation of powers in the UK constitution, that the office of Lord Chancellor had variously been said both to infringe and uphold the separation of powers.[102] Hartley and Griffith described the existence of the position as 'the living refutation of the doctrine of separation of powers in England'.[103] While Lord Irvine, holder of the office between 1997 and 2003, defended the position of Lord Chancellor as being:

> at a critical cusp in the separation of powers between Parliament, government and the judiciary. He is the natural conduit for communications between the judiciary and the executive, so that each fully understands the legitimate objectives of the other.[104]

Equally unsurprising, perhaps, are the contradictory assertions that the position of the Law Lords in Parliament both infringed separation of powers, and were held not to impact on the British interpretation of that doctrine. Placing himself very firmly in the latter camp, Lord Lloyd memorably suggested, 'it is sometimes said that for the Law Lords to sit in the Upper House is contrary to the theory of the separation of powers. I regard that as a nonsense argument.'[105]

While separation of powers clearly holds a disputed position in the constitution, the notion of judicial independence is, and has been, regarded

---

[99] See below pp.214–15.

[100] See generally: Woodhouse, *The Office of Lord Chancellor*, above n. 49.

[101] See below pp.216–18.

[102] For an account of the breaches of the separation of powers inherent in the office of Lord Chancellor, see: Woodhouse, *The Office of Lord Chancellor*, above n. 49, pp.12–13, 16–19.

[103] Hartley and Griffith, *Government and Law*, above n. 64, p.179.

[104] HL Debs, 25 November 1997, col. 934.

[105] Lord Lloyd of Berwick, HL Debs, 21 January 2003, col. 615. For defences of the position of the Lords of Appeal in Ordinary, see: Lord Cooke of Thorndon, 'The Law Lords: an

as fundamental. However, the very fact that a member of the executive branch was able to sit as a judge would appear to contradict the idea that the judicial branch should be institutionally independent of the executive. Similarly, the position of the Law Lords in Parliament would appear to sit uneasily with those other aspects of constitutional law and convention (discussed above) which appear to attempt to insulate judges from the controversies of party political debate. Considering that a number of commentators have held that separation of powers has been rendered virtually redundant in the UK due to its various anomalies, it is unusual that many have not been so quick to question judicial independence *itself,* based on the significant infringements of the principle that had been historically tolerated.

The longevity of the ideal of judicial independence in the UK constitution is slightly ironic, given the haste with which many commentators have dismissed the relevance of separation of powers. Yet judicial independence has achieved a fundamental significance in the British constitution, in the views of some, tantamount to entrenchment.[106] Even Geoffrey Marshall, whose sceptical views of separation of powers more generally have already been noted, recognised that 'the idea of separateness and independence of judicial power seems to have put up more resistance to the demands of the administrative state'.[107] This resistance can in part be attributed to statutory recognition of the independence of the judiciary in provisions such as those in the Act of Settlement, in part to the recognition at common law of the rule of law,[108] and of basic requirements of procedural fairness.[109] But the notion of judicial independence that has come to occupy a prominent place in British constitutional thought is a limited one which has prioritised the independence of individual judges and relegated the import that could be attached to the institutional independence of the judiciary as a component of government.

---

endangered heritage' (2003) 119 LQR 49; Royal Commission on Reform of the House of Lords, *A House for the Future*, Cm. 4534 (2000), evidence of Lord Wilberforce; HL Debs, 21 January 2003, col. 615 (Lord Lloyd of Berwick). For criticisms, see: Lord Bingham of Cornhill, *A New Supreme Court for the United Kingdom* (London: Constitution Unit, 2002); Lord Steyn, 'The case for a Supreme Court', above n. 97.

[106] Allan, *Constitutional Justice*, above n. 45, p.133.

[107] Marshall, *Constitutional Theory*, above n. 13, p.118.

[108] *Entick* v. *Carrington* (1765) 19 St Tr 1030.

[109] See e.g.: *Dimes* v. *The Proprietors of the Grand Junction Canal* (1852) 10 ER 301; *R* v. *Sussex Justices*, above n. 92, 259; *Ridge* v. *Baldwin* [1964] QC 40; *R* v. *Gough* [1993] AC 646; *Porter* v. *Magill* [2001] UKHL 67; [2002] 2 AC 357.

The contemporary separation of powers

Whatever separation of powers can be said to exist in the constitution has not been so diluted as to preclude its utility as a tool of judicial reasoning; historically, courts have relied upon the doctrine of separation of powers in cases concerning local authority spending,[110] the correct construction of the Trade Union and Labour Relations Act 1974,[111] and a ministerial decision not to publish a report by the Serious Fraud Office,[112] among others. What distinguishes such deployments of the separation of powers concept is not their tendency to support judicial activism, but their tendency to emphasise judicial restraint and the hierarchical division of power in the constitution under which Parliament is sovereign.[113] In this sense, separation of powers in the UK constitution primarily concerns the contours separating judicial, executive and legislative power. As we have already seen, those lines are in many cases unclear, may change over time, and – ultimately – may be subject to the mercy of legislative direction. Separation of powers in the contemporary constitution is at the very least, therefore, a dynamic, multidimensional, idea that is reflected in the status of, and interactions between, the institutions of government within the constitution and in the rules and principles by which those relationships are managed.

The purpose of this volume is to examine the dividing lines between the courts and the elected branches of government in the light of two of the most significant constitutional developments (in separation of powers terms) of recent times; the HRA 1998, and the CRA 2005. The HRA brings the courts into much closer relief with the actions of the political branches than hitherto permitted by the combined efforts of the sovereignty doctrine and the *Wednesbury* test of unreasonableness,[114] while the implementation of the CRA 2005 will only serve to enhance the independence of the judicial branch, and may come to be seen as having cemented the status of judicial independence as a constitutional fundamental in the UK constitution. First, for the reason – as Keith Ewing has written – that the HRA amounts to 'unquestionably the most significant formal

---

[110] *R v. Secretary of State for the Environment, ex parte Nottinghamshire County Council* [1986] AC 240, 250.

[111] *Duport Steel v. Sirs*, above n. 7.

[112] *R v. Secretary of State for Trade and Industry, ex parte Lonrho* [1989] 1 WLR 525.

[113] See e.g.: *R v. Secretary of State for the Home Department, ex parte Fire Brigades Union* [1995] 2 AC 513, 567 (Lord Mustill); *Duport Steel v. Sirs*, above n. 7, 157 (Lord Diplock).

[114] *Associated Provincial Picture Houses v. Wednesbury Corporation* [1948] 1 KB 223.

redistribution of political power in this country since [the Parliament Act] 1911, and perhaps since [the Bill of Rights] 1688'.[115] Second, for the reason that the requirements of the HRA were – in part, at least – the driving force behind the enactment of the CRA 2005. The cumulative effects of these two legislative initiatives are to extend the judicial role into spheres more frequently associated with the elected branches of government and to enhance the institutional separation of the judges from the executive and legislative branches. Taken together, the two can be seen to redefine the relationships between the judicial and elected branches of government, and, in so doing, revitalise the debate over the separation of powers in the contemporary constitution.

[115] K. D. Ewing, 'The Human Rights Act and parliamentary democracy' (1999) 62 MLR 79, 79.

2

The Human Rights Act 1998 and the separation of powers

Introduction

There are two distinct perspectives from which the contemporary separation of powers can be approached following the implementation of the HRA 1998 and the CRA 2005. Separation of powers might be analysed by examining the separation of, or distinctiveness of, governmental functions, or through an examination of the institutional divides or interactions among the three branches of government. The most visible change in the latter respect can be found in the increased institutional separation brought about by the CRA 2005, with the establishment of a Supreme Court for the United Kingdom being the most obvious indicator of an increased separation between the judicial and legislative branches. This separation of the judicial branch from the elected branches of government forms the subject of Part IV of this book, and centres on the changes driven by the requirement in Article 6(1) of the European Convention on Human Rights (ECHR, or the Convention) that, 'in the determination of his civil rights and obligations or of any criminal charge' an individual is entitled to a hearing before an 'independent and impartial tribunal'.

This chapter concerns the separation of function at the macro level – the specific roles that have been allocated to the judiciary, executive and Parliament by the HRA 1998 itself, and begins by introducing the controversy over extending the judicial role into the enforcement of human rights standards, and the mechanisms by which the HRA seeks to reconcile the enhanced protection for individual human rights with the maintenance of majority government. Later chapters will go on to examine the functional separation of powers at the micro level by examining how in practice the courts manage the boundary between considerations of policy and law, and of interpretation and judicial legislation.

Rights as questions of law and/or politics

As with the question of whether conceptions of separation of powers occupy a useful position within the UK constitution, questions of whether human rights are suitable for judicial determination[1] also polarise commentators.[2] Prior to the implementation of the HRA 1998, Parliament held primary responsibility for the domestic protection of human rights in the UK constitution. Indeed, it continues to do so: the HRA 1998 carefully insulates parliamentary legislation from overt challenge by the judicial branch, while even under the supervisory jurisdiction of the European Court of Human Rights, national authorities are considered to shoulder the primary burden of protecting the Convention rights.[3] Until October 2000, however, while the judiciary exercised the ability to determine questions of rights arising at law, in the absence of a general constitutional or legislative direction to the judges, the determination and protection of human rights had largely been the result of specific action undertaken by the elected legislature. As Sandra Fredman has commented, '[a] strong principle of Parliamentary sovereignty and a corresponding subordination of the judiciary establish a constitutional framework within which decisions about rights take place entirely through the political process'.[4]

In a number of legislative fields, Parliament had legislated to give effect to individual rights. Within the area of discrimination law, for example, a significant body of statute law had developed, granting positive rights to

---

[1] It is acknowledged that the distinction between 'law' and 'politics' as used in this chapter is a relatively rudimentary one, and does not do justice to the complex *relationships* which exist between the two spheres (see A. Tomkins, 'In defence of the political constitution' (2002) 22 OJLS 157, 166). Nevertheless, the debate over competence to determine questions of human rights has been dominated by the perhaps similarly rudimentary distinction between the elected and judicial power: that is, primarily 'political' institutions such as legislatures, and predominantly institutions of 'law' such as courts, and as such, forms an appropriate framework for the discussion which follows. Of course, as T. R. S. Allan has observed, a 'stark separation of legal rule from political principle' is 'ultimately incoherent' (T. R. S. Allan, *Law, Liberty and Justice: The Legal Foundations of British Constitutionalism* (Oxford: Clarendon Press, 1993), p.2). See further: W. Bagehot, *The English Constitution* (Oxford University Press, 2001); J. A. G. Griffith, 'The political constitution' (1979) 42 MLR 1; M. Loughlin, *Sword and Scales: An Examination of the Relationship between Law and Politics* (Oxford: Hart Publishing, 2000).

[2] Typically the debate is framed as being between the two apparently irreconcilable aspirations of democratic government and individual freedom. See e.g.: J. Allan, 'Bills of Rights and judicial power: a liberal's quandary' (1996) 16 OJLS 337.

[3] See e.g.: *Handyside* v. *United Kingdom* (1979–80) 1 EHRR 737, para.49.

[4] S. Fredman, 'Judging democracy: the role of the judiciary under the HRA 1998' (2000) 53 *Current Legal Problems* 99, 108.

individuals and groups.[5] The abolition of the death penalty[6] and legalisation of abortion[7] were achieved as a result of the legislative intervention of the Westminster Parliament, while the due process rights of suspected criminals[8] were similarly guaranteed through primary legislation. Since its accession to the ECHR in 1951, the UK's record in this sphere had been subject to the supervision of the Strasbourg organs. A number of judgments of the European Court of Human Rights – in which the UK had been found to be in breach of the terms of the Convention – had prompted further legislative change designed to safeguard that document's minimum standards.[9] By contrast, however, other areas of domestic law had become notorious for highlighting the failure of Parliament to enact positive measures to reinforce human rights against unwarranted infringement.[10] The limited protections offered by the common law for residual liberties – pitched against the powers of a sovereign Parliament – extended only so far as requiring the use of express words to limit the scope of certain recognised 'constitutional' rights.[11] Should Parliament choose to expressly limit a given individual right, then accountability for so doing would lie very firmly in the political – not the legal – domain; as Lord Hoffmann recognised in *R* v. *Secretary of State for the Home Department, ex parte Simms*, 'the principle of legality means that parliament must squarely confront what it is doing and accept the political cost'.[12]

But while a number of commentators lamented the state of liberty in the UK prior to the implementation of the HRA, it was by no means clear that there was unanimous support for the resolution to be found in a judicially enforced bill of rights.[13] As a result of the contestable nature

---

[5] See e.g.: Equal Pay Act 1970; Sex Discrimination Act 1975; Race Relations Act 1976; Disability Discrimination Act 1995.

[6] Murder (Abolition of Death Penalty) Act 1965.

[7] Abortion Act 1967.

[8] Police and Criminal Evidence Act 1984.

[9] See e.g.: Contempt of Court Act 1981 (passed in response to the decision of the European Court of Human Rights in *Sunday Times* v. *United Kingdom* (1979) 2 EHRR 245); Interception of Communications Act 1985 (implemented in response to *Malone* v. *United Kingdom* (1984) 7 EHRR 14).

[10] E.g., the lack of pre-HRA protection given by law to private information: *Malone* v. *Metropolitan Police Commissioner (No. 2)* [1979] Ch 344; *Kaye* v. *Robertson* [1991] FSR 62.

[11] See e.g.: *R* v. *Secretary of State for the Home Department, ex parte Leech (No. 2)* [1994] QB 198; *R* v. *Lord Chancellor, ex parte Witham* [1998] QB 575.

[12] *R* v. *Secretary of State for the Home Department, ex parte Simms* [2000] 2 AC 115, 131.

[13] For two particularly well-known examples displaying contrasting views on the suitability of judges to determine questions of human rights, see: R. Dworkin, *A Bill of Rights*

of human rights questions, and the issue of where to position the dividing line between their protection and the public interest, many commentators argue that determination of questions of human rights should continue to reside within the political realm. Discussion and determination of the range of different – and equally legitimate – responses that human rights disputes provoke, it is argued, should be a matter for representatives who may be removed by the electorate. Given the nature of the disagreements which may arise over the questions of, say, how to appropriately balance the privacy of individuals against the expressive rights of the press, or how to determine whether, or at which point, the right to life should offer protection to the unborn foetus, it is suggested that argument over the content of rights should take place in the open deliberative forum of Parliament. Indeed, on one reading at least, the determination of questions of the rights of individuals and groups is the very *raison d'être* of political institutions; as Martin Loughlin has written:

> politics must concern itself with the business of making choices between rival, sometimes incommensurable, goods and in circumstances for which there is no overarching rational or objective standard or principle for resolving that dispute.[14]

In resolving any dispute between an individual right and the public interest, or between two conflicting rights, the courts are therefore asked to choose between two such 'goods'. Political actors and parties can, of course, appeal to ideology or claim the support of the electorate in making such decisions; but the courts – being independent arbiters between the individual and the state – cannot. By asking the courts to resolve such disputes, sceptics therefore claim that not only will political institutions cede power to the unelected and unaccountable judges, but also that the courts will become politicised and their independence be lost as a result. Rights-sceptical arguments are therefore founded in a number of reasons related to both the *substance* of the 'human rights' to be guaranteed, and to the *processes* of judicial determination of how those rights should apply in practice.

Arguments against strong form judicial review of parliamentary legislation – that is, review which entitles the judiciary to overturn executive *and* legislative decisions – have proceeded on the basis of the effective disenfranchisement of the elected branches (and therefore of the electorate)

---

for Britain (London: Chatto and Windus, 1990); K. D. Ewing and C.A. Gearty, *Freedom Under Thatcher: Civil Liberties in Modern Britain* (Oxford: Clarendon Press, 1990).

[14] Loughlin, *Sword and Scales*, above n. 1, pp.123–4.

for the reason that decisions on human rights topics have the potential to be displaced by a small group of unelected, unaccountable judges.[15] This disenfranchisement occurs in a number of ways. First, the very issue of 'human rights' as substantive questions of law has provoked opposition. While Jeremy Bentham was able to ridicule natural rights theories as being 'nonsense on stilts', attempts to express human rights as positive statements of law have also drawn criticism. J. A. G. Griffith famously denounced Article 10 of the ECHR – the right to freedom of expression[16] – as a 'statement of a political conflict pretending to be a resolution of it'.[17] His point is illustrative of the contestable and contested nature of many human rights, and the controversies which surround their extent and application. As a result, it is argued that treating rights as being exclusively questions of law has the effect of enabling the judges to decide:

> controversial questions of social policy over which sincere, intelligent, well-meaning people disagree – questions about where to draw the line when it comes to abortion, privacy, free speech, police powers, religious practices, how refugee claimants are to be treated, who can marry, and much else.[18]

The *substance* of rights adjudication, therefore, is said to enable the unelected and unaccountable 'judges to unsettle decisions made in the

---

[15] See e.g.: J. Waldron, 'A rights-based critique of constitutional rights' (1993) 13(1) OJLS 18; Allan 'Bills of rights and judicial power', above n. 2; J. Waldron, 'The core of the case against judicial review' (2006) 115 *Yale Law Journal* 1346.

[16] Article 10 ECHR provides:
  1. Everyone has the right to freedom of expression. This right shall include freedom to hold opinions and to receive and impart information and ideas without interference by public authority and regardless of frontiers. This article shall not prevent States from requiring the licensing of broadcasting, television or cinema enterprises. 2. The exercise of these freedoms, since it carries with it duties and responsibilities, may be subject to such formalities, conditions, restrictions or penalties as are prescribed by law and are necessary in a democratic society, in the interests of national security, territorial integrity or public safety, for the prevention of disorder or crime, for the protection of health or morals, for the protection of the reputation or rights of others, for preventing the disclosure of information received in confidence, or for maintaining the authority and impartiality of the judiciary.

[17] Griffith, 'The political constitution', above n. 1, 14.

[18] J. Allan, 'A defence of the status quo' in T. Campbell, J. Goldsworthy and A. Stone, *Protecting Human Rights: Instruments and Institutions* (Oxford University Press, 2003), p.190. See also: M. Loughlin, *The Idea of Public Law* (Oxford University Press, 2003), p.129: 'Rights adjudication is intrinsically political; it requires judges to reach a determination on the relative importance of conflicting social, political and cultural interests in circumstances in which there is no objective – or even consensual – answer.'

political arena by the people's representatives and thereby frustrate the democratic process'.[19]

Further, the *process* of judicial reasoning from principles of human rights has also provoked opposition. It is argued that requiring judges to adjudicate on human rights issues involves inviting them to depart from textual analysis and the application of rules set down by the legislature, into the analysis and application of ever more 'woolly' principles.[20] Far from being absolute and inalienable, freedoms of association or expression or the right to a private life – for example – may be legally restricted in the pursuance of a 'legitimate aim', if the restriction is 'proportionate' and 'necessary in a democratic society'. The judges are asked therefore to interpret the compatibility of statutory language with human rights that are:

> always articulated in vague, amorphous, emotively stirring terms. They are pitched up in the Olympian heights of moral abstractions (for example, 'the right to freedom of expression', 'to life', 'to freedom of religion') in terms that in themselves do *not* resolve difficult policy decisions down in the quagmire of detail.[21]

The 'sanctity of the exact words of the statute'[22] which is characteristic of statutory interpretation under a sovereign Parliament is – critics argue – gradually abandoned, as judges invariably resort to reliance on their intuitive judgment in their attempts to give meaning to these vague and amorphous concepts. At the very least, the judge is required to 'draw on their philosophical understandings of equality and liberty, and to consider the appropriate role of the state in redressing social problems'.[23] At worst, the judge is drawn into decision making on the basis of

---

[19] K. D. Ewing, 'The bill of rights debate: democracy or juristocracy in Britain?' in K. D. Ewing, C. A. Gearty and B. A. Hepple, *Human Rights and Labour Law: Essays for Paul O'Higgins* (London: Mansell, 1994), p.156.

[20] Griffith, 'The political constitution', above n. 1, 14. Additionally, for Griffith, the 'illiberal instincts' of the English judges also made them unsuitable arbiters of rights. See: J. A. G. Griffith, *The Politics of the Judiciary* (5th edn) (London: Fontana Press, 1997).

[21] J. Allan, 'The Victorian Charter of Human Rights and Responsibilities: exegesis and criticism' (2006) 30 *Melbourne University Law Review* 906, 913. Such is the emphasis placed on 'human rights' as legal devices that:
> [w]hether or not the nature or scope of judicial review is made explicit, the adoption of a Bill of Rights is generally equated with the expectation that the judiciary will or should have primary responsibility for determining whether legislation imposes unjustified restrictions on rights' (J. Hiebert, 'Interpreting a bill of rights: The importance of legislative rights review (2005) 35 *British Journal of Political Science* 235, 237).

[22] G. Marshall, *Constitutional Theory* (Oxford: Clarendon Press, 1971), p.74.

[23] Hiebert, 'Interpreting a bill of rights, above n. 21, 238.

his or her own preferences and prejudices.[24] Therefore not only do bills of rights allow judges to strike down or amend decisions made in the political domain, but sceptics argue that they also encourage a departure from a style of legal reasoning which promotes and safeguards the legitimacy of the judicial method.

In short, it is argued that upon the adoption of a bill of rights, significant political power is transferred from the legislature to the judiciary. The objections of process and substance are brought into particularly sharp relief in those systems in which the judges possess the power to strike down parliamentary legislation. In systems – such as the United States or South Africa – which permit constitutional review, it is the judges who have the final say on whether measures which have been passed by the elected legislature are compatible with human rights standards.

On the other side of the spectrum, a number of commentators see the protection of human rights standards by the judicial branch as being entirely unobjectionable. Human rights, it is argued, are of such importance that they should be placed out of the reach of passing majorities, insulated from the pressures of party politics, and enshrined in a written, entrenched, document. So protected, human rights are given the status of *constitutional* guarantees and become something far more potent than the mere 'political claims' of individuals and groups.[25] Rights effectively become trumps which can – regardless of circumstance – defeat the potentially opposing claims of society at large.[26] Even if rights are not to be entrenched in such a way, others have argued that offering a degree of protection in law is a basic requirement of the rule of law, and that abandoning rights entirely to the political process would provide insufficient protection for the interests of the individual in the face of majority will.[27]

By drawing on their experience in the application of statute and common law – 'the ordinary law of the land' (Dicey's favoured mechanism for the protection of liberty)[28] – it is asserted that the courts are innately

---

[24] See e.g.: Justice A. Scalia, 'The bill of rights: confirmation of extant freedoms or invitation to judicial creation?' in G. Huscroft and P. Rishworth (eds), *Litigating Rights: Perspectives from Domestic and International Law* (Oxford: Hart Publishing, 2002), p.23; Allan, 'A defence of the status quo', above n. 18, p.183.

[25] Griffith, 'The political constitution', above n.1, 17.

[26] See e.g.: R. Dworkin, 'Rights as trumps' in J. Waldron (ed.), *Theories of Rights* (Oxford University Press, 1984).

[27] See e.g.: Lord Bingham, 'The rule of law' (2007) 66 CLJ 67, 75–7.

[28] A. V. Dicey, *Introduction to the Study of the Law of the Constitution* (Indianapolis: Liberty Fund, 1982), p.124.

suited to the task of determining human rights in practice.[29] Eric Barendt, for one, has written that:

> it is perfectly coherent to claim, for instance, that decisions on personal rights and liberties are inherently suitable for judicial resolution, and so must be made by a court, while the distribution of other goods and benefits may be regarded as a matter for administrative decision.[30]

On such a reading the courts, as the neutral arbiters of legal disputes between the individual and the state – the context in which human rights disputes classically arise[31] – are suited to independently determine such issues. That questions of rights may give rise to differing, but legitimately held views, should not act as a bar to judicial determination of legal disputes arising out of them – as T. R. S. Allan has written: 'the fact, for example, that people are likely to disagree over the proper balance between privacy and freedom of speech … does not show that the courts cannot fashion a reasonable balance as a matter of legal doctrine'.[32] For Allan, therefore, the potential for disagreement on a particular topic should not necessarily act as a bar to the development and application of legal standards – by courts – in that particular field. Other commentators are less sanguine regarding the possibility of judges determining what they would regard as vigorously contested issues of public policy.[33]

Practical considerations are also relevant. Due to executive dominance of the parliamentary timetable and the pressures associated with ensuring the implementation of government policy, commentators have also highlighted the inability of the legislative branch to act as a 'reliable guardian of human rights in practice'.[34] In a House of Commons dominated by a

---

[29] Cf. K. D. Ewing and C. A. Gearty, *The Struggle for Civil Liberties: Political Freedom and the Rule of Law in Britain, 1914–1945* (Oxford University Press, 2000), ch. 1; Ewing and Gearty, *Freedom under Thatcher*, above n. 13, ch.8. Griffith, *The Politics of the Judiciary*, above n. 20.

[30] E. Barendt, 'Separation of powers and constitutional government' [1995] PL 599, 605.

[31] Although see: A. Clapham, *Human Rights in the Private Sphere* (Oxford: Clarendon Press, 1993); I. Leigh and R. Masterman, *Making Rights Real: The Human Rights Act in its First Decade* (Oxford: Hart Publishing, 2008), ch.10.

[32] T. R. S. Allan, Review of R. Bellamy, *Political Constitutionalism: A Republican Defence of the Constitutionality of Democracy* (Cambridge University Press, 2007) in (2008) 67(2) CLJ 423, 425.

[33] See e.g.: J. Waldron, *Law and Disagreement* (Oxford: Clarendon Press, 1999); R. Bellamy, *Political Constitutionalism: A Republican Defence of the Constitutionality of Democracy* (Cambridge University Press, 2007), Allan, 'Bills of rights', above n. 2.

[34] T. Bingham, 'The European Convention on Human Rights: time to incorporate' (1993) 109 LQR 390, 393.

strong government, and a House of Lords hampered by the lack of a legislative veto and limited powers of legislative delay, the government's policy choices will more often than not become law.[35] Judicial enforcement of human rights tempers unrestrained majoritarianism by providing an additional layer of governmental accountability which allows individuals and groups to challenge executive (and possibly legislative) action.

By contrast with the suggested disenfranchisement of the electorate which occurs upon the adoption of a judicially enforced bill of rights, some commentators have argued that litigation on rights is in fact beneficial to the process of public debate over contested issues. The process of adjudication allows the individual an alternative route through which their views can be publicly aired, and may permit the individual or group to directly challenge the contested decision. Litigation on human rights disputes allows a wider range of viewpoints to be brought into the debate, including views which – paradoxically, considering the opinions of many rights-sceptical commentators – may not have come to light during the ordinary political process: those of the judges and the individuals or groups responsible for bringing the case to court. As to the first of those, Janet Hiebert has written:

> Political actors can benefit from exposure to the judgement of judges who have more liberty from the electoral, public and political pressures that may constrain political decision making and whose rulings may provide important insights into why legislation represents an inappropriate restriction on a protected right. This is particularly important for parliamentary systems where a majority government may not otherwise face serious constraints on legislative decisions.[36]

The increased ability of the courts to check the exercise of executive power where Parliament has been unable to do so is evident throughout the recent history of judicial review.[37] While the ability of groups and individuals to access the courts where the political process has otherwise proved too remote or unwilling to address their concerns is no substitute for more responsive democratic institutions, it certainly allows those with

---

[35] For a discussion of the ability of Parliament to influence and shape legislative proposals prior to their enactment, see: A. Brazier, S. Kalitowski and G. Rosenblatt, *Law in the Making: Influence and Change in the Legislative Process* (London: Hansard Society, 2008).

[36] Hiebert, 'Interpreting a bill of rights', above n. 21, 240.

[37] For two classic examples, see: *R v. Secretary of State for Foreign and Commonwealth Affairs, ex parte World Development Movement* [1995] 1 WLR 386; *R v. Secretary of State for the Home Department, ex parte Fire Brigades Union* [1995] 2 AC 513.

access to assert their views (and possibly obtain redress) in an alternative public forum.

The debate over reconciling individual freedom and the public interest has long been characterised as being one of irreconcilable differences. But the questions surrounding the design of bills of rights are no longer those relating to the all-or-nothing conflict between elected and judicial power. The judicial dominance of social policy decision making which is said to accompany the adoption of a bill of rights is no longer – if it ever was – guaranteed. This is especially the case in those countries which have seen the adoption of bills of rights which incorporate mechanisms that – when utilised – can ensure that the will of democratically elected institutions will not necessarily find itself subject to that of the judiciary.

The parliamentary bill of rights model

To address a number of the concerns over the anti-democratic tendencies of bills of rights, particularly those providing a judicial power to strike down primary legislation, alternate models have sought to accommodate the potential for disagreement between courts and legislatures over the interpretation of rights and freedoms and have sought to guard against the final word on rights issues necessarily belonging to the judicial branch. These bills of rights reject the finality of those instruments which provide for a power of judicial override, either by providing for a legislative power to legislate in avoidance of the terms of the bill of rights, or by instead allowing the courts to effectively refer particular issues of controversy back to the legislative branch. Some, such as the Canadian Charter of Rights and Freedoms, are entrenched, constitutional measures. The Charter, while providing a judicial power to disapply legislative provisions, permits the national and federal legislatures to legislate 'notwithstanding' the constitutional protections afforded by rights under its terms.[38]

A second model takes the form of a statutory bill of rights, that is, a legislative measure providing a limited protection for human rights standards within the framework provided for by parliamentary sovereignty. This latter design is known as the parliamentary, statutory or Commonwealth model bill of rights. The New Zealand Bill of Rights Act 1990, for example, only affords statutory protection to human rights – allowing the judiciary to adopt interpretations of statutory provisions

---

[38] Canadian Charter of Rights and Freedoms, s.33.

which are 'consistent' with those rights to which it gives effect[39] – contains no remedies clause,[40] and does not provide for a judicial power to question the legality of primary legislation.[41] Most recently, the Australian Capital Territory's Human Rights Act 2004 and the Victorian Charter of Rights and Responsibilities Act 2006 allow the courts to make non-coercive declarations in respect of statutes which, in the view of the judiciary, infringe human rights standards. As these declarations do not affect the continuing operation of the provision(s) in respect of which they are made, the sovereignty of the elected legislature is technically preserved.[42]

Statutory bills of rights eschew the judicial-centric model of interpretation as found in, for example, the US Bill of Rights, by promoting the parallel aim of enhancing the protection of rights throughout the policy-making and legislative process. As a result, it has been suggested that the value of such instruments 'is not the opportunity … for judges to set aside bad laws, but the incentives and pressures … for those developing legislation to give more attention to how their decisions affect rights'.[43] Judicial review runs in parallel with the accommodation of mechanisms of 'political rights review'[44] or 'non-judicial review'[45] into the political process. To this end, the Australian Capital Territory Human Rights Act and Victorian Charter of Rights and Freedoms make explicit provision for action to be taken during the legislative process to ensure that rights considerations are not simply bypassed during the parliamentary scrutiny of legislative and policy proposals.[46] The value of this model lies not only in

---

[39] New Zealand Bill of Rights Act 1990, s.6.

[40] Although see: *Simpson* v. *Attorney-General (Baigent's case)* [1994] 3 NZLR 667. On which, see: J. Allan, 'The effect of a statutory bill of rights where Parliament is sovereign: the lesson from New Zealand' in T. Campbell, K. D. Ewing and A. Tomkins, *Sceptical Essays on Human Rights* (Oxford University Press, 2001), pp.381–2; J. A. Smillie, '"Fundamental" rights, parliamentary supremacy and the New Zealand Court of Appeal' (1995) 111 LQR 209.

[41] New Zealand Bill of Rights Act, s.4. Although see: *Moonen* v. *Film and Literature Board of Review* [2000] 2 NZLR 9. On the New Zealand Bill of Rights Act generally, see: P. Rishworth, G. Huscroft, S. Optican and R. Maloney, *The New Zealand Bill of Rights* (Oxford University Press, 2003).

[42] The ACT Human Rights Act 2004 provides a power to make declarations of incompatibility (s.32) while the Victorian Charter provides for the making of declarations of inconsistent interpretation (s.36). On which, see: C. Evans and S. Evans, *Australian Bills of Rights: The Law of the Victorian Charter and the ACT Human Rights Act* (Chatswood, NSW: LexisNexis Butterworths, 2008).

[43] Hiebert, 'Interpreting a bill of rights', above n. 21, 242.

[44] J. L. Hiebert, 'Parliamentary bills of rights: an alternative model?' (2006) 69 MLR 7.

[45] M. Tushnet, 'Non-judicial review' in Campbell, Goldsworthy and Stone, above n. 18.

[46] See Australian Capital Territory Human Rights Act 2004, ss.37–9; Victorian Charter on Human Rights and Responsibilities Act 2006, ss.28–30.

providing alternatives to judicial review, but also in acknowledging and accommodating the potential for disagreement among the three branches of government over the scope and protection afforded to human rights:

> Whether they rely on ministerial statements of inconsistency, judicial declarations on incompatibility or on political invocation of a notwithstanding clause, they operate in a political environment that assumes political actors' disagreements with judicial perspectives will be significantly profound, and their commitments sufficiently robust, before being prepared to act contrary to judicial judgments. It is this inter-institutional dynamic that explains why many commentators characterise these new rights regimes as embodying dialogical potential.[47]

The UK's HRA 1998 falls within this trend by providing a limited statutory protection for rights under which the courts are not permitted to strike down legislative decisions or otherwise use human rights to conclusively defeat the democratic will of the legislature, *and* by providing that human rights considerations be built in to the policy-making and legislative process. It is for this reason that Lord Bingham was able, early in the life of the HRA, to say that '[j]udicial recognition and assertion of the human rights defined in the Convention is not a substitute for the processes of democratic government but a complement to them'.[48]

The Human Rights Act in the United Kingdom constitution

The debate over judicially enforced bills of rights very clearly influenced the design of the HRA. It is evident that the Act – while having the primary aim of providing the individual with an accessible remedy for the breach of Convention rights in domestic courts – was also designed to fit within the established general division of governmental power in the UK.[49] As a result, the then Lord Chancellor, Lord Irvine of Lairg, was able to describe the Human Rights Bill during the parliamentary debates as having been 'carefully drafted and designed to respect our traditional understanding of the separation of powers'.[50] Reduced to its bare minimum, this can be taken to mean that under the provisions of the HRA, while the reach and range of judicial review has been extended, the judges have no power to overturn statutes. As Jack Straw MP, then Home Secretary, also outlined during the parliamentary debates on the Human Rights Bill:

---

[47] Hiebert, 'Parliamentary bills of rights', above n. 44, 17.
[48] *Brown* v. *Stott* [2003] 1 AC 681, 703.
[49] For discussion, see: Leigh and Masterman, *Making Rights Real*, above n. 31, ch.1.
[50] HL Debs, vol.582, col.1228 (3 November 1997).

> The sovereignty of Parliament must be paramount. By that, I mean that Parliament must be competent to make any law on any matter of its choosing. In enacting legislation, Parliament is making decisions about important matters of public policy. The authority to make those decisions derives from a democratic mandate. Members of this place possess such a mandate because they are elected, accountable and representative … To allow the courts to set aside Acts of Parliament would confer on the judiciary a power that it does not possess, and which would draw it into conflict with Parliament.[51]

On its face, therefore, the HRA preserves the sovereignty of Parliament and eschews the strong form judicial review of legislation most typically seen in adjudication on the US Bill of Rights.[52] But to describe the separation of powers – as Lord Irvine and Jack Straw both did – as being synonymous with parliamentary sovereignty, does not fully explain the quite specific allocation of governmental power set down by the Act. The HRA envisages that all three branches of government should be actively involved in the protection of human rights in the UK. In other words, it envisages a very distinct separation of powers. The scheme established – while providing for a distinct and potentially powerful judicial role – also accommodates the potential for divergent views between the elected and judicial branches. The implementation of the HRA was manifestly not meant to fall within the sole responsibility of the courts: power on the face of the Act is divided between the judicial power of interpretation and the power of the elected branches to legislate and implement policy decisions. At the heart of the Act lie ss.3 and 4, the relationship between which is said to hold the key to the balance between parliamentary democracy and judicially enforced human rights.[53] It is clear, therefore, that the HRA makes human rights questions of *both* law and politics. (In this sense, the HRA marks a clear departure from the traditional parliamentary protection of human rights standards.) As the government indicated in the White Paper on the Human Rights Bill:

> The enforcement of Convention rights will be a matter for the courts, whilst the Government and Parliament will have the different but equally important responsibility of revising legislation where necessary. But it is

---

[51] HC Debs, vol.306, col.772 (16 February 1998).

[52] Although a number of rights-sceptical commentators have noted that this theory may not readily translate into practice. See e.g.: T. Campbell, 'Incorporation through interpretation', in Campbell, Ewing and Tomkins, *Sceptical Essays on Human Rights*, above n. 40, p.87. For discussion, see ch.6.

[53] See e.g.: C. A. Gearty, 'Reconciling parliamentary democracy and human rights' (2002) 118 LQR 248.

also highly desirable for the Government to ensure as far as possible that legislation which it places before Parliament in the normal way is compatible with the Convention rights, and for Parliament to ensure that the human rights implications of legislation are subject to proper consideration before the legislation is enacted.[54]

As a result, Parliament and the executive each play specific roles which are central to the effective functioning of the Act. As Hiebert has noted, the HRA model envisages three distinct stages of human rights review: 'executive-based rights review before legislation is introduced, followed by legislative rights review, and then [the possibility of] judicial review'.[55]

Integrating rights concerns into the legislative process

Parliamentary scrutiny of the Convention compatibility of legislative proposals is precipitated by the s.19 procedure. Upon introducing a bill at second reading, the responsible minister – under s.19(1)(a) – is directed to make a statement of compatibility of the proposed bill with the Convention rights. If the minister is unable to make such a statement – as happened, for example, in the case of the Communications Act 2003[56] – s.19(1)(b) entitles the minister to indicate that the government 'nevertheless wishes the House to proceed with the bill'. It is entirely in keeping with the sovereignty doctrine that Parliament retains the ability to legislate in explicit contravention of the Convention rights if it so chooses – indeed, it is implicit in the scheme of the HRA itself.[57] Parliamentary sovereignty – in respect of the domestic protection of human rights standards – is therefore reinforced by the fact that declarations of incompatibility give rise to no legal obligation enforceable against either the government or Parliament.[58] And in the event of a declaration of incompatibility being ignored or rejected by the elected branches, accountability for Parliament's decision to legislate in contravention of a Convention right would remain political – unless and until the UK was found to be in breach of the Convention by the European Court of Human Rights.

---

[54] *Rights Brought Home: The Human Rights Bill* (Cm. 3782, 1997), para. 3.1.

[55] Hiebert, 'Interpreting a bill of rights', above n. 21, 245.

[56] On which, now see: *R (on the application of Animal Defenders International)* v. *Secretary of State for Culture, Media and Sport* [2008] UKHL 15.

[57] In addition to the implications of ss.3(2) and 4(6), Parliament is expressly excluded from the definition of 'public authority' under the Act by s.6(3).

[58] Despite indicating that he thought it likely that s.4 declarations would be accepted and remedied in the 'overwhelming majority of cases', Jack Straw MP, the then Home Secretary,

The aim of the s.19 procedure is to integrate human rights concerns into both the pre-legislative and parliamentary processes without placing a substantive bar on the ability of Parliament to exercise legislative autonomy.[59] Section 19 is therefore designed to 'prevent Parliament from enacting legislation that inadvertently overrides human rights, without ultimately constraining political choice'.[60] The s.19 procedure has been complemented by the detailed scrutiny work undertaken by the Joint Committee on Human Rights which – since its establishment in the 2000–01 parliamentary session – has carried out wide-ranging and detailed inquiries into legislation and government policy with human rights implications.[61] But while the aim of s.19 appears to suggest a willingness to openly debate and respond to human rights concerns during the legislative process, in practice, however, it has been suggested that '[s]ection 19 statements have operated as a formal and procedural defence of a pre-determined policy, rather than an informative exercise in dialogue'.[62] If, then, there are doubts about the effectiveness of the political checks on human rights-relevant legislative proposals which are implemented by the HRA, it is reassuring that the s.19 and parliamentary scrutiny procedure does not appear to influence the role of the courts under the HRA. The strict legal question of Convention compatibility for the purposes of ss.3 and 6 HRA remains an issue for the domestic courts; as a result, s.19 statements have been held to carry little or no weight in a court of law.[63]

In addition to the ministerial obligation to provide a statement to Parliament under s.19, the executive branch is given various other specific functions under the Act. Most obviously, all public authorities are

was careful to remind Parliament during debates on the Human Rights Bill that, '[i]t is possible that the Judicial Committee of the House of Lords could make a declaration that … Ministers propose, and Parliament accepts, should not be accepted'. Mr Straw had in mind a decision which would cause 'very great controversy', giving the example of a hypothetical situation in which the Law Lords declared the UK's abortion regime to be incompatible with the Convention (HC Debs, vol. 317, col. 1301 (21 October 1998)).

[59] For a detailed discussion, see: Leigh and Masterman, *Making Rights Real*, above n. 31, pp.28–36.

[60] *Ibid.*, p.29.

[61] For discussion, see: Lord Lester, 'Parliamentary scrutiny of legislation under the Human Rights Act 1998' [2002] EHRLR 432; D. Feldman, 'Parliamentary scrutiny of legislation and human rights' [2002] PL 323; F. Klug and H. Wildbore, 'Breaking new ground: the Joint Committee on Human Rights and the role of Parliament in human rights compliance' [2007] EHRLR 231.

[62] Leigh and Masterman, *Making Rights Real*, above n. 31, p.48.

[63] *R* v. *A (No. 2)* [2001] 1 AC 45, 75, *per* Lord Hope: '[s.19 statements are] no more than expressions of opinion by the [responsible] minister. They are not binding on the court,

under an obligation to act compatibly with the Convention rights under
s.6(1) HRA. In addition, under s.5, the Crown has a right to intervene in
litigation under the Act in those cases where the court is considering the
making of a declaration of incompatibility. In those cases where a declaration of incompatibility has been issued by the courts, and when, in the
view of the responsible minister there exist 'compelling reasons for proceeding under' s.10, the minister 'may by Order [in Council] make such
amendments to the legislation as he considers necessary to remove the
incompatibility'.[64] The s.10 power is also available to the executive for the
purposes of bringing domestic law into line with the Convention jurisprudence following a decision of the European Court of Human Rights.[65]

Interpretations and declarations of incompatibility

Described by at least one former senior judge as the HRA's 'prime remedial measure',[66] s.3(1) provides an interpretative mechanism under which
statutes might be rendered compatible with the Convention rights.[67] As is
by now well known, s.3(1) of the HRA provides:

> So far as is possible to do so, primary legislation and subordinate legisla-
> tion must be read and given effect in a way which is compatible with the
> Convention rights.

This rule of statutory construction applies to legislation passed both
prior to and post the HRA,[68] and its application does not affect the 'validity, continuing operation or enforcement' of any legislation found to be
incompatible.[69] Parliamentary sovereignty appears to be simultaneously
undermined and preserved; on the one hand the provision purports to
control the interpretation of legislation not yet passed, on the other, the
continuing legality of any legislation which has been declared incompatible remains unquestioned.[70] While appearing to limit the judicial role
under the HRA to acts of interpretation, the terms of s.3(1) are vague
enough to harbour considerable scope for expansive and wide-ranging

---

nor do they have any persuasive authority.' This is contrary to the predictions of at least
one of the Law Lords: Lord Hoffmann, 'Human rights and the House of Lords' (1999)
62(2) MLR 159, 161–2.

[64] Section 10(2) HRA.   [65] Section 10(1)(b) HRA.

[66] *Ghaidan* v. *Godin-Mendoza* [2004] UKHL 30; [2004] 2 AC 557, para.46 (Lord Steyn).

[67] The 'Convention rights' are defined in s.1(1) HRA.

[68] Section 3(2)(a) HRA.

[69] Section 3(2)(b) HRA.

[70] For discussion, see: T. Hickman, 'Constitutional dialogue, constitutional theories and
the Human Rights Act' [2005] PL 306, 322–7.

'interpretations'.[71] Lord Hope captured the potential of s.3(1) in *ex parte Kebilene*, noting that it contained the possibility to 'subject the entire legal system to a fundamental process of review and, where necessary, reform by the judiciary'.[72]

While the courts are able – under s.3(1) – to interpret legislation to achieve compatibility with the 'Convention rights', they may also issue a non-coercive declaration of incompatibility in those cases where judicial interpretation is impossible.[73] The issue of a 'declaration of incompatibility' under s.4 HRA notifies the executive and legislature of the incompatibility and allows the elected branches the choice of whether or not to remedy the finding of incompatibility. As with the use of s.3(1), the issue of such a declaration 'does not affect the validity, continuing operation or enforcement of the provision in respect of which it is given', nor is it binding on the parties to the case.[74] In response to a judicially issued declaration, the executive may rely on the remedial order mechanism laid down in s.10 of the Act, which grants the responsible minister the power to amend the legislation in question by way of a statutory instrument.[75] However, the consequence of the non-binding nature of declarations of incompatibility – as was made clear by government ministers during the parliamentary debates on the Human Rights Bill[76] – is that there may be circumstances in which the government and Parliament are of the view that the 'incompatible' legislation should stand. This aspect of the HRA's scheme of rights protection appears distinctly weak; in remedial terms, a declaration of incompatibility can be seen as a 'booby prize'[77] for the (otherwise) successful litigant, as '[a]spirational human rights lose much of their significance if they do not encourage action to remedy specific evils'.[78] The declaration of incompatibility does not, therefore, compel the elected branches to repeal or amend the law in respect of which it is

---

[71] See pp.154–68.

[72] *R* v. *Director of Public Prosecutions, ex parte Kebilene* [2000] 2 AC 326, 374–5.

[73] Section 4 HRA. And see further pp.168–76.

[74] Section 4(6) HRA.   [75] Section 10 HRA.

[76] HC Debs, vol.317, col.1301 (21 October 1998). In spite of this, Lord Irvine of Lairg LC did indicate that 'we expect that the government and Parliament will in all cases almost certainly be prompted to change the law following a declaration of incompatibility' (HL Debs, vol.583, col.1139, (27 November 1997)). See also the White Paper, *Rights Brought Home: The Human Rights Bill*, Cm. 3782 (1997), 'A declatation [of incompatibility] ... will almost certainly prompt the Government and Parliament to change the law' (para. 2.10).

[77] I. Leigh, 'The UK's Human Rights Act 1998: an early assessment' in Huscroft and Rishworth (eds), *Litigating Rights*, above n. 24, p.324.

[78] Campbell, 'Incorporation through interpretation', above n. 52, p.91. See also: Hickman, 'Constitutional dialogue', above n. 70, 327.

made: the will of the elected branches is not necessarily subjected to that of the judicial branch.[79]

Described as such, the scheme established by the HRA *is* one which upholds the traditional basic conception of the separation of executive, legislative and judicial power – subject to a minor qualification. Parliament makes the laws and the courts interpret them, becomes Parliament makes the laws and the judiciary are empowered to interpret them – 'so far as is possible' – to be compatible with the Convention rights. On such an analysis, the courts' role appears to be purely interpretative, and it is clear that in the implementation of the Act, pre-HRA conceptions of the limitations of judicial power continue to resonate, with a number of cases demonstrating the continuing reluctance of the courts to act in a way which might be seen overtly to usurp the legislative function.[80] On this reading of the Act, therefore, Parliament's role as sovereign legislature is preserved. The Westminster Parliament – the representative body – appears to be given the final word. As such, the short-lived Department for Constitutional Affairs, in its 2006 review of the Act, felt able to issue the claim that 'arguments that the Human Rights Act has significantly altered the constitutional balance between Parliament, the executive and the judiciary have ... been considerably exaggerated'.[81] On such a reading, the potency of this new separation of powers, with its continuing attachment to legislative supremacy, is most certainly open to question – a system of checks and balances is considerably weakened where one branch effectively possesses the ability to opt out of being held in check.

Separation of powers at the macro level: an inter-institutional dialogue on rights?

Conor Gearty has written that the declaration of incompatibility – and the response it provokes – is the 'genius' of the HRA model, for the reason

---

[79] Even so, a number of critics remain sceptical of judicially issued declarations. As Ewing has noted, 'Parliament's position would have been stronger politically and constitutionally if incorporation of the ECHR had stopped short of giving the courts power to challenge primary legislation' (K. D. Ewing, 'The Human Rights Act and parliamentary democracy' (1999) 62 MLR 79, 99).

[80] See e.g.: *Re S (Children) (Care Order: Implementation of Care Plan); Re W (Children) (Care Order: Adequacy of Care Plan)* [2002] UKHL 10; [2002] 2 AC 291; *R (on the application of Anderson)* v. *Secretary of State for the Home Department* [2002] UKHL 46; [2003] 1 AC 837; *R (on the application of Ullah)* v. *Special Adjudicator; Do* v. *Immigration Appeal Tribunal* [2004] UKHL 26.

[81] Department of Constitutional Affairs, *Review of the Implementation of the Human Rights Act* (July 2006), 4.

that it invites 'the political back in to control the legal at just the moment when the supremacy of the legal discourse seems assured'.[82] In making the response to a declaration of incompatibility a matter of choice and not of compulsion, and in establishing mechanisms for human rights analysis in the policy-making and parliamentary processes, the HRA therefore possesses the two characteristics which Janet Hiebert has argued 'potentially represent a democratic rejoinder to sceptics'.[83] Hiebert suggests:

> This rejoinder arises from the model's capacity to generate broader and more reflective judgments on how rights should influence or constrain legislative decisions and its acceptance, in theory, of legitimate political dissent from judicial interpretations.[84]

The potential for disagreement between courts and legislatures over questions of the protection of rights finds parallels in the 'democratic dialogue' theory advanced by Hogg and Bushell in the context of the Canadian Charter.[85] Hogg and Bushell suggest that a court's power to review legislation on human rights grounds contributes a particular perspective to a broader debate over the legitimate exercise of state power *vis-à-vis* individual rights which would *not* be brought into the public domain were the courts not possessed of the power of judicial review and the legislature retained the sole authority of decisions of individual liberty.[86] As Hogg and Bushell observe:

> Where a judicial decision is open to legislative reversal, modification or avoidance, then it is meaningful to regard the relationship between the court and the competent legislative body as a dialogue … the judicial decision causes a public debate in which the *Charter* values play a more prominent role than they would if there had been no judicial decision. The legislative body is in a position to devise a response that is properly respectful of the *Charter* values that have been identified by the Court, but

---

[82] C. Gearty, *Can Human Rights Survive?* (Cambridge University Press, 2006), p.95.

[83] Hiebert, 'Parliamentary bills of rights', above n. 44, 9.

[84] *Ibid.*

[85] P. Hogg and A. Bushell, 'The *Charter* dialogue between courts and legislatures (or perhaps the *Charter of Rights* isn't such a bad thing after all' (1997) 35 *Osgoode Hall Law Journal* 75.

[86] See further: C. P. Manfredi and J. B. Kelly, 'Six degrees of dialogue: a response to Hogg and Bushell' (1999) 37 *Osgoode Hall Law Journal* 513; K. Roach, 'Constitutional and common law dialogues between the Supreme Court and Canadian Legislatures' (2001) 80 *Canadian Bar Review* 481; J. Debeljak, 'Rights protection without judicial supremacy: a review of the Canadian and British models of Bills of Rights' (2002) 26 *Melbourne University Law Review* 285; L. B. Tremblay, 'The legitimacy of judicial review: the limits of dialogue between courts and legislatures' (2005) 3 *International Journal of Constitutional Law* 617.

which accomplishes the social and economic objectives that the judicial decision has impeded.[87]

The dialogue model was originally conceived in the context of a jurisdiction which permitted judicial override of legislative measures – the United States – under which the courts' endorsement of the constitutionality of a given measure was seen as as important a contribution to the debate as the invalidation of a challenged measure.[88] In such a system, however, in the event of a finding that a measure is contrary to the constitution, a process of *constitutional* amendment is required to avoid the consequences of the judicial decision. It is for this reason that the dialogue metaphor can be said to hold more currency under a parliamentary, rather than a constitutional, bill of rights: the contested judicial decision 'can be reversed, modified, or avoided in the *ordinary* legislative process'.[89]

Strong form review by stealth?

It is clear also that a number of judicial advocates of the dialogic model view the increased propensity for the exchange of inter-institutional viewpoints as contributing to a more meaningful system of checks and balances. As Iacobucci J observed in the Supreme Court of Canada decision *Vriend* v. *Alberta*:

> To my mind, a great value of judicial review and this dialogue among the branches is that each of the branches is made somewhat accountable to the other. The work of the legislature is reviewed by the courts and the work of the court in its decisions can be reacted to by the legislature in the passing of new legislation … This dialogue between and accountability of each of the branches have the effect of enhancing the democratic process, not denying it.[90]

Nevertheless, critics of parliamentary bills of rights assert that the so-called parliamentary bill of rights model indirectly produces the type of strong form judicial review that it seeks to avoid; it is said that the elected branches may in practice be unable – for either practical or constitutional reasons – to overturn judicial interpretations of the meaning of rights

---

[87] Hogg and Bushell, 'The *Charter* dialogue between courts and legislatures', above n. 85, 79–80.

[88] A. M. Bickel, *The Least Dangerous Branch: The Supreme Court at the Bar of Politics* (Indianapolis: Bobbs-Merrill, 1962), ch.4.

[89] Hogg and Bushell, 'The *Charter* dialogue between courts and legislatures', above n. 85, 80 (emphasis added).

[90] *Vriend* v. *Alberta* [1998] 1 SCR 493, 566 (Iacobucci J).

and will unquestioningly endorse judicial declarations of incompatibility as a result, or they will otherwise seek to second-guess the courts and only propose readings of liberty which they believe will survive judicial scrutiny.[91]

The practical reasons why legislatures may be unable to reverse the interpretative rulings of courts lie in the pressures of party politics and the inability of a legislative programme dominated by the executive's policy choices to accommodate *ad hoc* responses to judicial decisions.[92] Practical objections to the operation of a dialogue between courts and legislatures are compounded by a constitutional dimension – as Grant Huscroft has argued: 'dialogue is meaningful only if disagreement with the decisions of the courts is not only possible but legitimate'.[93] Constitutionally, Tom Campbell has argued that the interpretative role of the courts is as established as the legislative powers of Parliament, and that as a consequence:

> the right of judges to interpret the law is as politically entrenched as the right of Parliament to make law. Interpretation is almost universally seen as the prerogative of the courts because it is part of adjudication, and that is taken to be their exclusive function. It is therefore not only politically difficult but also constitutionally questionable for parliaments to reject a court's particular interpretations or even question a court's interpretative methods.[94]

It is for this reason – among others – that the use of the notwithstanding clause in the Canadian Charter of Rights has been so rarely seen outside of Quebec.[95] Campbell's reliance on a 'politically entrenched' conception of separation of powers is, however, revealing, for it appears to suggest that – even within a system of parliamentary supremacy – there is a division of governmental competence which appears to have a degree of normative force.

Further, and perhaps less obviously, the potential for meaningful dialogue is said to be hampered by the juridification of the political process which takes place when the elected branches of government begin to adopt

[91] R. Bellamy, *Political Constitutionalism: A Republican Defence of the Constitutionality of Democracy* (Cambridge University Press, 2007), p.48.

[92] G. Huscroft, 'The trouble with living tree interpretation' (2006) 25 *University of Queensland Law Journal* 3, 19–22.

[93] G. Huscroft, 'Rights, bills of rights and the role of courts and legislatures' in Huscroft and Rishworth (eds), *Litigating Rights*, above n. 24, p.14.

[94] Campbell, 'Incorporation through interpretation', above n. 52, p.87.

[95] See: P. Hogg, *Constitutional Law of Canada* (Scarborough, Ont: Thomson Canada, 2004), ch.36; C. P. Manfredi, *Judicial Power and the Charter: Canada and the Paradox of Liberal Constitutionalism* (2nd edn) (Ontario: Oxford University Press, 2001).

legalistic views of human rights – that is, when 'respect for human rights is equated with replicating judicial assumptions' about those rights[96] – and seek to make their legislation and policy choices review-proof by adopting measures which they believe will survive judicial scrutiny. In this scenario, a 'culture of compliance'[97] develops in which legislators and politicians are increasingly driven only to propose solutions to policy questions that they believe will survive judicial scrutiny.[98] On this reading, the separation of powers brought into being under the HRA is a much more potent concept under which judicial views of questions of human rights hold considerable legal and political force, regardless of whether the courts utilise s.3 or s.4.

Operating in the shadow of Strasbourg

The potential for any such inter-institutional dialogue to take place in the context of the operation of the HRA is, of course, constrained by the fact that the UK is subject to the supervision of the European Court of Human Rights. The HRA does not create rights standards anew, but instead establishes a regime under which an existing body of international rights standards might be given 'further effect' in domestic law. The UK, as a signatory to the Convention, is subject to the ultimate authority of the European Court of Human Rights. As a result of these ties to the Strasbourg institutions, domesticated readings of the 'Convention rights' – whether proposed by Parliament, executive or courts – are potentially subject to review, and possibly override, by the Strasbourg organs.

Under s.2(1) of the HRA, UK courts – in 'determining a question which has arisen in connection with a Convention right' – are directed to take account of 'relevant' decisions of the enforcement bodies of the Convention.[99] The approach of UK courts to the domestic application of the Convention standards has seen a general tendency to place quite

---

[96] Hiebert, 'Parliamentary bills of rights', above n. 44, 23.
[97] D. Nicol, 'The Human Rights Act and the politicians' (2004) 24 LS 451, 472–3; Lord Steyn, 'Democracy through law' [2002] EHRLR 725, 735.
[98] See e.g.: Bellamy, *Political Constitutionalism*, above n. 91, pp.47–8.
[99] Section 2(1) HRA provides:

> A court or tribunal determining a question which has arisen in connection with a Convention right must take into account any – judgment, decision, declaration or advisory opinion of the European Court of Human Rights, opinion of the Commission given in a report adopted under Article 31 of the Convention, decision of the Commission in connection with Article 26 or 27(2) of the Convention, or decision of the Committee of Ministers taken under Article 46 of the Convention, whenever made

heavy reliance on the findings of the Strasbourg institutions. Domestic courts have, in effect, read the requirement that relevant decisions be 'taken into account' to mean that clear authority should be followed,[100] and have been hesitant to find meaning in the Convention which cannot be clearly traced back to a Strasbourg decision or decisions.[101] While this relationship between the Strasbourg jurisprudence and domestic law undoubtedly contributes to greater certainty for the victim of a purported infringement – in the sense that they could relatively confidently predict that clear Strasbourg reasoning would be adopted by a domestic court – it undoubtedly also limits the ability of the domestic courts to engage in a 'dialogue' on the meaning of the Convention rights as given effect under the HRA. Indeed, the position of the UK as a signatory to the Convention also places restrictions on the ability of the elected branches to engage in free thinking on the meaning of the Convention rights: even if the doctrine of parliamentary sovereignty has survived the passing of the HRA unscathed, the ultimate meaning of those 'Convention rights' is *not* an area in which the authority of Parliament is insulated from future challenge at Strasbourg. As the Appellate Committee of the House of Lords has indicated – even if national authorities seek to expand on, or interpret the Convention's provisions in the domestic context – the Convention remains 'an international instrument, the correct interpretation of which can be authoritatively expounded only by the Strasbourg court'.[102] To present the HRA as offering an opportunity for blue-sky thinking on rights generally is to misconstrue the nature of the HRA, and the position of national authorities under the Convention.[103] Any contribution to be made to such a 'dialogue' – by either courts or legislature – necessarily

---

or given, so far as, in the opinion of the court or tribunal, it is relevant to the proceedings in which that question has arisen. See further pp.191–202.

[100] See e.g.: *R (on the application of Alconbury Developments Ltd) v. Secretary of State for the Environment, Transport and the Regions* [2001] UKHL 23, para.26; *R (on the application of Anderson) v. Secretary of State for the Home Department,* above n. 80, para.18.

[101] *R (on the application of Ullah) v. Special Adjudicator; Do v. Immigration Appeal Tribunal,* above n. 80, para.20, *per* Lord Bingham. For commentary, see: R. Masterman, 'Aspiration or foundation? The status of the Strasbourg jurisprudence and "Convention rights" in domestic law' in H. Fenwick, G. Phillipson and R. Masterman, *Judicial Reasoning under the UK Human Rights Act* (Cambridge University Press, 2007).

[102] *R (on the application of Ullah) v. Special Adjudicator; Do v. Immigration Appeal Tribunal,* above n. 80, para. 20, *per* Lord Bingham.

[103] Nicol, for one, alludes favourably to the 'potential for unrestrained debate' that the HRA could foster (D. Nicol, 'Law and politics after the Human Rights Act' [2006] PL 722, 748). For a response to Professor Nicol's article, see: T. Hickman, 'The courts and politics after the Human Rights Act: a comment' [2008] PL 84.

takes place within the context of, and is ultimately subject to, the jurisdiction of the European Court of Human Rights.

The separation of powers implications of the dialogic model

The dialogue metaphor is therefore somewhat disingenuous for a number of reasons. For rights sceptics, the difficulty with the declaration of incompatibility is that, just as it is Parliament's constitutional role to make the law, it is the role of the courts to interpret and give effect to that law in the cases that come before them. To fully accept that either the HRA institutes a 'dialogue' concerning the protection of rights in which each partner has a legitimate right to proffer its preferred reading of the compatibility – or incompatibility – of a given measure also requires us to reassess our expectations of the judicial function.

While those who are sceptical of the judicial determination of questions of rights have criticised the juridification of political debate, comparatively little attention has been given to the opposing phenomenon; the politicisation, not of the judiciary, but of the judicial process. As Tom Hickman has written, an unquestioning acceptance that the courts are involved in a 'dialogue' over the limits of human rights in a parliamentary system reduces their judgments to the status of mere advisory opinions, or the actions of a 'privileged pressure group', in the political process.[104] The natural consequence of this would effectively be to give the elected branches the option of whether or not to accept a judicial finding or the meaning of the law, which would strip judicial decisions of much of their normative authority.

As a result, the dialogue metaphor asks us to accept that judicial decisions are *both* binding findings of the content and meaning of legal rights, *and* contributions to an inter-institutional discussion from which the legislature, and possibly the executive, can depart if they so choose. The notion of 'dialogue' may therefore be additionally problematic for the reason that it raises expectations that not only will the *issue* of 'declarations of incompatibility' be 'routine and unproblematic',[105] but that so, too, will be the *refusal* of the elected branches unquestioningly to adopt the asserted grounds of incompatibility. While the HRA has undoubtedly reconfigured the separation of powers, it cannot have been intended to mandate a departure from the constitutional guarantee that the executive

---

[104] Hickman, 'Constitutional dialogue', above n. 70, 309–10.
[105] Campbell, 'Incorporation through interpretation', above n. 52, p.99.

obey the law as a matter of necessity, rather than grace.[106] Even under a constitution in which sovereignty is said to be preserved, if we accept Campbell's argument over the politically entrenched right of judges to interpret the law, then the dialogue metaphor compels a reassessment of the judicial function, and may require a downgrading of the normative value of judicial decisions. The idea of dialogue promotes the notion of a free and frank exchange of views – something which sits entirely uneasily with the idea that a judicial decision is not something that the government or an individual can opt into if they fortuitously happen to agree with it. Martin Loughlin has argued that if incorporating rights into the language and practice of society is itself controversial, then allowing the judiciary to determine the outcome of disputes over those rights only serves to compound the controversy:

> handing the task of explicating those rights to an institution whose entire *modus operandi* is rooted in a conviction that there are right answers to all disputes in law and that such answers are revealed through the deployment of some unique legal logic must be doubly contentious.[107]

The hesitancy of a number of senior judges to openly commit to such a dialogue was evident in an early appearance before the fledgling Joint Parliamentary Committee on Human Rights. Giving evidence to the Committee, Lord Bingham was dismissive of the idea that the judiciary would be involved in a dialogue with the elected branches of government, saying:

> I would not myself think in terms of a dialogue at all. *The business of the judges is to listen to cases and give judgment.* In doing that, of course, they will pay attention to the arguments that are addressed to them and one hopes they will be alive to the currents of thought which are prevalent in the community, but I do not myself see it as the role of the judges to engage in dialogue.[108]

On this reading, therefore, the primary role of the courts would remain that of deciding those cases which appear before them, independently, and on the basis of the law. Such an approach is not indicative of a branch of government engaged in a dialogue of any but the most abstract sort. While the architecture of the HRA may accommodate the potential for

---

[106] *M* v. *Home Office* [1994] 1 AC 377, 395 (Lord Templeman).
[107] Loughlin, *The Idea of Public Law*, above n. 18, p.130.
[108] Joint Committee on Human Rights, Oral Evidence (21 March 2001), 78 (emphasis added).

disagreement, it is unclear whether the judicial process itself is open to such modification.

In reality – as the experience in the UK demonstrates – while declarations of incompatibility may be issued by the courts with a degree of frequency, it will be wholly unusual for Parliament to refuse to accept the declaration and take the necessary steps to remedy it.[109] Again, this does not necessarily herald the undisputed supremacism of the judiciary in the determination of questions of human rights. Parliament enjoys a broad discretion to determine the manner of the response; declarations of incompatibility are by no means self-executing. And, as indicated above, the government's acceptance of s.4 declarations can at least in part be explained by the position of the UK as a signatory to the ECHR.[110] However, it is equally clear that the declaration of incompatibility does possess a degree of political – if not legal – potency.[111] (This is particularly well illustrated by those instances where the courts and Parliament, or perhaps more realistically the executive, have been portrayed as being diametrically opposed to each other.[112]) The prediction of the Labour administration in its White Paper on the Human Rights Bill – that the issue of '[a] declaration [of incompatibility] … will almost certainly prompt the Government and Parliament to change the law' – has been realised.[113] It may be a step too far to suggest that the government and Parliament would *never* dispute the findings of a declaration of incompatibility; as Jeffrey Goldsworthy has written: '[t]here is clearly a difference between

---

[109] At the time of writing, all of the judicially made declarations under s.4 HRA have been accepted by the UK government and had either been remedied, or steps had been taken indicating a response would be forthcoming. Remedial action to address the incompatibility highlighted by *Smith* v. *Scott* 2007 SC 345, however, has yet to materialise. See pp.175–6.

[110] Although it should also be noted that the UK government's record – to date – of accepting judicial declarations of incompatibility has not been sufficient to persuade the European Court of Human Rights that the s.4 declaration provides an 'effective remedy' for the victim of a violation for the purposes of Article 13 of the ECHR (see: *Burden and Burden* v. *United Kingdom* (2007) 44 EHRR 51, para.39).

[111] See e.g.: HC Debs, vol.307, col.780 (16 February 1998); HL Debs, vol.582, col.1231 (3 November 1997); Ewing, 'The Human Rights Act and parliamentary democracy', above n. 79, 99.

[112] E.g., in the sphere of counter-terrorism; on which see: *A (FC) and others (FC)* v. *Secretary of State for the Home Department* [2004] UKHL 56; and Leigh and Masterman, *Making Rights Real*, above n.31, ch. 8.

[113] *Rights Brought Home*, above n. 76, para.2.10. These comments were echoed in Parliament by Lord Irvine, who said that, 'we expect that the government and Parliament will in all cases almost certainly be prompted to change the law following a declaration of incompatibility' (HL Debs, vol.583, col.1139 (27 November 1997)).

relinquishing or disabling one's power to make certain kinds of decisions, and declining – even routinely – to exercise it'.[114] Yet it is undeniable that to entirely avoid the consequences of a declaration of incompatibility, then the elected branches would have to articulate carefully considered reasons for so doing, and would have to face the political consequences of rejecting a judicially declared assessment of what the law requires. On this reading, borne out by the experience of the HRA to date, the coercive powers of the courts over questions of rights are significant, with a judicial declaration of incompatibility difficult to overturn.

Second, the dialogue metaphor sidesteps the fact that the judicial determination of questions of rights under the HRA model is not unconstrained. At the domestic level, judicial decisions necessarily take place within either the legislative framework laid down by Parliament, or the common law. And while it has been recognised that the courts possess a greater discretion as to the interpretation and application of the latter,[115] common law decision making is by no means unconstrained. At the supranational level, judicial determination of the meaning of 'the Convention rights' is constrained by over half a century's worth of jurisprudence from the Strasbourg institutions. And it is to the influence of that jurisprudence that we now turn.

---

[114] J. Goldsworthy, 'Judicial review, legislative override and democracy' in T. Campbell, J. Goldsworthy and A. Stone, *Protecting Human Rights: Instruments and Institutions* (Oxford University Press, 2003), p.268.

[115] *R (on the application of Animal Defenders International)* v. *Secretary of State for Culture, Media and Sport*, above n. 56, para.53.

3

The Strasbourg influence

Introduction

The influence of the Convention and the Strasbourg case law on the domestic separation of governmental powers has a number of distinct dynamics. As Clapham has noted, '[t]he European Court of Human Rights is not seeking to harmonize constitutional traditions but to ensure international protection for the rights contained in the Convention'.[1] Yet the influence of the jurisprudence of the European Court of Human Rights quite clearly brings with it a strong adherence to the values of constitutionalism and limited government. This is most obviously evident in the commitment shown by the Convention to the rule of law.[2] The Convention therefore reflects the spirit of checked and limited government, even if it prescribes no specific template for how such an objective might be achieved. So while the European Court of Human Rights has been able to consistently state that the Convention does not demand the maintenance of any specific 'theoretical constitutional concepts as such',[3] the notion of the separation of executive, legislative and judicial power can also be said to have achieved a certain prominence in the case law of the Strasbourg court. For example, in *Stafford* v. *United Kingdom*, the 'growing importance' of the notion of the separation of governmental powers was noted,[4] while in *Benjamin and Wilson* v. *United Kingdom* the idea was referred to as being 'fundamental'.[5] More specifically, perhaps, the Strasbourg jurisprudence

---

[1] A. Clapham, *Human Rights in the Private Sphere* (Oxford: Clarendon Press, 1992), p.181.

[2] S. Grosz, J. Beatson and P. Duffy, *Human Rights: The 1998 Act and the European Convention* (London: Sweet and Maxwell, 2000), p.169:

> The Convention uses the words 'law' and 'lawful' 39 times. The preamble refers to the 'common heritage of … the rule of law' which the States parties share, and which the court has described as 'one of the fundamental principles of a democratic society, [which] is inherent in all the Articles of the Convention.'

[3] *McGonnell* v. *United Kingdom* (2000) 30 EHRR 289, para.51.

[4] *Stafford* v. *United Kingdom* (2002) 35 EHRR 32, para.78.

[5] *Benjamin and Wilson* v. *United Kingdom* (2003) 36 EHRR 1, para.36.

has seen the separation of judicial and executive power acknowledged as a 'legitimate aim' to be pursued by domestic authorities.[6] The emphasis placed on the importance of separated governmental institutions by the Strasbourg institutions has not gone unnoticed in domestic courts; in *R (on the application of Anderson)* v. *Secretary of State for the Home Department*, Lord Bingham observed that the European Court of Human Rights had been correct to 'describe the complete functional separation of the judiciary from the executive as "fundamental" since the rule of law depends on it',[7] with Lord Hutton adding that such a separation is an 'essential part of a democracy'.[8]

Second, and in spite of the Court's assertion that the Convention does not require adherence to any 'theoretical constitutional concepts',[9] the effect of the Convention has on occasion required a *de facto* separation of particular governmental powers. It is clear, for instance, that the Convention envisages that courts discharge certain constitutional functions.[10] And in its application of the right to a fair hearing before an 'independent and impartial tribunal', the Strasbourg court has required a separation of – for example – executive involvement in sentencing functions,[11] and judicial involvement in legislative functions[12] where, in the objectively assessed circumstances of the case, doubt can be raised as to the impartiality of the judicial procedures adopted. As a result, a separation of judicial power from that of the legislature or executive may effectively be compelled by the Strasbourg jurisprudence where the protection of one of the Convention rights is at issue. Separation of powers is neither the aim nor the objective of the Strasbourg court, but may nevertheless be the result.

Third, the requirement that restrictions on Convention rights be proportionate has required a marked departure from the *Wednesbury* standard of unreasonableness and cemented a more intensive standard of review in domestic law.[13] While adoption of the proportionality standard of review had been mooted by various judges in the recent history of

---

[6] *A* v. *United Kingdom* (2003) 36 EHRR 51, para.77.

[7] *R* v. *Secretary of State for the Home Department, ex parte Anderson* [2003] 1 AC 837, 882.

[8] *Ibid.*, 899.

[9] *McGonnell* v. *United Kingdom*, above n. 3, para.51.

[10] For clear examples, see the text of Articles 5 and 6, and the discussion at pp.74–6.

[11] *Stafford* v. *United Kingdom*, above n. 4. Cf. *Wynne* v. *United Kingdom* (1995) 19 EHRR 333.

[12] *Procola* v. *Luxembourg* (1996) 22 EHRR 193; *McGonnell* v. *United Kingdom*, above n. 3.

[13] For a survey, see: I. Leigh and R. Masterman, *Making Rights Real: The Human Rights Act in its First Decade* (Oxford: Hart Publishing, 2008), ch.6.

judicial review[14] – and had been utilised by British judges determining cases in the Judicial Committee of the Privy Council[15] – the common law had long resisted the wholesale importation of the test of proportionality into administrative law for at least two reasons. First, on the ground that bringing tests into domestic law that were so intimately linked to the provisions of the European Convention would usurp the legislative function, and would in effect bring the Convention itself into domestic law via the back door.[16] Second, judges had been hesitant to apply principles of proportionality for fear that it would invite them to scrutinise and possibly question the merits of executive decisions.[17] Judicial review had studiously maintained a distinction between review and appeal, which was perhaps most famously noted by Lord Greene in the *Wednesbury* case:

> The power of the court to interfere in each [judicial review] case is not as an appellate authority to override a decision of the local authority, but as a judicial authority which is concerned, and concerned only, to see whether the local authority have contravened the law by acting in excess of the powers which Parliament has confided in them.[18]

The significance of Lord Greene's dicta was visible throughout administrative law during the twentieth century. Indeed, it remains influential: the HRA has certainly not marked the complete abandonment of *Wednesbury* principles of review.[19] Prior to the Act's implementation, while judicial review had come to recognise a more intensive standard of review would apply where individual rights were at stake[20] – culminating in the 'anxious scrutiny' approach adopted in cases such as *ex parte Smith*[21] – detailed proportionality analysis had not been specifically adopted as a ground which would justify the judicial interference

---

[14] Most famously, perhaps, by Lord Diplock in *Council of Civil Service Unions* v. *Minister for the Civil Service* [1985] AC 374, 410.

[15] See e.g.: *De Freitas* v. *Permanent Secretary of Ministry of Agriculture, Fisheries, Lands and Housing* [1999] 1 AC 69.

[16] See e.g.: *R* v. *Secretary of State for the Home Department, ex parte Brind* [1991] 1 AC 696, 762–3 (Lord Ackner).

[17] *Ibid.*, and see also 722 (Lord Donaldson).

[18] *Associated Provincial Picture Houses Ltd* v. *Wednesbury Corporation* [1948] 1 KB 223, 234.

[19] I. Leigh, 'The standard of judicial review after the Human Rights Act' in H. Fenwick, G. Phillipson and R. Masterman, *Judicial Reasoning under the UK Human Rights Act* (Cambridge University Press, 2007), pp.198–200.

[20] See e.g.: *R* v. *Secretary of State for the Home Department, ex parte Bugdaycay* [1987] AC 514, 531 (Lord Bridge of Harwich).

[21] *R* v. *Ministry of Defence, ex parte Smith* [1996] QB 517, 554–6 (Sir Thomas Bingham MR).

with executive discretion.[22] Judicial review of executive action therefore remained a largely procedural guarantee, and – prior to the implementation of the HRA – to invite the judges to assess the proportionality of administrative decisions, it was argued, would invite them to cross 'the constitutional Rubicon into merits review'.[23]

The standard of review and requirement of proportionate interference

In the seminal decision of *Associated Provincial Picture Houses* v. *Wednesbury Corporation*, Lord Greene MR stated that a court would be able to intervene in the exercise of executive discretion when the decision taken was 'so unreasonable that no reasonable authority could have come to it'.[24] Since the *Wednesbury* decision, a number of attempts had been made to restate the threshold at which substantive unreasonableness would permit judicial intervention. The most famous of these re-formulations is, of course, that provided in the *GCHQ* decision, where Lord Diplock stated that the court would be able to intervene on grounds of unreasonableness when the decision taken was:

> so outrageous in its defiance of logic or of accepted moral standards that no sensible person who had applied his mind to the question to be decided could have arrived at it.[25]

The *Wednesbury* standard was certainly not monolithic.[26] For instance, in decisions involving the allocation of public finance, statements of *Wednesbury* unreasonableness had arguably become pitched at a (virtually unreachable) level of manifest absurdity, reflecting the judges' traditional hesitancy to unsettle decisions seen as falling squarely within

---

[22] Although Jowell has pointed to examples of the courts having adopted more vague 'proportionality' requirements which 'ask ... abstractly whether "a steamhammer has been used to crack a nut", or whether the "punishment fits the crime"' (J. Jowell, 'Beyond the rule of law: towards constitutional judicial review' [2000] PL 671, 679). For examples of domestic courts engaging with proportionality, see: *R* v. *Burnley Metropolitan Borough Council, ex parte Hook* [1976] 1 WLR 1052; *R* v. *Secretary of State for Transport, ex parte Pegasus Holdings (London) Ltd* [1988] 1 WLR 990.

[23] Leigh and Masterman, *Making Rights Real*, above n. 13, p.295.

[24] *Associated Provincial Picture Houses Ltd* v. *Wednesbury Corporation*, above n. 18, 230.

[25] *Council for Civil Service Unions* v. *Minister for the Civil Service*, above n. 14, 408 (Lord Diplock).

[26] For discussion, see: Sir J. Laws, '*Wednesbury*' in C. Forsyth and I. Hare, *The Golden Metwand and the Crooked Cord: Essays on Public Law in Honour of Sir William Wade QC* (Oxford: Clarendon Press, 1998).

the competence of the elected branches. As Lord Scarman suggested in
R v. *Secretary of State for the Environment, ex parte Nottingham County
Council*, the court might overturn an administrative decision only where
that decision was 'so absurd' that the decision maker 'must have taken leave
of his senses'.[27] Lord Bridge – in *R* v. *Secretary of State for the Environment,
ex parte Hammersmith and Fulham London Borough Council* – echoed
the sentiment that public body decision making should not be interfered
with in cases of resource allocation 'short of the extremes of bad faith,
improper motive or manifest absurdity'.[28]

In cases engaging individual rights, however, it is certainly arguable
that the courts had sought to apply a more rigorous standard of review.[29]
In *Bugdaycay*, Lord Bridge had argued that in cases where individuals'
rights were at stake, the 'basis of the decision must surely call for the most
anxious scrutiny'.[30] While, in *ex parte Smith*, Sir Thomas Bingham MR
endorsed an approach to the test of unreasonableness that would require
more strict scrutiny of the official explanation put forward for the decision in question:

> The more substantial the interference with human rights, the more the
> court will require by way of justification before it is satisfied that the deci-
> sion is reasonable.[31]

As *Smith* itself illustrated, however, in a dispute engaging questions
of rights and questions of policy over which the elected branches could
claim a mandate (however questionable) even the most 'anxious scrutiny'
might not actually furnish the courts with the ability to provide a remedy
in the individual case. As a result, the feeling remained widely held that
Wednesbury review remained 'one of the weakest forms of judicial review
known to the common law'.[32]

---

[27] *R* v. *Secretary of State for the Environment, ex parte Nottinghamshire County Council*
[1986] AC 240, 247 (Lord Scarman).

[28] *R* v. *Secretary of State for the Environment, ex parte Hammersmith and Fulham London
Borough Council* [1991] 1 AC 521, 597 (Lord Bridge).

[29] For a survey, see: Lord Browne-Wilkinson, 'The infiltration of a bill of rights' [1992] PL
397.

[30] *R* v. *Secretary of State for the Home Department, ex parte Bugdaycay*, above n. 20, 531
(Lord Bridge of Harwich).

[31] *R* v. *Ministry of Defence, ex parte Smith*, above n. 21, 554 (Sir Thomas Bingham MR, quot-
ing from the submissions of David Pannick, counsel for the applicants).

[32] B. Goold, L. Lazarus and G. Swiney, *Public Protection, Proportionality and the Search for
Balance* (Ministry of Justice Research Series 10/07), September 2007, p.9, n.8.

The inadequacy of Wednesbury *review*

While the Convention bodies do not *require* member states to amend domestic laws to allow citizens to directly assert the Convention rights in domestic courts[33] – for the reason that member states are permitted to give effect to the Convention's requirements 'in accordance with the rules of [their] national legal system'[34] – whatever remedial structures are in operation should meet the requirements of Article 13. For the Strasbourg institutions, an effective remedy for the purposes of Article 13 must allow the domestic court to consider the substance of the Convention arguments put forward, and must also be competent to make an appropriate award in the event of the finding of a breach.[35] The European Court of Human Rights, in a series of cases brought against the UK, had held that judicial review fulfilled the requirements of Article 13, as scope for raising Convention arguments could be found within the existing head of irrationality.[36] These findings had, however, come in for a degree of criticism. Murray Hunt, for one, argued that in finding that *Wednesbury* unreasonableness provided an effective remedy, the European Court of Human Rights was too ready to concede that the ability to raise an argument was to be equated with the actual detailed consideration of its substance.[37] In fact, Hunt considered the inability to consider the substance of Convention-based arguments at the domestic level was only one of a number of grounds on which *Wednesbury* review could have been argued to fail to satisfy the Convention requirement of an effective remedy. Writing in research published in 1997, Hunt argued:

> it is no surprise that the greatest controversy has arisen over whether the present law of judicial review satisfies even the minimal requirements of Article 13 … The judicial insistence on preserving the supposed distinction between the 'manner' in which a decision is made and 'the merits'; the preservation of the high threshold *Wednesbury* test for irrationality challenges; and the refusal, so far, to give practical effect to the concept of proportionality as part of English law, or even, in the case of some judges, to

---

[33] *Ireland* v. *United Kingdom* (1979–80) 2 EHRR 25, para.239.

[34] D. J. Harris, M. O'Boyle, E. P. Bates and C. M. Buckley, *Law of the European Convention on Human Rights* (2nd edn) (Oxford University Press, 2009), p.26.

[35] *Silver* v. *United Kingdom* (1983) 5 EHRR 347, para.113.

[36] *Soering* v. *United Kingdom* (1989) 11 EHRR 439; *Vilvarajah* v. *United Kingdom* (1991) 14 EHRR 248, paras.125–6.

[37] M. Hunt, *Using Human Rights Law in English Courts* (Oxford: Hart Publishing, 1997), p.317.

countenance the possibility, are all potential obstacles to the effectiveness
of judicial review as a remedy for the purposes of Article 13.[38]

However, in the European Court of Human Rights decision in *Smith and
Grady* v. *United Kingdom*, the Court held that the blanket prohibition on
homosexuals serving as members of the armed forces was an infringement of Articles 8 and 13 of the Convention.[39] As to the latter, the Court
noted that even the 'anxious scrutiny' approach to *Wednesbury* unreasonableness fell short of the Convention requirement to provide an effective remedy, for the reason that the threshold at which the policy could be
found to have been irrational was so high that:

> it effectively excluded any consideration by the domestic courts of the
> question of whether the interference with the applicants' rights answered
> a pressing social need or was proportionate to the national security and
> public order aims pursued, principles which lie at the heart of the Court's
> analysis of complaints under Article 8 of the Convention.[40]

In other words, the structure of *Wednesbury* review prevented the court
from engaging in any meaningful way with the requirements of the
Convention that legitimate restrictions on the Convention rights be justified for reason of being in pursuance of a specified and legitimate aim and
necessary in a democratic society. At the heart of this justification analysis in the jurisprudence of the Strasbourg institutions lies the principle
of proportionality.

Proportionate interference

In respect of those Articles of the Convention which are qualified – in
other words, which can be restricted in the interests of a 'democratic
society' – the requirement of proportionate interference is most obvious.
As the European Court of Human Rights noted in the *Handyside* decision, '[e]very "formality", "condition", "restriction" or "penalty" imposed
[restricting the enjoyment of a Convention right] must be proportionate
to the legitimate aim pursued'.[41] Proportionality, however, should not be

---

[38] *Ibid.*, pp.315–16.
[39] *Smith and Grady* v. *United Kingdom* (2000) 29 EHRR 493.
[40] *Ibid.*, para.138. See also: *HL* v. *United Kingdom* (2005) 40 EHRR 32, para.139: 'pre-incor-
poration judicial review of necessity in accordance with "the super-*Wednesbury*" criteria
was not sufficiently intrusive to constitute an adequate examination of the merits of the
relevant … decisions'.
[41] *Handyside* v. *United Kingdom* (1979–80) 1 EHRR 737, para.49.

thought of solely as a component of the rights to privacy, expression, association, and so on. As the European Court of Human Rights observed in the case of *Soering* v. *United Kingdom*:

> inherent in the whole of the Convention is a search for a fair balance between the demands of the general interest of the community and the requirements of the protection of the individual's fundamental rights.[42]

At a very basic level of analysis, to require courts to assess whether the balance between the individual and public interest is proportionate to the aims pursued – to determine where the dividing line should be struck between potentially equally meritorious claims – is to ask them to do the very thing that critics of bills of rights claim that courts are ill-suited to doing.[43] It is argued here, however, that proportionality analysis also arguably provides courts with the necessary framework for analysis which ensures that such a 'balancing act' is not simply reduced to an *ad hoc* exercise in which individual judicial preference is equally as important a consideration as the degree of intrusion and the reasons articulated to justify the restriction.[44]

The specific requirements of the Convention giving rise to its requirement of proportionality can be found most obviously in the text of Articles 8–11 and Article 1 of Protocol No. 1. Article 10(2), for instance, provides that the Convention right to freedom of expression:

> may be subject to such formalities, conditions, restrictions or penalties as are prescribed by law and are necessary in a democratic society, in the interests of national security, territorial integrity or public safety, for the prevention of disorder or crime, for the protection of health or morals, for the protection of the reputation or rights of others, for preventing the disclosure of information received in confidence, or for maintaining the authority and impartiality of the judiciary.

Hence, to justifiably restrict freedom of speech within the bounds of the Convention, the limitation must be prescribed by law, in pursuance of a legitimate aim, and necessary in a democratic society. As to the latter of these tests – that a measure be 'necessary in a democratic society' – the European Court of Human Rights has offered some assistance in defining the meaning of this nebulous phrase, ruling out the 'flexibility of such expressions as "admissible", "ordinary", "useful", "reasonable"

---

[42] *Soering* v. *United Kingdom*, above n. 36, para.89. See also: *Gaskin* v. *United Kingdom* (1989) 12 EHRR 36, para.42.

[43] See above pp.34–42. [44] See pp.139–42.

or "desirable"' and noting that it implied the existence – rather circuitously – of a 'pressing social need'.[45] As Lord Steyn noted in *Daly*, the increased intensity of review is therefore 'guaranteed by the twin requirements that the limitation of the right was necessary in a democratic society, in the sense of meeting a pressing social need, and the question whether the interference was really proportionate to the legitimate aim being pursued'.[46] Or, as the European Court of Human Rights has put it, '[t]here must be a reasonable relationship of proportionality between the means employed and the aim pursued'.[47]

The requirement of proportionality also places an evidential burden on the state – to demonstrate an attempt to find a balance between the interests of society and the individual right at issue – and falls under the general requirement that the rights under the Convention be 'practical and effective' rather than 'theoretical and illusory':[48]

> A limitation upon a right, or steps taken positively to protect or fulfil it, will not be proportionate, even allowing for a margin of appreciation, where there is no evidence that the state institutions have balanced the competing individual and public interests when deciding on the limitations or steps, or where the requirements to be met to avoid or benefit from its application in a particular case are so high as not to permit a meaningful balancing process.[49]

The first of those requirements represents a marked departure from the *Wednesbury* standard of review. To legitimate the restriction of a Convention right, a decision maker will have to display evidence of having considered alternative responses, and undertaken an assessment of the relative impact of each of those proposed alternatives. The onus of proof therefore falls on the decision maker to justify the measures taken, with the result that public authority decision makers will 'no longer be able to hide behind the *Wednesbury* shield'.[50] As Hale LJ – as she then was – noted, in the context of HRA review, even 'super-*Wednesbury* is not enough'.[51]

---

45 *Handyside* v. *United Kingdom*, above n. 41, para.48.
46 *R (on the application of Daly)* v. *Secretary of State for the Home Department* [2001] 2 AC 532; [2001] 3 All ER 433, para.27.
47 *Immobiliare Saffi* v. *Italy* (2000) 30 EHRR 756, para.49.
48 *Artico* v. *Italy* (1981) 3 EHRR 1, para.33.
49 Harris, O'Boyle, Bates and Buckley, *Law of the European Convention on Human Rights*, above n. 34, p.11
50 Jowell, 'Beyond the rule of law' above n. 22, 681.
51 *R (on the application of Wikinson)* v. *Broadmoor Hospital* [2001] EWCA Civ 1515; [2002] 1 WLR 419, para.83 (Hale LJ).

Given that the Convention itself makes no explicit reference to the requirement that legitimate interferences with the Convention rights be subject to a requirement of proportionality, it is striking that the test of proportionality has been held to have such a pervasive influence over the construction of the Convention as a whole. Tom Hickman has rightly observed that one consequence of this is that the implementation of the Convention rights via the HRA does not of itself *compel* domestic courts to adopt and apply principles of proportionality.[52] However, given that domestic courts are obligated by s.2(1) to 'take into account' the Strasbourg jurisprudence, which in broad terms places proportionality at the heart of the processes of interpreting the Convention,[53] then some transplantation of the requirement of proportionate interference into domestic law was unavoidable. The difficulty arising out of this, however, is that the approach of the European Court of Human Rights to assessing the proportionality of measures has been argued to be unpredictable and manifestly lacking 'a consistent or uniform set of principles' to be applied.[54]

The obvious consequences of this for the standard of review applied by the Strasbourg court are compounded where the margin of appreciation is in play. In those cases where the margin of appreciation has been invoked, as Fenwick and Phillipson have written in the context of direct action protest, the standard of review adopted by the Court is reminiscent of the least rigorous *Wednesbury* standard:

> Review of the 'necessity' of State interferences is not intensive, at times appearing to be confined to ensuring actions were taken in good faith and were not manifestly unreasonable ... States are typically not required to demonstrate that lesser measures than those actually taken would have been inadequate to deal with the threats posed ... the effect of this 'light touch' review may also be seen in the tendency to deal with crucial issues – typically proportionality, but also in some cases the scope of the primary right – in such a brusque and abbreviated manner that explication of the findings is either non-existent or takes the form of mere assertion.[55]

---

[52] T. Hickman, 'The substance and structure of proportionality' [2008] PL 194, 194.

[53] *Soering* v. *United Kingdom* above n. 36, para.89; *Gaskin* v. *United Kingdom*, above n. 42, para.42.

[54] See e.g.: *R* v. *Shayler* [2002] UKHL 11; [2003] AC 247, para.60 (Lord Hope); R. Clayton, 'Regaining a sense of proportion: the Human Rights Act and the proportionality principle' [2001] EHRLR 504, 510–12.

[55] H. Fenwick and G. Phillipson 'Direct action, Convention values and the Human Rights Act' (2001) 21 LS 535, 553–4.

Arguably, then, the mere adoption of a test of proportionality would not compel the application of a more intensive standard of review across all areas of public law – so long as domestic courts did not slip below the minimum standard as required by the Convention jurisprudence – and the potential for a variable standard of review, reflecting the policy discretion of public bodies, would be preserved.[56]

The Strasbourg jurisprudence on separated governmental functions

In the view of the Strasbourg institutions, the requirements that member states 'secure to everyone within their jurisdictions the rights and freedoms'[57] defined in the Convention are directed towards the national authorities of the member states. For the purposes of the European Court of Human Rights, the obligations imposed by the Convention need not therefore be discharged – for the most part – by any particular one of the three branches of government. As Baroness Hale has observed, where, for example, the Strasbourg institutions find that a certain decision would fall within the margin of appreciation afforded to member states, the judgment of how to strike the balance between the individual right and the public interest 'must be one for the national authorities'.[58] However, Strasbourg does not – as a general rule – dictate which specific branch of government, if any, should be responsible. While the Court indicates that 'national authorities' possess a discretion over where the balance should lie:

> that does not answer the question of whether the judgment should be made by the courts or by the legislature. Strasbourg is no help with this; it is concerned only with the end product, not who made it.[59]

What is clear, however, is that while Strasbourg's direction to national authorities does not generally stipulate which arm of government should be responsible for specific activity in this sense, nor does it exempt any particular arm of government from shouldering the burden of realising the Convention rights. Prior to the coming into force of the HRA, Murray Hunt drew a parallel with the position of domestic courts in the European Union context, arguing that:

---

[56] T. Poole, 'The reformation of English administrative law' (2009) 68 CLJ 142, 146.
[57] Article 1 ECHR.
[58] *In Re P (Adoption: Unmarried Couples)* [2008] UKHL 38; [2009] 1 AC 173, para.118.
[59] *Ibid.*, para.119.

it was recognised by the ECJ [in *Von Colson*[60]] that courts are 'national authorities' for the purposes of the relevant Treaty Articles, and therefore share responsibility with the political branches for ensuring that Community obligations are carried out. Under the ECHR, not only are courts required under Article 13 to ensure that effective remedies are available for violations of Convention rights, but they are also public authorities for the purpose of all the other rights in the Convention, and are equally as capable of infringing those rights as are the political branches. As the *Sunday Times*[61] litigation demonstrates, court judgments engage a state's liability under the Convention, in the sense that a judicial interpretation of the common law may infringe the rights protected under the Convention.[62]

For the purposes of the Convention organs, it is therefore not only on the executive or legislative branches that the burden of securing the Convention standards falls; as Judge Martens, formerly of the European Court of Human Rights, has observed, the role of the domestic judiciary under the Convention system runs in parallel with that of the domestic executive and legislature for the reason that 'the ECHR's injunction to further realise human rights and fundamental freedoms contained in the preamble is also addressed to domestic courts'.[63]

However, as far as the Strasbourg organs are concerned, a wide margin of appreciation will be afforded to those decisions of national authorities which involve the 'consideration of political, economic and social issues on which opinions in a democratic society may reasonably differ widely'.[64] In the consideration of such decisions, particularly those concerning 'social and economic policies', the European Court of Human Rights:

> will respect the legislature's judgment as to what is 'in the public interest' unless that judgment be manifestly without reasonable foundation. In other words, although the court cannot substitute its own assessment

---

[60] 14/83, *Von Colson and Kamann* v. *Land Nordrhein Westfalen* [1984] ECR 1891.

[61] *Sunday Times* v. *United Kingdom* (1979–80) 2 EHRR 245.

[62] Hunt, *Using Human Rights Law in English Courts*, above n. 37, p.319.

[63] Judge S. K. Martens, 'Incorporating the European Convention: the role of the judiciary' [1998] EHRLR 5, 14.

[64] *James* v. *UK* (1986) 8 EHRR 123, para.43. See also: *Hatton* v. *United Kingdom* (2003) 37 EHRR 611, para.97:

> the court reiterates the fundamentally subsidiary nature of the Convention. The national authorities have direct democratic legitimation and are, as the court has held on many occasions, in principle better placed than an international court to evaluate local needs and conditions. In matters of general policy, on which opinions within a democratic society may reasonably differ widely, the role of the domestic policy maker should be given a special weight.

for that of national authorities, it is bound to review the contested measures ... and, in so doing, to make an inquiry into the facts with reference to which the national authorities acted.[65]

Two points are made clear by this statement. First, in social policy decisions taken by national authorities with implications for the allocation of public funds, the Strasbourg court will be hesitant to intervene, and the test for proportionality may be reduced to one of 'manifest unreasonableness'. Second, however, that in respect of social policy decisions – while a wide margin of appreciation *may* be afforded[66] – the 'political' nature of the decision itself will not amount to a ground on which to defer completely to the judgment of national authorities. While the margin of appreciation may require the application of a lower intensity of review, the Court nevertheless retains the ability to find a state in breach of the Convention. The extent to which national authorities make public funds available to enable the individual to enjoy a Convention right, for example, is a matter for political, rather than judicial, institutions.[67] However, the determination of whether the Convention standards themselves have been breached is a matter, ultimately, for the Court.[68]

The justification for the European Court of Human Rights affording member states a wide margin of appreciation in respect of such decisions is, of course, founded on the basis of a national legislature's 'direct and continuous contact with the vital forces of their countries'.[69] While it may be appropriate for the European Court of Human Rights to rely on their relative remoteness from national political and legal systems as a justification for non-intensive intervention, it would rarely – if ever – be appropriate for a domestic authority to invoke similar grounds for institutional restraint. Accordingly, in recognition of the status of the margin of appreciation as an international standard unsuitable for direct application by a domestic court, Lord Hope noted in *Kebilene* that it should

[65] *Ibid*. See also: *Immobiliare Saffi* v. *Italy*, above n. 47, para.49; *JA Pye (Oxford) Ltd* v. *United Kingdom* (2008) 46 EHRR 45, para.75.
[66] See e.g.: *Marzari* v. *Italy* (1999) EHRR CD175; *Penticova* v. *Moldova* (2005) 40 EHRR SE23.
[67] See e.g.: *Chapman* v. *United Kingdom* (2001) 33 EHRR 18, para.99, where the Court noted, in the context of Article 8, 'whether the state provides funds to enable everyone to have a home is a matter for political not judicial decision'.
[68] *Ibid*., para.100. See also: *Handyside* v. *United Kingdom*, above n. 41, para.49; *Bladet Tromsø and Stensaas* v. *Norway* (2000) 29 EHRR 125, para.79; *VgT Verein gegen Tierfabriken* v. *Switzerland* (2002) 34 EHRR 4, para.67.
[69] *Handyside* v. *United Kingdom*, above n. 41, para.48.

not be open to national courts to afford a margin of appreciation in the domestic context.[70]

However, the text of the Convention itself also reveals some quite specific indications that certain functions be discharged by particular branches of government. In the first instance it is clear, for example, that the Convention envisages that courts be competent to determine the extent of an individual's 'civil rights and obligations' and of any 'criminal charge' levelled against the individual by the state.[71] Similarly, under the provisions of Article 5(1)(a) of the Convention, detention of an individual may be rendered lawful 'after conviction by a competent court'. Detentions effected by officers of the state – under Article 5(1)(c) – of those who are, *inter alia*, under a 'reasonable suspicion of having committed an offence', are only lawful if the individual is 'brought promptly before a judge or other officer authorised by law to exercise judicial power'.[72] And under the same Article, the following guarantee is provided to all of those who have suffered a deprivation of liberty at the hands of the state:

> Everyone who is deprived of his liberty by arrest or detention shall be entitled to take proceedings by which the lawfulness of his detention shall be decided speedily by a court and his release ordered if the detention is not lawful.[73]

The Convention further indicates that those bodies exercising judicial functions of the type indicated above – courts and tribunals – should possess a number of quite specific institutional characteristics, the most obvious of these being their 'independence and impartiality'.[74]

---

[70] R v. *Director of Public Prosecutions, ex parte Kebilene* [2000] 2 AC 326, 380–1. However, the extent to which domestic courts have sought to disentangle the margin of appreciation from Strasbourg decisions when giving effect to them in the domestic context is open to question. As Fenwick and Phillipson have noted:
> In numerous appellate decisions under the HRA, the courts have paid lip service to the notion that the margin of appreciation has no role to play in domestic decision-making. In nearly every case … the courts have then gone on to apply Strasbourg case law heavily determined by that doctrine, thus precisely applying the margin of appreciation.
(H. Fenwick and G. Phillipson, *Media Freedom under the Human Rights Act* (Oxford University Press, 2006), p.146.)

[71] Article 6(1) ECHR.

[72] Article 5(3) ECHR.

[73] Article 5(4) ECHR.

[74] The relevant text of Article 6(1) ECHR reads:
> In the determination of his civil rights and obligations or of any criminal charge against him, everyone is entitled to a fair and public hearing within a reasonable time by an independent and impartial tribunal established by law.
See below pp.79–84.

Two specific areas of governmental decision making involving an arguable overlap of executive and judicial responsibility have come under particular scrutiny at the Strasbourg level: namely, the extent to which members of the executive branch might be involved in criminal sentencing, and the question of whether a right of judicial review in respect of certain administrative decisions might be available as of right.

Executive involvement in 'judicial' decisions – sentencing

One area in which the Strasbourg jurisprudence has had an evident effect on the exercise of governmental functions in domestic law concerns the involvement of the executive in sentencing decisions. A series of cases at Strasbourg – concerning the role of the Home Secretary in the sentencing of adult and juvenile offenders convicted of murder – demonstrated both that the Convention is indeed a 'living instrument',[75] and that the Court has increasingly come to regard the separation of executive and judicial roles in respect of certain governmental decisions as being integral to the Convention.

Following the Murder (Abolition of Death Penalty) Act 1969, the only sentence a court may impose on a convicted murderer is a mandatory life sentence. While the sentence itself was imposed by a court under the Act, the actual length of time a convicted murderer might spend in prison was effectively determined by a politician: the Home Secretary. The Home Secretary effectively determined the minimum period of the life sentence that would be served before the prisoner became eligible for release, otherwise known as the tariff. While the trial judge and Lord Chief Justice both made recommendations to the Home Secretary on the tariff to be served in individual cases, the minister was free to depart from those recommendations. Indeed, it was not unusual for the minister to depart from the judicial recommendation and set a lengthier tariff.[76] Beyond this, once the prisoner became eligible for release, the Home Secretary held the power to set the release date, on the recommendation of the Parole Board.[77] This questionable executive involvement in individual proceedings was the subject of a number of challenges in domestic courts, and at

---

[75] *Tyrer* v. *United Kingdom* (1979–80) 2 EHRR 1, para.31.

[76] S. Shute, 'Punishing murderers: release procedures and the "tariff", 1953–2004' [2004] Crim LR 873, 885.

[77] For a summary, see: A. Ashworth, *Sentencing and Criminal Justice* (4th edn) (Cambridge University Press, 2005), pp.116–18.

the European Court of Human Rights. It is the approach of the latter that is of relevance here.[78]

In *Wynne* v. *United Kingdom*,[79] the European Court of Human Rights found no objection to the role played by the Home Secretary in determining the minimum tariff to be served by mandatory life prisoners convicted of murder. In the case of mandatory life sentences, the Court held, the requirements of Article 5(4) were satisfied by the judicial processes of the original trial procedure,[80] and that 'the release of the prisoner is entirely a matter within the discretion of the Secretary of State who is not bound by the judicial recommendation as to the length of the tariff period'.[81] As a result, the European Court of Human Rights appeared to be able to tolerate a degree of executive involvement in individual sentencing decisions.

However, in *V and T* v. *United Kingdom*,[82] the Court began to move towards a more clear separation of executive and judicial functions on the basis of Article 6(1). *V and T* was a case brought by the convicted killers of the child Jamie Bulger who contended that, *inter alia*, the involvement of the Home Secretary in determining the length of time that they would be detained at Her Majesty's pleasure amounted to an infringement of their right to a fair trial.[83] As with adult prisoners, the Home Secretary had the ability – under s.43(2) of the Criminal Justice Act 1991 – to set the tariff to be served by juvenile killers detained at Her Majesty's pleasure. The circumstances of the case had already given rise to judicial review proceedings in domestic courts, in which the House of Lords held that, having taken into account and placed reliance on the public clamour for a lengthy sentence, the Home Secretary had misdirected himself in the exercise of his power, and as a result, had acted *ultra vires*.[84] For present purposes, it is the Court's findings in respect of the alleged violation of Article 6(1) – the right to a fair trial – that are germane.

In respect of Article 6(1), the applicants contended that the ability of the Home Secretary to set the tariff was akin to a sentencing function that – as a part of the trial process – should attract the protection of Article 6(1)

---

[78] Although see pp.229–31.

[79] *Wynne* v. *United Kingdom*, above n. 11.

[80] *Ibid.*, para.36.   [81] *Ibid.*, para.35.

[82] *V and T* v. *United Kingdom* (2000) 30 EHRR 121.

[83] Arguments were also raised by the applicants that the trial process itself violated Articles 3 and 6 of the Convention, and Article 6 read with Article 12, and that the sentence imposed violated Article 3.

[84] See *R* v. *Secretary of State for the Home Department, ex parte Venables and Thompson* [1998] AC 407. See pp.229–30.

of the Convention and therefore should be carried out by an independent and impartial tribunal. The Court agreed, and accordingly held that Article 6(1) was applicable to the setting of the tariff.[85] It followed that, as the Home Secretary quite clearly could not be regarded as being independent of the executive, the Court found that there had been a breach of Article 6(1).[86]

While in *V and T* the Court attempted to distinguish between cases involving juvenile and adult offenders, 'it was only a matter of time before this fragile distinction collapsed'.[87] *Stafford* v. *United Kingdom*[88] effectively extended the findings of the Court in *V and T* to cases involving adult offenders. Noting the developments in this area at both the domestic and Strasbourg levels, the European Court of Human Rights was able to point to the 'growing perception that the tariff-fixing function was closely analogous to a sentencing function'[89] and to the 'steady erosion of the scope of the Secretary of State's decision-making power in this field'.[90] As a result, the Court found that tariff fixing was indeed a 'sentencing exercise'[91] and therefore more appropriately carried out by a competent court, rather than an elected politician. While at first glance the decision of the European Court of Human Rights was a case of fair process, and the right to a sentencing procedure carried out by an independent and impartial body, the decision in *Stafford* also possesses another aspect. It is also a case about constitutional principle. The Court was at pains not only to stress that the sentencing powers of the Home Secretary had infringed the applicant's right to a fair trial, but also to suggest that 'the continuing role of the Secretary of State in fixing the tariff and in deciding on a prisoner's release following its expiry has become increasingly difficult to reconcile with the notion of separation of powers between the executive and the judiciary'.[92]

Judicial review of 'administrative' decisions

Article 6(1) of the Convention requires that 'in the determination of his civil rights and obligations or of any criminal charge against him, everyone is entitled to a fair and public hearing' by an independent and

---

[85] *V and T* v. *United Kingdom*, above n. 82, para.111.
[86] *Ibid.*, para.114.
[87] Ashworth, *Sentencing and Criminal Justice*, above n. 77, p.116.
[88] *Stafford* v. *United Kingdom*, above n. 4.
[89] *Ibid.*, para.72.   [90] *Ibid.*, para.71.
[91] *Ibid.*, para.79.   [92] *Ibid.*, para.78.

impartial tribunal. While the meanings of 'criminal charge' and 'civil rights and obligations' are the source of a wide-ranging jurisprudence at the Strasbourg level,[93] one issue of particular import for the separation of executive and judicial functions at the domestic level is how far Strasbourg requires access to an independent and impartial tribunal in respect of the judicial review of administrative decisions taken by a member, or members, of the executive. Would the influence of Article 6 require domestic administrative structures based on efficiency and expediency to be reconfigured to provide more substantive due process rights across administrative decision making?[94]

The position of the Strasbourg court is that, in respect of administrative decisions that are 'directly decisive' of civil rights and obligations as construed by the Court, Article 6 will apply. The specific requirements of the Article will, however, depend on the circumstances of the case. At the most straightforward level, Article 6 requires that:

> there must be the possibility of judicial review, or in some cases an appeal on the merits, of administrative decisions that are directly decisive for civil rights and obligations by a body that complies with Article 6.[95]

While the Strasbourg court had recognised that the 'demands of flexibility and efficiency'[96] which were characteristic of administrative decisions meant that the entire administrative process need not be Article 6 compliant, defects in administrative processes that were determinative of rights and obligations could be remedied on appeal to a court of full jurisdiction.[97] It is for this reason that the Strasbourg case law – prior to the coming into operation of the HRA – had already made itself felt in English administrative law; judicial review had already been held to amount to an inadequate remedy, for the reason that it precluded review of the initial administrative process on the merits.[98]

More difficult, however, are questions relating to the exercise of what the European Court of Human Rights has referred to as 'the classic exercise of administrative discretion'.[99] As Harris *et al.* have commented:

---

[93] For a survey, see: Harris, O'Boyle, Bates and Buckley, *Law of the European Convention on Human Rights*, above n. 34, pp.204–23.

[94] For a general introduction, see: A. Boyle, 'Administrative justice, judicial review and the right to a fair hearing under the European Convention on Human Rights' [1984] PL 89.

[95] *Le Compte, Van Leuven and De Meyere* v. *Belgium* (1981) 4 EHRR 1, para.51.

[96] *Ibid.*

[97] *Albert and Le Compte* v. *Belgium* (1983) 5 EHRR 533, para.29.

[98] *W* v. *United Kingdom* (1988) 10 EHRR 29, paras.82–3.

[99] *Kingsley* v. *United Kingdom* (2001) 33 EHRR 13, para.53.

> In such cases, there may be policy considerations that suggest that the final decision on the merits should rest with the executive rather than the court, despite the impact on a person's 'civil rights and obligations' that the decision may have.[100]

In other words, the European Court of Human Rights has recognised that in some circumstances in which the requirements of Article 6 would otherwise require the determination of an issue by a judicial body, the political content of a particular decision may require that the executive has the final say over that decision in the domestic context.[101] In such cases, review of the legality of the decision is adequate, so long as the administrative procedure itself has accorded with the requirements of Article 6.[102]

The separation of powers implications of this line of cases are twofold. First, they raise the suggestion of Article 6 extending the reach of the common law in requiring procedurally fair decision-making processes in questions engaging the Convention rights. Second, the cases also show that, within the framework of Article 6, allowance may still be made for the superior knowledge or expertise of the executive branch in determining questions with policy implications: the 'classic exercise of administrative discretion' – so long as notionally Article 6 compliant – need not be subjected to judicial override.

The Strasbourg jurisprudence on separated institutions

As has been noted, the Strasbourg court has consistently argued that protection of the Convention rights requires adherence to no particular theoretical constitutional structure or design. A separation of governmental institutions is not, therefore, a *general* requirement of the Convention itself, nor any of its individual provisions. However, Article 6 of the Convention does require that, in the determination of their civil rights and obligations, or of a criminal charge, an individual is entitled to a fair trial conducted by a court that is both independent of the executive and parties to the case,[103] and impartial, in both an objective and subjective sense.[104] So while separation of powers as a general principle appears not to be required of member

---

[100] Harris, O'Boyle, Bates and Buckley, *Law of the European Convention on Human Rights*, above n. 34, p.230.

[101] As Harris *et al.* have also commented, the recognition of this area of executive discretion dilutes the effects of Article 6 in certain public law decisions (*ibid.*, p.232).

[102] *Bryan* v. *United Kingdom* (1995) 21 EHRR 342, para.47.

[103] *Ringeisen* v. *Austria* (1979–80) 1 EHRR 455, para.95.

[104] *Sigurdsson* v. *Iceland* (2005) 40 EHRR 15, para.37.

states by the Convention, Article 6 provides a very clear indication that an independent and impartial judicial branch should be regarded as an essential component of a democratic state under the Convention.

An independent and impartial tribunal

In the jurisprudence of the Strasbourg court, the standards of independence and impartiality are closely linked;[105] accordingly, there is a degree of interchange between the language used to describe the tests. In *Findlay v. United Kingdom*, the European Court of Human Rights outlined the requirements of independence and impartiality in the following terms:

> In order to establish whether a tribunal can be considered as 'independent', regard must be had inter alia to the manner of appointment of its members and their term of office, the existence of guarantees against outside pressures and the question whether the body presents an appearance of independence.
>
> As to the question of 'impartiality', there are two aspects to this requirement. First, the tribunal must be subjectively free of personal prejudice or bias. Secondly, it must also be impartial from an objective viewpoint, that is, it must offer sufficient guarantees to exclude any legitimate doubt in this respect.[106]

In determining 'independence', regard must be had 'to the manner of appointment of [the court's] members and their term of office, the existence of safeguards against outside pressures and the question whether it presents an appearance of independence'.[107] What can be said with some certainty is that Article 6(1) requires not only that the court or tribunal be independent of the parties to the case, but also of the executive.[108] On its face, this would suggest that the contemporaneous holding of executive and judicial office would automatically be in breach of Article 6(1):

> in practice, however, the Convention organs have been reluctant to conclude that a court coming under their supervision lacks independence. Such a finding would cast doubt on the contracting state's adherence to the rule of law and the common political traditions which underline co-operation with the Council of Europe.[109]

---

[105] *Findlay* v. *United Kingdom* (1997) 24 EHRR 221, para.73.
[106] *Ibid.*   [107] *Ibid.*
[108] See e.g.: *Ringeisen* v. *Austria*, above n. 103, para.95; *De Wilde, Ooms and Versyp* v. *Belgium (No. 1)* (1979–80) 1 EHRR 373, para.78.
[109] S. Grosz, J. Beatson, and P. Duffy, *Human Rights: The 1998 Act and the European Convention* (London: Sweet and Maxwell, 2000), pp.240–1.

As to the requirement that a court or tribunal be impartial, the European Court of Human Rights has interpreted this as requiring both a subjective and an objective element:

> First, the tribunal must be subjectively free of personal prejudice or bias. Secondly, it must also be impartial from an objective viewpoint, that is, it must offer sufficient guarantees to exclude any legitimate doubt in this respect. Under the objective test, it must be determined whether, quite apart from the judge's personal conduct, there are ascertainable facts which may raise doubts as to their impartiality. In this respect even appearances may be of a certain importance.[110]

The Strasbourg jurisprudence on the compatibility of holding both judicial and legislative office with the fair trial guarantees in Article 6(1) of the Convention displays two strands of reasoning. The first – and most common – is that the ability to exercise judicial and legislative power will not of itself amount to a breach of Article 6(1). This strand requires that there be a degree of proximity between the roles played in each sphere before it can be said that a legitimate doubt as to the impartiality of a court will have been established. The second strand of jurisprudence, however, seems to suggest that a strict separation of judicial and legislative function is required, and appears to allow no scope for argument over the relationship between the holding of two offices in a given set of circumstances. As a result, the dual exercise of judicial and legislative power will of itself amount to a breach of Article 6(1) by creating the legitimate doubt as to the court's impartiality.

The circumstantial approach to impartiality

Evidence of what might be called the circumstantial approach can be found in the decision of the European Court of Human Rights in *McGonnell* v. *United Kingdom*,[111] and more recently in the opinions of the majorities of the Strasbourg court in *Kleyn* v. *Netherlands*[112] and *Pabla KY* v. *Finland*.[113] A lack of clear institutional divisions between judicial and legislative power will not be immediately indicative of a breach of Article 6; the facts of the case must be considered. As the Court outlined in *McGonnell*:

> any direct involvement in the passage of legislation, or of executive rules, is likely to be sufficient to cast doubt on the judicial impartiality of a

---

[110] *Pabla KY* v. *Finland* (2006) 42 EHRR 34, para.27.
[111] *McGonnell*, above n.3.
[112] *Kleyn* v. *Netherlands* (2004) 38 EHRR 14.
[113] *Pabla KY* v. *Finland*, above n. 110.

person subsequently called to determine a dispute over whether reasons exist to permit a variation from the wording of the legislation or rules at issue.[114]

But as to the question of whether this demanded a strict separation of powers, the Court added:

> neither Article 6 nor any other provision of the Convention requires States to comply with any theoretical constitutional concepts as such. The question is always whether, in a given case, the requirements of the Convention are met.[115]

As such, the test appears to turn on the issue of proximity; should the advisory or legislative role played be sufficiently related to the issue decided upon judicially, then the test of objective impartiality might be satisfied. The mere ability to exercise the two roles will not be sufficient. Thus, in *McGonnell*, the Bailiff of Guernsey had adjudicated on a planning appeal which concerned the island's development plan, the passage of which he had presided over in the island's legislature. The European Court of Human Rights held that there was sufficient proximity between the legislative and judicial roles to create a doubt as to the impartiality of the court.

By contrast, in *Kleyn* the applicant claimed that the Administrative Jurisdiction Division of the Council of State was not an independent and impartial tribunal for the reason that it had given advice on draft planning legislation, but had subsequently judicially decided a dispute over the route of a proposed railway in which that legislation was relevant. The majority of the court ruled that the two actions – the giving of an advisory opinion on the draft legislation and the adjudication over the routing decision – could not 'be regarded as involving "the same case" or "the same decision" ', and as such there had been no breach of Article 6(1).[116]

Perhaps the most ringing endorsement of the proximity or circumstantial approach can be found in the decision of *Pabla KY v. Finland*.[117] In that case, the applicant alleged that the Finnish Court of Appeal which had heard his case had lacked the independence and impartiality required by

---

[114] *McGonnell*, above n.3, para.55.

[115] *Ibid.*, para.51.

[116] *Kleyn*, above n. 112, para.200. The decision that there was no breach of Article 6(1) was reached by twelve votes to five. Two of the dissenting judges – Judge Thomassen and Judge Zagrebelsky – felt that the advisory role and judicial decision *were* in respect of the 'same case' or 'same decision'. The dissenting judgment of the remaining three judges is discussed below.

[117] *Pabla KY*, above n.110.

Article 6(1), as one of its members had contemporaneously been a member of the Finnish Parliament. The applicant contended that this exercise of 'both legislative functions as a member of Parliament and judicial functions on the Court of Appeal' was in violation of his Article 6 rights. *Pabla KY* however, can be distinguished from *McGonnell* on the grounds that there had been no active legislative or advisory involvement in the passing of the provision in question, and as such:

> [t]he judicial proceedings therefore cannot be regarded as involving 'the same case' or 'the same decision' in the sense which was found to infringe Article 6(1) in [*McGonnell* v. *United Kingdom*].[118]

The challenge was therefore made on the grounds that concurrent holding of legislative and judicial office *alone* would violate Article 6(1). The majority, however, found that a degree of proximity to the legal issue in question is necessary before it can be found that a violation had occurred:

> the Court is not persuaded that the mere fact that MP was a member of the legislature at the time when he sat on the applicant's appeal is sufficient to raise doubts as to the independence and impartiality of the Court of Appeal. While the applicant relies on the theory of the separation of powers, this principle is not decisive in the abstract.[119]

This line of cases can be seen to be consistent with the findings of the Court of Human Rights in *V and T* and *Stafford*: while not going so far as to require a strict separation of the judicial branch from the legislative, the Court acknowledges that institutional overlaps *may* be sufficient ground to find a breach of Article 6, based on the lack of objective impartiality of the body under scrutiny.

The strict separation approach to impartiality

The second strand of reasoning seems to suggest that the mere exercise of judicial and legislative roles by the same person will of itself amount to a breach of Article 6(1). According to the proponents of this approach, the context of the overlap between functions, or circumstances of that overlap, is irrelevant. Therefore, this position seems to demand a separation of both function and personnel; no individual should be a member of more than one branch of government. This approach has evidenced itself, most recently, in the dissenting opinions of Judges Tsata-Nikolovska and

---

[118] *Ibid.*, para.34.   [119] *Ibid.*

Borrego Borrego in *Kleyn* and *Pabla KY*, respectively, but is also arguably apparent in the earlier unanimous judgment of the Court in *Procola* v. *Luxembourg*,[120] ironically one of the cases – along with *McGonnell* – which is most frequently cited in support of a judgment endorsing the first strand of jurisprudence, outlined above. The European Court of Human Rights in *Procola* noted that:

> four members of the *Conseil d'Etat* carried out both advisory and judicial functions in the same case. In the context of an institution such as Luxembourg's *Conseil d'Etat* the mere fact that certain persons successively performed these two types of function in respect of the same decisions is capable of casting doubt on the institution's structural impartiality. In the instant case, Procola had legitimate grounds for fearing that the members of the Judicial Committee had felt bound by the opinion previously given. That doubt in itself, however slight its justification, is sufficient to vitiate the impartiality of the tribunal in question ...[121]

This stance seems to suggest that the very ability to exercise such functions – regardless of the context or nature of the advice given – would amount to a breach of Article 6(1). Cornes' analysis of *Procola* suggests that, in determining that the dual role of the *Conseil d'Etat* as legislative and judicial body amounted to a 'structural impartiality' in breach of Article 6(1), the judgment 'may imply that Art.6(1) requires a formal separation of powers, regardless of the facts of each case'.[122] However, as indicated above, the decision in *McGonnell*, and the majority opinions in *Kleyn* and *Pabla KY*, seem to take a step back from this reading of *Procola*.

The dissenting judgments in *Kleyn* and *Pabla KY*, however, explicitly endorse the strict conception of the separation of powers as a principle of human rights law under the Convention – a reading of Article 6(1) which would in effect see interaction between the arms of government as a breach of the Convention. Under the strict approach, the minimum requirement that the applicant should have an objectively justified, or legitimate, fear concerning the impartiality of the court or tribunal in question would be satisfied by the very fact of the ability to exercise both legislative and judicial functions. In *Kleyn*, the dissenting judgment of Judge Tsata-Nikolovska reads as follows:

---

[120] *Procola* v. *Luxembourg*, above n. 12.

[121] *Ibid.*, para.45.

[122] R. Cornes, '*McGonnell* v. *United Kingdom*, The Lord Chancellor and the Law Lords' [2000] PL 166, n.13. See also: M. Russell and R. Cornes, 'The Royal Commission on Reform of the House of Lords: a House for the future?' (2001) 64(1) MLR 82, 93.

the exercise of both advisory and judicial functions by the same person is, as a matter of principle, incompatible with the requirements of Article 6, *regardless of the question of how remote or close the connection is between these functions.* A strict and visible separation between the legislative and executive authorities on the one hand and the judicial authorities on the other is indispensable for securing the independence and impartiality of judges and thus the confidence of the general public in its judicial system. Compromise in this area cannot but undermine this confidence.[123]

The dissenting judgment of Judge Borrego Borrego in *Pabla KY* v. *Finland* similarly endorses the strict separation approach. In that opinion it was stated – *without* regard to the particular factual circumstances of the case – that the doctrine of separation of powers is an 'essential component of a state based on the rule of law'.[124] Judge Borrego Borrego reviewed the case law of the European Court of Human Rights, finding that, 'as far back as 1980 the European Commission stated: "the term independent appearing in Article 6 ... [means] that the courts must be independent both of the executive and of the parties, and the same independence must be established in respect of the legislature" '.[125] Bolstering this argument by reference to Montesquieu, Judge Borrego Borrego concluded that the independence of the judiciary from the legislature or Parliament must at all times be one of fact, and should not be a question of the degree of proximity between the two roles in the circumstances of the dispute at issue.[126]

Conclusion

The various separation of powers dynamics evident at the Strasbourg level demonstrate the significant potential for the Convention rights to play a role in delineating the relationships between governmental institutions at the national level. Therefore, in spite of the claims of the European Court of Human Rights that the Convention does not require adherence to any specific 'theoretical constitutional concepts as such',[127] the practical realities of the influence of the Convention may well be to influence the relationships among the three branches of government. The coercive effects of the Convention case law contain the potential to enhance both the range and intensity of the courts' powers to review the activities

---

[123] *Kleyn,* above n.112, para.O-III7.
[124] *Pabla KY* v. *Finland,* above n.110, dissenting opinion of Judge Borrego Borrego.
[125] *Ibid.*   [126] *Ibid.*
[127] *McGonnell* v. *United Kingdom,* above n. 3, para.51.

of the political branches. In addition, the Convention – most obviously through its Article 6(1) case law – also shows the potential to touch on the structural relationships among the three branches of government at the national level. The dissenting judgments in *Kleyn* and in *Pabla KY* demonstrate that beyond the bare application of the Convention rights themselves, constitutional principle provides a discernible undercurrent to the Convention decisions in which the interplay between judicial, executive and legislative roles is at issue.[128] The Convention, and its transplantation into domestic law, contained considerable potential to spur the transformation of separation of powers from a descriptive, political aspiration, to something more readily asserted by courts as a legal, and an enforceable, principle.[129]

---

[128] Draft Resolution of the Parliamentary Assembly of the Council of Europe, 'Office of Lord Chancellor in the Constitutional System of the United Kingdom' (Document 9798, 28 April 2003), para.2: 'separation of powers has become a part of the common basic constitutional traditions of Europe, at the very least insofar as it concerns the attribution of the judicial office to an independent state institution'.

[129] A. Tomkins, 'The rule of law in Blair's Britain' (2007) 26 *University of Queensland Law Journal* 255, 260.

PART II

Judicial engagement with the 'political' branches

4

Justiciability

The extended range of review

Looking beyond the narrow and simplistic view of the separation of powers which holds that the status quo is maintained, and sovereignty unscathed, by the enactment of the HRA, it is apparent that a significant realignment of governmental, specifically judicial, power has occurred.[1] Prior to the implementation of the HRA – and in spite of pressures to the contrary, especially in judicial review cases – the ability of the courts to place reliance on the Convention rights and case law was quite strictly limited.[2] Even in common law cases, where judges were rightly acknowledged to possess a greater creative role, the reluctance of the courts to usurp the legislative function had traditionally been marked.[3] As Francesca Klug has argued, however, under the HRA, the courts have quite clearly been given powers of review which they simply did not possess prior to October 2000:

> [as] they can now review the decisions and actions of ministers and officials in substantive, human rights terms and they can even consider the compatibility of primary legislation with the Convention rights in the HRA, something they were effectively constitutionally barred from doing before.[4]

It is the recognition of such a reality, that informs the assertion that the HRA has brought about a significant redistribution of political power which has empowered the judiciary at the expense of the elected branches

---

[1] House of Lords Select Committee on the Constitution, *Relations between the Executive, the Judiciary and Parliament* (HL 151), July 2007, para.32 (citing the evidence of Professor Anthony Bradley).

[2] *R* v. *Secretary of State for the Home Department, ex parte Brind* [1991] 1 AC 696.

[3] *Malone* v. *Metropolitan Police Commissioner (No. 2)* [1979] Ch 344; *Kaye* v. *Robertson* [1991] FSR 62.

[4] F. Klug, 'The Human Rights Act – a "third way" or "third wave" bill of rights' [2001] EHRLR 361, 370.

of government.[5] As we have already seen, however, it is an oversimplification to barely suggest that the HRA empowers the courts to the detriment of the executive and Parliament; the Act envisages quite specific roles for *each* branch of government. But to say that the power of the courts has been extended significantly is also undeniable. Perhaps the most obvious evidence of this expansion of the courts' jurisdiction can be seen in the ability to review the acts (and omissions) of public authorities for compatibility with the Convention rights under s.6 of the HRA; the effect of this section being to add a statutory ground of illegality to the well-known substantive heads of judicial review.[6] Add to this the direction under s.3(1) that all legislation be interpreted in a Convention-compatible manner – a power that has been likened to one of *constitutional* review[7] – and the potential for the development of the common law in the light of the Convention rights,[8] and it becomes apparent that the HRA has the potential to reach virtually every sphere of judicial decision making.

The significance of this extended range of review can perhaps most clearly be seen in the judicial engagement with those areas of government decision making which were previously seen as being at the periphery of judicial competence; decisions with resource allocation implications, decisions made in the interests of national security, and executive use of prerogative powers in areas of 'high' policy-making – in other words, so-called 'non-justiciable' issues.

The justiciability of the Convention rights

Questions of justiciability are perennial in the sphere of public law decision making. Geoffrey Marshall has observed that use of the term justiciable can connote two differing meanings. First, justiciability in the 'fact-stating' sense concerns an assertion that an issue *is not*, as a matter of law, open to determination by courts. Second, justiciability in the 'prescriptive' sense concerns an assertion that an issue *should not* be open

---

[5] See e.g.: K. D. Ewing, 'The Human Rights Act and parliamentary democracy' (1999) 62 MLR 79, 79.

[6] See: P. Craig, *Administrative Law* (6th edn) (London: Sweet and Maxwell, 2008), pp.565–85; I. Leigh, 'Taking rights proportionately: judicial review, the Human Rights Act and Strasbourg' [2002] PL 265, 265.

[7] A. Kavanagh, *Constitutional Review under the UK Human Rights Act* (Cambridge University Press, 2009). See Ch.6.

[8] See e.g.: C. Gearty, 'Tort law and the Human Rights Act' in T. Campbell, K. D. Ewing and A. Tomkins (eds), *Sceptical Essays on Human Rights* (Oxford University Press, 2001). See pp.181–91.

to determination by the courts.[9] Just as the HRA itself made questions pertaining to 'the Convention rights' justiciable, so too it opened up to judicial scrutiny those circumstances in which disputes over those rights arose. Hence, further engagement with areas of policy, and of political choice, which were previously said to be outside of the sphere of judicial competence were brought conclusively – by specific legislative direction – within the sphere of judicial influence. The HRA itself, therefore, puts an end to the suggestion that the Convention rights fall without the jurisdiction of the courts. However, as Marshall has also noted, bringing a particular area of policy within the range of judicial review – while in a sense ending the technical debate over the justiciability of a given issue in a fact-stating sense – may not put an end to further debates over the suitability of courts, as opposed to other fora, resolving such questions.[10] It is unsurprising, therefore, that arguments persist that certain areas of policy-making should be placed entirely out of reach of judicial scrutiny, irrespective of the legislative direction provided by the HRA itself.[11] At least part of the challenge faced by the courts in the HRA age has therefore been to wrestle with questions concerning the legitimate exercise of these extended powers of review.

The justiciability of the Convention rights given effect under s.1 of the HRA is no longer in doubt.[12] In making the Convention rights recognised and enforceable legal standards in domestic law, the HRA has significantly narrowed those areas of executive policy and decision making which could previously have been said to fall outside the range of effective judicial scrutiny. While the particular area of policy-making itself may call for a degree of judicial deference to the superior knowledge or expertise of the elected branches, this is not, and should not be regarded as being, the same as rendering a topic non-justiciable in its entirety. Therefore, as Baroness Hale has recognised, following the implementation of the HRA, 'it is now common ground that if a Convention right requires the court to

[9] G. Marshall, 'Justiciability' in A. G. Guest (ed.), *Oxford Essays in Jurisprudence* (Oxford: Clarendon Press, 1961), pp.265–9.

[10] *Ibid.*, p. 268. And see: K. D. Ewing, 'The futility of the Human Rights Act' [2004] PL 829 and K. D. Ewing and J.-C. Tham, 'The continuing futility of the Human Rights Act' [2008] PL 668 for sustained critiques of the judicial record under the HRA.

[11] See the representations made on behalf of the government in *R (on the application of Gentle and another)* v. *Prime Minister* [2008] UKHL 20; [2008] 1 AC 1356, 1361–3 and in *R (on the application of Bancoult)* v. *Secretary of State for Foreign and Commonwealth Affairs (No. 2)* [2008] UKHL 61; [2009] 1 AC 453, 466–7.

[12] S. Beatson, S. Grosz, T. Hickman, R. Singh and S. Palmer, *Human Rights: Judicial Protection in the United Kingdom* (London: Sweet and Maxwell, 2008), pp.436, 439.

examine and adjudicate upon matters which were previously regarded as non-justiciable, then adjudicate it must'.[13] Section 6(1) of the Act is quite clear in this regard, providing simply that, '[i]t is unlawful for a public authority to act in a way which is incompatible with a Convention right'. Therefore, if one of the Convention rights is prima facie engaged by an exercise of executive power, even in those areas of 'high policy' traditionally thought to lie outside the sphere of legitimate judicial intervention, then the HRA requires that the role of the court is to adjudicate on the question of engagement, and on the legality of the purported restriction or infringement.

The passing of the HRA therefore opened up the possibility that *all* exercises of statutory or prerogative power might be subject to judicial review.[14] It is for this reason in particular that the persistence of non-justiciability doctrines may be regarded as being highly unsound where the Convention rights are engaged. First, as Baroness Hale's observations highlight, such an approach would amount to an abandonment of the unambiguous statutory direction in the HRA that decisions in which Convention rights are engaged are open to judicial resolution. Further, it would raise an effective obstacle to enforcement of the Convention against public bodies for which no support can be found in the Strasbourg case law.[15] Beyond this, however, the judicial invocation of non-justiciability doctrines in Convention rights adjudication may be regarded as being objectionable on broader grounds. A practical objection may be levelled on the basis of the potentially far-reaching consequences of a finding of non-justiciability in this area: as Jeff King has written, '[t]he precedential force of a non-justiciability finding can be extremely strong and potentially sweeping. It is a rather nuclear option.'[16] The effects of such a finding may be to exclude not only the decision in question, but future cases based on similar facts, from judicial analysis, regardless of the merits of the claim and of potential developments in the Strasbourg case law. Further, a judicial finding that certain areas of governmental decision making are non-justiciable may also contravene the rule of law. As a result

---

[13] *R (on the application of Gentle)* v. *Prime Minister* [2008] UKHL 20, para.60. See also: *International Transport Roth GmbH* v. *Secretary of State for the Home Department* [2003] QB 728, para.27 (Simon Brown LJ): 'Judges nowadays have no alternative but to apply the Human Rights Act 1998.'

[14] R. Clayton and H. Tomlinson, *The Law of Human Rights* (2nd edn) (Oxford University Press, 2009), para.5.139; Lord Woolf, J. Jowell and A. Le Sueur, *De Smith's Judicial Review* (London: Sweet and Maxwell, 2007), paras.1.025, and 1.026–1.036.

[15] Beatson, Grosz, Hickman, Singh and Palmer, *Human Rights*, above n. 12, p.439.

[16] J. A. King, 'Institutional approaches to judicial restraint' (2008) 28 OJLS 409, 421.

of the requirement that 'all aspects of government are conducted within the law ... it follows that the possibility of judicial review, in appropriate cases, should not be lightly excluded'.[17]

Public resources

Questions involving the distribution of public authority resources have historically been seen to lie on the fringes of justiciability, whether at the level of national economic policy[18] or at the level of specific spending decisions with a direct impact on an identifiable individual.[19] In the context of the latter, as Sir Thomas Bingham MR – as he then was – noted in *R* v. *Cambridge Health Authority, ex parte B*:

> Difficult and agonising judgments have to be made as to how a limited budget is best allocated to the maximum advantage of the maximum number of patients. That is not a judgment that a court can make.[20]

Concerns over the engagement of courts with decisions impacted in the allocation of resources have traditionally highlighted the lack of judicial accountability to the electorate for the consequences of those decisions, and the unsuitability of the courtroom to determine 'polycentric'[21] issues concerning how best to deploy public monies in pursuance of a particular policy or legislative objective. Cases concerning the appropriate allocation of resources by governmental bodies in pursuance of specific party political objectives have also had the unfortunate consequence of provoking some of the most well-known instances of overt political bias in judicial decision making.[22] It is clear, then, that judicial involvement in decisions with resource implications contains the potential for controversy.

---

[17] T. R. S. Allan, *Law, Liberty and Justice: The Legal Foundations of British Constitutionalism* (Oxford: Clarendon Press, 2003), pp.211–12. See also: J. Jowell, 'Parliamentary sovereignty under the new constitutional hypothesis' [2006] PL 562, 578.

[18] *Nottinghamshire County Council* v. *Secretary of State for the Environment* [1986] AC 240; *R* v. *Secretary of State for the Environment, ex parte Hammersmith and Fulham London Borough Council* [1991] 1 AC 521.

[19] *R* v. *Cambridge Health Authority, ex parte B* [1995] 2 All ER 129.

[20] *Ibid.*, 137.

[21] L. Fuller, 'The forms and limits of adjudication' (1978–9) 92 *Harvard Law Review* 353. On which, see: J. A. King, 'The pervasiveness of polycentricity' [2008] PL 101.

[22] See e.g.: *Roberts* v. *Hopwood* [1925] AC 578, 594 (Lord Atkinson):
The council would, in my view, fail in their duty if, in administering funds ... they ... allowed themselves to be guided in preference by some eccentric principles of socialistic philanthropy, or by a feminist ambition to secure the equality of the sexes in the matter of wages in the world of labour.

However, the crucial test for justiciability in this sphere is now the engagement of one or more of the Convention rights. However, given that issues concerning resource allocation are frequently accompanied by an electoral mandate, the courts – rightly – remain sensitive to issues of accountability and legitimacy in respect of their decision making in the social policy sphere.[23] As Lord Woolf noted in the *Poplar Housing* decision:

> The economic and other implications of any policy in this area are extremely complex and far-reaching. This is an area where, in our judgment, courts must treat the decisions of Parliament as to what is in the public interest with particular deference.[24]

However, the HRA makes clear that the question for *judicial* resolution is not one of the exclusivity of the legislative or executive power to determine how resources should be allocated. The role of the court is to assess whether the decision in question amounts to an unjustifiable infringement of one or more of the Convention rights, not to question the decision to allocate, or fail to allocate funds in any other specified way. As a result, the exercise of the jurisdiction of the courts in this sphere does not amount to a usurpation of the powers of the elected branches:

> The allocation of scarce resources is a matter for which primary responsibility must lie with the political branches of government; but any complaint of illegality must be examined on its own terms.[25]

The courts have therefore recognised that where the Convention rights are engaged, their prescribed role – under the direction of the HRA – is to adjudicate on the legality of the purported restriction.[26] It is perhaps an over-simplification to say, as Laws LJ did in *ex parte Begbie*, that the more an issue can be said to lie in the 'macro-political' field, the 'less intrusive will be the court's supervision',[27] for this runs the risk of a uniform low-intensity review being applied in all cases where the executive exercises a

---

[23] See e.g.: *R (on the application of Alconbury Developments Ltd) v. Secretary of State for the Environment* [2003] 2 AC 295, para.60 (Lord Nolan); *A and others v. Secretary of State for the Home Department* [2004] UKHL 56; [2005] 2 AC 68, para.38 (Lord Bingham).

[24] *Poplar Housing and Regeneration Community Association Ltd v. Donoghue* [2001] EWCA Civ 595; [2002] QB 48, 71. See also: *R (on the application of Hooper) v. Secretary of State for Work and Pensions* [2003] EWCA Civ 813; [2003] 1 WLR 2623, paras.63–4.

[25] T. R. S. Allan, 'Human rights and judicial review: a critique of "due deference"' (2006) 65 CLJ 671, 693.

[26] *Ghaidan v. Godin-Mendoza* [2004] UKHL 30; [2004] 2 AC 557, para.19 (Lord Nicholls).

[27] *R v. Secretary of State for Education and Employment, ex parte Begbie* [2000] 1 WLR 1115, 1131 (Laws LJ).

policy choice, regardless of the severity of the impact of that policy choice on the concerned parties.[28] And – just as with *Wednesbury* in the sphere of administrative law more generally – the influence of *ex parte B* remains visible; as Laws LJ confirmed in *Wells* v. *Parole Board*, the courts were ill-suited to determine *competing* claims to public funds: '[i]t is well-settled that the courts are generally in no position to make judgments upon competing claims for the allocation of scarce public resources, and will decline to do so'.[29] However, the mere presence of concerns over public resources in cases in which Convention considerations are in play will not, it seems, displace the obligation of the court to analyse the compatibility of a given decision or action. As Lord Phillips of Worth Matravers noted bluntly in *R (Walker)* v. *Secretary of State for Justice*, interference with the Convention rights will not be justified by a shortage of funds: 'limitations of resources [are] no answer; it [is] the obligation of the state to organise its legal system so as to comply with the Convention obligations'.[30]

The award of damages as a remedy against public authorities has long raised similar concerns over the impact of such awards on the authority's broader responsibilities.[31] As Lord Browne-Wilkinson noted in *X* v. *Bedfordshire County Council*, 'if a liability in damages were to be imposed, it might well be that the local authorities would adopt a more cautious approach to their duties'.[32] In making damages available against public bodies for their failures to act compatibly with the Convention rights, the HRA puts an end to debates over another potential area of questionable justiciability and provides the judges with a potential potent tool of enforcement in the protection of those rights.[33] However, reflective of continuing concerns over the knock-on effects of making damages readily available as a remedy for a breach of the Convention rights, the courts have made such awards in only a handful of cases since the passing of the HRA, and in assessing the quantum of such awards have been careful not to exceed the amount strictly

---

[28] See pp.132–5.

[29] *Wells* v. *Parole Board* [2007] EWHC 1835, para.39 (Laws LJ).

[30] *R (Walker)* v. *Secretary of State for Justice* [2008] EWCA Civ 30; [2008] 1 WLR 1977 (endorsing the findings of the Court of Appeal in *R (Noorkoiv)* v. *Secretary of State for the Home Department* [2002] EWCA Civ 770; [2002] 1 WLR 3284).

[31] For a survey, see: M. Fordham, 'Reparation for maladministration: public law's final frontier' [2003] *Judicial Review* 104.

[32] *X (Minors)* v. *Bedfordshire County Council* [1995] 2 AC 633, 750.

[33] J. A. King, 'The justiciability of resource allocation' (2007) 70 MLR 197, 211–12. And for a survey of the case law, see: I. Leigh and R. Masterman, *Making Rights Real: The Human Rights Act in its First Decade* (Oxford: Hart Publishing, 2008), pp.273–82.

necessary to achieve 'just satisfaction'.[34] In considering whether to award damages, the courts have made significant attempts to balance their obligations to enforce the Convention rights with the abilities of public bodies effectively to manage their own spending, being particularly hesitant to impose further financial burdens on public bodies even in cases where a clear breach is shown.[35]

National security

Prior to the implementation of the HRA, the *GCHQ* case had made resoundingly clear the point that the jurisdiction of the courts would not be excluded solely on the basis of the source of a governmental power, and that the subject matter of a decision would govern the extent of the courts' ability to intervene.[36] *GCHQ*, however, also resoundingly illustrated that certain areas of policy-making fell well outside the scope of judicial competence. Despite finding that the employees of GCHQ were entitled to legitimately expect that they would be consulted prior to any change to the conditions of their employment, the House of Lords held that the national security concerns advanced on behalf of the government effectively trumped whatever procedural fairness obligations were owed. Lord Diplock remarked that:

> National security is the responsibility of the executive government … It is *par excellence* a non-justiciable question. The judicial process is totally inept to deal with the sort of problems it involves.[37]

While the rigidity of Lord Diplock's assessment was subsequently shown to be open to question,[38] the ability of courts to exercise powers of review over national security decisions was hampered, first, by the justiciability hurdle, and second, by the degree of deference generally afforded in the

---

[34] The area is now governed by the leading case of *R (Greenfield)* v. *Secretary of State for the Home Department* [2005] UKHL 14; [2005] 1 WLR 673. On which, see: R. Clayton, 'Damage limitation: the courts and Human Rights Act damages' [2005] PL 429.

[35] *Anufrjieva* v. *Southwark London Borough Council* [2003] EWCA Civ 1406; [2004] QB 1124, para.56 (Lord Woolf).

[36] *Council of Civil Service Unions* v. *Minister for the Civil Service* [1985] AC 374, 407 (Lord Diplock). Cf. Lord Roskill, who argued that, the 'nature and *subject matter*' of some prerogative powers would render them 'as not to be amenable to the judicial process' (*ibid.*, at 418).

[37] *Ibid.*, 412 (Lord Diplock). Cf. *Secretary of State for the Home Department* v. *Rehman* [2001] UKHL 47; [2003] 1 AC 153, para.31 (Lord Steyn).

[38] See e.g.: *R* v. *Secretary of State for the Home Department, ex parte McQuillan* [1995] 4 All ER 400.

arena of national security law, which had significantly undermined the rigour with which the courts applied *Wednesbury* standards in practice.[39]

Following the implementation of the HRA, early indications were of little change in the approach of the courts to matters engaging national security concerns. In *Secretary of State for the Home Department* v. *Rehman* – concerning the deportation of a Pakistani national on grounds of a potential threat to national security – the House of Lords unanimously deferred to the executive assessment of the risk.[40] As Lord Hoffmann noted:

> In matters of national security, the cost of failure can be high. This seems to me to underline the need for the judicial arm of government to respect the decisions of ministers of the Crown on the question of whether support for terrorist activities in a foreign country constitutes a threat to national security. It is not only that the executive has access to special information and expertise in these matters. It is also that such decisions, with serious potential results for the community, require a legitimacy which can be conferred only by entrusting them to persons responsible to the community through the democratic process. If the people are to accept the consequences of such decisions, they must be made by persons whom the people have elected and whom they can remove.[41]

Lord Hoffmann's comments raise the possibility of a 'spatial' approach to the separation of governmental functions which appears to preclude – or at least severely curtail – the possibility of meaningful judicial scrutiny, regardless of the nature of the impact of the particular decision or action on the individual's Convention rights, where the decision in question is in an area deemed to fall within the expertise of the executive.[42]

Since *Rehman*, however, the weight of authority against such a clear division of competence between the executive and judicial branches has steadily grown. Indeed, since the passage of the HRA, the number of cases in which executive, and legislative, measures taken in the name of national security have been subject to judicial analysis and found to be wanting in

---

[39] See e.g.: *Liversidge* v. *Anderson* [1942] AC 206; *R* v. *Secretary of State for the Home Department, ex parte Hosenball* [1977] 1 WLR 766; [1977] 3 All ER 452. And for a survey, see: L. Lustgarten and I. Leigh, *In From the Cold: National Security and Parliamentary Democracy* (Oxford: Clarendon Press, 1994).

[40] *Secretary of State for the Home Department* v. *Rehman*, above n. 37.

[41] *Ibid.*, paras.50–4, and para.62 (Lord Hoffmann).

[42] For criticism of the adoption of such 'spatial metaphors', see: M. Hunt, 'Sovereignty's blight: why contemporary public law needs the concept of "due deference"' in N. Bamforth and P. Leyland (eds), *Public Law in a Multi-Layered Constitution* (Oxford: Hart Publishing, 2003).

human rights terms, is nothing short of striking.[43] Perhaps none more
so than *A v. Secretary of State for the Home Department*, decided by a
panel of nine Law Lords in December 2004.[44] As is by now well known,
A concerned the compatibility of s.23 of the Anti-Terrorism, Crime and
Security Act 2001[45] – which sanctioned the indefinite detention without
trial of non-UK citizens suspected of involvement in terrorist activities –
with Article 5, read with Article 14, of the Convention. The Law Lords
held, by an 8:1 margin, that the provision was incompatible, and issued a
declaration to that effect under s.4 of the HRA. In the context of this discussion, it is not perhaps the outcome of the case that is the most striking
result. Indeed, the limited remedial function of the declaration of incompatibility in this instance is well illustrated by the fact that the court could
not compel the release of the detained prisoners. But in making the decision to issue such a declaration, the House of Lords arguably abandoned
the overly deferential tones of previous decisions concerned with national
security issues.

Lord Bingham highlighted the inaccuracy of regarding human rights
issues which impacted on national security decisions as falling outside
the competence of the courts, instead emphasising the differing nature of
the judicial and executive tasks in respect of dealing with such issues:

> It is of course true that the judges in this country are not elected and are
> not answerable to Parliament. It is also of course true … that Parliament,
> the executive and the courts have different functions. But the function of
> independent judges charged to interpret and apply the law is universally
> regarded as a cardinal feature of the modern democratic state, a corner-
> stone of the rule of law itself. The Attorney-General is fully entitled to
> insist on the proper limits of judicial authority, but he is wrong to stigma-
> tise judicial decision-making as in some way undemocratic.[46]

The then Senior Law Lord regarded the suggestion that the courts lacked
a 'very specific, wholly democratic, mandate' in adjudication under the

---

[43] See e.g.: *A and others* v. *Secretary of State for the Home Department*, above n. 23; *A
v. Secretary of State for the Home Department (No. 2)* [2005] UKHL 71; [2006] 2 AC
221; *Secretary of State for the Home Department* v. *JJ* [2007] UKHL 45; [2008] 1 AC 385;
Secretary of State for the Home Department v. *AF* [2009] UKHL 28; [2009] 3 WLR 74. For
discussion, see: Leigh and Masterman, *Making Rights Real*, above n. 33, ch.8.

[44] *A and others* v. *Secretary of State for the Home Department*, above n. 23. On which, see: A.
Tomkins, 'Readings of *A* v. *Secretary of State for the Home Department*' [2005] PL 259.

[45] On which, see: A. Tomkins, 'Legislating against terror: the Anti-Terrorism, Crime and
Security Act 2001' [2002] PL 205; H. Fenwick, 'The Anti-Terrorism, Crime and Security
Act 2001: a proportionate response to 11 September?' (2002) 65 MLR 724.

[46] *A and others* v. *Secretary of State for the Home Department*, above n. 23, para.42.

HRA as being 'particularly inappropriate'.[47] As an indicator of the interplay between executive and judicial power in this area of law and policy, Lord Bingham's statement is particularly revealing. On his analysis, power to determine questions which concern national security is not seen as being separated in an absolute sense. This is not a strict separation of function by subject matter – as had been hinted at in cases such as *Rehman*, for example.[48] Rather, the spheres of executive authority and judicial authority overlap, and are separated by the constitutional obligations of, and processes of decision making undertaken by, the arms of government in question:

> The judges are constrained … rightly, by the fact that their role is reactive; they cannot initiate; all they can do is apply principle to what is brought before them by others. Nothing could be more distinct from the duty of political creativity owed to us by Members of Parliament.[49]

This much remains the same following the implementation of the HRA – while the subject matter of decisions taken by judges, legislators and officials will necessarily overlap, the processes of decision making adopted by each are necessarily different, as are the aims and objectives of each in making the decision in question.

'High policy' and prerogative powers

Just as *GCHQ* had opened the door to judicial investigation of certain exercises of the prerogative, it had seemingly closed the door on others. The speech of Lord Roskill, in particular, highlighted 'the making of treaties, the defence of the realm, the prerogative of mercy, the grant of honours, the dissolution of Parliament and the appointment of ministers' as being effectively non-justiciable 'because their nature and subject matter are such as not to be amenable to the judicial process'.[50] While subsequent cases revealed that the apparent exclusion of these areas of decision making was not immune from judicial reconsideration[51] – especially where

---

[47] *Ibid.*
[48] See above n.37.
[49] Sir J. Laws, 'Law and democracy' [1995] PL 72, 93.
[50] *Council of Civil Service Unions* v. *Minister for the Civil Service*, above n. 36, 418 (Lord Roskill).
[51] See e.g.: *R* v. *Secretary of State for Foreign and Commonwealth Affairs, ex parte Everett* [1989] QB 811 (issue and renewal of passports); *Secretary of State for the Home Department, ex parte Bentley* [1993] 4 All ER 442 (prerogative of mercy); *R* v. *Ministry of Defence, ex parte Smith and others* [1996] QB 517 (whether homosexuals might serve in the armed forces).

the challenged decision was administrative in character – others had remained apparently impervious to judicial scrutiny.[52] Questions of 'high policy', for example, the deployment of the armed forces[53] and the foreign relations prerogatives of the executive, fell squarely within the latter camp. The HRA has not, however, prompted a wholesale revision of the judicial tendency towards caution in the oversight of certain high policy powers.[54] In the context of the UK constitution, the difficulty of this for a comprehensive system of checks and balances is that, while the judiciary may exercise restraint, the ability of Parliament to scrutinise ministerial action is in many respects also limited.[55]

Deployment of the armed forces

The ability of the executive to deploy the armed forces in the absence of 'reliable' legal advice was at issue in *R (on the application of Gentle and another)* v. *Prime Minister*. In *Gentle*, the applicants were the mothers of two members of the armed forces who had been killed while on active service in Iraq. The applicants argued that the Convention placed the government under an enforceable legal obligation to establish an inquiry into the circumstances surrounding – and legality of – the deployment of British armed forces in Iraq in 2003.[56] Their argument was not based on questions of the public interest in establishing such an inquiry,[57] but on the requirements of Article 2 of the Convention, the right to life. The applicants contended that Article 2 imposed a duty on member states to protect the lives of citizens – a duty which extends to those citizens who may be exposed in the course of their work to a risk of death. As a result

---

[52] See e.g.: *McWhirter* v. *Attorney-General* [1972] CMLR 882 (power to enter into treaties); *ex parte Molyneaux and others* [1986] 1 WLR 331 (power to enter into treaties).

[53] On which, see: Select Committee on the Constitution, *Waging War: Parliament's Role and Responsibility* (HL 236-I), 2006.

[54] *R* v. *Jones (Margaret)* [2006] UKHL 16; [2007] 1 AC 136, para.30 (Lord Bingham):
      there are well-established rules that the courts will be very slow to review the exercise of prerogative powers in relation to the conduct of foreign affairs and the deployment of the armed services, and very slow to adjudicate upon rights arising out of transactions entered into between sovereign states on the plane of international law.

[55] Public Administration Select Committee, *Taming the Prerogative: Strengthening Ministerial Accountability to Parliament* (HC 422), 2004, para.12. Although see now: Ministry of Justice, *The Governance of Britain* (Cm. 7170), July 2007, ch.1 (on the suggestion that Parliament be responsible for the exercise of certain prerogatives); Constitutional Reform and Governance Act 2010, Part 2 (on parliamentary involvement in the ratification of treaties).

[56] *R (on the application of Gentle and another)* v. *Prime Minister*, above n. 11, para.2.

[57] *Ibid.*

of this suggested duty, the parents argued that the government was under an obligation to obtain 'reliable legal advice before committing its troops to armed conflict'. Had the government obtained such legal advice, it was argued, it may not have taken the decision to invade Iraq, and Fusilier Gentle and Trooper Clarke may not have been killed.[58]

The differences between the Court of Appeal and the House of Lords on the question of justiciability were marked. The Court of Appeal found that, notwithstanding the terms of the Convention rights and of the HRA itself, there are certain areas of policy that fall within 'the *exclusive* discretion of the state',[59] and that accountability for decisions taken in such areas of policy 'must be aired at what is sometimes called the bar of public opinion and resolved at the ballot box'.[60] As a result, the primary ground for the Court of Appeal's dismissal of the applicants' claim, was the non-justiciability of the issues raised.

By contrast, the House of Lords' approach treated the question of whether the government was under an enforceable legal obligation to hold a general inquiry into the circumstances surrounding the invasion of Iraq to be justiciable,[61] but found that Article 2 could not impose the procedural obligations argued for by the applicants, in the absence of its being substantively engaged on the facts.[62] While neither the Court of Appeal nor the House of Lords was able to provide the applicants with the remedy sought, the decision of the Law Lords is to be preferred to that of the Court of Appeal. For the reasons outlined above, invoking effective non-justiciability doctrines in those cases where the Convention rights are *prima facie* engaged is open to question. The consequences of raising the artificial procedural hurdle of non-justiciability may not only be to prevent full judicial examination of the legal issues raised in argument, but also to stifle future judicial decision making on similar factual grounds.

Foreign relations and the power to enter into treaties

Some areas of prerogative power, however, appear to have been untouched by the passage of the HRA. In the Court of Appeal decision in *Abassi*, the Court was asked to require the Foreign Secretary to make representations to the government of the United States on behalf of several British

---

[58] *Ibid.*, para.3.
[59] *R (Gentle and Another)* v. *Prime Minister* [2006] EWCA Civ 1689, para.43.
[60] *Ibid.*
[61] Specific inquests into the deaths of Fusilier Gordon Gentle and Trooper David Clark were conducted in 2007.
[62] *R (on the application of Gentle and another)* v. *Prime Minister*, above n. 11, para.6 (Lord Bingham).

citizens who were detained without trial in the legal 'black hole'[63] of
Guantanamo Bay.[64] The Court of Appeal noted its 'deep concern' that the
detention of Abassi and the other applicants was at the exclusive discretion of the US executive and entirely outside the range of judicial supervision. Nevertheless, the Court felt unable to make the orders claimed,
as, *inter alia*:

> On no view would it be appropriate to order the Secretary of State to make
> any specific representations to the United States, *even in the face of what
> appears to be a clear breach of a fundamental human right*, as it is obvious
> that this would have an impact on the conduct of foreign policy, and an
> impact on such policy at a particularly delicate time.[65]

The Court of Appeal in *Abassi*, therefore, – for practical as well as political reasons[66] – felt unable to provide the remedy sought by the applicants. Importantly, however, the Court also endorsed proportionality as
the appropriate standard of review, even in Convention rights cases where
foreign policy prerogatives are in play.[67]

Extending the range of the courts' powers of review in cases where
the Convention rights are engaged has not, however, resulted in a clear
extension of the courts' powers where those rights are *not* at issue. The
prerogative power to enter into treaties was again engaged in the case of
Wheeler v. Prime Minister, in which the applicant sought a finding that,
in failing to hold a referendum on the ratification of the Lisbon Treaty,
the government had frustrated the applicant's legitimately held expectation that a referendum would be held.[68] At permission stage, the case
was distinguished from *direct* challenges to exercises of the prerogative
power to enter into treaties on the basis of this arguable legitimate expectation. Previous challenges to such exercises of the prerogative had been
rejected on the basis of the non-justiciability of the prerogative power to
enter into treaties,[69] or the failure of the applicants to advance a specific

---

[63] Lord Steyn, 'Guantanamo Bay: the legal black hole' (2004) 53 ICLQ 1.

[64] *R (on the application of Abassi) v. Secretary of State for Foreign and Commonwealth
Affairs* [2002] EWCA Civ 1598; [2003] UKHRR 76. For a case on similar factual grounds
brought by non-British citizens, see: *R (on the application of Al Rawi) v. Secretary of State
for Foreign and Commonwealth Affairs and Secretary of State for the Home Department*
[2006] EWCA Civ 1279; [2008] QB 289.

[65] *Ibid.*, para.107 (emphasis added).

[66] *Ibid.*, para.67.   [67] *Ibid.*, para.65.

[68] *Wheeler v. Prime Minister* [2008] EWHC 936 (Admin), paras.3–8.

[69] See: *McWhirter and Gouriet v. Secretary of State for Foreign and Commonwealth Affairs*
[2003] EWCA Civ 384.

legal issue for resolution.[70] However, in *Wheeler*, the legitimate expectation issue – as submitted by counsel for the applicants – prompted the
conclusion that the 'case [was] not political in character but about the rule
of law'.[71] Yet, the court in *Wheeler* was nevertheless able to find that the
essentially 'political' nature of the issues raised made them unsuitable for
judicial determination.[72] At the very best, the court stated, due in part to
the lack of a clearly engaged right, the decision not to hold a referendum
on the Lisbon Treaty was a 'matter to be approached on a *Wednesbury*
basis'.[73] Ultimately, however, as the decision to hold a referendum would
be made by Parliament rather than the government, the issues raised lay
'so deep in the macro-political field that the court should not enter the
relevant arena at all'.[74]

Importantly, the decision in *Abassi* does not appear to place a blanket injunction on the judicial consideration of foreign policy decisions,
seeming to leave such decisions susceptible to review in alternative, perhaps less delicate, circumstances. Instead, the intensity of review will be
dependent on the engagement of one or more of the Convention rights – if
a question of compatibility is raised, the appropriate standard of review
will be dictated by the proportionality test.[75] This aside, however, as *Abassi*
demonstrates, there are still areas of policy which remain substantially
immune from judicial interference, despite raising *prima facie* justiciable
issues under the HRA. The separation of judicial powers from that of the
executive and Parliament is therefore variable rather than spatial, with
circumstances and the severity of the intrusion determining the intensity
with which the courts might intervene.

The withering of non-justiciability doctrines

Just as Taylor LJ was able to suggest in *ex parte Everett* that the courts' ability to review the exercise of executive discretion 'cannot be ousted merely
by invoking the word "prerogative"',[76] nor can the jurisdiction of the

---

[70] *R (Southall)* v. *Secretary of State for Foreign and Commonwealth Affairs* [2003] EWCA Civ
1002; [2003] 3 CMLR 18.
[71] *R (on the application of Wheeler)* v. *Prime Minister and Secretary of State for Foreign and
Commonwealth Affairs* [2008] EWHC 1409 (Admin), para.18.
[72] *Ibid.*, paras.34, 41 and 43.
[73] *Ibid.*, para.37.   [74] *Ibid.*, para.43.
[75] *R (on the application of Bancoult)* v. *Secretary of State for Foreign and Commonwealth
Affairs*, above n. 11, para.131 (Lord Carswell).
[76] *R* v. *Foreign Secretary, ex parte Everett*, above n. 51, 820.

courts now be called into question by referring to 'high policy', 'national security' or 'resource allocation'.

The cases discussed above indicate that even in areas of high policy – which may previously have been regarded as being on the periphery of the courts' jurisdiction – engagement of one or more of the Convention rights will put an end to questions of justiciability in its 'fact-stating' sense. As such, 'the idea of a judicial "no-go area" encapsulated in the non-justiciability doctrine has effectively been replaced with a more flexible and pragmatic test of deference'.[77] It is the variable standard of deference which allows the courts to afford a degree of respect to the decisions of elected bodies and which has come to mean that while action taken at what might have been called the fringes of justiciability may be reviewable *per se*, it may not necessarily be subject to intensive review in practice. In separation of powers terms, the consequence of these developments has been a considerable narrowing of those spheres within which executive action may only be subject to parliamentary and popular scrutiny. This narrowing represents a considerable strengthening of the separation of powers as a system of checks and balances. In the sphere of the exercise of prerogative powers, these advances of legal accountability – taken alongside recent attempts to strengthen the powers of Parliament in this regard[78] – amount to a significant step towards plugging the 'accountability gap' in which executive activity is subject to neither meaningful parliamentary nor judicial examination.

Before turning to questions of deference, however, an important obstacle to the complete abandonment of a non-justiciability doctrine in cases where Convention rights are at issue should be discussed. Writing in an article published in 1995, Laws LJ, then a High Court judge, observed that 'save as regards the Queen in Parliament, there is in principle always jurisdiction in the court to review the decisions of public bodies'.[79] One important exception remains to this general presumption that public decision-making powers will be justiciable: the *legality* of Acts of Parliament.

---

[77] King, 'The justiciability of resource allocation', above n. 33, 224. See also: Beatson, Grosz, Hickman, Singh and Palmer, *Human Rights*, above n. 12, p.444.

[78] Ministry of Justice, *The Governance of Britain – Draft Constitutional Renewal Bill* (Cm. 77342-II), March 2008. See now: Constitutional Reform and Governance Act 2010, Part II. Proposals to make the deployment of the armed forces conditional on parliamentary endorsement – contained in the draft Bill – did not make it onto the statute book.

[79] Laws, 'Law and democracy', above n. 49, 76.

Towards legislative review?

While the HRA itself makes specific provision for a power to review the *compatibility* of Acts of Parliament with the Convention rights, and allows the courts to issue declarations of incompatibility where such interpretation is not possible,[80] the classic example of a non-justiciable issue in the UK constitution remains a challenge to the *legality* of an Act of Parliament.[81] The lack of a general judicial power to strike down Acts of the Westminster Parliament acts as authority for the enduring supremacy of Parliament at its most absolute in the contemporary constitution. As a result, the fundamental pillar of parliamentary supremacy seems to ensure the ultimate dominance of the political over the legal in the constitution,[82] and that parliamentary legislation remains substantially immune from judicial review.

Perhaps, therefore, the most significant – and telling – example of the courts' extended range of review can be found in the case of *Jackson* v. *Attorney-General*, in which the House of Lords openly considered the 'legality' of Parliament's deployment of legislative power under the Parliament Acts.[83] As is now well known, the case concerned a challenge to the validity of the Hunting Act 2004 – an Act passed using the Parliament Acts procedure – brought by members of the Countryside Alliance.[84] The challenge proceeded on the argument that the Parliament Act 1911, by removing the necessity of gaining the consent of the House of Lords in the legislative process, implemented a new mechanism for the creation of delegated legislation.[85] It was contended that the Parliament Act 1949, itself passed under the terms of the Parliament Act 1911, was therefore a piece of delegated legislation, and was also unlawful, as it entailed the House of Commons unilaterally expanding the powers delegated to it without the express authorisation of the delegating instrument. As a result, it

---

[80] See Ch.6.
[81] *Cheney* v. *Conn* [1966] 1 WLR 242, 247; *Madzimbamuto* v. *Lardner-Burke* [1969] 1 AC 645, 723; *Pickin* v. *British Railways Board* [1974] AC 765, 798.
[82] J. A. G. Griffith 'The political constitution' (1979) 42 MLR 1.
[83] *Jackson and others* v. *Her Majesty's Attorney-General* [2005] UKHL 56; [2006] 1 AC 262.
[84] For commentary, see: M. Elliott, 'The sovereignty of Parliament, the hunting ban and the Parliament Acts' (2006) 65 CLJ 1; A. Young, 'Hunting sovereignty: *Jackson* v. *Attorney-General*' [2006] PL 187; J. Jowell, 'Parliamentary sovereignty under the new constitutional hypothesis' [2006] PL 562; T. Mullen, 'Reflections on *Jackson* v. *Attorney-General*: questioning sovereignty' (2007) 27 LS 1.
[85] See: H. W. R. Wade, 'The basis of legal sovereignty' (1955) 13 CLJ 172, 193–4.

was argued that any subsequent legislation – including the Hunting Act 2004 – passed under the Parliament Acts procedure was also invalid.[86]

While the arguments of the Countryside Alliance were ultimately rejected by the Court of Appeal and the House of Lords, both courts were forced to acknowledge the unusual circumstances in which the case had arisen. The then Senior Law Lord, Lord Bingham, recognised the 'sense of strangeness' in being asked to adjudicate over the legality of Acts passed under the Parliament Acts procedure.[87] And while the Lords were keen to stress that the precedent set down by *Pickin* v. *British Railways Board* – that 'the courts in this country have no power to declare enacted law to be invalid'[88] – was 'unquestioned',[89] there was a distinct air of unreality to this assertion, given that the invalidation of enacted legislation was the very thing that the Law Lords were being asked to do in the case in hand.[90] The Court of Appeal in *Jackson* was perhaps more candid, noting that they were clearly exercising a 'constitutional' jurisdiction, and openly acknowledging that in so doing they were operating in an entirely unprecedented manner.[91]

The decision of the House of Lords in *Jackson* is notable for the varying degrees to which the nine Law Lords envisaged a modified reading of the sovereignty doctrine under which legislative supremacy may be subject to an unspecified degree of judicial oversight. At the Diceyan end of the spectrum lay Lord Bingham, who noted that sovereignty remains the 'bedrock of the British constitution' and regarded it as unnecessary for the purposes of the issue at hand to make any further comment.[92] Next, as Lord Nicholls noted, '[t]he proper interpretation of a statute is a matter for the courts, not Parliament'.[93] While Parliament may legislate on a given issue, he argued, it is the courts that possess the definitive say on how that legislative direction is to be interpreted, and by extension, given effect.

---

[86] *Jackson and others* v. *Her Majesty's Attorney-General*, above n. 83, 264–8 (for a summary, see para.7 (Lord Bingham)).

[87] *Ibid.*, para.27 (Lord Bingham).

[88] *Pickin* v. *British Railways Board*, above n. 81, 789 (Lord Simon).

[89] *Jackson and others* v. *Her Majesty's Attorney-General*, above n. 83, para.27 (Lord Bingham).

[90] *Ibid.*, paras.49–51 (Lord Nicholls).

[91] *R (on the application of Jackson and others)* v. *Her Majesty's Attorney-General* [2005] QB 579, para.12, where the then Lord Chief Justice acknowledged that the court was acting as a 'constitutional court' and that there was 'no precise precedent' for its so doing.

[92] *Jackson and others* v. *Her Majesty's Attorney-General*, above n. 83, para.9 (Lord Bingham).

[93] *Ibid.*, para.51 (Lord Nicholls).

Others went further still. Lord Hope, while acknowledging the continuing dominance of the sovereignty doctrine in the constitution, asked whether the absolutism of the doctrine could be sustained,[94] and – crucially – was prepared to countenance a specific role for the courts in regulating the exercise of Parliament's legislative power; noting enigmatically that the 'courts have a part to play in defining the limits of Parliament's legislative sovereignty'.[95]

In making these observations in the context of a usage of the Parliament Acts procedure, *Jackson* marked a notable – if strictly limited[96] – extension of the courts' powers to scrutinise the legality of primary legislation. However, important dicta from two of the Law Lords hinted at something much more potent than an authoritative general power to interpret statutory legislation, and pointed towards a marked judicial resistance to the legislative insulation of areas of governmental activity from judicial scrutiny. Lord Steyn was perhaps most forthright on the issue, openly acknowledging the troubling consequences of recognising that the Parliament Acts procedure could be invoked in all but the narrow circumstances specified in s.2 of the 1911 Act, and the concurrent endorsement of unbridled executive power that this would bring about.[97] The result of such a finding, Lord Steyn suggested, would be that:

> the 1949 Act could be used to introduce oppressive and wholly undemocratic legislation. For example, it could theoretically be used to abolish judicial review of flagrant abuse of power by a government or even the role of the ordinary courts in standing between the executive and citizens.[98]

While parliamentary sovereignty may well continue to be the '*general* principle of our constitution', he argued, unchecked *executive* power does not hold such sway.[99] Lord Steyn went on to assert that the constitution is not 'uncontrolled' – as a Diceyan reading of parliamentary supremacy might

---

[94] *Ibid.*, para.104.   [95] *Ibid.*, para.107.

[96] The Parliament Acts procedure had – until recently – only been used sparingly, and even given the recent increase in the willingness of the House of Commons to resort to the Acts, has only ever been used to enact seven statutes. Those statutes enacted under the Parliament Acts procedure are: Welsh Church Act 1914; Home Rule Act 1914; Parliament Act 1949 (enacted under the provisions of the Parliament Act 1911); War Crimes Act 1991; European Parliamentary Elections Act 1999; Sexual Offences (Amendment) Act 2000; Hunting Act 2004.

[97] *Jackson and others* v. *Her Majesty's Attorney-General*, above n. 83, para.101.

[98] *Ibid.*, at para.102.

[99] A viewpoint previously addressed in Lord Steyn's extrajudicial writings, see: Lord Steyn, 'The weakest and least dangerous department of government' [1997] PL 84, 87.

claim – and that sovereign power is now effectively 'divided' among the Westminster Parliament, the devolved administrations and the courts.[100] As a result, an attempt by Parliament to render specific exercises of governmental power non-justiciable may, Lord Steyn suggested, be rejected by the judges:

> In exceptional circumstances involving an attempt to abolish judicial review or the ordinary role of the courts, the Appellate Committee of the House of Lords or a new Supreme Court may have to consider whether this is a constitutional fundamental which even a sovereign Parliament acting at the behest of a complaisant House of Commons cannot abolish.[101]

Baroness Hale also speculated on the effects of a parliamentary direction that the courts' jurisdiction be expressly limited where human rights were at stake. While she recognised that 'in general ... the constraints upon what Parliament can do are political and diplomatic rather than constitutional', she also noted that:

> [t]he courts will treat with particular suspicion (and might even reject) any attempt to subvert the rule of law by removing governmental action affecting the rights of the individual from judicial scrutiny.[102]

While *Jackson* itself was not an HRA case,[103] the Act was nevertheless used by both Lord Steyn and Baroness Hale to contextualise their observations on the gradual inroads that had been made into Parliament's legislative supremacy.[104] Alongside devolution and the UK's membership of the European Union, the HRA marked a 'further qualification' of the Diceyan conception of parliamentary sovereignty[105] and a significant strengthening of the rule of law.[106]

Such judicial – and academic – musings on the limits of Parliament's power are not now uncommon.[107] And although claims as to the courts'

---

[100] *Jackson and others* v. *Her Majesty's Attorney-General*, above n. 83, para.102. On the issue of divided sovereignty, see: *X* v. *Morgan Grampian Ltd* [1991] AC 1, 48 (Lord Bridge of Harwich) and Sir Stephen Sedley, 'The sound of silence: constitutional law without a constitution' (1994) 110 LQR 270.

[101] *Jackson and others* v. *Her Majesty's Attorney-General*, above n. 83, para.102.

[102] *Ibid.*, para.159.

[103] For details of the (ultimately unsuccessful) challenge to the Hunting Act 2004 lodged on the basis of Article 8 ECHR, see: *R (on the application of the Countryside Alliance)* v. *Her Majesty's Attorney-General* [2007] UKHL 52; [2008] 1 AC 719.

[104] *Jackson and others* v. *Her Majesty's Attorney-General*, above n. 83, para.102 (Lord Steyn) and para.159 (Baroness Hale).

[105] *Ibid.*, para.105 (Lord Steyn).   [106] *Ibid.*, para.107.

[107] See e.g.: Lord Woolf, 'Droit public – English style' [1995] PL 57, 69; Laws, 'Law and democracy', above n. 49, 84–90; G. Wilson, 'The courts, law and convention' in M. P. Nolan

ability to check the power of Parliament may be without a pedigree that postdates the Civil War,[108] it is difficult to reject their validity on such grounds alone. Similarly, while the remaining Law Lords in *Jackson* neglected to engage with the constitutional speculation of Lord Steyn and Baroness Hale, the concerns of the latter over the insulation of executive action from judicial scrutiny should not simply be rejected as insignificant dicta.

Lord Steyn's suggestion that the courts may be required to revisit the common law acceptance of parliamentary sovereignty in the context of an 'exceptional' usage of the Parliament Acts procedure is worthy of serious consideration, for it is in those circumstances – when an executive-dominated Commons can bypass the objections of the House of Lords – that the potential for unchecked executive power is at its most evident. It is as an encapsulation of those circumstances in which the checking and balancing functions of both Commons and Lords are largely ineffective in the face of executive authority that Lord Hailsham's phrase 'elective dictatorship' is most appropriately used.[109] In other areas, the courts have been willing to scrutinise – and invalidate – executive action where Parliament has proven unable or unwilling to constrain ministerial discretion,[110] and, as has been argued, there is a broader discernible trend towards limiting unchecked executive power.[111] A parallel can be drawn between the sentiments expressed by Lord Steyn and Baroness Hale in *Jackson* and those highlighted by Lord Hoffmann in *Bancoult*. In the latter decision, Lord Hoffmann – in the context of holding that prerogative legislative powers are in principle subject to judicial review – made clear a degree of

---

and S. Sedley, *The Making and Remaking of the British Constitution* (London: Blackstone Press, 1997), p.116. Cf. C. Gearty, 'Are judges now out of their depth?', JUSTICE Tom Sargant Memorial Annual Lecture 2007 (available at: www.justice.org.uk/publications/listofpublications/index.html).

[108] As Lord Coke (in)famously noted in *Dr Bonham's Case* (1610) 8 Co Rep 113b, 118a:

In many cases, the common law will control Acts of Parliament, and sometimes adjudge them to be utterly void: for when an Act of Parliament is against common right and reason, or repugnant, or impossible to be performed, the common law will control it, and adjudge such Act to be void.

[109] Lord Hailsham, *The Dilemma of Democracy: Diagnosis and Prescription* (London: Collins, 1978).

[110] For two classic examples, see: *R v. Secretary of State for Foreign and Commonwealth Affairs, ex parte World Development Movement* [1995] 1 WLR 386; *R v. Secretary of State for the Home Department, ex parte Fire Brigades Union* [1995] 2 AC 513.

[111] See pp.103–4. And see the decision of the House of Lords in *R (on the application of Bancoult) v. Secretary of State for Foreign and Commonwealth Affairs*, above n. 11.

scepticism over the executive's ability to implement legislative measures absent parliamentary supervision:

> The principle of the sovereignty of Parliament ... is founded upon the unique authority Parliament derives from its representative character. An exercise of the prerogative lacks this quality, although it may be legislative in character, it is still an exercise of power by *the executive alone*.[112]

It is at least arguable that action taken by the executive branch under the Parliament Acts, beneath a veneer of legislative authority, should also be open to judicial scrutiny. Indeed, in checks and balances terms, opening up uses of the Parliament Acts to judicial scrutiny may be regarded as being entirely unobjectionable, so that executive power might not be exercised entirely absent of effective legal and political supervision. A reading of *Jackson* which would endorse the possibility of judicial scrutiny of legislative measures implemented under the Parliament Acts procedure would not be obviously inconsistent with a separation of powers that values judicial checks on virtually unbridled executive power. It is in the potential for the judiciary to revisit their acceptance of sovereignty in the face of a legislative measure endorsed by *both* the House of Commons and House of Lords that Steyn's and Hale's dicta is, of course, most controversial. A more expansive reading of this dicta – seeming to suggest a residual judicial competence to reject primary legislation which the courts hold to be inconsistent with the requirements of the rule of law – is more difficult to sustain. Even so, such a possibility was seemingly not ruled out by either of the Law Lords.[113]

To illustrate that significance of the comments of Lord Steyn and Baroness Hale, a more practical parallel can be drawn with claims made both by parliamentarians, commentators and – extrajudicially – by judges during the passage of the Asylum and Immigration (Treatment of Claimants etc) Bill 2004. The Bill, as originally introduced into Parliament, contained an ouster clause, which would have had the effect of excluding decisions on the status of asylum seekers from the jurisdiction of the courts in judicial review proceedings subsequent to the (effectively final) findings of the Asylum and Immigration Tribunal. The effect of the clause, Rick Rawlings has argued, would have been to 'neuter the

---

[112] *Ibid.*, para.35 (Lord Hoffmann) (emphasis added).
[113] See: D. Jenkins, 'Common law declarations of unconstitutionality' (2009) 7 *International Journal of Constitutional Law* 183.

judicial role in the constitution' with the effect of casting 'administrative law back to the sleepy days of the 1950s'.[114]

The proposed ouster clause – unsurprisingly – provoked considerable opposition both within and without Parliament, which eventually caused the government to remove the provision from the draft legislation. While the successes of *parliamentary* and *popular* pressure in bringing about the removal of the ouster clause should be welcomed, the *judicial* contribution to the broader debate, extrajudicially and within Parliament, should not be understated.[115] Within the legislature the government's proposal was variously described – with notable contributions from one former Lord Chancellor, and another former Law Lord – as 'a serious affront to the rule of law', 'a constitutional outrage' and the 'worst threat to the rule of law since [the passing of] Magna Carta'.[116] While extrajudicially, Lord Woolf, then Lord Chief Justice, speculated that, had the clause been implemented, 'it would have been so inconsistent with the spirit of mutual respect between the different arms of government that it could have been the catalyst for a campaign for a written constitution'.[117] Objections from other branches of the legal establishment were no less robust. Most striking – perhaps for saying outright what many others were thinking – was the suggestion from Michael Fordham that the response of the courts to such a blatant and excessive denial of jurisdiction might be to recognise 'the role and responsibility of the court to strike down such an enactment as unconstitutional'.[118]

The cumulative effect of the House of Lords decision in *Jackson* and of the 2004 Asylum and Immigration Bill episode is to highlight a further potential faultline in the theory of parliamentary supremacy. The extent of this weakness has not yet been seriously tested.[119] The available evidence would appear, at first glance, to support the continuing ability of

---

[114] R. Rawlings, 'Review, revenge and retreat' (2005) 68 MLR 378, 378–9. And for details of further attempts to reduce the availability of judicial review in this sphere, see: A. Le Sueur, 'Three strikes and it's out: the UK government's strategy to oust judicial review from immigration and asylum decision making' [2004] PL 225.

[115] Rawlings, 'Review, revenge and retreat', above n. 114, 379.

[116] HL Debs, 15 March 2004, vol.659 cols.67 (Lord Mackay of Clashfern), 72 (Lord Donaldson of Lymington) and 82 (Earl Russell).

[117] Lord Woolf, 'The rule of law and a change in the constitution' (2004) 63 CLJ 317, 329.

[118] M. Fordham, 'Common law illegality of ousting judicial review' [2004] JR 86, 93. See also: A. Lester QC, 'Beyond the powers of Parliament' [2004] JR 95. Cf. Rawlings, 'Review, revenge and retreat' above n. 114, 404–6.

[119] For a failed attempt to advance a similar argument, pre-*Jackson*, see: *McWhirter and Gouriet v. Secretary of State for Foreign and Commonwealth Affairs*, above n. 69.

Parliament to legislate in whatever manner, and terms, it chooses. As we have already seen, structural respect for parliamentary sovereignty is an inherent feature of the HRA itself – as Lord Millett, dissenting, argued in *Ghaidan* v. *Godin Mendoza*, while the sovereignty doctrine is not 'sacrosanct ... any change in a fundamental constitutional principle should be the consequence of deliberate legislative action and not judicial activism, however well meaning'.[120] At common law, the courts have conceded that – in spite of the limited protections afforded through the fundamental rights jurisdiction[121] – 'Parliament can, if it chooses, legislate contrary to fundamental principles of human rights.'[122] And finally, outside of the sphere of influence of European Union law, no court in modern times has attempted to disapply primary legislation, either in its entirety or even in part.[123]

Yet, in spite of the evidence to the contrary, a question-mark hangs over the potential consequences of Parliament's ability to legislate in flagrant contravention of the Convention rights or constitutional principle, no matter how clear the wording used. As Jeffrey Jowell observed in 2004:

> [i]t is no longer self-evident, therefore, that our courts would inevitably concede parliament's right to ride roughshod over fundamental rights and ... constitutional principles. And the issue that is most likely to provoke the courts finally to question parliament's paramount rule is an attack on the courts' own constitutional duty to hear out people claiming injustice.[124]

If, as a part of a broader 'dialogue' on the limits of parliamentary power, such judicial dicta exerts influence – however limited – at a legislative level, then ultimately its potential normative force cannot be denied in its entirety. If this can be accepted, then the threat of a *potential* judicial response to a particularly oppressive measure in direct contravention of the Convention rights – or other established constitutional standards – becomes an effective checking and balancing tool in the broader political debates over the merits of such legislative proposals, which may

---

[120] *Ghaidan* v. *Godin-Mendoza*, above n. 26, para.57 (Lord Millett). See pp.162–3.
[121] See: *R* v. *Secretary of State for the Home Department, ex parte Leech (No. 2)* [1994] QB 198; *R* v. *Lord Chancellor, ex parte Witham* [1998] QB 575.
[122] *R* v. *Secretary of State for the Home Department, ex parte Simms* [2000] 2 AC 115, 131.
[123] *R* v. *Secretary of State for Transport, ex parte Factortame (No. 2)* [1991] 1 AC 603.
[124] J. Jowell, 'Immigration wars', *The Guardian*, 2 March 2004.

prompt the government and Parliament to reconsider the wisdom of their proposed actions.[125]

Conclusion

It is a sign of just how far the constitutional balance has been tipped in recent times that discussions of the fringes of justiciability now verge on including the constitutionality of specific legislative directions rather than the questions of resource allocation, national security and so on. Discussions of justiciability in this sphere have largely been replaced by discussions over the degree of deference to be afforded, and of the proportionality of a given intrusion. While the engagement of one or more of the Convention rights may have put a stop to the *complete* exclusion of some areas of executive activity – foreign affairs, for example – from judicial scrutiny, the standard of review applied may be such as to preserve the virtual autonomy of executive decision making. Victories for the ability of the courts to subject executive power to the demands of the rule of law in this regard may rightly be regarded as being pyrrhic;[126] while a particular power may be found to be reviewable in principle, the remedy sought by the applicant may be less frequently forthcoming. The practical significance of the withering of non-justiciability doctrines should not, however, simply be discounted as failing to bring any practical benefit for even the partially successful litigant. The ability of the courts to consider a range of 'political' disputes which might previously have been regarded as being non-justiciable is of significance in itself, for it lends credence to the idea that the scope within which the executive is able to act outside the supervisory jurisdiction of the courts is gradually diminishing. The decision of the House of Lords in *Bancoult* adds weight to this suggestion, by confirming that prerogative legislation – long thought to fall outside the scope of judicial scrutiny[127] – in an area to which the HRA did not extend, could be subject to judicial review.[128] In addition – as can be seen perhaps most obviously in the area of national security – the range of executive

---

[125] For a discussion of more direct contributions by courts to the business of constitutional politics, see pp.168–76 and 179–80.

[126] M. Elliott and A. Perreau-Saussine, 'Pyrrhic public law: *Bancoult* and the sources, status and content of common law limitations on prerogative power' [2009] PL 697.

[127] M. Cohn, 'Judicial review of non-statutory executive powers after *Bancoult*: a unified anxious model?' [2009] PL 260, 269.

[128] *R (on the application of Bancoult)* v. *Secretary of State for Foreign and Commonwealth Affairs*, above n. 11, para.35 (Lord Hoffmann).

decisions to which the courts will afford particularly wide latitude is also becoming increasingly narrow, leaving open the possibility that the gravity of the infringement will weigh as heavily on the court as the potential degree of deference owed to the executive. In separation of powers terms, this system of judicial checks and balances may not be comprehensive, but signs are emerging that no governmental power may be regarded as being entirely immune from review.

5

Deference and proportionality

Introduction

By bringing questions arising in connection with the Convention rights clearly into the jurisdiction of the courts, the HRA has considerably altered the division of governmental power in the constitution. But it is not simply the judicial determination of questions of human rights *simpliciter* that has fuelled calls that the judicial branch has been empowered at the expense of the elected branches. It has already been noted that the circumstances in which disputes over rights arise frequently call for courts to consider and adjudicate over competing 'goods' which are said to be more appropriately considered in political fora. While the judicial review jurisdiction has long held to the notion that review of administrative action should not amount to review of the merits of a given decision,[1] it has been argued that – in asking that the courts review instances where individual rights should be proportionately balanced against the public interest – courts are brought into much closer relief with the merits of individual governmental decisions.[2] It is therefore the legal tests associated with rights adjudication that have provoked objection from rights sceptics, as much as adjudication over human rights themselves.

This chapter examines the related issues of deference and proportionality. Deference allows a variable degree of weight to attach to the decisions of public bodies, and to the justifications put forward by those bodies in defence of a particular policy or course of action. Deference therefore ensures respect for the realities of political decision making by acknowledging the differences between the processes of decision making adopted by the executive and the legislature and those adopted by the courts, and ensuring that judges remain sensitive to the fact that those

---

[1] *Associated Provincial Picture Houses Ltd* v. *Wednesbury Corporation* [1948] 1 KB 223, 228.

[2] See e.g: *R* v. *Secretary of State for the Home Department, ex parte Brind* [1991] 1 AC 696, 762–3 (Lord Ackner), 766–7 (Lord Lowry).

differences may produce differing conclusions in practice. Adherence to the test of proportionality, meanwhile, guarantees that judicial engagement with matters of political controversy proceeds on the basis of a structured, defined, series of legal questions, rather than on the basis of *ad hoc* assessments of rationality or reasonableness. Taken together, deference and proportionality effectively regulate the degree to which the courts can intervene in decisions taken by political actors in those instances where the Convention rights are engaged.

Deference

At first glance, the division of power under the HRA appears clear-cut; the courts remain 'interpreters' of the law, and any legislative amendment which may be thought necessary to achieve Convention compatibility is a matter of parliamentary choice. Thus, parliamentary sovereignty is preferred to judicial supremacy. Through this nominal preservation of parliamentary sovereignty – even in the event of the courts making a declaration of incompatibility – the Act makes explicit provision for a degree of respect for the decisions of the elected arms of the state. In this sense at least, the HRA does not mark a radical departure for the UK constitution, as deference to the elected branches – in particular, Parliament – has long been an established feature of judicial review,[3] and indeed lay at the heart of the reluctance of the courts to use the common law to enforce the Convention rights in domestic law prior to the enactment of the HRA.[4] The following extract – from the judgment of Sir John Donaldson in *ex parte Smedley* – is typical of the constitutional importance attached by the judges to this particular aspect of the separation of powers dynamic:

> Although the United Kingdom has no written constitution, it is … of the highest importance that the legislature and the judicature are separate and independent of one another, subject to certain ultimate rights of Parliament over the judicature which are immaterial for present purposes.

[3] Most obviously evidenced in the work of those who argue that the *ultra vires* principle provides the constitutional underpinnings of judicial review, e.g.: W. Wade and C. Forsyth, *Administrative Law* (10th edn) (Oxford University Press, 2009), ch.2; C. Forsyth, 'Of fig leaves and fairy tales: the *ultra vires* doctrine, the sovereignty of Parliament and judicial review' (1996) 55 CLJ 122. Cf. D. Oliver, 'Is the *ultra vires* rule the basis of judicial review?' [1987] PL 543; C. Craig, 'Competing models of judicial review' [1999] PL 428. And see generally: M. Elliott, *The Constitutional Foundations of Judicial Review* (Oxford: Hart Publishing, 2001).

[4] *R* v. *Secretary of State for the Home Department, ex parte Brind*, above n. 2, 718 (Lord Donaldson of Lymington MR), 762–3 (Lord Ackner).

> It therefore behoves the courts to be ever sensitive to the paramount need
> to refrain from trespassing on the province of Parliament.[5]

It is clear, therefore, that enacting the HRA, and the attendant re-evaluation of the judicial role which its enforcement would require, would not simply collapse the established divisions between executive, legislative and judicial power. These conventional divisions are in a sense preserved by the development of notions of deference – otherwise referred to as the discretionary area of judgment[6] – that courts have, to varying degrees, afforded decisions of Parliament and the executive following the implementation of the HRA.

Deference or a margin of appreciation?

At the Strasbourg level, a parallel can be found in the margin of appreciation doctrine, under which the European Court of Human Rights allows a discretion to national authorities over how the minimum standards found in the Convention are to be realised, taking into account the prevailing circumstances in that state,[7] though ultimately subject to a Strasbourg supervision.[8] The justifications for this, occasionally non-interventionist, approach can be traced back to the decision of the European Court of Human Rights in *Handyside*:

> the machinery of protection established by the Convention is subsidiary to the national systems regarding human rights ... by reason of their direct and continuous contact with the vital forces of their countries, State authorities are in principle in a better position than the international judge to give an opinion on the exact content of those requirements as well as on the 'necessity' of a 'restriction' or 'penalty' intended to meet them.[9]

However, from the earliest decisions under the HRA, it became evident that domestic courts would not – and indeed *should* not – apply the margin of appreciation doctrine undiluted to rights adjudication in the domestic context. To do so, it was suggested, would result in a less-than-rigorous standard of review at the domestic level, and would allow margins

---

[5] *R* v. *HM Treasury, ex parte Smedley* [1985] QB 657, 666 (Sir John Donaldson MR).
[6] Lord Lester of Herne Hill and D. Pannick, *Human Rights Law and Practice* (London: Butterworths, 1999), pp.73–6.
[7] Although – in the words of the Commission – those circumstances 'cannot of themselves be decisive' (*Dudgeon* v. *United Kingdom* (1981) 3 EHRR 40, para.114).
[8] *Handyside* v. *United Kingdom* (1979–80) 1 EHRR 737, para.49.
[9] *Ibid.*, para.48.

of appreciation designed for other member states to creep into domestic law.[10] Recognising that the arguments based on grounds of geographical remoteness employed by the European Court of Human Rights would not carry weight in the domestic context, Lord Hope stated in *Kebilene* that the margin of appreciation is 'not available to the national courts when they are considering Convention issues arising within their own countries'.[11] Nevertheless, it was also recognised that the *spirit* of the margin of appreciation – and the deference that it afforded the decisions of national legislatures and executives – would be reflected in the decision-making processes of domestic courts under the HRA.[12] Conscious of the respect for the decisions of the elected branches which is inherent in the design of the HRA – and no doubt of the views of critics who feared that the Act would herald the introduction of strong form review by way of the back door – the courts were eager to stress that introduction of the HRA did not introduce government by judges:

> While a national court does not accord a margin of appreciation … it will give weight to the decisions of a representative legislature and a democratic government within the discretionary area of judgment accorded to those bodies.[13]

The existence, and parameters, of the degree of deference afforded to the relevant decision maker have provided some of the most debated issues arising out of adjudication under the HRA.[14] What degree of latitude – if

---

[10] See e.g.: H. Fenwick and G. Phillipson, 'Direct action, Convention values and the Human Rights Act' (2001) 21 LS 535, 553–4. Fenwick and Phillipson have since been critical of the attempts of domestic courts to disentangle the margin of appreciation from those aspects of the Strasbourg case law which are applicable at the domestic level:
> [i]n numerous appellate decisions under the HRA, the courts have paid lip service to the notion that the margin of appreciation has no role to play in domestic decision-making. In nearly every case … the courts have then gone on to apply Strasbourg case-law heavily determined by that doctrine, thus precisely applying the margin of appreciation.

(H. Fenwick and G. Phillipson, *Media Freedom under the Human Rights Act* (Oxford University Press, 2006), p.146.)

[11] *R* v. *Director of Public Prosecutions, ex parte Kebilene* [2000] 2 AC 326, 380–1.

[12] D. Pannick, 'Principles of interpretation of Convention rights under the Human Rights Act and the discretionary area of judgment' [1998] PL 545, 549:
> Just as there are circumstances in which an international court will recognise that national institutions are better placed to assess the needs of society, and to make difficult choices between competing considerations, so national courts will accept that there are circumstances in which the legislature and the executive are better placed to perform those functions.

[13] *Brown* v. *Stott* [2001] 2 WLR 817, 835 (PC).

[14] For a sample of the voluminous literature, see: R. Edwards, 'Judicial deference under the Human Rights Act' (2002) 65(6) MLR 859; F. Klug, 'Judicial deference under the Human

any[15] – the courts should afford the elected arms of the state informs the intensity of review to which the scrutinised decision will be subject. The question is one of separation of powers in the sense that deference conditions the rigour with which courts will scrutinise decisions made in the political arena; deference indirectly affects the ability of the courts to intervene, or challenge, decisions taken by the elected branches of government. As a result, one commentator has described the discretionary area of judgment as 'the classic separation of powers device articulated in the post-Human Rights Act era'.[16]

Constraining judicial power under a statutory bill of rights

While the debates over the separation of elected and judicial power under a judicially enforced bill of rights have traditionally emphasised the restrictions placed on the powers of the executive and legislature to curb individual freedom, a corresponding emphasis on limiting the powers of the judicial branch in policing the protected rights has been significantly lacking. As Janet Hiebert has argued:

> Most view a Bill of Rights as an explicit restraint on legislative and executive powers … this emphasis on granting protection from state-imposed constraints often reflects only a partial view of the state, one that treats the

Rights Act' [2003] EHRLR 125; M. Hunt, 'Sovereignty's blight: why contemporary public law needs a concept of "due deference"' in N. Bamforth and P. Leyland, *Public Law in a Multi-Layered Constitution* (Oxford: Hart Publishing, 2003); J. Jowell, 'Judicial deference: servility, civility or institutional capacity?' [2004] PL 592; Lord Steyn, 'Deference: a tangled story' [2005] PL 346; C. O'Cinneide, 'Democracy and rights: new directions in the human rights era' [2004] 57 *Current Legal Problems* 175; T. Hickman, 'Constitutional dialogue, constitutional theories and the Human Rights Act 1998' [2005] PL 306; T. R. S. Allan, 'Human rights and judicial review: a critique of "due deference"' [2006] CLJ 671; A. Kavanagh, 'Deference or defiance? The limits of the judicial role in constitutional adjudication' in G. Huscroft (ed.), *Expounding the Constitution: Essays in Constitutional Theory* (Cambridge University Press, 2008); A. L. Young, 'In defence of due deference' (2009) 72 MLR 554.

[15] One school advances the view that there is no further need for a 'discretionary area of judgment' to be afforded to the legislative enactments of Parliament due to the deference integral to the design of the HRA itself. Francesca Klug has argued that for this reason there is 'no need for judges, legal practitioners or academics to develop complex theories of judicial deference if the scheme of the Act is properly appreciated and appropriately applied' (Klug, 'Judicial deference under the Human Rights Act', above n. 14. See further: G. Phillipson, 'Deference, discretion and democracy in the Human Rights Act era' (2007) 60 *Current Legal Problems* 40.

[16] S. Tierney, 'Determining the state of exception: what role for Parliament and the courts?' (2005) 68 MLR 668, 670.

judiciary as the umpire or neutral arbiter of conflicts and not as a potential source of rights violations. Most commentators on Bills of Rights do
not think it is necessary to envisage similar constraints on the judiciary
itself, despite the fact that when making legal rules, developing the common law and interpreting the constitution, the judiciary also exercises
state power.[17]

As has already been seen, critics of bills of rights emphasise the extension
of judicial power into the sphere of political decision making that rights
adjudication will prompt. While the structure of the HRA itself attempts
to mitigate against decisions affecting rights taken by Parliament and
the executive being entirely at the mercy of the judicial branch, judicial
deference provides an additional measure of institutional self-restraint.
Deference allows the judicial branch to take account of the relative institutional competence and expertise of the decision maker, and allows the
court to afford a degree of respect to both the decision maker and to the
grounds on which a given decision was made. In short, deference allows
the judicial process to accommodate the ability of political processes of
decision making to produce differing outcomes from those which may
have resulted had the same issues been considered in the court room.

Conor Gearty has drawn a distinction in this regard between what he
argues should rightly be referred to as 'judicial restraint' and 'judicial
deference'. Gearty has argued that in cases where the Convention rights
are in play, courts may exercise both restraint *and* deference. The former
'derives more from an awareness of the limitations of the judicial function
than it does from respect for parliamentary sovereignty as such'.[18] And as
Gearty argues, '[i]t may be that judicial restraint relates to areas where
the executive is rightly the lead agent (e.g. foreign policy), and judicial
deference to those subject matters that Parliament has taken onto itself'.[19]
Part of the difficulty with such an assessment is, as we have already seen,
that Parliament has specifically placed partial responsibility for enforcement of the Convention rights within judicial competence. Arguments
that Parliament or the executive may rightly be the 'lead agent' in respect
of certain issues should not be taken as suggesting that the judicial role
be completely ousted. This is for the reason that the Act makes questions
concerning, say, both national security and Convention rights, a matter in

---

[17] J. Hiebert, 'Interpreting a bill of rights: the importance of legislative rights review' (2005)
35 *British Journal of Political Science* 235, 236.
[18] C. Gearty, *Principles of Human Rights Adjudication* (Oxford University Press, 2004),
p.120.
[19] *Ibid.* p.134.

which both arms of government are competent to make decisions. It is the nature of the decision – and of the decision-making processes adopted – that will differ, rather than the topic in respect of which the decision is made.

Deference therefore allows courts to take account of the relative position of the elected branches in the constitution *and* the nature of legislative and executive decision-making processes *vis-à-vis* those of the courts. It can therefore be seen as a tool of institutional self-restraint which mitigates against a potentially uniform (and robust) standard of review across all prima facie justiciable issues. Deferential concerns therefore enable human rights review to be receptive to judicial moderation – and thus sensitive to the justifications articulated in defence of a decision by elected officials – within a framework which undoubtedly contains the potential for wide-ranging and rigorous subjection of those decisions to judicial control.

Deference under the Human Rights Act

From the earliest decisions under the HRA, it has been evident that 'national courts may accord to the decisions of national legislatures some deference *where the context justifies it*'.[20] Such a position makes clear two basic points of principle: the status of a decision maker alone should not immunise a decision from judicial analysis or the potential intervention of the courts, nor should the giving of prima facie justificatory reasons prompt an abandonment of scrutiny on HRA grounds. Deference – in excess of any minimalistic notions of inter-institutional comity[21] – is therefore not an obligation *owed* by courts to the elected branches, irrespective of the circumstances in which a dispute has arisen.

Nevertheless, the courts have recognised that certain governmental decisions may demand greater respect than others. An early attempt to outline the general principles under which the courts would afford deference to the elected branches was provided by Lord Hope in *Kebilene*. As to the circumstances when courts might afford a degree of latitude to the primary decision maker, as Lord Hope noted:

> It will be easier for such [a discretionary] area of judgment to be recognised where the Convention itself requires a balance to be struck, much less so where the right is stated in terms which are unqualified. It will be

---

[20] *Brown* v. *Stott* [2003] 1 AC 681, 711 (emphasis in original).
[21] See: Kavanagh, 'Deference or defiance?', above n. 14, pp.191–3.

easier for it to be recognised where the issues involve questions of social or economic policy, much less so where the rights are of high constitutional importance or are of a kind where the courts are especially well placed to assess the need for protection.[22]

Laws LJ sought to expand on this analysis in *International Transport Roth GmbH v. Secretary of State for the Home Department.*[23] In that case, Laws LJ outlined four general principles under which the courts would acknowledge the legitimacy of decisions taken by Parliament and the executive. First, he said, 'greater deference is to be paid to an Act of Parliament than to a decision of the executive or subordinate measure … where the decision-maker is not Parliament, but a minister or other public or governmental authority exercising power conferred by Parliament, a degree of deference will be due on democratic grounds' for the reason that 'the decision-maker is Parliament's delegate'.[24] Second, 'there is much more scope for deference "where the Convention itself requires a balance to be struck, much less so where the right is stated in terms which are unqualified" '.[25] Hence, where the qualified rights of the Convention are at issue, the courts should be mindful of the legitimacy of the decision maker's assessment of what action is deemed to be 'necessary in a democratic society'. Laws LJ continued:

> [t]he third principle is that greater deference will be due to the democratic powers where the subject matter in hand is peculiarly within their constitutional responsibility, and less when it lies more particularly within the constitutional responsibility of the courts. The first duty of government is the defence of the realm. It is well settled that executive decisions dealing directly with matters of defence, while not immune from judicial review (that would be repugnant to the rule of law) cannot sensibly be scrutinised by the courts on grounds relating to their factual merits … The first duty of the courts is the maintenance of the rule of law. That is exemplified in many ways, not least by the extremely restrictive construction always placed on no-certiorari clauses.[26]

And finally, Laws LJ noted that the fourth principle held that:

> greater or lesser deference will be due according to whether the subject matter lies more readily within the actual or potential expertise of the

---

[22] *R v. Director of Public Prosecutions, ex parte Kebilene*, above n. 11, 381 (Lord Hope).

[23] *International Transport Roth GmbH v. Secretary of State for the Home Department* [2002] EWCA Civ 158; [2003] QB 728.

[24] *Ibid.*, para.83.

[25] *Ibid.*, para.84, citing Lord Hope of Craighead in *Kebilene v. Director of Public Prosecutions* [2000] 2 AC 326, 381.

[26] *International Transport Roth GmbH*, above n. 23, para.85.

democratic powers or the courts. Thus, quite aside from defence, government decisions in the area of macro-economic policy will be relatively remote from judicial control ...[27]

At first glance, these principles may appear relatively uncontroversial. Yet, in spite of a clear grounding in the structural design of the HRA itself, and an obvious heritage in the history of administrative law, the notion of deference has been subject to a degree of criticism. This criticism lies, in part, in the 'overtones of servility, or perhaps gracious concession' that accompany use of the term deference,[28] in part, in the suspicion that deference may be used as a fig leaf for non-justiciability.[29]

'...servility, or perhaps gracious concession'?

The first of these criticisms is perhaps most obviously evident in the speech of Lord Hoffmann in *R v. British Broadcasting Corporation, ex parte ProLife Alliance*. Lord Hoffmann argued in his speech that:

> although the word 'deference' is now very popular in describing the relationship between the judicial and the other branches of government, I do not think that its overtones of servility, or perhaps gracious concession, are appropriate to describe what is happening. In a society based upon the rule of law and the separation of powers, it is necessary to decide which branch of government has in any particular instance the decision-making power and what the legal limits of that power are. That is a question of law and must therefore be decided by the courts.[30]

In many respects, criticisms of the notion of deference based on the acknowledgement that the courts occupy a less-dominant position in the constitution relative to Parliament should not be surprising – if Parliament retains sovereign power, then the institutional position of the courts is undeniably inferior. Yet a number of commentators argue that it would be entirely inappropriate for a court to defer to the decision of a public body – whether executive or Parliament – on the basis of that body's constitutional status alone.[31] In his speech in *ProLife Alliance*, Lord Hoffmann attempted to capture the nature of the judicial exercise

---

[27] *Ibid.*, para.87.
[28] *R v. British Broadcasting Corporation, ex parte ProLife Alliance* [2003] UKHL 23; [2004] 1 AC 185, para.75 (Lord Hoffmann).
[29] Allan, 'Human Rights and Judicial Review', above n. 14.
[30] *R v. British Broadcasting Corporation, ex parte ProLife Alliance*, above n. 28, para.75 (Lord Hoffmann).
[31] See e.g.: Jowell, 'Judicial deference', above n. 14.

of determining the holder and extent of a particular legal power as a question of separation of powers, and a task for the courts.[32] Lord Hoffmann's articulation of this specific legal responsibility is worth reproducing in full:

> The principles upon which decision-making powers are allocated are principles of law. The courts are the independent branch of government and the legislature and executive are, directly and indirectly respectively, the elected branches of government. Independence makes the courts more suited to deciding some kinds of questions and being elected makes the legislature or executive more suited to deciding others. The allocation of these decision-making responsibilities is based upon recognised principles. The principle that the independence of the courts is necessary for a proper decision of disputed legal rights or claims of violation of human rights is a legal principle. It is reflected in article 6 of the Convention. On the other hand, the principle that majority approval is necessary for a proper decision on policy or allocation of resources is also a legal principle. Likewise, when a court decides that a decision is within the proper competence of the legislature or executive, it is not showing deference. It is deciding the law.[33]

For Lord Hoffmann, then, the branches of government may each display distinct institutional characteristics which might arguably make them most apt to make a particular decision. The determination of the extent of a specific legal right is, for example, on Lord Hoffmann's analysis, clearly one for the courts, while the determination and implementation of a policy is a matter for the elected branches. Such a robust approach, at first glance, is certainly reflective of a clearly defined separation of functions which would appear to be 'enforceable by the courts'.[34] However, the application of this approach in practice appears to have led Lord Hoffmann to draw overly strict lines between areas of, for example, legislative and judicial competence, which seemed to preclude judicial analysis of the specific limitation on freedom of expression at issue in *ProLife*.[35] And as a result, on the basis that Parliament had determined where the balance should lie between freedom of expression and the

---

[32] *R v. British Broadcasting Corporation, ex parte ProLife Alliance*, above n. 28, para.75 (Lord Hoffmann).

[33] *Ibid.*, para.76 (Lord Hoffmann).

[34] E. Barendt, 'Separation of powers and constitutional government' [1995] PL 599, 605.

[35] For criticism of this decision, see: E. Barendt, 'Free speech and abortion' [2003] PL 580; Phillipson, 'Deference, discretion and democracy in the Human Rights Act era', above n. 15, 71–4.

public interest, Lord Hoffman found that the court should not readily intervene in the substance of the specific decision to censor the ProLife Alliance's election broadcast.[36]

At least part of the difficulty with such an approach, as we have already seen, is that our constitution has not traditionally drawn such bright lines between executive, judicial and legislative functions.[37] A further – more pressing – problem lies in the fact that the HRA provides that policy issues engaging the Convention rights *should* fall within judicial competence. The absolutism of Lord Hoffmann's analysis provides little or no room to accommodate the interplay between legal rights and questions of policy. As Sandra Fredman has written of continued attempts to compartmentalise 'law' and 'policy' where the Convention rights are at issue:

> The democratic dilemma posed by human rights adjudication ... cannot be resolved by creating separate spheres for 'political' and 'legal' decision-making, since policy-making has clear human rights implications and vice versa.[38]

A clear separation of powers categorised by subject matter, described in terms of 'spatial metaphors', is therefore unsustainable in the HRA era.[39] Instead, the separation of judicial, legislative and executive functions must be achieved by the maintenance of distinctive institutional processes of decision making adopted by courts and elected officials.

A fig leaf for non-justiciability?

While Lord Hoffmann found that the considerations associated with deference were an aspect of a (relatively rigid) separation of powers,[40] other commentators have not been prepared to treat the idea of deference as being reflective of such a separation. In an important critique, T. R. S. Allan, rather than seeing deference as a manifestation of a contemporary separation of powers, sees it as being potentially damaging to a central

---

[36] *R* v. *British Broadcasting Corporation, ex parte ProLife Alliance*, above n. 28, para.76 (Lord Hoffmann). Cf. the dissenting view of Lord Scott, paras.83–100 and the extrajudicial criticisms of Lord Steyn, 'Deference', above n. 14.

[37] See pp.16–20.

[38] S. Fredman, 'From deference to democracy: the role of equality under the Human Rights Act 1998' (2006) 122 LQR 53, 80.

[39] See further: Hunt, 'Sovereignty's blight', above n. 14.

[40] For a more detailed outline of Lord Hoffmann's views on the issue of separation of powers, see: 'The COMBAR lecture 2001: separation of powers' [2002] JR 137.

characteristic of that separation properly understood,[41] the independence of the judiciary. Allan argues that:

> A judge who allows his own view on the merits of any aspect of the case to be displaced by the contrary view of public officials – bowing to their greater expertise or experience or democratic credentials – forfeits the neutrality that underpins the legitimacy of constitutional adjudication.[42]

He refers to this as an 'illegitimate species of deference by abstention'.[43] Although through his use of terminology Allan hints at a 'legitimate' form of deference, in truth, the alternative position – a judge finding that, as a matter of law, the official's account and the requirements of the law are in accord – is not really a species of deference at all.

Allan likens the search for a coherent '*theory* or *doctrine*' of deference to the search for a chimera, and further argues that deference holds the potential to foreclose on intensive judicial review in the HRA era, just as notions of justiciability did so prior to its enactment.[44] Principles of deference, Allan suggests, exercising normative force independently of the distinct facts of the case at hand, run the risk of disengaging the outcome of a judicial decision from the specific circumstances and characteristics of the legal problem before the court.[45] For Allan, the preferred alternative is almost blindingly simple:

> the decisions of the 'political' branches of government should be loyally accepted insofar as they are consistent with the constitutional rights enshrined in the general law; and such decisions should be rejected where, in the court's best judgment, they violate those rights. The only 'deference' called for, in a liberal democracy worthy of the name, is obedience to rules or decisions that comply with the constitutional constraints that competent legal analysis identifies.[46]

On occasion, the courts have shown a marked reluctance to rigorously scrutinise legislative schemes for Convention compatibility – almost to the extent of suggesting that as Parliament may have indicated in a legislative scheme where the balance should lie, the courts have no further scrutiny role to perform.[47] This may, at least in part, be attributable to

---

[41] That is, a separation of powers which flows from, and is conditioned by the requirements of the rule of law: T. R. S. Allan, *Constitutional Justice: A Liberal Theory of the Rule of Law* (Oxford University Press, 2001).

[42] Allan, 'Human rights and judicial review', above n. 14, 676.

[43] *Ibid.*, 681.   [44] *Ibid.*, 671–2 (emphasis in original).

[45] *Ibid.*, 674–5.   [46] *Ibid.*, 673.

[47] See e.g.: *R (on the application of ProLife Alliance)* v. *British Broadcasting Corporation* [2004] 1 AC 185. The view persists among some commentators that excessive deference

traditional judicial reluctance to engage in review of the merits of governmental actions based on a hierarchical conception of the separation of powers in which the sovereignty of Parliament is overwhelmingly dominant. Equally, as the above discussion of *Rehman* shows,[48] the courts have also, on occasion, failed to subject executive decisions to detailed HRA analysis as a result of supposed institutional competence.[49] But while Dicey undoubtedly continues to wield considerable influence, and while the executive branch may well ultimately be better equipped to determine matters of national interest, *unquestioning* acceptance of either parliamentary or executive judgment is in clear tension with the role of the courts as prescribed by the HRA. As Jowell has written, in implementing the Act, Parliament has entrusted the courts with the task of 'delineating the boundaries of a rights-based democracy'.[50] More realistic, therefore, is the view put forward by Lord Woolf in *R* v. *Lambert*:

> The courts … are entitled to and should, as a matter of constitutional principle pay a degree of deference to the view of Parliament as to what is in the interest of the public generally when upholding the rights of the individual under the Convention. The courts are required to balance the competing interests involved.[51]

Allan's argument is certainly persuasive, and has been seen to have a resonance with the courts.[52] As Lord Bingham suggested, on behalf of a unanimous House of Lords, in *Huang*:

> The giving of weight to factors such as these is not, in our opinion, aptly described as deference: it is performance of the ordinary judicial task of weighing up the competing considerations on each side and according appropriate weight to the judgment of a person with responsibility for a given subject matter and access to special sources of knowledge and advice.[53]

---

has effectively neutered the HRA's ability to effectively protect individual rights (see K. D. Ewing, 'The futility of the Human Rights Act' [2004] PL 829, 843. Cf. A. Lester, 'The utility of the Human Rights Act: a reply to Keith Ewing' [2005] PL 249).

[48] pp.97–8.   [49] See: *R (on the application of ProLife Alliance)* v. *BBC*, above n. 47.

[50] Jowell, 'Judicial deference', above n. 14, 597. See also the comments of Lord Bingham in *A and other* v. *Secretary of State for the Home Department* [2004] UKHL 56; [2005] 2 AC 68, para.42.

[51] *R* v. *Lambert* [2002] QB 1112, para.16.

[52] M. Hunt, 'Against bifurcation' in D. Dyzenhaus, M. Hunt and G. Huscroft, *A Simple Common Lawyer: Essays in Honour of Michael Taggart* (Oxford: Hart Publishing, 2009), p.116.

[53] *Huang* v. *Secretary of State for the Home Department* [2007] UKHL 11; [2007] 2 AC 167, para.16.

Such a position illustrates the reluctance of the Law Lords to embrace an independent 'doctrine' or 'theory' of deference, but certainly leaves the door open to decisions being taken which are influenced by deferential concerns. It is for this reason that deference should not be regarded as enjoying an autonomous existence, outside of the relevant range of questions that a court should ask in determining whether a public authority has acted in accordance with the Convention rights.

An autonomous or an integrated concept?

Deference to the elected branches of government allows courts to acknowledge the greater institutional competence, expertise or legitimacy of the elected branches of government in a particular area of governmental decision making.[54] Deference should not allow a wholesale abdication of rigorous standards of review; it is not, or should not be, a non-justiciability doctrine in disguise. As Lord Rodger recognised in *A* v. *Home Secretary*, 'due deference does not mean abasement'.[55] Indeed, it is certainly arguable that deference should not be rightly regarded as being an 'autonomous concept'[56] at all, as in reality it cannot be separated in its entirety from the judicial decision-making process as prescribed by the HRA. Indeed, regarding the idea of deference as existing, and exercising influence, outside of the range of relevant legal considerations available for judicial consideration in decisions under the Act would – as Allan suggests – seem to heighten the likelihood of courts' abdicating their constitutional role.

Affording a degree of latitude to the range of responses available to the decision maker, recognising the differing nature of the decision-making process and the reasons articulated in support of a given policy decision, all allow the courts to acknowledge the distinct constitutional roles of the legislature and executive *without* abandoning the structural requirements of judicial review set down by the HRA. Each of these considerations enables a court to give weight to the views of the elected branches within the context of the specific dispute. By contrast, an unquestioning acceptance of a legislative or executive decision afforded solely on the basis of the status of the individual decision maker should not be regarded as being

[54] See: Kavanagh, 'Deference or defiance?', above n. 14; Jowell, 'Judicial Deference', above n. 14.

[55] *A and others* v. *Secretary of State for the Home Department*, above n. 50, para.176 (Lord Rodger of Earlsferry).

[56] B. Goold, L. Lazarus and G. Swiney, *Public Protection, Proportionality and the Search for Balance* (Ministry of Justice Research Series 10/07), September 2007, p.49.

appropriate. Deferring exclusively on the basis of the constitutional position of the decision maker would run the risk of insulating the parliamentary or executive decision from meaningful judicial scrutiny informed by the circumstances of the individual case (even though, in the context of parliamentary direction at least, this would be the natural consequence of a continuing acceptance of an undiluted sovereignty doctrine). Such an approach based solely on the 'relative authority of legislature, executive and judiciary' appears to have been rejected by the House of Lords in the decision in *Huang*.[57]

In short, deference should not stand alone as a ground for a particular judicial decision, but may be a part of the process in coming to that decision. As the Court of Appeal rightly recognised in *Wilson* v. *First County Trust*, deference is intimately linked with the process of determining whether a given policy or decision is justifiable:

> unless deference is to be equated with unquestioning acceptance, the argument ... recognises ... the need for the court to identify the particular issue of social policy which the legislature or the executive thought it necessary to address, and the thinking which led to that issue being dealt with in the way that it was. It is one thing to accept the need to defer to an opinion which can be seen to be the product of reasoned consideration based on policy; it is quite another thing to be required to accept, without question, an opinion for which no reason of policy is advanced.[58]

Key, then, is the judge's ability to formulate their own view as to the merits of the arguments deployed on behalf of the executive. Affording a degree of latitude to the status of the decision maker, the decision-making process and the reasons articulated in support of a given policy decision, should allow the courts to recognise the strengths and shortcomings of legislative, executive and judicial decision-making processes *without* abandoning the structure of judicial review set down by the HRA. It is to the structural aspect of HRA review that we now turn.

Proportionality and the intensity of review

Over fifteen years after Lord Diplock in *GCHQ* speculated that a fourth substantive head of judicial review might develop over time, the unanimous decision of the House of Lords in *R (on the application of Daly)* v. *Secretary of State for the Home Department* confirmed the place of

---

[57] Young, 'In defence of due deference', above n. 14, 573.
[58] *Wilson* v. *First County Trust* [2001] EWCA Civ 633; [2002] QB 74, para.33.

proportionality analysis in the domestic law of judicial review, where either common law, or Convention-based rights are in play.[59] Although *Daly* was nominally a case concerning rights existent at common law, the influence of the HRA in bringing about this development is undeniable, with Lord Steyn's speech being instructive in demonstrating the significance – in separation of powers terms – of the judicial adoption of this new test of legality.

In his judgment in *Daly*, while Lord Steyn indicated that there would exist an 'overlap between the traditional grounds of review and the approach of proportionality'[60] – and that in many instances the outcome of the case may well not differ no matter which approach the court adopts – crucially he also noted that 'the intensity of the review is somewhat greater' when proportionality review is employed.[61] Three specific differences were identified in Lord Steyn's speech. First, under a proportionality approach, the court may have to assess the grounds on which the decision in question was made, not simply whether it was within a range of reasonable responses available to the decision maker. Second, the proportionality approach might allow the court to assess the 'relative weight accorded to interests and considerations'.[62] Third, in questions involving rights, the Convention requires that the court make an assessment of whether the policy or decision in question pursues a 'pressing social need' and is proportionate to the policy or decision's legitimate purpose.[63]

Adopting the test of proportionality set down by the Judicial Committee of the Privy Council in *De Freitas*,[64] Lord Steyn indicated that a court should assess whether:

(i)   the legislative object is sufficiently important to justify limiting a fundamental right;

(ii) the measures designed to meet the legislative objective are rationally connected to it; and

(iii) the means used to impair the right or freedom are no more than is necessary to accomplish the objective.[65]

Proportionality analysis on the *Daly* reading, therefore, requires that courts assess the necessity of the given measure, the suitability of the measure to satisfy the stated objective, and whether or not the measure

---

[59] *R (on the application of Daly)* v. *Secretary of State for the Home Department* [2001] 2 AC 532; [2001] 3 All ER 433.

[60] *Ibid.*, para.27.   [61] *Daly*, above n. 59.   [62] *Ibid.*   [63] *Ibid.*   [64] *Ibid.*

[65] *De Freitas* v. *Permanent Secretary of Ministry of Agriculture, Fisheries, Lands and Housing* [1999] 1 AC 69, 80 (Lord Clyde).

imposes an excessive burden on the individual.[66] The balance struck between the individual right in question and the broader public interest is central to this structured test.[67] The structure of the domestic proportionality review closely mirrors the approach of the European Court of Human Rights to the assessment of whether a measure is 'necessary in a democratic society'.[68]

While the adoption of a test of proportionality in administrative law and in review under the HRA has been publicly welcomed by a number of senior judges, it has not simultaneously brought about the demise of *Wednesbury* review. In *Daly*, Lord Cooke noted his suspicion that:

> the day will come when it will be more widely recognised that *Associated Provincial Picture Houses* v. *Wednesbury Corporation* ... was an unfortunately retrogressive decision in English administrative law, insofar as it suggested that there are degrees of unreasonableness and that only a very extreme degree can bring administrative action within the legitimate scope of judicial invalidation.[69]

That day appears not to have come about. The Court of Appeal has held that – outside the scope of European Union law and those cases in which the Convention rights are at issue – there remains a legitimate role for *Wednesbury* review,[70] and has indicated that only the House of Lords could hammer the final nail into the *Wednesbury* coffin.[71] Neither the House of Lords nor Supreme Court has – yet – dealt the final blows.[72] But while the formal demise of *Wednesbury* has yet to be confirmed,[73] even if

---

[66] P. Craig, *Admininistrative Law* (6th edn) (London: Sweet and Maxwell, 2008), pp.627–8.

[67] *R (on the application of Daly)* v. *Secretary of State for the Home Department*, above n. 59, para.27 (Lord Steyn). Although a number of commentators have suggested that the question of whether a 'fair balance' has been struck is, in fact, a free-standing fourth branch of the proportionality analysis (see e.g.: J. Rivers, 'Proportionality and variable intensity of review' (2006) 65 CLJ 174, 181; Wade and Forsyth, *Administrative Law*, above n. 3, pp.306–7.

[68] pp.66–70.

[69] *R (on the application of Daly)* v. *Secretary of State for the Home Department*, above n. 59, para.32 (Lord Cooke).

[70] *R (Association of British Civilian Internees: Far East Region)* v. *Secretary of State for Defence* [2003] EWCA Civ 473; [2003] QB 1397, para.37 (Dyson LJ). For discussion of the residual role of *Wednesbury*, see: A. Le Sueur, 'The rise and ruin of unreasonableness?' [2005] JR 32.

[71] *R (Association of British Civilian Internees)*, above n. 70, para.35.

[72] One commentator has speculated that the House of Lords – in refusing leave to appeal in the *British Civilian Internees* case – has consciously avoided the opportunity to confirm the demise of *Wednesbury*: M. Fordham, 'Wednesbury' [2007] JR 266, 267.

[73] For recent examples of the continuing relevance of *Wednesbury* review, see: *R (on the application of Bancoult)* v. *Secretary of State for Foreign and Commonwealth Affairs*

it were, the new theoretically more rigorous standard of proportionality review[74] still harbours the potential to be applied in varying degrees of intensity where deferential considerations arise.[75]

The structure of proportionality review

Proportionality requires of courts a more exacting standard of review. Whereas *Wednesbury* permitted significant discretionary latitude – so long as the decision remained within the four corners of the jurisdiction available to the decision maker – proportionality analysis requires courts to ask not only whether a decision fell within a range of 'reasonable' responses, but also whether there were less intrusive means by which the decision could have been carried into effect. Therefore, not only should a decision fall within the legitimate jurisdiction of the decision maker, but a court's assessment of that decision should also accommodate analysis of whether alternative options would have produced a less marked impact on the rights of the individual. In theory, then, proportionality analysis brings considerations of the impact of a given measure on the individual into the centre stage of a judicial review proceeding.[76]

Approaches to HRA review which simply seek to ascertain whether the correct 'balance' has been achieved between individual rights and the broader public interest, are therefore inappropriate. First, reducing proportionality to an assessment of 'fair balance' runs the risk of perpetuating *Wednesbury*-intensity review by paying lip-service to the demands of the Convention without requiring judicial engagement with, for example,

---

(No. 2) [2008] UKHL 61; [2009] 1 AC 453, para.131 (Lord Carswell) and perhaps more controversially – due to the engagement of the Convention rights – *RB (Algeria)* v. *Secretary of State for the Home Department; OO (Jordan)* v. *Secretary of State for the Home Department* [2009] UKHL 10, para.73 (Lord Phillips) and para.216 (Lord Hope). For discussion of the continuing utility of *Wednesbury* in non-human rights cases see: M. Taggart, 'Proportionality, deference, *Wednesbury*' (2008) NZLR 423. (Cf. Hunt, 'Against bifurcation', above n. 52.)

[74] *R (on the application of Begum)* v. *Governors of Denbigh High School* [2006] UKHL 15; [2007] 1 AC 100, para.30 (Lord Bingham).

[75] See: I. Leigh, 'The standard of judicial review after the Human Rights Act' in H. Fenwick, G. Phillipson and R. Masterman, *Judicial Reasoning under the UK Human Rights Act* (Cambridge University Press, 2007), pp.198–200.

[76] As Tom Poole has argued, prior to the coming into force of the HRA, 'the individual was marginal to the business of the court, providing a trigger for an action but not necessarily the focal point of legal analysis and argument' (T. Poole, 'The reformation of English administrative law' (2009) 68 CLJ 142, 142).

the rational objective of the measure, or whether it amounts to the least intrusive means by which the same effect could have been engineered. In *Samaroo*, for example, Dyson LJ suggested that applying the test of proportionality requires that:

> the court must decide whether a fair balance was struck between the demands of the general interest of the community and the requirements of the protection of the individual's fundamental rights.[77]

Dyson LJ was, of course, correct to note in *Samaroo* that 'the striking of a fair balance lies at the heart of proportionality'.[78] As much has been confirmed by the House of Lords as being entirely consistent with the aims and objectives of the Convention itself: in *Huang* v. *Secretary of State for the Home Department* the Law Lords noted that applying the test of proportionality will necessarily involve assessing the needs of society as a whole with those of the individual or group in question.[79] However, the striking of a fair balance does not, of itself, provide a clear indication of the strict proportionality of a given measure or decision. As the European Court of Human Rights noted in *Sporrong and Lönnroth* v. *Sweden* – the very case cited by Dyson LJ in support of the 'fair balance' approach – such a balance would not be legitimate if the affected individual bore an 'excessive burden'.[80] Second, then, a further concern of equating 'proportionality' with a straightforward assessment of the 'fair balance' of a decision is that it collapses the structured reasoning process of the former into a simple assessment of where the judge thinks that an appropriate – or perhaps reasonable – balance might lie. As a result, equating proportionality with fair balance runs the risk of obscuring one of the potential benefits of proportionality strictly construed: that is, increased openness and clarity in judicial decision making. As Tom Poole has observed:

> whereas *Wednesbury* required nothing more than a Delphic utterance of 'unreasonable' or 'not unreasonable', proportionality at least requires judges to show their 'workings out'. By requiring courts to specify whether or not there was a 'sufficient' connection between the measures adopted

---

[77] *R (on the application of Samaroo)* v. *Secretary of State for the Home Department* [2001] EWCA Civ 1149, para.26 (Dyson LJ).

[78] *Ibid.*

[79] *Huang* v. *Secretary of State for the Home Department*, above n. 53, para.19. See also: *R (Razgar)* v. *Secretary of State for the Home Department* [2004] UKHL 27; [2004] 2 AC 368, para 20: '[an assessment of the proportionality of a measure] must always involve the striking of a fair balance between the rights of the individual and the interests of the community which is inherent in the whole of the Convention'.

[80] *Sporrong and Lönnroth* v. *Sweden* (1983) 5 EHRR 35, para.73.

and a (legitimate) aim, the test seems to demand more from judges by way of articulation and elaboration.[81]

While balance may therefore underpin proportionality, it should not be taken to exclude judicial assessment of the specific limbs of the *Daly* test in practice.

Other approaches have shown a tendency on the part of the judges to fail to engage with the structured approach to proportionality by isolating one of the three stages of proportionality analysis to the exclusion of the others. In the House of Lords decision in *Marper*, for instance, emphasis was placed on the fact that the policy of retaining DNA data for the purpose of combating crime was 'objectively justified'.[82] The structure of the proportionality test set down in *Daly* was therefore reduced to an assessment of the objective justification of the policy. In *R (on the application of Gillan)* v. *Commissioner of Police for the Metropolis*, the Law Lords found that the use of police stop and search powers under the Terrorism Act 2000 was not in breach of the Convention rights.[83] Emphasis was placed on the extent of the interference[84] – described by Lord Bingham as being 'superficial'[85] – but in other respects the proportionality analysis of the Law Lords amounted to little more than an assessment of whether the stop and search measures pursued a legitimate aim, and had been used in pursuance of that aim.[86] The difficult aspect of the *Gillan* decision – admittedly a decision made in circumstances in which a degree of deference was due to the assessment made by Parliament and the executive as to the necessity of the steps taken to counter the threat of terrorism – is that rather than emphasise the need for the elected branches to justify the necessity of the interference, reliance appears to have been placed on the failure of the applicants to disprove that necessity.[87] Given the nature of the obligation imposed by the Convention rights – to require *the state* to

---

[81] T. Poole, 'Tilting at windmills? Truth and illusion in "the political constitution"' (2007) 70 MLR 250, 268.

[82] *R (on the application of S)* v. *Chief Constable of South Yorkshire Police; R (on the application of Marper)* v. *Chief Constable of South Yorkshire Police* [2004] UKHL 39; [2004] 1 WLR 2196, paras.40, 54–5 (Lord Steyn).

[83] *R (on the application of Gillan)* v. *Commissioner of Police for the Metropolis* [2006] UKHL 12; [2006] 2 AC 307.

[84] *Ibid.*, para.63 (Lord Scott).   [85] *Ibid.*, para.28 (Lord Bingham).

[86] *Ibid.*, para.29 (Lord Bingham).

[87] *Ibid.*, paras.63–4 (Lord Scott). 'Reliance was placed on the fact that the applicants had made no attempt to contradict evidence based on intelligence material of the value of such searches, despite an invitation to do so through a closed hearing process' (I. Leigh and R. Masterman, *Making Rights Real: The Human Rights Act in its First Decade* (Oxford: Hart Publishing, 2008), p.218).

justify, on specified grounds, the necessity of a given interference – this seems an unnecessarily onerous burden to place on an applicant.[88]

This latter aspect of proportionality analysis has proved particularly troublesome for the judges: as Sandra Fredman has written, '[c]ourts are especially reluctant to insist that there was some less intrusive alternative than that chosen by policy makers'.[89] In many ways this can be seen as understandable, as courts have long chosen to place reliance on the separation of 'law' and 'policy',[90] and will doubtless be mindful of the claims of critics that the HRA invites unelected judges to play an active role in the policy-making process.[91] Yet a proper application of the proportionality test should not require a creative deployment of judicial thinking in this regard – courts are not being asked to formulate *their own* alternative, less intrusive, response. Rather, as proportionality requires a heightened standard of justification from public bodies, it is those bodies themselves that are asked to demonstrate that their policy or decision amounted to the least intrusive of the range of available responses. The role of the courts in this regard is to adjudicate over whether, on an objective assessment of the evidence brought before them, the public body's claims as to the justification of the policy are made out.

The integration of proportionality and deference

The HRA was designed to promote a culture of rights in which 'our public institutions are habitually, automatically, responsive to human rights considerations'.[92] The aspiration of a 'culture of human rights' in turn lends credence to the idea of an inter-institutional dialogue on the content, meaning and application of rights in which the views of public officials, as

---

[88] It is worth noting that, by contrast with the findings of the House of Lords, the European Court of Human Rights found in both *Marper* and *Gillan* that the Convention rights had been violated. See *S* v. *United Kingdom* (2009) 48 EHRR 50; *Gillan* v. *United Kingdom* (4158/05), 12 January 2010.

[89] Fredman, 'From deference to democracy', above n. 38, 55. See e.g.: *R (Williamson and others)* v. *Secretary of State for Education and Employment* [2005] UKHL 15; [2005] 2 AC 246.

[90] See: J. A. King, 'Institutional approaches to judicial restraint' (2008) 28 OJLS 409, 415–19.

[91] See e.g.: M. Bevir, 'The Westminster model, governance and judicial reform' (2008) 61 *Parliamentary Affairs* 559, 573. Cf. R. Masterman, 'Juridification, sovereignty and separation of powers' (2009) 62 *Parliamentary Affairs* 499, 499–500.

[92] Joint Committee on Human Rights, *Minutes of Evidence*, 19 March 2001, 38 (Lord Irvine).

well as of the legislature, as to the requirements of those rights should be treated as relevant considerations in the adjudicative process. While the reasons articulated by elected officials in support of their decisions are of course material, it is now becoming clear that, ultimately, certain issues are regarded as matters of law for the determination of the courts. This is for the reason that elements of the judicial decision-making process under the HRA do not lend themselves to the application of notions of deference. In order to assess the merits of deferential concerns, and what practical use (if any) they should serve, it is necessary to examine which stages of the judicial decision-making procedure under the HRA might be susceptible to deference to the elected, or political, branches.

In the process of determining that a public body has acted unlawfully under the Act, a court must first determine whether or not one of the Convention rights is actually engaged. The question of engagement – of whether a certain practice, decision or omission falls within the scope of a Convention right – cannot be one on which the courts should defer to the view of the executive, or Parliament. The role of the court must be to 'take into account' the decisions of the Strasbourg organs in the determination of whether or not on the facts, a Convention right has been, engaged. Nor should deference be afforded to a public body's view of whether a given right – as a matter of law – has been interfered with. The Convention rights clearly possess meaning and content that is independent of the decisions and provisions to which they are meant to apply, and the HRA makes clear that questions of engagement and interference are necessarily matters for *judicial* resolution. Section 3(1) confirms that the compatibility of a given legislative provision is a matter for judicial determination. Section 6(1) requires courts to determine the legality, or otherwise, of the actions of public bodies against the requirements of the Convention rights: '[d]omestic courts must themselves form a judgment whether a Convention right has been breached'.[93] If the HRA is to have its intended effect, both Parliament and the executive should have taken steps to guard against implementing measures, or taking decisions, that are manifestly incompatible with the Convention rights (although the Act provides that such outcomes are indeed ultimately possible). But, if the ability of the courts to bring certainty to a legal dispute under the rule of law is to be preserved, then the judges should possess the power to determine whether or not a given exercise of public power does, or does not, engage with one or more of the Convention rights, and whether or

---

[93] *R v. Secretary of State for the Home Department, ex parte Daly* [2001] 2 AC 532, para.23 (Lord Bingham).

not that exercise of power amounts to a prima facie interference with those rights.

It is to the assessment of a measure's necessity in a democratic society that a court would be most inclined to afford a degree of respect to the decisions of an elected branch of the state. It is at this stage of the analysis to which a decision must be subject that the public body in question should articulate grounds and justification for the relevant decision. Deference may, rightly, be afforded at this stage of the judicial decision-making process, for the reason that it is not the role of the court to second-guess the grounds on which executive or legislative decisions have been taken. Even then, however, affording a degree of respect to such a decision, or the grounds on which such a decision has been taken, should not be equated with endorsement of the decision itself. It remains the duty of the court to assess, and pass judgment on, whether the infringement of the Convention right is justified in the circumstances. In carrying out this analysis, executive assessments of fact should be distinguished from the executive's own assessment of proportionality based on those facts. While considerations of institutional competence may allow courts to defer to particular expert analyses of certain factual considerations, this deference should not extend to the determination of normative questions concerning whether or not the Convention standards have been satisfied.[94]

In the final analysis, therefore, the human rights compatibility of public authority decision making under the Act is a matter of after-the-fact assessment by the courts. As the House of Lords confirmed in the decision in *Belfast City Council* v. *Miss Behavin' Ltd*,[95] the central question for the courts must always be to adjudge whether the relevant decision infringed the victim's Convention rights. Even in adjudication over those Convention rights with 'procedural content':

> the question is still whether there has actually been a violation of the applicant's Convention rights and not whether the decision-maker properly considered the question of whether his rights would be violated or not.[96]

As Lord Hoffmann indicated, 'no display of human rights learning' by public authorities could render compatible a decision which in the view

---

[94] Phillipson, 'Deference, discretion and democracy in the Human Rights Act era', above n. 15, 72–4.

[95] *Belfast City Council* v. *Miss Behavin' Limited* [2007] UKHL 19; [2007] 1 WLR 1420.

[96] *Ibid.*, at para.15. Cf. the views of Baroness Hale, at para.37:

of the court violated the applicant's rights.[97] While the requirements of proportionality require public authority decision makers to analyse and assess the potential impact of alternatives to the proposed policy response or decision, this analysis need not impose an undue burden on public authorities. While it may be open to public bodies to consider the potential impact of a particular policy or decision in substantive human rights terms – and while there may be good reasons for them to do so – it is not a requirement of the decision-making process. Section 6(1) of the HRA does not therefore require public authorities to engage with the *substance* of the Convention rights themselves during the decision-making process; it is the outcome of the process which the courts will assess for Convention compliance. This reading of the role of courts under the HRA, as Poole has recognised, proceeds from the premise that, 'for the HRA to have real legal purchase, it must be up to the courts to make authoritative determinations as to what Convention rights require'.[98] In other words, it relies on a separation of powers under which the legal application and determination of what the Convention rights require is ultimately a matter for the courts.

While public bodies should address certain questions by engaging Convention-like analyses,[99] courts will retain the determinative say over the Convention compatibility of such a decision. This is not to say that the decision-making process adopted by the public authority is not relevant, more that it cannot be determinative. As Lord Neuberger put it in *Miss Behavin'*:

> it seems to me … that where a council has properly considered the issue in relation to a particular application, the court is inherently less likely to conclude that the decision ultimately infringes the applicant's rights.[100]

> The views of the local authority are bound to carry less weight where the local authority has made no attempt to address that question [of the impact of a decision on the Convention right at issue]. Had the Belfast City Council expressly set itself the task of balancing the rights of individuals to sell and buy pornographic literature and images against the interests of the wider community, a court would find it hard to upset the balance that the local authority had struck.

[97] Ibid., at [13]. See also: *R (on the application of Begum)* v. *Governors of Denbigh High School*, above n. 74, at paras.26–31.

[98] Poole, 'The reformation of English administrative law', above n. 76, 160.

[99] See e.g.: *R* v. *Secretary of State for the Home Department, ex parte Razgar* [2004] UKHL 27; [2004] 2 AC 368, para.17 (Lord Bingham).

[100] *Belfast City Council* v. *Miss Behavin' Ltd*, above n. 95, para.91 (Lord Neuberger). This point is echoed by Baroness Hale at para.37.

The relevance of the public body's decision-making processes becomes apparent as a part of the justificatory analysis that courts must undertake to assess the proportionality of a given measure. It is at this point that the courts should rightly afford a degree of latitude to the decision maker and a degree of respect to the reasons articulated in support of the given policy or decision (especially in those cases where the courts are poorly placed to question or assess the specific factual or evidential grounds on which a given decision has been taken). While a court's acknowledgement of an available degree of latitude in respect of the decisions of elected officials and administrators would at first glance appear to fit within a dialogical approach to HRA adjudication, cases such as *Miss Behavin'* demonstrate that this dialogue has not undermined the judicial ability to make determinative rulings as to the requirements of the law. Where the substance of the Convention rights has been taken into account in public body decision making, this is something to which the courts should rightly have regard, but as the *Miss Behavin'* decision makes clear, ultimately, questions of Convention compatibility are to be determined by the courts.

While deference is the mechanism through which the courts are able to accord respect to the views of the decision maker, this respect should be an acknowledged aspect of the proportionality analysis of a given decision, rather than a free-standing aspect of judicial decision making. Proportionality is a flexible enough tool to accommodate considerations of superior institutional expertise, just as it is malleable enough to permit the courts to consider the merits of a decision, without reviewing the decision on those merits alone.

Proportionality, legitimacy and merits review

Richard Bellamy, in his book, *Political Constitutionalism: A Republican Defence of the Constitutionality of Democracy*, argues that 'the test of a political process is not so much that it generates outcomes we agree *with* as that it produces outcomes that we can all agree *to*, on the grounds that they are legitimate'.[101] It is the process by which governmental decisions are made, rather than their outcome, which is crucial. The same is true, of course, of decisions of the courts. It is a constitutional expectation that judicial decisions be adequately and clearly reasoned and offer justifications for choosing to follow, or distinguish, relevant authorities. There is

---

[101]   R. Bellamy, *Political Constitutionalism: A Republican Defence of the Constitutionality of Democracy* (Cambridge University Press, 2007), p.164.

an increased burden on those decisions which closely engage with those areas of 'policy' which might naturally be said to fall within the domain of the elected branches of government. Thus, in adjudicating over a decision with, say, resource implications, there is an increased onus on the judge to ensure the legitimacy of both the process of reasoning adopted *and* the outcome of the case.

Judicial review remains a largely procedural guarantee which preserves the autonomy of the elected branches to make decisions within their areas of competence on the basis of considerations which are not open to deliberation in a court of law. As T. R. S. Allan has noted, the distinction between review and appeal, therefore, 'reflects a conception of limited judicial authority, recognising that in most cases a public authority may exercise a genuine choice between competing public policy objectives and contrasting methods of implementation'.[102] While HRA review requires courts to be more closely engaged with the merits of a given policy or decision than was previously the case, the notion of deference allows weight to be given to a public body's justifications for the decision, recognising the 'genuine choice' that public bodies should have in determining decisions involving competing goods, the allocation of resources, and so on. The difference made by proportionality analysis should be that the scope of the legal choices available to the decision maker is narrower than under the traditional *Wednesbury* standard.

Proportionality analysis does not, however, compel merits review – the test 'allows sufficient latitude to the decision-maker so that one could argue that, overall, the process of judicial reasoning does not focus solely on the merits'.[103] This is for the reason that 'the defining characteristic of the proportionality test is that it requires a court to undertake a *structured* analytical exercise'.[104] An adherence to the structural test for proportionality will guard against the courts reviewing decisions solely on their merits and will preserve the separation of executive and adjudicative decision-making processes. While proportionality analysis requires a greater engagement with the merits of administrative decisions, it simultaneously requires that judicial decisions answer certain prescribed questions relating to the substance of the impugned decision. The strength

---

[102] Allan, 'Human rights and judicial review', above n. 14, 679.

[103] I. Leigh, 'Taking rights proportionately: judicial review, the Human Rights Act and Strasbourg' [2002] PL 265, 284. See: *R (on the application of Begum)* v. *Governors of Denbigh High School*, above n. 74, para.30 (Lord Bingham).

[104] R. Clayton and H. Tomlinson, *The Law of Human Rights* (2nd edn) (Oxford University Press, 2009), para.6.91. See also: S. Beatson, S. Grosz, T. Hickman, R. Singh and

of an adherence to the requirements of proportionality, therefore, is that it avoids the real danger of so-called merits review: that is, the judicial assessment of the substance of an administrative decision unguided by questions of principle.[105] Proportionality analysis, in other words, has the capacity to legitimate judicial intervention in policy, political, or borderline non-justiciable matters, by regulating the scope of the judicial inquiry through stipulating consideration of certain key issues, while rejecting the consideration of extraneous considerations which would jeopardise the legitimacy of the judicial method. While proportionality analysis permits *engagement* with the merits of a governmental decision, it should not be equated with *review* on the basis of those merits alone.

Conclusion

While the spheres of judicial, executive and parliamentary decision making obviously overlap, the differing tasks carried out by each branch require a functional separation of powers. Just as it is not the task of the courts to design policy (though they may legitimately engage with it in judicial review cases), it is not the task of the executive to determine, with finality, whether a given proposal or policy is Convention compliant (though they may legitimately articulate reasons in support of a particular decision to which the courts might attach a greater or lesser degree of weight). Therefore, provided that judicial review does not mutate into pure merits review, then judicial and executive decision-making processes will remain separated at a constitutional level. It is here that the structural importance of proportionality becomes apparent. In this respect, in those cases in which the Convention rights are engaged, what is therefore clear is that while the subject matter of the policy decision *may* condition the intensity of the review which follows – and less controversially, *should* be considered in determining the proportionality of a given restriction – it cannot insulate the decision in its entirety from

---

S. Palmer, *Human Rights: Judicial Protection in the United Kingdom* (London: Sweet and Maxwell, 2008), p.559:

> The role of UK courts under the HRA and devolution statutes remains that of ensuring that state action does not overstep legal bounds: it is not to dictate decisions to local or central government, or to Parliament. Courts judge, they do not and should not govern. The proportionality test affirms the principle that it is for the government and Parliament to decide how the country is to be run and that the courts' position is only supervisory.

[105] See: N. Blake, 'Importing proportionality: clarification or confusion' [2002] EHRLR 19, 26.

judicial analysis.[106] The relative institutional competence or expertise of Parliament and/or the executive should not therefore be used to displace the constitutional obligation of the courts to determine the legality of the purported exercise of public power in cases where the Convention rights are engaged, nor their own obligation to act compatibly with the Convention rights.[107]

If, as T. R. S. Allan argues, 'the familiar *Wednesbury* doctrine of review of administrative action, preserving an "absolute" freedom within the "four corners" of the agency's "jurisdiction", is simply an expression of the separation of powers inherent in the rule of law',[108] then we must also accept that considerations or legal formulae – such as deference and proportionality – must similarly be expressions of such a separation.[109]

---

[106] See e.g: *International Transport Roth GmbH* v. *Secretary of State for the Home Department*, above n. 23, para.27 (Simon Brown LJ): 'the court's role under the 1998 Act is as the guardian of human rights. It cannot abdicate this responsibility.'

[107] Section 6(1) HRA.

[108] T. R. S. Allan, *Constitutional Justice*, above n. 41, p.162.

[109] A point acknowledged in Rivers, 'Proportionality and variable intensity of review', above n. 67, 176; R. Clayton, 'Judicial deference and "democratic dialogue": the legitimacy of judicial intervention under the HRA 1998' [2004] PL 23, 40.

PART III

The creative powers of courts

6

Statutory interpretation and declarations of incompatibility

Introduction

As has already been noted, much of the uncertainty surrounding separation of powers in the UK constitution can be traced back to the myriad interpretations of the doctrine that have, over time, been proposed. Yet the idea that judges should not be seen to *legislate* – to create law rather than to interpret it – has historically provided one of the more certain dividing lines between the respective functions of the three branches of government in the constitution of the UK. The tradition of what Stevens has termed 'substantive formalism', which dominated judicial attitudes and method for much of the twentieth century, ironically gave rise to a relatively rigid conception of separated governmental functions under which 'the function of the legislature is to make the law, the function of the administration is to administer the law and the function of the judiciary is to interpret and enforce the law'.[1]

It is, of course, central to the Diceyan understanding of parliamentary supremacy that no other constitutional body possesses legal power which can challenge that of Parliament; as such, the judiciary have no generally applicable competence to strike down or question the authority of primary legislation,[2] nor do the judges have power to act in a way which would otherwise usurp the legislative function.[3] As we have seen, the HRA attempts, in theory, to preserve Parliament's role as sovereign legislature and therefore preserve the constitutional equilibrium. As a result of this – at least rhetorical – adherence to the demands of parliamentary

---

[1] W. Greene, 'Law and progress' (1944) 94 *Law Journal* 349, 351 (quoted in R. Stevens, *Law and Politics: The House of Lords as a Judicial Body, 1800–1976* (London: Weidenfeld and Nicolson, 1979), p.357, and on the 'formalist' tradition generally, see chs.10 and 11).

[2] *Edinburgh and Dalkeith Railway Co* v. *Wauchope* (1842) 8 Cl & F 710; *Pickin* v. *British Railways Board* [1974] AC 765.

[3] E.g., by giving domestic effect to the terms of an unincorporated treaty: *R* v. *Secretary of State for the Home Department, ex parte Brind* [1991] 1 AC 696, 718 (Lord Donaldson of Lymington MR), 762–3 (Lord Ackner).

supremacy, the Department for Constitutional Affairs was able to issue the claim in 2006 that the HRA had not 'significantly altered the constitutional balance between Parliament, the executive and the judiciary'.[4] On the face of the Act, therefore, the judicial branch is not explicitly given a 'legislative' role.[5]

Yet s.3(1) of the Act – which provides that 'so far as it is possible to do so, primary legislation and subordinate legislation must be read and given effect in a way which is compatible with the Convention rights' – undoubtedly brings courts into much closer relief with matters of parliamentary competence than had been countenanced by those of a formalist persuasion. The exercise of the s.3(1) power is, however, only one of a number of ways in which the courts might play a creative, or law-making, role under the HRA. This chapter and the next examine three spheres in which the judges might be seen to contribute to the process of making law in adjudication under the HRA. First, the degree to which the exercise of the courts' interpretative powers under s.3(1) involves the judiciary in matters of legislative choice will be considered, alongside the coercive effects of the HRA's parallel remedial device, the declaration of incompatibility. In the next chapter, the influence of the Convention on law making at common law will be examined. And finally, the ability of the courts to creatively influence the meaning of 'the Convention rights' under the HRA will be charted. First, however, it is necessary to briefly scope the controversy surrounding the idea of judicial legislation.

The judge as law-maker

The idea of the judge as maker of law is anathema to ideals of democratic, or even representative, law making.[6] Judges cannot be said to

---

[4] Department of Constitutional Affairs, *Review of the Implementation of the Human Rights Act* (July 2006), p.4.

[5] See e.g.: *R (on the application of Pretty)* v. *Director of Public Prosecutions* [2001] UKHL 61; [2002] 1 AC 800, para.2 (Lord Bingham): 'In discharging the judicial functions of the House, the Appellate Committee has the duty of resolving issues of law properly brought before it ... The Committee is not a legislative body.'

[6] See: A. V. Dicey, 'Judicial Legislation' in *Lectures on the Relationship between Law and Public Opinion in England during the Nineteenth Century* (London: Macmillan, 1914); Lord Reid, 'The judge as law maker' (1972–3) 12 *Journal of the Society of the Public Teachers of Law* 22; Lord Devlin, 'Judges and law-makers' (1976) 39 MLR 1; Lord Mackay, 'Can judges change the law?' Maccabaean Lecture (1987) LXXIII *Proceedings of the British Academy* 285; Lord Lester, 'English judges as law makers' [1993] PL 269; Sir A. Mason, 'Legislative and judicial law-making: can we locate an identifiable boundary?' [2004] *Adelaide Law Review* 15.

be directly accountable to, or representative of the electorate, except in only the most tenuous sense – via the possibility of their removal on an address by both Houses of Parliament.[7] This aspect of the constitutional position of the judiciary is, of course, a strength: their independence of government, and impartiality between parties, is central to the effective discharge of their function as arbiters of legal disputes. The potential to compromise this independence provides a further objection to judge-made law; to adopt Lord Reid's terminology, the 'real difficulty about judges making law' is the potential for them, by so doing, to compromise their independence by appearing to support one (potentially political and/or controversial) viewpoint in favour of another.[8] Further, the adversarial context of adjudication – often involving debate on narrow and technical points of law – provides an unsatisfactory basis for the design of legal principles, which may range much wider than may be countenanced in the context of a dispute between parties. The courts cannot take account of the various perspectives on a given issue that would be aired in the less confined debates of Parliament, the press and civil society.[9] As Frankfurter J famously argued in *Dennis* v. *United States*, courts 'are not designed to be a good reflex of a democratic society. Their judgment is best informed, and therefore most dependable, within narrow limits.'[10]

Yet to paint a picture of judicial decisions as mechanical applications of perpetually clear legal rules would also be a mistake. Choice is also a central element of the judicial role. As H. L. A. Hart wrote:

> in the vast majority of cases that trouble the courts, neither statutes nor precedents in which the rules are allegedly contained allow of only one result. In the most important cases there is always a choice. The judge has to choose between alternative meanings to be given to the words of

---

[7] The Act of Settlement provides that 'judges commissions be made *quamdiu se bene gesserint* and their salaries ascertained and established; but upon an address of both houses of Parliament it may be lawful to remove them'. See also: Supreme Court Act 1981, s.11(3); Appellate Jurisdiction Act 1876, s.6; Constitutional Reform Act 2005, s.33.

[8] Lord Reid, 'The judge as law maker', above n. 6, 23. See also: *Duport Steel* v. *Sirs* [1980] 1 WLR 142, 169 (Lord Scarman):
> if people and Parliament come to think that the judicial power is to be confined by nothing other than the judge's sense of what is right (or, as Selden put it, by the length of the Chancellor's foot), confidence in the judicial system will be replaced by fear of it becoming uncertain and arbitrary in its application.

Cf. J. A. G. Griffith, *The Politics of the Judiciary* (5th edn) (London: Fontana Press, 1997).

[9] Lord Devlin, 'Judges and law-makers', above n. 6, 11–12.

[10] *Dennis* v. *United States* (1951) 341 US 494.

a statute or between rival interpretations of what a precedent 'amounts to.' It is only the tradition that judges 'find' and do not 'make' law that conceals this, and presents their decisions as if they were deductions smoothly made from clear pre-existing rules without intrusion of the judge's choice.[11]

In the UK, the relationship between legislation and its judicial interpretation is conditioned by the doctrine of parliamentary sovereignty, with the degree of choice available to the judge restricted by the form of words in which legislative decisions are presented, and by a respect for – or deference to – those decisions as made by the democratic legislative body.[12] In his book, *Constitutional Theory*, Geoffrey Marshall wrote that the theory underpinning statutory interpretation held that:

> Parliament, in the United Kingdom … is the sovereign master. Its instructions are subject to no constitutional reservations and this, perhaps, gives rise to a belief in the sanctity of the exact words of the statute.[13]

In practice, he added that principles of statutory interpretation have been based on one of two propositions: first, that the words employed by legislators provide evidence of their objectives or intentions; second, that the objectives or intentions of legislators provides evidence of the meaning to be given to the words chosen.[14] The first approach might be called literal, the second purposive. On *either* analysis, the actual form of words chosen by the legislator is central to any legitimate judicial interpretation of statutory meaning. Yet the dominant approach to the construction of statutes was, until relatively recently, very firmly wedded to the former, with a focus on the search for the 'ordinary', 'natural' or 'literal' meaning

---

[11] H. L. A. Hart, *The Concept of Law* (2nd edn) (Oxford: Clarendon Press, 1997), p.12. See also: J. Webber, 'Supreme Courts, independence and democratic agency' (2004) 24 LS 55, 64–5.

[12] See e.g.: *Duport Steel* v. *Sirs*, above n. 8, 168–9 (Lord Scarman):
> the judge's duty is to interpret and to apply the law, not to change it to meet the judge's idea of what justice requires. Interpretation does, of course, imply in the interpreter a power of choice where differing constructions are possible. But our law requires the judge to choose the construction which in his judgment best meets the legislative purpose of the enactment. If the result be unjust but inevitable, the judge may say so and invite Parliament to reconsider its provision. But he must not deny the statute. Unpalatable statute law may not be disregarded or rejected, merely because it is unpalatable. Only if a just result can be achieved without violating the legislative purpose of the statute may the judge select the construction which best suits his idea of what justice requires.

[13] G. Marshall, *Constitutional Theory* (Oxford: Clarendon Press, 1971), p.74.

[14] *Ibid.*, pp.74–5. See also: J. Steyn, 'Does legal formalism hold sway in England?' (1996) 49 *Current Legal Problems* 43, 50.

of statutory words.[15] To suggest otherwise, the argument goes, would be to undermine the function of Parliament, and as such would amount to a judicial, and constitutional, heresy.[16] As Lord Steyn has observed, until the latter years of the twentieth century, the legal formalism of the literal approach to interpretation held sway in the domain of statutory construction.[17]

Significant developments in the latter part of the twentieth century, however, pointed towards a judicial branch prepared to accommodate greater flexibility at the expense of legal certainty, and to allow statutory interpretation to be guided by contextual information relating to the intent of the framer of legislation. In 1966, the Appellate Committee of the House of Lords issued a *Practice Statement* indicating that they would no longer be required to follow their own precedents; the then Lord Chancellor, Lord Gardiner, indicating that 'too rigid an adherence to precedent may lead to injustice in a particular case and also unduly restrict the proper development of the law'.[18] This was followed in 1993 by the seminal House of Lords decision in *Pepper* v. *Hart*.[19] In that case, the House of Lords held that *Hansard* could be employed as an aid to statutory construction where the legislation in question was ambiguous, obscure, or led to an absurdity, and where the statements sought to be relied on were both clear and made by the relevant minister or other promoter of the Bill; that is, 'where such material clearly discloses the

---

[15] For a synopsis, see: D. Greenberg (ed.), *Craies on Legislation* (8th edn) (London: Sweet and Maxwell, 2004), ch.17. For a detailed and specific analysis of the role of parliamentary intent in HRA adjudication, see: A. Kavanagh 'The role of parliamentary intention in adjudication under the Human Rights Act 1998' (2006) 26 OJLS 179.

[16] Lord Lester, 'English judges as law makers', above n. 6, 272. Cf. *Magor and St Mellons Rural District Council* v. *Newport Corporation* [1950] 2 All ER 1226, 1236 (Lord Denning) and *Magor and St Mellons Rural District Council* v. *Newport Corporation* [1952] AC 189, 191 (Lord Simonds). In the former, Lord Denning argued in the Court of Appeal that '[the role of the court is to] find out the intention of Parliament and of Ministers and carry it out, and we do this better by filling in the gaps and making sense of the enactment than by opening it up to destructive analysis'. On appeal to the House of Lords, Lord Simonds responded that such an approach would amount to a 'naked usurpation of the legislative function under the thin guise of interpretation'.

[17] Steyn, 'Does legal formalism hold sway in England?', above n. 14. See also: R. Stevens, 'Judges, politics, politicians and the confusing role of the judiciary' in K. Hawkins (ed.), *The Human Face of Law: Essays in Honour of Donald Harris* (Oxford: Clarendon Press, 1997); M. Zander, *The Law-Making Process* (Cambridge University Press, 2004), pp.132–47.

[18] *Practice Statement (Judicial Precedent)* [1966] 1 WLR 1234. See also: Lord Denning, *From Precedent to Precedent* (Oxford: Clarendon Press, 1959).

[19] *Pepper (Inspector of Taxes)* v. *Hart* [1993] AC 593.

mischief aimed at or the legislative intention lying behind the ambiguous or obscure words'.[20] More broadly, such developments were accompanied by a gradual movement away from the overly literal approach to statutory construction under which it became commonplace for the judiciary to seek to apply a statute in the light of its purpose, to do so in context of its aims, or to subject it to common law presumptions of parliamentary intent.[21] The certainty said to be offered by the literal approach to statutory interpretation was slowly yielding ground to the flexibility of a more purposive style of reasoning.

Contemporaneously, Parliament was allowing inroads to be made into its supposedly unconstrained ability to legislate. The European Communities Act 1972 committed Parliament (and the courts) to accepting the supremacy of European Community law, and while it may have taken some time for the inevitable to happen, the House of Lords decision in *Factortame (No. 2)* resoundingly illustrated that while the UK enjoys membership of the European Community, in a direct conflict between domestic and Community law, the latter would prevail.[22] The devolution of (notionally limited) legislative power to devolved bodies in Northern Ireland, Scotland and Wales,[23] has raised similar concerns over the continuing ability of the Westminster Parliament to unilaterally exercise its legislative will in the devolved areas.[24] Each development – in differing ways – has undermined Parliament's claim to exercise a legislative monopoly within the constitution. The ability of courts to review the compatibility of primary legislation with the Convention rights – whose source is to be found in a specific *external* source of law – amounts to a further limitation to the Diceyan conception of Parliament's ability to legislate subject to 'no constitutional reservations'.[25]

---

[20] *Ibid.*, 634.

[21] For a survey, see: Kavanagh, 'The role of parliamentary intention in adjudication under the Human Rights Act 1998', above n. 15, 183–7. And see in particular: *R* v. *Lord Chancellor, ex parte Witham* [1997] 1 WLR 104 and *R* v. *Secretary of State for the Home Department, ex parte Simms* [2000] 2 AC 115.

[22] *R* v. *Secretary of State for Transport, ex parte Factortame (No. 2)* [1991] 1 AC 603. See also: *Pickstone* v. *Freemans* [1989] AC 66; *Litster* v. *Forth Dry Dock and Engineering Co* [1990] 1 AC 546.

[23] Northern Ireland Act 1998; Scotland Act 1998; Government of Wales Act 1998. See also Government of Wales Act 2006.

[24] V. Bogdanor, 'Devolution: decentralisation or disintegration?' (1999) 70 *Political Quarterly* 185, 186–9.

[25] Marshall, *Constitutional Theory*, above n. 13, p.74. For a more detailed analysis of recent challenges to parliamentary supremacy, see M. Elliott, 'Parliamentary sovereignty and the new constitutional order: legislative freedom, political reality and convention' (2002)

Interpretative latitiude under the human rights act

The debate over the judicial determination of human rights standards – as well as engaging the constitutional balance between judicial and elected power in a broad sense – has also touched on the more prosaic world of statutory interpretation. J. A. G. Griffith, for example, famously argued that a textual representation of a human right was a 'statement of a political conflict pretending to be a resolution of it',[26] adding with unconcealed cynicism that the judicial determination of such standards would involve the courts in the 'happy and fruitful exercise of interpreting woolly principles and even woollier exceptions'.[27] From the perspective of the literalist, this accusation carries weight, for it highlights the fact that 'bills of rights' are arguably not capable of sustaining literal interpretation. It is in the nature of rights instruments that they are drafted in a 'broad and ample style'[28] and that, as a result, they are arguably not suited to 'relatively strict methods of interpretation'.[29] Writing prior to the coming into force of the HRA, Lord Irvine wrote that the Act would 'necessarily leave the judges with a significant margin of interpretative autonomy'.[30] Involving the judiciary in the legal determination of questions of rights *requires* a further departure from the literalistic approach to interpretation:[31] the HRA scheme appears to mandate this departure, while attempting to guard against the simultaneous dilution of Parliament's sovereign power.

The design of the HRA sets down a system of rights protection which appears able to reconcile the judicial enforcement of human rights norms with the preservation of parliamentary sovereignty. Section 3(1) requires the judiciary to adopt and apply a Convention-compatible interpretation of a statute, so far as such a reading is possible. If such an interpretation is possible, it *must* be given effect to. If such a reading is not possible, the higher courts may issue a declaration of incompatibility – a

---

22 LS 340; M. Elliott, 'Parliamentary sovereignty under pressure' (2004) 2 *International Journal of Constitutional Law* 545.

[26] J. A. G. Griffith, 'The political constitution' (1979) 42 MLR 1, 14.   [27] *Ibid.*

[28] *Minister of Home Affairs* v. *Fisher* [1980] AC 319, 328 (Lord Wilberforce).

[29] Lord Steyn, 'The new legal landscape' [2000] EHRLR 549, 550.

[30] Lord Irvine, 'Activism and restraint: human rights and the interpretative process' in his *Human Rights, Constitutional Law and the Development of the English Legal System* (Oxford: Hart Publishing, 2003), p.64 (originally published at [1999] EHRLR 350).

[31] Campbell has gone so far as to suggest that s.3(1) of the HRA amounts to an 'invocation to change the fundamentals of statutory interpretation' (T. Campbell, 'Incorporation through interpretation' in T. Campbell, K. D. Ewing and A. Tomkins (eds), *Sceptical Essays on Human Rights* (Oxford University Press, 2001), p.98).

legally non-coercive order informing the elected branches of the incompatibility of the provision in question. However, in either case, the 'validity, continuing operation or enforcement' of the legislation in question remains unquestioned.[32] Under s.3(1), therefore, the limits of the courts' interpretative role seem to fall short of mounting a formal legal challenge to the validity of a statute or statutory provision, and as a result the traditional judicial role as interpreters of parliamentary intent is also seemingly preserved. Lord Hope's speech in *Lambert* appears to endorse such a suggestion:

> Section 3(1) preserves the sovereignty of Parliament. It does not give power to the judges to overrule decisions which the language of the statute shows have been taken on the very point at issue by the legislator … [T]he interpretation of a statute by reading words in to give effect to the presumed intention must always be distinguished carefully from amendment. Amendment is a legislative act. It is an exercise which must be reserved to Parliament.[33]

Nevertheless, the processes of adjudication under ss.3 and 4 invite argument on the compatibility of Acts of Parliament with the UK's treaty obligations. The authority of Acts of Parliament which engage with the Convention rights is no longer a matter for judicial assumption. While, strictly speaking, the *legality* of challenged Acts remains unquestioned, the difference between a direct power of strike down, and the potential for a declaration of incompatibility to undermine the political authority of a statute or its provisions, may be a fine one. As Anthony Bradley has argued:

> The fact that the HRA does not give power to the courts to quash primary legislation on Convention grounds is a limitation on the remedy that the courts provide, not on the substance of what may be argued in court and if necessary decided.[34]

In practice, therefore, it is widely acknowledged that the HRA provides the judiciary with much broader powers of interpretation than provided for by the traditional canons of statutory construction.[35] The application

---

[32] Sections 3(2)(b) and 4(6) HRA.

[33] *R* v. *Lambert* [2001] UKHL 37; [2002] 2 AC 545, paras.79 and 81.

[34] House of Lords Select Committee on the Constitution, *Relations between the Executive, the Judiciary and Parliament* (HL 151), July 2007, p.79 (evidence of Professor Anthony Bradley).

[35] *R* v. *A (No. 2)* [2002] 1 AC 45; [2001] 3 All ER 1, para.44 (Lord Steyn) and para.108 (Lord Hope). On statutory construction generally, see: Greenberg (ed.), *Craies on Legislation*, above n. 15, Part IV.

of s.3(1) is not subject to the relevant statute containing an ambiguity, nor is its application restricted to those enactments passed earlier in time relative to the HRA: it applies to 'primary legislation and subordinate legislation whenever enacted'.[36] The number of choices which the domestic judge can make in seeking to give effect to ss.3 and 4 HRA is therefore considerable. At the most basic level of reasoning, the judge will have to ask: is a Convention right engaged? If so, is there a prima facie incompatibility with the statute at issue? Can the incompatibility be remedied by way of an interpretation? What degree of interpretation is 'possible' in the circumstances? Is a declaration of incompatibility the more appropriate response?

If it is accepted that reasoning under judicially enforced rights instruments offers more scope for judicial interpretative latitude than the interpretation of other forms of legislative enactment, then – bearing in mind the traditional arguments against judge-made law – it must also be conceded that rights adjudication offers a corresponding potential for the independence of the judiciary to be put in jeopardy. T. R. S. Allan has suggested that:

> the separation of powers would be undermined – and the independence of the judiciary made more vulnerable – if the interpretative function were to permit wholesale judicial revision of statutes which infringed fundamental rights.[37]

Allan's comment was, of course, written prior to the enactment of the HRA and its accompanying general direction on statutory interpretation, and envisages 'wholesale judicial revision' based on judicial engineering alone 'in the absence of a tradition of judicial review of primary legislation'.[38] Nevertheless, a similar sentiment is reflected in Griffith's lamentation that the HRA will *require* the judiciary to exercise yet further political functions:

> so open-textured are the incorporated provisions that the judges will be obliged to exercise their political judgments in the process of interpretation much more widely than in the past.[39]

As in the sphere of challenges to public authority action under s.6 of the HRA, the ability of the courts to interpret legislation or to declare

---

[36] Section 3(2)(a) HRA.
[37] T. R. S. Allan, *Law, Liberty and Justice: The Legal Foundations of British Constitutionalism* (Oxford: Clarendon Press, 1993), p.62.
[38] *Ibid.*
[39] J. A. G. Griffith, 'The brave new world of Sir John Laws' (2000) 63 MLR 159, 170.

it incompatible with the Convention rights reflects the constitutional dilemma of reconciling parliamentary government with a judicially enforced rights instrument. While it is undeniable that the HRA amounts to a considerable extension of judicial power *vis-à-vis* the legislative competence of Parliament, the application of human rights standards under it is not, however, something which is to be assessed by reference to metaphorical 'Chancellor's foot'. While allowing judicial interpretation of statutes which are prima facie incompatible with the Convention rights, the HRA scheme attempts to guard against judicial independence being compromised in a number of ways. First, the general direction that legislation be interpreted in a way which is compatible with the Convention rights is a statutory, rather than judge-made, rule of construction. As Lord Bingham has therefore recognised, the HRA provides the judges with a 'very specific, wholly democratic, mandate' – where possible – to interpret primary legislation compatibly with the Convention rights.[40] Further, the power to interpret statutes under s.3(1) is, by its own terms, limited; interpretations must not only be 'possible', they must also be compatible with the *Convention rights*. As a result, whatever constructions of the Convention rights are adopted in the domestic context should not be products of the judicial imagination, but of a considered application of the Convention text and its accompanying case law which – under s.2(1) – the courts are bound to 'take into account'.[41] Finally, the HRA provides an alternative to judicially designed interpretations: the declaration of incompatibility.[42] The availability of this substitute to the creative interpretative role sanctioned by s.3(1) indicates that while the interpretative power is undoubtedly broad, it is not limitless. It is within this framework that the law-making power of the judiciary under the HRA should be re-examined.

Interpretative law-making on the Human Rights Act model

In respect of the judicial power to review legislation for compatibility with the Convention rights, the uneasy balance between judicial and elected power under the HRA is reflected in its key provisions – ss.3 and 4.[43] For the Labour architects of the Act, curtailing the judicial role in the

---

[40] *A and others* v. *Secretary of State for the Home Department* [2004] UKHL 56; [2005] 2 AC 68, para.42.

[41] See pp.191–202.   [42] Section 4 HRA.

[43] For a sample of the – now vast – literature on ss.3 and 4 see: C. Gearty, 'Reconciling parliamentary democracy and human rights' (2002) 118 LQR 248; G. Phillipson,

protection of human rights was central to preserving the status quo in separation of powers terms:[44] Parliament makes the laws and the courts interpret them, became Parliament makes the laws and the judiciary are empowered to interpret them – 'so far as is possible' – to be compatible with the Convention rights.

The broader scheme employed by the HRA re-enforces the point. Key here is s.4(6) of the Act, which states that even in the event of a declaration of incompatibility being issued by one of the higher courts, the relevant 'incompatible' provision remains valid and enforceable.[45] Crucially, therefore, Parliament is not obliged to remedy the judicial determination of incompatibility. While the declaration by a higher court that a statutory provision is incompatible with the Convention rights will wield considerable political force,[46] it remains vital that the response – should there be one – from Parliament and the executive is a matter of choice and not of compulsion.

Hence, on the terms of the HRA itself, the courts may declare a statute to be incompatible with the Convention rights, but they may not strike it down, or otherwise directly contest its legality. As a result, the most radical form of judicial law making (or unmaking) is apparently precluded on the HRA model.[47] For Conor Gearty, this rejection of the 'orthodox precedents' of other bills of rights represents the 'genius' of the HRA.[48]

'(Mis-)Reading section 3 of the Human Rights Act' (2003) 119 LQR 183; C. Gearty, 'Revisiting section 3 of the Human Rights Act' (2003) 119 LQR 551; A. Kavanagh, 'The elusive divide between interpretation and legislation under the Human Rights Act 1998' (2004) 24(2) OJLS 259; D. Nicol, 'Statutory interpretation and human rights after *Anderson*' [2004] PL 274; A. Kavanagh, 'Statutory interpretation and human rights after *Anderson*: a more contextual approach' [2004] PL 537; A. Kavanagh, 'Unlocking the Human Rights Act: the "radical" approach to section 3(1) revisited' [2005] EHRLR 259; D. Feldman, 'Institutional role and meanings of "compatibility" under the Human Rights Act 1998' in H. Fenwick, G. Phillipson and R. Masterman (eds), *Judicial Reasoning under the UK Human Rights Act* (Cambridge University Press, 2007); A. Kavanagh, 'Choosing between sections 3 and 4 of the Human Rights Act 1998: judicial reasoning after *Ghaidan* v. *Mendoza*' in Fenwick, Phillipson and Masterman (eds), *Judicial Reasoning under the UK Human Rights Act*, above.

[44] HL Debs, vol.582, col.1228, 3 November 1997 (Lord Irvine); HC Debs, vol.306, col.772, 16 February 1998 (Jack Straw MP).

[45] Section 4(6) HRA provides that 'a declaration under this section ... (a) does not affect the validity, continuing operation or enforcement of the provision in respect of which it is given; and (b) is not binding on the parties to the proceedings in which it is made'. See also s.3(2)(b) HRA.

[46] See e.g.: HC Debs, vol.307, col.780 (16 February 1998); HL Debs, vol.582, col.1231 (3 November 1997); K. D. Ewing, 'The Human Rights Act and parliamentary democracy' (1999) 62 MLR 79, 99.

[47] Although see the discussion above at pp.168–76.

[48] C. Gearty, *Can Human Rights Survive?* (Cambridge University Press, 2006), pp.94–8. Gearty writes (at p.95) that the HRA 'deliberately undermines its own authority, inviting

Recognition of this limitation on the powers of the courts under the Act can be found in the frequently repeated direction that courts should not effectively 'legislate' through their use of s.3(1).[49] However, we have already seen that the bald assertion that parliamentary supremacy remains unscathed following the implementation of the HRA offers an inadequate explanation of the reality of the judicial role in the constitution. So while the emerging case law on s.3(1) displays a rhetorical adherence to the demands of parliamentary sovereignty, judicial utilisation of the 'interpretative' techniques sanctioned by the HRA has also led the courts to openly acknowledge their ability to amend or modify primary legislation in the name of achieving compatibility with the Convention rights. Recognising this, Kavanagh has argued that 'the activity of interpretation involves, rather than eschews, judicial law-making',[50] while Alison Young has written that the leading case, *Ghaidan* v. *Godin-Mendoza*, provides an example of 'acceptable judicial legislation'.[51]

A power of invalidation through interpretation?

Before examining the range of legitimate uses of the courts' interpretative power under the HRA, it is illustrative to examine one suggested, but ultimately unsuccessful, deployment of s.3(1). In *R* v. *Secretary of State for the Home Department, ex parte Anderson*, a seven-strong panel of Law Lords declined to employ s.3(1) to read down the Home Secretary's sentencing power under s.29, of the Crime (Sentences) Act 1997 in order to achieve compatibility with Article 6 ECHR.[52] Under s.29, the Home Secretary had a discretionary power to determine the minimum tariff to be served by adult prisoners convicted of murder, and the date of their eligibility for release on licence. The unanimous House of Lords held that a declaration of incompatibility be issued on the grounds that it would be impossible to read s.29 as allowing the Home Secretary *no* discretion

---

the political back in to control the legal at just the moment when the supremacy of the legal discourse seems assured'.

[49] See e.g.: *R* v. *Director of Public Prosecutions, ex parte Kebilene* [2000] 2 AC 326, 367; *R* v. *Lambert* [2002] 2 AC 545, para.79; *Re S (Children) (Care Order: Implementation of Care Plan); Re W (Children) (Care Order: Adequacy of Care Plan)* [2002] UKHL 10; [2002] 2 AC 291, para.39; *A and others* v. *Secretary of State for the Home Department* [2004] UKHL 56, para.220.

[50] Kavanagh, 'The Elusive Divide', above n. 43, 261.

[51] A. Young, '*Ghaidan* v. *Godin-Mendoza*: avoiding the deference trap' [2005] PL 23, 27.

[52] *R (on the application of Anderson)* v. *Secretary of State for the Home Department* [2002] UKHL 46; [2003] 1 AC 837.

over the effective length of time to be served by mandatory life prisoners following conviction, without effectively depriving the provision of meaning. Lord Bingham argued that to use s.3(1) to attribute a meaning to a legislative provision 'quite different from that which Parliament intended … would go well beyond any interpretative process sanctioned by section 3 of the 1998 Act',[53] and which – given the nature of the change necessary to achieve compatibility – would have amounted to 'judicial vandalism'.[54] As a result, the s.3(1) power would appear to fall short, not only of an overt power to strike down legislative provisions, but also of enabling judges to effectively invalidate statutory provisions under the guise of interpretation.[55]

Two other cases, however – both heard early in the life of the HRA – demonstrate how the interpretative power of s.3(1) *can* be used to significantly amend how a statutory provision takes effect. The Court of Appeal decision in *R* v. *Offen*[56] provides an example of the radical potential of s.3(1) in practice. *Offen* concerned the interpretation of s.2 of the Crime (Sentences) Act 1997, a requirement of which was that persons convicted of a 'second serious offence'[57] should serve a mandatory life sentence of imprisonment, and courts would only be entitled not to impose such a sentence where they could demonstrate that there were 'exceptional circumstances' relating to either of the offences which would 'justify its not doing so'.

In *R* v. *Offen*, the Court of Appeal was concerned that – given the 'restrictive' readings of the phrase 'exceptional circumstances' which had predominated prior to the HRA[58] – it was possible that the section could be applied in an 'arbitrary and disproportionate' manner in contravention of Article 5, and possibly Article 3, of the Convention.[59] Giving the judgment of the Court, Lord Woolf said very little about the scope or requirements of s.3(1), disarmingly stating that, '[t]he consequence of section 3 is that legislation which affects human rights is required to be construed in a manner which conforms with the Convention wherever this is possible'.[60] Flowing from this, the Court of Appeal felt able to suggest that 'section 2 of the 1997 Act will not contravene Convention rights if courts

---

[53] *Ibid.*, para.30 (Lord Bingham).   [54] *Ibid.*
[55] C. A. Gearty, 'Reconciling parliamentary democracy and human rights' (2002) 118 LQR 248, 255–6.
[56] *R* v. *Offen* [2001] 1 WLR 253 (CA).
[57] 'Serious offences' were defined in s.2(5)–(7) Crime (Sentences) Act 1997.
[58] See e.g.: *R* v. *Kelly (Edward)* [2000] QB 198.
[59] *R* v. *Offen*, above n. 56, paras. 95–6.   [60] *Ibid.*, para.92.

apply the section so that it does not result in offenders being sentenced to life imprisonment when they do not constitute a significant risk to the public'.[61]

Lord Woolf downplayed the significance of the interpretation adopted, stating that under its terms, 'the 1997 Act will still give effect to the intention of Parliament. It will do so, however, in a more just, less arbitrary and more proportionate manner.'[62] Conor Gearty was less generous, commenting that 'however it is dressed up or explained away, the *Offen* case has effectively disembowelled a particularly savage legislative intervention', so that, 'even opponents of judicial activism find themselves applauding the result while diverting their eyes from how it was brought about'.[63] The reading adopted by the Court of Appeal was unmistakably a considerable liberalisation of the approach to be taken to the provision in question, and one which amply demonstrates the stark difference between the natural meaning of legislative language and its Convention-compliant interpretation.

The first House of Lords decision on the scope of s.3(1) was the controversial case of *R* v. *A (No. 2)*.[64] *R* v. *A* concerned the construction of s.41 of the Youth Justice and Criminal Evidence Act 1999; a provision designed to prevent the submission of evidence based on the complainant's previous sexual history in rape proceedings, except in closely defined circumstances. The Law Lords' concern over the provision – which Lord Slynn referred to as 'disproportionately restrictive'[65] – was that the virtual blanket exclusion of such materials could preclude the submission of evidence which would guarantee the defendant's right to a fair trial under Article 6 of the Convention. Lords Slynn, Steyn, Clyde and Hutton were all of the view that beyond this concern lay the potential for the application of s.41 to lead to a prima facie incompatibility with Article 6(1).[66] The key question for the Law Lords was whether the remedy of such an 'incompatibility' would be 'possible' under s.3(1). In deciding that it was, Lord Steyn held that:

> It is ... possible under section 3 to read section 41, and in particular section 41(3)(c), as subject to the implied provision that evidence or questioning

---

[61] *Ibid.*, para.97.   [62] *Ibid.*, para.99.

[63] C. A. Gearty, *Principles of Human Rights Adjudication* (Oxford University Press, 2004) p.77.

[64] *R* v. *A (No. 2)* [2001] UKHL 25; [2002] 1 AC 45.   [65] *Ibid.*, para.13.

[66] *Ibid.*, paras.10, 43, 136 and 161, respectively. Lord Hope, on the other hand, felt that 'it has not been shown that ... the provisions of section 41 which are relevant to the respondent's case are incompatible with his Convention right to a fair trial' (at para.106).

which is required to ensure a fair trial under Article 6 of the Convention should not be treated as inadmissible.[67]

As Nicol has noted, the difference between the natural meaning of the provision, and the Convention-compatible interpretation adopted by the House of Lords, is stark: '[i]t is difficult to see [the interpretation adopted] as bearing any relationship either to the wording of section 41(3)(c) or to Parliament's intention in enacting it'.[68]

Although a unanimous decision of the House of Lords, the more circumspect approach of Lord Hope highlights the significance of the interpretation adopted. Use of the s.3 power – he argued – should not allow judges to displace *specific* decisions made by the legislature. As a result, interpretation under s.3 should not be possible if 'the legislation contains provisions which expressly contradict the meaning which the enactment would have to be given to make it compatible'.[69] In the context of s.41, therefore, Lord Hope felt that what was 'possible' would be constrained by the intentions of Parliament passing the provision in question; to adopt an interpretation – such as that suggested by Lord Steyn – 'would not be possible, without contradicting the plain intention of Parliament'.[70] As Lord Hope noted, 'the whole point of the section … was to address the mischief which was thought to have arisen due to the width of the discretion which had previously been given to the trial judge'.[71] In other words, such use of s.3(1) would bring back the possibility for mischief which Parliament had specifically sought to avoid.

Both *Offen* and *R v. A* show the courts utilising their interpretative power to restore judicial discretion in an area where Parliament had sought to reduce it. It is no surprise that both concerned an area of the law where arguments over deference to the legislator are less than persuasive; as Richard Clayton has argued, 'in the criminal field, the courts will intervene unhesitatingly if they take the view that a judicial discretion is being circumscribed on unpersuasive grounds'.[72] What distinguishes *Offen* and *R v. A* from the suggested use of s.3(1) in *Anderson* is that the contested provisions were not effectively invalidated by way of interpretation. In both *Offen* and *R v. A*, the 'interpreted' provisions

---

[67] *Ibid.*, para.45.
[68] D. Nicol, 'Are Convention rights a no-go zone for Parliament?' [2002] PL 438, 443.
[69] *R v. A (No. 2)*, above n. 64, para.108.
[70] *Ibid.*, para.109.   [71] *Ibid.*
[72] R. Clayton, 'The limits of what's possible: statutory construction under the Human Rights Act' [2002] EHRLR 559, 560.

remained meaningful, albeit with an effect in practice which differs – arguably significantly – from that which would be the result of the natural interpretation of the statutory language. Under the interpretation of s.2 of the Crime (Sentences) Act 1997 which was adopted in *Offen*, persons convicted of a 'second serious offence' would continue to be sentenced to life imprisonment so long as they posed a 'significant risk to the public'. Similarly, on the interpretation of s.41 of the Youth Justice and Criminal Evidence Act 1999 adopted in *R* v. *A*, evidence relating to the victim's previous sexual history would not be admissible, unless refusal to admit such evidence posed a threat to the fair trial rights of the accused. By contrast, had the suggested s.3 interpretation been adopted in *Anderson*,[73] then s.2 of the Crime (Sentences) Act would have been rendered meaningless, as the discretionary power of the Home Secretary would have been interpreted out of existence.

It would seem, then, that s.3(1) does not permit judicial interpretations which would render statutory provisions inoperable or meaningless. As much was to be expected; given that the HRA does not provide for an explicit power to invalidate statutes, it would have been a radical application indeed that permitted the same result under a facade of interpretative power. Yet in spite of this, the interpretative latitude available to the courts remains considerable.

Implied terms and additional words

Perhaps the most obvious indicator of the scope of the courts' interpretative power can be found in their ability, under s.3, to adopt interpretations which depart from the natural meaning of the statutory language, or to modify that language through the implication of terms or provisions. In *R* v. *A*, Lord Steyn argued that under the interpretative approach sanctioned by s.3(1):

> it will sometimes be necessary to adopt an interpretation which linguistically may appear strained. The techniques to be used will not only involve the reading down of express language in a statute but also the implication of provisions.[74]

Compatibility was achieved in that case by adopting the implied proviso that evidence relating to the victim's sexual history would not be deemed

---

[73] *R (on the application of Anderson)* v. *Secretary of State for the Home Department*, above n. 52, para.30.
[74] *R* v. *A (No. 2)*, above n. 35, para.44.

inadmissible where to do so would jeopardise the fair trial rights of the accused.[75] Following soon after, *Re S; Re W* also concerned a less controversial – but equally striking – implication of provisions.[76]

In *Re S; Re W*, the House of Lords overturned a decision of the Court of Appeal which had made 'two major adjustments and innovations in the construction and application of the Children Act' 1989 in the name of achieving compatibility with Article 8 of the Convention.[77] The first was to broaden the margin of discretion available to a judge considering making an interim or final care order. The second – and in the words of Lord Nicholls in the House of Lords, the 'more radical' – was to set down a new scheme of 'starred' care plans, the supervision of which would be undertaken by the court. The Court of Appeal – by 'reading into' the statute a system of starred care plans – in effect had created a new supervisory jurisdiction.

In the view of Lord Nicholls – with whose speech the remaining Law Lords agreed – not only was this innovation 'radical', but it was also the polar opposite of parliamentary intent as evidenced in the Children Act; 'where a care order is made the responsibility for the child's care is with the [local] authority rather than the court. The court retains no supervisory role ... That was the intention of Parliament.'[78] In interpreting the Children Act in this way, Lord Nicholls noted that the Court of Appeal had departed from a 'cardinal principle' of that Act,[79] and, in doing so, had 'crossed the boundary between interpretation and amendment'.[80] Additionally, the Court of Appeal had strayed from legitimate interpretation into the realms of illegitimate legislative amendment for the reason that its decision would have had 'important practical repercussions which the court is not equipped to evaluate'.[81] The court in *Re S; Re W* was not competent to make the wholesale changes required to provide the remedy desired. Additionally, the scheme devised by the Court of Appeal would have run counter to the intent of Parliament as evidenced in the Children Act. In consequence, Parliament, and not the courts, should be the appropriate author of whatever steps were necessary to achieve compatibility in this sphere.

---

[75] *Ibid.*, para.45.

[76] *Re S (Children) (Care Order: Implementation of Care Plan) Re W (Children) (Care Order: Adequacy of Care Plan)*, above n. 49.

[77] *Ibid.*, para.1.   [78] *Ibid.*, para.25.

[79] Lord Nicholls repeatedly uses this phrase, at paras. 23, 27, 28, and 42.

[80] *Re S (Children) (Care Order: Implementation of Care Plan); Re W (Children) (Care Order: Adequacy of Care Plan)*, above n. 49, para.40 (Lord Nicholls).

[81] *Ibid.*

More recently, however, the decision of the House of Lords in *Ghaidan* v. *Godin-Mendoza* has confirmed the breadth of the power to read in words and provisions to remedy incompatibilities in primary legislation, so long as those words go 'with the grain of the legislation' at issue.[82] According to the majority in *Ghaidan*, subject to the express limitation that interpretations adopted under s.3(1) be 'possible', and the implied restrictions that the court should not 'adopt a meaning inconsistent with a fundamental feature of the legislation' nor engage in decision making which would more readily fall within the expertise of the elected branches, the courts enjoy a wide discretion in the discharge of their functions under s.3(1).[83] Parliamentary intent clearly continues to play a role – as an analysis of the purpose of the contested provision is required – but is certainly no longer the courts' sole concern.

In *Ghaidan*, Lord Nicholls accepted that Parliament – through the enactment of s.3(1) of the HRA – intended that courts should be able to 'modify the meaning, and hence the effect, of primary and secondary legislation'.[84] Tackling the supposed constraints of statutory language, his Lordship noted that the courts should have regard not only to the specific language in question, but also to the 'concept expressed in that language',[85] further adding that s.3(1) might require a court to depart from the unambiguous wording of a statute in order to achieve compatibility.[86] Lord Nicholls continued that if this is accepted – in other words, if it can be accepted that *unambiguous* words can be 'interpreted' in order to achieve compatibility – then 'it becomes impossible to suppose that Parliament intended that the operation of section 3 should depend critically upon the particular form of words adopted by the parliamentary draftsman'.[87]

The point was echoed by Lord Rodger: while acknowledging that the importation of terms into a statutory provision to achieve compatibility may result in the appearance that a court has 'amended' the provision in question, he added that, so long as the 'court implies words that are consistent with the scheme of the legislation', then the addition of words would remain an act of interpretation.[88] He continued:

> if the implication of a dozen words leaves the essential principles and scope of the legislation intact but allows it to be read in a way which is

[82] *Ghaidan* v. *Godin-Mendoza* [2004] 2 AC 557.
[83] *Ibid.*, para.33.   [84] *Ibid.*, para.32.   [85] *Ibid.*, para.31.
[86] Cf. Nicol, 'Are Convention rights a no-go zone for Parliament?', above n. 68.
[87] *Ghaidan* v. *Godin-Mendoza*, above n. 82, para.31.
[88] *Ibid.*, para.121. See also para.40 (Lord Steyn).

compatible with Convention rights, the implication is a legitimate exercise of the powers conferred by s.3(1).[89]

In the not too distant past, such utterances would have been unthinkable. As a consequence, while the will of Parliament as expressed in statutory language may be an important consideration in adjudication under the HRA, it is questionable whether, following *Ghaidan*, even clear and unambiguous terms could be used to preclude the potential reinterpretation of a provision under s.3(1).[90]

For advocates of the literal, parliamentary sovereignty-driven, approach to interpretation, the difficulties of adopting an interpretation which implies words or provisions into a statute are clear – the words deliberated over and chosen by the legislature may no longer be determinative of how a statute ought to take effect. Lord Nicholls acknowledged as much in *Ghaidan*, in saying that s.3(1) enables the judiciary to 'modify the meaning, and hence the effect' of primary legislation.[91] As a result, s.3(1) has undoubtedly put increasing strain on – and possibly consigned to history – the approach to legislative interpretation which denies a creative role to the judge.

Deference to the legislature and the limitations of judicial interpretation

In failing to create a power of judicial strike-down and in upholding the primacy of Parliament even in the event of a declaration of incompatibility, a respect for legislative decisions taken by Parliament is clearly inherent in the design of the HRA.[92] At the level of judicial decision making, this structural deference is compounded by the terms of s.3(1) itself – particularly the stipulation that the judicial task should remain one of 'interpretation' – and it is further limited by the wider judicial recognition that 'national courts may accord to the decisions of national legislatures some deference *where the context justifies it*'.[93] In the sphere of the

---

[89] *Ibid.*, para.122.

[90] Further evidence of this significant departure from the traditional approach to statutory construction can be seen from the judgment of Simon J in *R* v. *Holding*, in which it was noted that 'the precise form of words read in for the purpose of section 3 is of *no significance*' ([2006] 1 WLR 1040, para.47) (emphasis added).

[91] *Ghaidan* v. *Godin-Mendoza*, above n. 82, para.32.   [92] See pp.151–3.

[93] *Brown* v. *Stott* [2003] 1 AC 681, 711 (emphasis in original). See also: *International Transport Roth GmbH* v. *Secretary of State for the Home Department* [2002] 3 WLR 344; *Huang* v. *Secretary of State for the Home Department* [2007] UKHL 11.

interpretation of legislation under the HRA, it is perhaps unsurprising that there has been recognition that 'greater deference is to be paid to an Act of Parliament than to a decision of the executive or a subordinate measure'[94] as the former has the 'imprimatur of democratic approval'.[95] But – as with deference to decisions of the executive – this 'direct deference'[96] should not be used as a ground on which to displace the judicial analysis of the compatibility of a given statutory scheme on the facts of the stated case.[97] Nor is deference to the legislator a one-size-fits-all concession to the view of Parliament as expressed in legislation; the degree of deference to which a statute may be subject is a variable standard. While the scheme of the Act ensures that no piece of parliamentary legislation may be excluded from HRA review, the willingness of courts to deploy the s.3(1) interpretative power – and the nature of the linguistic amendments they feel able to propose – may well vary according to the circumstances of the individual case.

Hence, two of the most creative deployments of the s.3(1) power – *R v. Offen* and *R v. A* – are, for example, argued to have been justified on the basis that their subject matter directly engaged judicial expertise and discretion. By contrast, a declaration of incompatibility was the preferred remedy in the House of Lords decision in *Bellinger v. Bellinger*.[98] In that case, a declaration was sought by Mrs Bellinger, a post-operative male to female transsexual, that s.11(c) of the Matrimonial Causes Act 1973 – which provided that parties to a marriage must be 'respectively male and female' – was incompatible with Articles 8 and 12 of the ECHR. The House of Lords, in the light of clear authority from the European Court of Human Rights,[99] unanimously endorsed the making of a declaration of incompatibility. As Lord Hope noted in *Bellinger*, quite simply, s.11(c) of the Matrimonial Causes Act was 'not capable of being given the extended meaning' of the sort which had been sought by Mrs Bellinger.[100]

---

[94] *International Transport Roth GmbH v. Secretary of State for the Home Department*, above n. 93, 376–8.

[95] *Huang v. Secretary of State for the Home Department*, above n. 93, para. 17.

[96] I. Leigh, 'The standard of review after the Human Rights Act' in Fenwick, Phillipson and Masterman (eds), *Judicial Reasoning under the UK Human Rights Act*, above n. 43, p.194.

[97] As was arguably the case in *R (on the application of ProLife Alliance) v. British Broadcasting Corporation* [2003] UKHL 23; [2004] 1 AC 185.

[98] *Bellinger v. Bellinger* [2003] UKHL 21; [2003] 2 AC 467.

[99] *Goodwin v. United Kingdom* (2002) 35 EHRR 18.

[100] *Bellinger v. Bellinger*, above n. 98, para.56. Lord Hobhouse added that to interpret the provision in the way suggested by Mrs Bellinger 'would … not be an exercise in

Considering this linguistic issue in isolation, it is arguable that giving an extended definition to the word 'female' would indeed have been possible.[101] However, for the House of Lords in *Bellinger*, the discrete nature of the linguistic interpretation was not their sole concern:

> the recognition of gender re-assignment for the purposes of marriage is part of a wider problem which should be considered as a whole and not dealt with in piecemeal fashion. There should be a clear, coherent policy. The decision regarding recognition of gender reassignment for the purpose of marriage cannot sensibly be made in isolation from a decision on the like problem in other areas where a distinction is drawn between people on the basis of gender.[102]

While the linguistic change may have been 'possible' in the sense envisaged by s.3(1), addressing the wider ramifications of such an interpretation was felt to be beyond the constitutional competence of the court.[103] The specific reasons for this, however, lay within the broader context surrounding the specific dispute.

The legal recognition of acquired gender had been the subject of a series of cases before the European Court of Human Rights.[104] This series of cases had culminated in the decision of the Court in *Goodwin* v. *United Kingdom*, signalling a movement towards the 'legal recognition of the ... sexual identity of post-operative transsexuals'.[105] In response to *Goodwin*, the government had announced the imminent publication of draft legislation concerning the legal recognition of acquired gender.[106] Against this backdrop – and in the light of a concession made by counsel for the government that *Goodwin* effectively rendered s.11(c) of the Matrimonial Causes Act incompatible with Articles 8 and 12 of the Convention[107] – the House of Lords unanimously found in favour of issuing a declaration

---

interpretation, however robust. It would be a legislative exercise of amendment making a legislative choice as to what precise amendment was appropriate' (para.78).

[101] Especially considering the subsequent case of *Ghaidan* v. *Godin-Mendoza* in which the House of Lords had felt able to interpret the words 'as his husband or wife' to include same-sex partners [2004] UKHL 30; [2004] 2 AC 557. For discussion, see pp.162–3 and G. Phillipson, 'Deference, discretion and democracy in the Human Rights Act era' (2007) 60 *Current Legal Problems* 40, 63–8.

[102] *Bellinger* v. *Bellinger*, above n. 98, para.45.

[103] For a challenge to this viewpoint see: Phillipson, 'Deference, discretion and democracy in the Human Rights Act era', above n. 101.

[104] E.g.: *Rees* v. *United Kingdom* (1987) 9 EHRR 56; *Cossey* v. *United Kingdom* (1991) 13 EHRR 622.

[105] *Goodwin* v. *United Kingdom*, above n. 99, para.85.

[106] Subsequently enacted as the Gender Recognition Act 2004.

[107] *Bellinger* v. *Bellinger*, above n. 98, paras.25–7.

of incompatibility. While the decision of the House of Lords in *Bellinger* undoubtedly displays a respect for the decision-making domain of the elected branches, it also can be viewed as evidence of the limits of the law-making power of the judiciary under the HRA and of a judicial conscious-ness of the wider context within which their rights jurisdiction operates.

This jurisdiction, whatever the degree of latitude afforded to the pri-mary decision maker, is not one which the courts can 'abdicate'.[108] In short, while it might have been possible to suggest that intensive review was not a historical characteristic of judicial decisions in certain fields – national security,[109] social policy and/or resource allocation,[110] for example – deci-sions under the HRA demonstrate that those areas are no longer neces-sarily subject to light touch review, and that statutory language is not exempt from (potentially radical) judicial interpretation.[111] Section 3(1) ensures that parliamentary legislation is as susceptible to judicial review on human rights grounds as executive action. The degree of deference afforded to the legislator will not only directly relate to the question of whether a judicial interpretation is possible or impossible under s.3(1), but also to the potential for a greater (or lesser) degree of judicial creativ-ity in the use of that interpretative power. Importantly, and as we have already seen in the context of review of executive action, deference will not be owed in the process of gauging compatibility.

The reality of judicial power under the HRA as evidenced in cases such as *R* v. *A* and *Ghaidan*, makes it increasingly difficult to sustain the once unqualified truth that Parliament continues to exercise unfettered legis-lative discretion; while Parliament could legislate in clear and unequivo-cal language on a given topic, that would not insulate the words chosen from subsequent judicial refinement under s.3(1). Mindful of the poten-tial within s.3(1) to significantly interfere with legislative objectives, the courts have sought to articulate grounds on which this legislative power can be called upon, have allowed a degree of latitude to the policy choices of the elected branches as manifested in legislation[112] and have sought to safeguard a degree of certainty through an adherence to the doctrine of

---

[108] *International Transport Roth GmbH* v. *Secretary of State for the Home Department* [2003] QB 728, para.27 (Simon Brown LJ).

[109] See e.g.: *Liversidge* v. *Anderson* [1942] AC 206; *R* v. *Secretary of State for the Home Department, ex parte Hosenball* [1977] 1 WLR 766; [1977] 3 All ER 452.

[110] See e.g.: *R* v. *Cambridge Health Authority, ex parte B* [1995] 1 WLR 898.

[111] See e.g.: *A and others* v. *Secretary of State for the Home Department*, above n. 40; *Ghaidan* v. *Godin-Mendoza* [2004] UKHL 30; [2004] 2 AC 557.

[112] For a recent example, see: *R (on the application of Animal Defenders International)* v. *Secretary of State for Culture, Media and Sport* [2008] UKHL 15.

precedent.[113] As such, judicial law making on the HRA model is therefore more certain and legitimate where the change is discrete or incremental,[114] rather than sweeping or wholesale.[115] In this sense, parallels can be drawn with the development of the common law prior to the implementation of the HRA.[116] In many cases, the s.3(1) power of interpretation may not be available to the courts at all.[117] However, the breadth of the judicial law-making power under s.3(1) is confirmed by those decisions in which the judges feel confident to assert their interpretative authority,[118] and by the degree to which *Ghaidan* suggests that the courts are able to effectively 'amend' statutory provisions to achieve compatibility so long as the variance or importation of words is consistent with the 'grain of the legislation' in question.

However it is presented, the experience of judicial decision making under s.3(1) of the Act marks a further significant departure from the traditional literal approach to the interpretation of legislation passed by the sovereign Parliament. While the formal role of the judiciary remains to interpret the law as passed by Parliament, such is the width of the judicial discretion under s.3(1) that it seems increasingly implausible to seek to deny that judges possess significant creative power, and that the sovereignty of Parliament has been entirely undisturbed by the passing of the HRA. Nowhere, perhaps, is this refinement of the separation of powers clearer than in those instances in which the courts have used s.3 to refine statutory provisions which post-date the HRA.[119] In those instances, Parliament has legislated with the *explicit* knowledge of the human rights implications of a given measure under the procedure laid down by s.19 of the Act: yet, as Lord Cooke has asked, '[c]an the United Kingdom Parliament of 2000 be classified as sovereign if, by virtue of an Act of

---

[113] *Kay* v. *London Borough of Lambeth; Leeds City Council* v. *Price* [2006] UKHL 10.

[114] *Ghaidan* v. *Godin-Mendoza*, above n. 82.

[115] *Re S (Children) (Care Order: Implementation of Care Plan); Re W (Children) (Care Order: Adequacy of Care Plan)*, above n. 49; *Bellinger* v. *Bellinger*, above n. 98.

[116] As Lord Reid, for example, indicated in *Steadman* v. *Steadman*, judges should hesitate to make law in those cases where the ramifications of their so doing are unclear, or where it would be 'impracticable to foresee all the consequences of tampering with it' ([1976] AC 536, 542C). See also: Kavanagh, 'Choosing between sections 3 and 4 of the Human Rights Act 1998, above n. 43.

[117] See e.g.: *Bellinger* v. *Bellinger*, above n. 98; *A and others* v. *Secretary of State for the Home Department* [2004] UKHL 56.

[118] *R* v. *Offen*, above n. 56; *R* v. *A (No. 2)*, above n. 35.

[119] *Secretary of State for the Home Department* v. *MB* [2007] UKHL 46; [2007] 3 WLR 681. See also: *AG's ref number 4 of 2002; Sheldrake* v. *DPP* [2004] UKHL 42.

an earlier Parliament, it was powerless to achieve its intention, however clearly articulated?'[120]

Democratic dialogue in practice: parliamentary and executive responses to incompatibility

If the use of s.3(1) is presented as having the potential at least to further dilute the powers of a supposedly sovereign legislature, then s.4 – the declaration of incompatibility – has typically been presented as the 'escape-hatch' for the sovereignty doctrine.[121] Yet we have already seen criticisms of the suggestion that the mere provision of the declaration of incompatibility tool provides the necessary safeguards to guarantee that political autonomy over the content of legislative decisions would be substantially preserved,[122] and early indications were that recourse to s.4 might be infrequent at best. In *R* v. *A (No. 2)*, Lord Steyn, considering the issue of the appropriate judicial response to a prima facie incompatibility with the Convention rights, indicated that the declaration of incompatibility should operate as a 'measure of last resort' which 'must be avoided unless it is plainly impossible to do so'.[123] While it might be argued that such an approach is in keeping with the intentions of the framers of the HRA,[124] it also contains the potential to upset the careful balance between elected and judicial power which has seen the Act supported by those sceptical of stronger-form judicial review.[125] In his speech in *R* v. *A*, Lord Steyn in fact went further, arguing that the *only* circumstance in which it would be necessary to issue a declaration of incompatibility would be where a 'clear limitation on Convention rights' was 'stated in terms' in the debated provision(s).[126] Subsequent cases were to weigh against the establishment of an overriding preference in favour of adopting s.3(1) interpretations

---

[120] Lord Cooke of Thorndon, 'The myth of sovereignty' (2007) 11 *Otago Law Review* 377, 380.

[121] I. Leigh, 'The UK's Human Rights Act 1998: an early assessment' in G. Huscroft and P. Rishworth (eds), *Litigating Rights: Perspectives from Domestic and International Law* (Oxford: Hart Publishing, 2002), p.324.

[122] See pp.44–6.

[123] *R* v. *A (No. 2)*, above n. 35, para.44.

[124] HL Debs, 3 November 1997, col.1231 (Lord Irvine of Lairg).

[125] Compare, for example, Professor Gearty's reservations over judicially enforceable bills of rights in K. D. Ewing and C. A. Gearty, *Freedom under Thatcher: Civil Liberties in Modern Britain* (Oxford: Clarendon Press, 1990) and K. D. Ewing and C. A. Gearty, 'Rocky foundations for Labour's new rights' [1997] EHRLR 146 with his pro-HRA stance in Gearty, *Principles of Human Rights Adjudication*, above n. 63 .

[126] *R* v. *A (No. 2)*, above n. 35, para.44.

in all but the most explicit of limitations on Convention rights.[127] But while cases such as *Re S; Re W, Anderson* and *Bellinger* may illustrate that recourse to s.3(1) might be precluded under certain circumstances,[128] debate over the *cumulative* effect of these cases disguises the fact that a *single* usage of the s.3(1) power may well constitute a significant inroad into the legislative discretion of Parliament.

In *Ghaidan* v. *Godin-Mendoza*, Lord Steyn indicated that:

> If Parliament disagrees with an interpretation by the courts under section 3(1), it is free to override it by amending the legislation and expressly reinstating the incompatibility.[129]

Such a position is – as a matter of law – clearly consistent with the idea of legal sovereignty, and clearly also consistent with the idea that the HRA itself makes no concrete effort to prevent Parliament legislating in a way that is incompatible with the Convention rights. Yet the technical legal position readily ignores the potential difficulties – and political cost – associated with a rejection by Parliament or the executive of either a judicial finding of incompatibility or a s.3(1) interpretation. As has already been seen, Tom Campbell has argued that even in the event of the balance on the face of the HRA being translated into practice – that is, where declarations of incompatibility are made as a matter of routine – the interpretative powers of the courts are so well established as to be 'politically entrenched'.[130] The consequence of this is that due to the normative authority which attaches to a judicial reading of compatibility, it may be particularly difficult in practice – though not impossible – for the elected branches to overturn or reject either a s.3(1) interpretation, or a declaration of incompatibility. This reluctance on the part of Parliament or the executive to challenge the views of the courts might correctly be appreciated as deference to the judicial role, and to the courts' authority as interpreters of the law. Such respect may be manifest in differing ways: either – as sceptics might contend – in an overt and consistent reluctance to depart from a judicial interpretation of the requirements of the HRA and the Convention rights; or otherwise, in a more flexible

---

[127] See: *Re S (Children) (Care Order: Implementation of Care Plan); Re W (Children) (Care Order: Adequacy of Care Plan)*, above n. 49; *R (on the application of Anderson)* v. *Secretary of State for the Home Department*, above n. 52; *Bellinger* v. *Bellinger*, above n. 98.

[128] On which, see: Nicol, 'Statutory interpretation and human rights after *Anderson*', above n. 43; Kavanagh, 'Statutory interpretation and human rights after *Anderson*: a more contextual approach', above n. 43.

[129] *Ghaidan* v. *Godin-Mendoza*, above n. 101, para.43 (Lord Steyn).

[130] Campbell, 'Incorporation through interpretation', above n. 31, p.87.

acknowledgement of the relative institutional competence and expertise of the courts as interpreters of the compatibility of statutory provisions with the requirements of the Convention rights. Either approach may be thought of as being consistent with a separation of powers in which the role of the courts is a potent check on the power of executive *and* legislature, though the latter ultimately allows for the political will to prevail. No judicial use of s.3(1) has – to date – been legislatively reversed during the life of the HRA.

Those who argue that the HRA initiates a 'dialogue' between the institutions of government, claim that the coercive force of a declaration of incompatibility – by contrast to an interpretation under s.3 – is limited to making a contribution to this broader dialogue on the meaning and requirements of the Convention rights. As Tom Hickman has observed, those who claim that the declaration of incompatibility contains the potential to effectively temper the potentially far-reaching impact of s.3(1), advocate a 'radical reconceptualisation of the separation of powers' which 'repositions the courts within the forum of ordinary politics, providing not a check or balance, but counsel'.[131] Such a viewpoint may find some support in the text of the Act itself, which provides that a declaration of incompatibility does not affect the 'validity, continuing operation or enforcement' of the provisions in respect of which it is made.[132] Sceptics, on the other hand, stress the improbability of the elected branches failing to act positively in response to a declaration of incompatibility, and liken the process created to one of an indirect judicial power of strike-down.[133]

In practice, the executive and Parliament have – to date – responded positively to each of the declarations of incompatibility issued by the higher courts (or have, at the least, indicated a willingness to do so). Opinions vary on the cumulative impact of this pattern of responses. For Aileen Kavanagh, the experience to date is categorised as a 'practice' under which the 'elected branches do not reject' declarations of incompatibility.[134] For the European Court of Human Rights, however, even if the parliamentary and executive responses to declarations of incompatibility to date can be categorised as an emerging practice, it is not one

---

[131] T. Hickman, 'Constitutional dialogue, constitutional theories and the Human Rights Act' [2005] PL 306, 309–10.

[132] Sections 3(2)(b) and 4(6) HRA.

[133] K. D. Ewing, 'The Human Rights Act and parliamentary democracy' (1999) 62 MLR 79, 92.

[134] A. Kavanagh, 'Deference or defiance? The limits of the judicial role in constitutional adjudication' in G. Huscroft (ed.), *Expounding the Constitution: Essays in Constitutional Theory* (Cambridge University Press, 2008), p.214.

which offers sufficient certainty for the recipient of the declaration that the offending provision(s) will be amended. As a result, the Court held – in its decision in *Burden and Burden* v. *United Kingdom* – that the declaration of incompatibility does not amount to an effective remedy for the purposes of Article 13 of the Convention, for the reason that it does not place the relevant minister under an obligation to amend the provision under scrutiny.[135] The pattern to date of declarations of incompatibility being acted upon by the elected branches has been insufficient to convince the European Court of Human Rights of the existence of a convention, or an 'established practice', that such action will become a matter of routine.[136] While the Joint Committee on Human Rights has also encouraged the government to adopt a 'much clearer policy on systematically responding to declarations of incompatibility',[137] the consequence of such a 'convention' emerging would be a seeming strengthening of the judicial hand in determining questions of compatibility.

For the time being, and notwithstanding the trend in responding positively to declarations of incompatibility, the position remains that it is open to government and/or Parliament to reject a judicial finding of incompatibility. The emergence of a convention to the effect that declarations of incompatibility would be responded to, positively, as a matter of course, would strengthen the grip of the judges over definitional and interpretative issues in a manner that would arguably upset the apparent balance on the face of the HRA. Yet, from a separation of powers perspective, such a development may not be seen as being entirely objectionable. It will be recalled that one of the perceived weaknesses of the HRA can be found in the potential – inherent in s.4 – to 'decouple rights from remedy',[138] or, in other words, to leave the recipient of a declaration of incompatibility, an otherwise successful claimant, without a remedy to speak of. The adoption or development of a convention whereby declarations of incompatibility *are* responded to in a strategic manner would undoubtedly enhance the remedial capacity of the HRA, and concurrently point to a robust, judicially policed, respect for human rights within a separation of powers where judicial decisions were not simply treated as 'principle proposing'[139]

---

[135] *Burden and Burden* v. *United Kingdom* (2007) 44 EHRR 51, para.39.
[136] *Ibid.*
[137] Joint Committee on Human Rights, *Monitoring the Government's Response to Court Judgments Finding Breaches of Human Rights* (HL 128/HC 728), 2006–7, paras.109–21.
[138] Hickman, 'Constitutional dialogue, constitutional theories and the Human Rights Act', above n. 131, 327.
[139] See e.g.: Campbell, 'Incorporation through interpretation', above n. 31.

contributions to a dialogue between institutions.[140] Even in the absence of such a convention, if we are to take seriously the ability of the courts to authoritatively determine the requirements of the law[141] – including the interpretation and application of the Convention Rights in the domestic context – then the ability of the executive and Parliament to ignore, or otherwise fail to act upon a declaration of incompatibility, should be regarded as being an entirely extraordinary response.

It is suggested that this deference to the courts might be evident in cases in which either s.3 or s.4 is invoked, and should be seen, not as an unjustifiable inroad into the constitutional competence of the elected branches, but as evidence of the authoritative interpretative powers of the courts under the separation of powers. If it is correct that, 'for the HRA to have real legal purchase, it must be up to the courts to make authoritative determinations as to what Convention rights require',[142] then this authority should not be diminished dependent on whether the judges chose to utilise either s.3(1) or to issue a declaration of incompatibility under s.4. It is for this reason that deference to the legislature remains a central component of the reasoning processes in statutory interpretation cases, for without *any* notion of deference to the choices of legislators to offset the undoubted potency of judicial use of s.3(1) and of s.4, the idea that the HRA has ushered in an age of judicial supremacism becomes more credible.

It is clear, then, that the potential of the courts to contribute to legislative development lies not only in the creative possibilities of s.3, but in the more indirect contribution to constitutional politics inherent in the issue of a declaration of incompatibility. If, as emerging practice appears to indicate, an executive or parliamentary response to a declaration of

---

[140] For discussion, see: Hickman, 'Constitutional dialogue, constitutional theories and the Human Rights Act', above n. 131.

[141] Lord Steyn, 'The weakest and least dangerous department of government' [1997] PL 84, 86.

[142] T. Poole, 'The reformation of English administrative law' (2009) 68 CLJ 142, 160. See pp.137–9. From the earliest legislative review cases under the HRA, one avenue of potential dialogue between the executive and Parliament has seemingly been closed down: by determining that ministerial statements of compatibility made under s.19 of the HRA are of no binding or persuasive status in adjudication concerning questions of statutory compatibility, the judges have arguably sought to minimise the potential exchange of institutional viewpoints between executive, legislature and courts. As Lord Hope noted in *R* v. *A*, s.19 statements are 'no more than expressions of opinion by the [responsible] minister' (*R* v. *A (No. 2)* [2001] 1 AC 45, 75.) Instead, the text of the Act itself, and its application in the context of the case, must provide the courts with the relevant evidence on which to assess the measure's compatibility. Though for a seeming exception to this,

incompatibility will be a matter of likelihood, if not of routine, then significant force evidently continues to attach to the judicial statement of the requirements of the Convention rights as evidenced in that declaration. If this is so, then – consistent with statements made by the Labour government during the parliamentary debates on the Human Rights Bill[143] – it would take particularly forceful arguments to displace the expectation that the declaration should be acted upon by the executive and/or Parliament.[144] While a practice of adherence to the judicial assessment of compatibility does not signal the abandonment of the power to depart from the findings of a declaration of incompatibility,[145] it clearly signals the normative force which continues to attach to judicial readings of the requirements of the law, regardless of the invocation of dialogue metaphors and their apparent implications for the authority of judicial power.

Evidence of judicial awareness of the potency of a declaration of incompatibility can be found in the decision of the House of Lords in *R (on the application of Animal Defenders International)* v. *Secretary of State for Culture, Media and Sport*.[146] In *Animal Defenders International*, the House of Lords was asked to issue a declaration of incompatibility in respect of s.321(2) of the Communications Act 2003. Section 321(2) imposed a ban on the broadcast of political advertisements on television, the blanket nature of which had caused doubts as to the proportionality of the restriction imposed by the provision on freedom of expression. As a result of these doubts, the government had been unable to make a statement of compatibility in respect of the measure upon its introduction to Parliament. The House of Lords was faced with two relevant decisions of the European Court of Human Rights. The first of these decisions – *VgT Verein gegen Tierfabriken* v. *Switzerland*[147] – seemed to indicate that

where the relevant minister felt unable to make a statement of compatibility, see the discussion of *R (on the application of Animal Defenders International)* v. *Secretary of State for Culture, Media and Sport*, above n. 112, at pp.173–5.

[143] See above, n. 58, pp.46–7.

[144] A. L. Young, *Parliamentary Sovereignty and the Human Rights Act* (Oxford: Hart Publishing, 2009), p.143.

[145] As Jeffrey Goldsworthy has written: '[t]here is clearly a difference between relinquishing or disabling one's power to make certain kinds of decisions, and declining – even routinely – to exercise it' (J. Goldsworthy, 'Judicial review, legislative override and democracy' in T. Campbell, J. Goldsworthy and A. Stone, *Protecting Human Rights: Instruments and Institutions* (Oxford University Press, 2003), p.268).

[146] *R (on the application of Animal Defenders International)* v. *Secretary of State for Culture, Media and Sport* [2008] UKHL 15; [2008] 1 AC 1312.

[147] *VgT Verein gegen Tierfabriken* v. *Switzerland* (2002) 34 EHRR 4.

a blanket ban on advertising for political ends would be a disproportionate interference with freedom of expression. The second relevant decision – *Murphy* v. *Ireland*[148] – suggested that a similar restriction placed on advertising for religious purposes would fall within the range of reasonable responses available to states as a result of the margin of appreciation doctrine. While *VgT* was arguably the more relevant decision on the facts, the House of Lords found that the two cases, when taken together, demonstrated no clear consensus on the issue and provided evidence that the judgment of a state legislature would be likely to fall within the margin of appreciation granted by the European Court of Human Rights.[149]

While the grounds on which the House of Lords determined that greater weight should be placed on the Court's decision in *Murphy* may be open to criticism,[150] our concern here is with the Law Lords' treatment of the suggestion that a declaration of incompatibility should be awarded. In failing to grant the declaration sought, Lord Bingham – with whom in determining the outcome of the case the remaining Law Lords agreed[151] – stated that 'great weight' should be afforded to the considered opinion of Parliament in implementing the measure in question, particularly as the government had felt unable to make a s.19 statement of compatibility at the point of introducing the Communications Bill into Parliament.[152] At first glance, given the structure of the HRA and the explicit language of ss.3(2) and 4(6), Parliament's ability to enact legislation which may be incompatible with Convention rights is clearly countenanced. As a result, perhaps Lord Bingham felt it necessary to have regard to the executive's failure to make a statement of compatibility due to the fact that Parliament, notwithstanding concerns over the compatibility of the ban on political advertising with Article 10, had nevertheless chosen to enact such a provision. The circumstances of the case at hand, while envisaged by the framers of the Act, were arguably exceptional enough to merit the court taking notice of the legislative history of the provision under scrutiny. Perhaps, then, *Animal Defenders International* could be taken as illustrative of the deference owed to a specific legislative decision taken following explicit consideration of its Convention implications.

---

[148] *Murphy* v. *Ireland* (2004) 38 EHRR 13.

[149] *R (on the application of Animal Defenders International)* v. *Secretary of State for Culture, Media and Sport*, above n. 112, para.35.

[150] C. J. S. Knight, 'Monkeying around with free speech' (2008) 124 LQR 557.

[151] Though see the discussion at p.194.

[152] *R (on the application of Animal Defenders International)* v. *Secretary of State for Culture, Media and Sport*, above n. 112, para.33. Though no explanation is given for the apparent inconsistency between giving 'great weight' to a ministerial *failure* to make a statement

However, a closer inspection of the language chosen by Lord Bingham seems to reveal an underlying concern over the consequences of granting the remedy sought by the applicants. In his speech, Lord Bingham repeatedly alluded to the implications of granting the relief sought. First, he argued, the judgment of Parliament 'should not be lightly *overridden*'.[153] Further, he went on to say that, in the balancing of competing interests:

> a line must be drawn, and it is for Parliament to decide where. The drawing of a line inevitably means that hard cases will arise falling on the wrong side of it, but that should not be held to *invalidate* the rule if, judged in the round, it is beneficial.[154]

The language used by Lord Bingham is striking. It is the vocabulary of the *constitutional* review of primary legislation. Yet in *Animal Defenders International*, the House was not being asked to 'override' the provision in question, nor was it being asked to 'invalidate' it. Instead, the House was being asked to declare it incompatible with Article 10 of the Convention which, in theory at least, is a far less radical proposition.

So what are we to make of Lord Bingham's startling turn of phrase? Does he deliberately overstate the consequences of issuing a declaration of incompatibility in the light of Parliament's decision to enact the ban notwithstanding the failure of the government to make a statement of compatibility under s.19? Given the previous record of the courts in failing to attach any significance to the issue of a ministerial statement of compatibility,[155] this seems unlikely. Given also the assumption that 'great weight' should attach to *any* legislative decision taken by Parliament, the failure of the government to make a statement of compatibility in respect of the particular statute should not be of any material significance to a court considering whether or not to issue a declaration of incompatibility. We are left, then, with the conclusion that *Animal Defenders International* provides clear evidence of judicial awareness of the political potency of a declaration of incompatibility, and of the fact that – exceptional circumstances aside – such a declaration will cause the amendment or replacement of the primary legislation or provisions at issue.

It is not the only example to be found in the case law. In *R (on the application of Chester)* v. *Secretary of State for Justice*, Burton J declined to make a declaration of incompatibility in respect of s.3 of the Representation of

---

of compatibility under s.19 and the House of Lords' previously stated position that an actual statement of compatibility should be treated as being of no persuasive authority whatsoever (see n. 142 above).

[153] *Ibid.* (emphasis added). [154] *Ibid.* (emphasis added). [155] Above n. 142.

the People Act 1983. Section 3 of the Act disenfranchised serving prisoners from voting in any election in the UK during the course of their sentence. The provision had already been the subject of an earlier declaration, granted in *Smith* v. *Scott*[156] as a result of the incompatibility between the prohibition and Article 3 of Protocol 1 to the Convention, in reliance on the decision of the Grand Chamber of the European Court of Human Rights in *Hirst* v. *United Kingdom*.[157] In the intervening period, the government had indicated a willingness to address the incompatibility, and had opened the issue to consultation, though no draft legislation had been published.[158] In *Chester*, however, Burton J declined to grant the remedy sought, in part on the basis that a declaration of incompatibility had 'already been made', in part for the reason that the government had begun to take steps to address the incompatibility, and in part – but arguably most notably – for the fact that the declaration already granted was '*binding* on the UK government'.[159]

Conclusion

Outside the sphere of influence of the HRA, the judicial role in respect of statutory interpretation retains at least some of the vestiges of a more formalist approach to statutory construction; as Lord Collins noted in one of the final appeals heard by the Appellate Committee of the House of Lords, 'it is not the role of the court to re-write legislation … there is a difference between legitimate purposive construction and impermissible judicial legislation'.[160] Yet in cases where the Convention rights are in play, as Lord Nicholls demonstrated in *Ghaidan*, the courts are able to play a limited legislative role where statutory language, and the intention

---

[156] *Smith* v. *Scott* 2007 SC 345; 2007 SLT 137.

[157] *Hirst* v. *United Kingdom* (2006) 42 EHRR 41.

[158] Department of Constitutional Affairs, *Voting Rights of Convicted Prisoners Detained within the United Kingdom*, CP29/06 (December 2006); Ministry of Justice, *Voting Rights of Convicted Prisoners Detained within the United Kingdom*, CP6/09 (April 2009).

[159] *R (on the application of Chester)* v. *Secretary of State for Justice* [2009] EWHC 2923 (Admin), para.34 (emphasis added). See also: M. Elliott, 'Parliamentary sovereignty and the new constitutional order: legislative freedom, political reality and convention' (2002) 22 LS 340, 349.

[160] *Transport for London (London Underground Ltd)* v. *Spirerose Ltd* [2009] UKHL 44, para.131 (Lord Collins). Cf. Campbell, 'Incorporation through interpretation', above n. 31, p.87, who argues that the 'textually relaxed' and 'morally purposive' approach to interpretation adopted under a legal rights instrument is 'not easily confined to the interpretation of those rights themselves, so that there will be a major impact on legal interpretation in general'.

behind it, is arguably no longer the overriding concern. Rather, as Aileen Kavanagh has written:

> Under s.3(1), the overriding aim of the interpretative process is to find a Convention-compatible meaning of the legislative provision, rather than to ascertain the intention of Parliament when it enacted the provision in a particular context.[161]

If this is accepted, then in human rights adjudication it becomes impossible to sustain the argument that parliamentary language (beyond that utilised in s.3(1)), or intention (beyond that to find Convention-compliant meaning) however construed, remains determinative of how a statute should take effect. Section 3(1) therefore provides the central test of statutory interpretation where the Convention rights are at issue, and any question as to the statutory language adopted, or the intent of Parliament in passing the disputed provision, is of only secondary importance. As Lord Nicholls noted in *Ghaidan*:

> in the ordinary course the interpretation of legislation involves seeking the intention reasonably to be attributed to Parliament in using the language in question. Section 3 may require the court to depart from this legislative intention, that is, depart from the intention of the Parliament which enacted the legislation.[162]

It should not be suggested that, prior to the HRA coming into force, judicial decisions did not adopt controversial or disputable readings of statutory wordings; as Griffith has argued, cases such as *Padfield*,[163] *Pergau Dam*[164] and *Al-Fayed*,[165] among others, could be interpreted as 're-defining the purpose of a statute so as to reverse its meaning'.[166] So, too, *Fitzpatrick* v. *Sterling Housing Association Ltd*[167] – decided in 2000 before the Act came into force – hinted at the interpretative techniques later

---

[161] Kavanagh, 'The role of parliamentary intention in adjudication under the Human Rights Act 1998', above n. 15, 196.

[162] *Ghaidan* v. *Godin-Mendoza*, above n. 82, para.33. See also: *Attorney-General's Reference No. 4 of 2002*; *Sheldrake* v. *Director of Public Prosecutions*, above n.119, para.28 (Lord Bingham).

[163] *Padfield* v. *Minister of Agriculture, Fisheries and Food* [1968] AC 997.

[164] *R* v. *Secretary of State for Foreign and Commonwealth Affairs, ex parte World Development Movement* [1995] 1 WLR 386.

[165] *R* v. *Secretary of State for the Home Department, ex parte Al-Fayed (No. 1)* [1997] 1 All ER 228.

[166] J. A. G. Griffith, 'The brave new world of Sir John Laws' (2000) 63 MLR 159, 172.

[167] [2001] 1 AC 27.

deployed in *Ghaidan* v. *Godin-Mendoza*.[168] Prior to the HRA, however, while the literal approach to interpretation remained dominant, such approaches to statutory construction were certainly not the orthodoxy. The difference, post-HRA, is that *all* statutes are potentially susceptible to judicial (re-)interpretation on human rights grounds and that this limited judicial law-making function has at least indirect parliamentary sanction. As we have seen, however, the creative influence of the courts does not extend only to s.3(1) interpretations, for the ability of the courts to authoritatively determine whether a statutory provision meets the standards of legality required by the HRA is also reflected in the declaration of incompatibility. The continuing ability of Parliament to override a judicial decision – whether taken under s.3(1) or s.4 – is undeniable, but the experience to date illustrates that such a response will be wholly exceptional.

This is not, of course, to say that judicial decision making on human rights topics is immune from the legitimate criticisms of the political branches. Far from it. The readiness of courts to 'read in' implied conditions and terms into ostensibly clear legislative provisions has, in particular, drawn criticism from the influential Joint Parliamentary Committee on Human Rights. In its 2008 report into *Counter Terrorism Policy and Human Rights*, the Joint Committee noted with surprise the willingness of the Law Lords to read words into statutory provisions in order to render them compatible.[169] More specifically, the Joint Committee considered that the use of s.3(1) *in Secretary of State for the Home Department* v. *MB*[170] was particularly hard to defend. *MB* concerned the compatibility of the system of special advocates adopted in control order cases under ss.2 and 3(1)(a) of the Prevention of Terrorism Act 2005 with Article 6(1) of the Convention. By a four-to-one majority,[171] the House of Lords held that the case should be referred back to the trial judge, relying on s.3(1) to subject the provisions to the requirements of procedural fairness inherent in Article 6(1) of the Convention.

Given its own interpretation of the overall scheme of the HRA, the Joint Committee felt that the application of s.3(1) in *MB* was difficult to justify; the Committee argued:

---

[168] Kavanagh, 'Choosing between sections 3 and 4 of the Human Rights Act, above n. 43, pp.137–42.

[169] Joint Committee on Human Rights, *Counter Terrorism Policy and Human Rights* (HL 50/HC 199), 7 February 2008, para.46.

[170] *Secretary of State for the Home Department* v. *MB* [2007] UKHL 46; [2008] 1 AC 440.

[171] Lord Hoffmann dissenting (at paras.45–55).

the Human Rights Act deliberately gives Parliament a central role in deciding how best to protect the rights protected in the EHCR. Striking the balance between sections 3 and 4 of the Human Rights Act is crucial to the scheme of democratic rights protection. In our view it would have been more consistent with the scheme of the Human Rights Act for the House of Lords to have given a declaration of incompatibility, requiring Parliament to think again about the balance it struck in the control order legislation between the various competing interests.[172]

A focus on specific invocations of ss.3 and 4 of the HRA of course bypasses a further notable contribution; the broader effects of human rights litigation on the political process – that is, the influence of judicial decisions on debates outside the confines of the courtroom, beyond the implications of the individual decision.[173] While the concrete effects of such influence may be less readily discernible, it is not doubted that the judicial decision-making process provides a distinctive contribution to wider discussion:

> Deliberative decision-making based on human rights values and principles, on the instigation of litigants who contribute to the shape and content of the debate, is a unique judicial contribution. This is democratic insofar as it sets high standards of legislative and executive accountability through the requirement of transparency and the insistence on taking into account groups which would otherwise have no say in the political arena.[174]

The indirect impact of judicial decisions may not be immediately obvious, but it can reasonably be speculated that human rights adjudication under the HRA has indirectly influenced the broader debates over, among other things, adoption, acquired gender recognition, immigration and asylum policy, freedom of expression and hate speech, sentencing and criminal justice, the rights of squatters, and – as will be seen in a later chapter – the structure of government itself. This broader influence may not necessarily be a direct result of the outcome of an individual case, but may result from the debate which accompanies its hearing, or indeed is generated by the tone of a particular decision. As Tom Poole has observed, such has been the impact of the *Belmarsh* detainees decision, where the tenor of the House of Lords decision – if not its actual result – has come to have broader resonance through contributing judicial weight to the ongoing

---

[172] Joint Committee on Human Rights, above n. 169, para.47.

[173] J. Hiebert, 'Interpreting a bill of rights: the importance of legislative rights review' (2005) 35 *British Journal of Political Science* 235, 240.

[174] S. Fredman, 'From deference to democracy: the role of equality under the Human Rights Act 1998' (2006) 122 LQR 53, 80.

parliamentary debates over anti-terrorism measures and strategy.[175] As the criticisms by the Joint Committee on Human Rights of the House of Lords decision in *MB* demonstrate, this indirect influence contains the potential to work both ways. It is here, perhaps – in the less tangible realm of constitutional politics – that the dialogue metaphor is most appropriately used, for, as we have seen, the misleading suggestion that the concrete effects of adjudication are merely to propose principles of little normative worth seems not to have been carried into the practical arena.

The debate over the limits of what is possible under s.3(1) and the coercive properties of declarations of incompatibility is also, however, only one branch of the discussion over the limits of acceptable judicial law making under the HRA, and it is to the creative influence of the judges in common law adjudication and in defining the meaning of the Convention rights in domestic law that we now turn.

---

[175] T. Poole, 'Tilting at windmills? Truth and illusion in "the political constitution"' (2007) 70 MLR 250, 271.

7

Developing the common law and the meaning of 'the Convention rights'

Introduction

While the interplay between ss.3 and 4 of the HRA provides the most obvious examples of judicial engagement with law-making – both directly via s.3 and indirectly via the legislative adoption of a court's reading of compatibility – it is by no means the only way in which the courts might play a distinctive role in the development of legal norms in human rights adjudication. While the judicial role in developing the common law has long been acknowledged, the HRA provides an additional creative impetus to reshape established causes of action at common law in the name of achieving Convention compatibility. Less pronounced, but by no means less significant for the protection of human rights within the constitution, is the potential for judges to influence the meaning and scope of the Convention rights as given effect in domestic law. Each will be examined in turn.

The incremental nature of common law development

The historical tradition of substantive formalism in statutory interpretation – and the rigid demarcation of legislative functions as parliamentary matters to which it gave rise – appeared to place strict limitations on the creative powers of the courts. Even in the context of common law adjudication – perceived more properly as the domain of the judges – such was the influence of this aspect of legislative sovereignty theory that the illusion persisted that the judges did not *create* the law, they *declared* it. By the 1970s, Lord Reid was prepared to explode the myth:

> Those with a taste for fairy tales seem to have thought that in some Aladdin's cave there is hidden the common law in all its splendour and that on a judge's appointment there descends on him knowledge of the magic words *Open Sesame*. Bad decisions are given when the judge has

muddled the password and the wrong door opens. But we do not believe in
fairy tales any more.[1]

Any recognition of a creative judicial role in respect of the common law
must also naturally acknowledge its limits. Even if a suitable case makes
its way before the courts, the common law has traditionally not been seen
as the appropriate mechanism by which to design and implement wholesale legal change.[2] In part, this can be attributed to the responsive nature
of common law decision making; due to the case-by-case nature of common law adjudication, any change to be engineered will be incremental. It
may also, of course, be subject to parliamentary override. As Lord Devlin
has written, even if it could be said that the judges possess a 'general war-
rant for judicial law making' in the common law sphere:

> This warrant is an informal and rather negative one, amounting to a will-
> ingness to let the judges get on with their traditional work on two con-
> ditions – first, that they do it in the traditional way, i.e. in accordance
> with precedent, and second, that parliamentary interference should be
> regarded as unobjectionable.[3]

This general tenor of judicial restraint is recognition that 'the common
law is a process of law-making developed in a pre-democratic era, and
maintained by a non-democratic form'[4] – in separation of powers terms,
recognition that it is primarily the constitutional function of Parliament to
act as legislator. This tendency towards restraint has not, however, resulted
in the stagnation of the common law.[5] Progress may generally be slow, but
the cumulative effects of this judicial law-making are extensive, and considering the body of common law that has developed in the fields of – for

---

[1] Lord Reid, 'The judge as law maker' (1972–73) 12 *Journal of the Society of the Public Teachers of Law* 22.

[2] See e.g.: *Malone v. Metropolitan Police Commissioner* [1979] 1 Ch 344, 372 (Sir Robert Megarry VC):

> It is no function of the courts to legislate in a new field. The extension of the existing laws and principles is one thing, the creation of an altogether new right is another. At times judges must, and do, legislate; but as Holmes J once said, they do so only interstitially, and with molecular rather than molar motions ... anything beyond that must be left for legislation. No new right in the law, fully-fledged with all the appropriate safeguards, can spring from the head of a judge deciding a particular case: only Parliament can create such a right.

[3] Lord Devlin, 'Judges and law-makers' (1976) 39 MLR 1, 9.

[4] K. D. Ewing, 'A theory of democratic adjudication: towards a representative, accountable and independent judiciary' (2000) 38 *Alberta Law Review* 708, 711.

[5] Lord Devlin, 'Judges and law-makers', above n.3, 12: 'The judges who made the common law must not abrogate altogether their responsibility for keeping it abreast of the times.' As Dicey recognised, however, this responsiveness comes with clear limits: 'If a statute ... is apt to reproduce the public opinion not so much of today as of yesterday, judge-made

example – contract, tort, equity and judicial review, it had become increasingly difficult to sustain the notion that these laws already existed in the ether, ready to be plucked out and applied when the appropriate case arose.

The Human Rights Act and law-making at common law

The potential for the implementation of the HRA to spur reform of domestic causes of action at common law – and therefore exercise an effect on the legal relationships between private persons and bodies, as well as between individuals and the state – was acknowledged during the parliamentary debates on the Human Rights Bill. Most prominently featured in those debates were the discussions centring on the possible development of an action for breach of privacy based on the existing common law doctrine of breach of confidence.[6] While subsequent judicial modifications to the breach of confidence action have notably fallen short of creating a freestanding tort of invasion of privacy,[7] the metamorphosis of the confidence doctrine amply illustrates the transformative influence that the Convention rights may exert over the substance of common law causes of action.

The interpretation and extent of s.6 of the HRA is of central importance to the capacity of the courts to remould existing common law causes of action in the light of the perceived requirements of the Convention. Section 6(1) provides that 'it is unlawful for a public authority to act in a way which is incompatible with a Convention Right', while s.6(3) provides that courts fall within the scope of 'public authorities' for the purposes of the section. It is the nature of the obligation imposed on courts by s.6 that informs the debate over horizontal effect, and it is the judicial interpretation of that obligation that in turn shapes the extent to which the Convention rights might drive reform, amendment, or complete redesign of the common law.

The transformative potential of models of horizontality

The arguments over the potential for horizontal application of the Convention rights which took place on the eve of the Act's coming

---

law occasionally represents the opinion of the day before yesterday.' (A. V. Dicey, 'Judicial Legislation' in *Lectures on the Relationship between Law and Public Opinion in England during the Nineteenth Century* (London: Macmillan, 1914), p.369).

[6] HL Debs, vol.595, cols.784–6, 24 November 1997 (Lord Irvine). And see also: H. Fenwick and G. Phillipson, 'Confidence and privacy: a re-examination' (1996) 55 CLJ 447; H. Fenwick and G. Phillipson, 'Breach of confidence as a privacy remedy in the Human Rights Act era' (2000) 63 MLR 660.

[7] *Wainwright* v. *Home Office* [2003] UKHL 53; [2004] 2 AC 406.

into effect have already been alluded to.[8] At opposing ends of the spectrum lay positions advocated by Sir Richard Buxton, who argued that
the Convention rights – being instruments designed to be of vertical
application only – should have no horizontal effect whatsoever,[9] and Sir
William Wade, who argued that the HRA would prompt the creation of
a common law cause of action, enforceable against private individuals,
of breach of the Convention rights.[10] Buxton, therefore, argued for no
horizontal effect, Wade in favour of direct horizontal effect. A policy of
no horizontal effect would have minimised the transformative potential
of the HRA for decision making at common law, one of direct horizontal
effect would have maximised it. Both positions, however, seemed slightly
untenable.

The difficulty for Buxton's argument was that the European Court
of Human Rights had already begun to articulate the circumstances in
which the Convention rights might impose obligations on the state to
regulate the relationships between private persons and bodies.[11] As a
result, the European Court of Human Rights – whose case law courts
were to be directed to 'take into account' in the domestic context[12] – had
already begun to undermine the suggestion that the Convention rights
had *no* influence over the private law sphere. Further, the HRA itself
clearly envisaged that the Convention rights would be of some horizontal
effect: s.3(1) is of general application, and does not discriminate between
legislation with private and public law effects,[13] nor does s.2(1) draw distinctions in respect of which cases the Convention jurisprudence should
be 'taken into account'.[14]

At the opposing end of the spectrum, the main obstacle to Wade's
argument in favour of direct horizontal application lay in the terms of the
HRA itself. While the Act imposed a legal obligation on public bodies, and

---

[8] See above, n. 31, p.40.
[9] R. Buxton, 'The Human Rights Act and private law' (2000) 116 LQR 48.
[10] H. W. R. Wade, 'The United Kingdom's bill of rights' in Cambridge Centre for Public
Law, *Constitutional Reform in the United Kingdom: Practice and Principles* (Oxford: Hart
Publishing, 1998), pp.62–4; H. W. R. Wade, 'Horizons of horizontality' (2000) 116 LQR 217.
[11] See e.g.: *X and Y* v. *Netherlands* (1986) 8 EHRR 235; *Earl Spencer* v. *United Kingdom* (1998)
25 EHRR CD105. For a survey of the development of the European Court of Human
Rights jurisprudence on this issue, see: A. Clapham, *Human Rights in the Private Sphere*
(Oxford: Clarendon Press, 1993), ch.7.
[12] Section 2(1) HRA. See pp.191–202.
[13] For a survey of this 'statutory horizontality', see: I. Leigh and R. Masterman, *Making Rights
Real: The Human Rights Act in its First Decade* (Oxford: Hart Publishing, 2008), ch.9.
[14] Section 2(1) directs that Convention jurisprudence be taken into account by courts when
'determining a question which has arisen in connection with a Convention Right'.

those private persons exercising 'public' functions, to act compatibly with the Convention rights,[15] and created a new cause of action under which the legality of a public authority's actions or inactions could be tested on human rights grounds,[16] it contained no parallel provision obliging private individuals exercising private functions to respect the Convention rights, nor did it make specific provision for actions to be brought against such private individuals for breach of the Convention rights. The 'clear implication' of this, as Murray Hunt has written, 'is that there are persons who are *not* bound to act compatibly with the Convention at all'[17] – namely, private persons exercising non-public functions. In terms of the specific effects of the Convention in private common law, the HRA itself was largely silent. Wade's argument was therefore reliant on the courts taking immediate, and radical, steps to fill the statutory void by engineering a parallel common law cause of action allowing private individuals to bring actions for breach of the Convention rights against other non-public persons and bodies.

Between these positions lay the potential for the HRA to give indirect horizontal effect to the Convention rights via the common law. In a 1998 article, Hunt argued in favour of a model of indirect horizontal effect which – reliant on s.6 – would place courts under a duty to 'act compatibly with the Convention, including when they decide purely private disputes between private parties governed solely by the common law'.[18] The consequences of this 'unequivocal duty to act compatibly with the Convention rights' would require courts to actively 'modify or develop the common law' in order to achieve compatibility.[19] As a result, the discretionary power of the courts to modify or develop the common law when required by the interests of clarity or justice, would be replaced by an obligation to amend the common law where necessary to achieve compatibility with the Convention rights. Indeed, to utilise the word 'develop' in the context of the potential comprehensive reformulation of the common law – as might be required under the Hunt model – might be inappropriate: as Gavin Phillipson has noted, the complete jettisoning of established features of the common law, including its incremental processes of development, that would result from the courts' adoption of a *duty* to develop the law consistently with the Convention, would be a staggering consequence of an Act which 'conspicuously omits *any* mention of private common law' whatsoever.[20]

---

[15] Section 6(1) and 6(3)(b) HRA.   [16] Section 7 HRA.

[17] M. Hunt, 'The "horizontal effect" of the Human Rights Act' [1998] PL 423, 438 (emphasis in original).

[18] *Ibid.*, 440.   [19] *Ibid.*, 441.

[20] G. Phillipson, 'The Human Rights Act, "horizontal effect" and the common law: a bang or a whimper?' (1999) 62 MLR 824, 839 (emphasis added).

Phillipson, therefore, proposed an alternate model of indirect horizontal effect, which – rather than placing courts under a duty to modify the common law to render it Convention compatible – would allow them a discretion to do so.[21] Under Phillipson's model, in the adjudication of common law causes of action between private bodies, the Convention rights would 'figure only as principles to which the courts must have regard' rather than rules which the courts must apply.[22] Such an approach would have the benefits of not exposing private bodies to wide-ranging new areas of legal liability, and would allow the courts to provide Convention-compatible outcomes while preserving the distinctively 'domestic' qualities of common law causes of action.

The modification of breach of confidence

From the earliest cases brought under the HRA, the influence of the Convention rights in common law adjudication between private parties was evident. Without explicitly adopting one particular specific model of indirect horizontal effect, the courts clearly gave effect to the view that their own duty under s.6 required them – at the very least – to apply existing common law principles in a Convention-compatible manner. In *Venables and Thompson*, Butler-Sloss P felt able – as a result of s.6(1) and 6(3)(a) of the Act – to assert that while the applicants could not rely on a 'free-standing application under the Convention',[23] the court itself was under an obligation to act compatibly with the Convention rights. This duty, she outlined, 'includes both a positive and a negative obligation'.[24] In other words, not only was the court to seek to avoid the infringement of rights, it could also impose measures actively designed to protect them. The extent of this obligation – as demonstrated by the unprecedented award of injunctions *contra mundum* in *Venables and Thompson* – clearly encompassed the deployment of novel remedies to ensure a Convention-compatible outcome in the case at hand. At a stroke, the polarised views of Buxton and Wade were rejected.

Perhaps the most significant early indication of the common law's acceptance of, and willingness to respond to the Convention rights,

---

[21] Phillipson, 'The Human Rights Act, "horizontal effect" and the common law', above n. 20.

[22] *Ibid.*, 848.

[23] *Venables* v. *News Group Newspapers; Thompson* v. *News Group Newspapers* [2001] Fam 430, 447.

[24] *Ibid.*, 446.

came in *Douglas* v. *Hello!*[25] In that case, all three Court of Appeal judges noted the potential for the Convention to have a significant impact on the common law. Both Brooke LJ and Keene LJ were relatively circumspect, noting, respectively, 'the ability of the common law to adapt to new situations'[26] and the potential for the s.6 duty of the courts to extend to 'their activity in interpreting and developing the common law'.[27] More confident, however, was Sedley LJ, who was able to note that the common law and the Convention rights, 'now run in a single channel' as a result of the combined effects of s.2 and s.6.[28] The ability of the courts to develop the law on the basis of this obligation was implicit in Sedley LJ's assertion that the HRA provided the 'final impetus to the recognition of a right of privacy in English law'.[29]

Prior to the implementation of the HRA, the requirements of the breach of confidence action had been set down by the case of *Coco* v. *AN Clark (Engineers) Ltd.*[30] The three stages of the test were as follows: first, the information which formed the subject of the action 'must be of a confidential nature';[31] second, the 'information must have been communicated in circumstances importing an obligation of confidence';[32] and finally, there 'must be an unauthorised use of the information to the detriment of the person communicating it'.[33]

Through a series of cases which melded consideration of the Convention rights with the domestic confidence action – which arguably yielded mixed results for those seeking an enhanced protection of privacy in domestic law[34] – the courts demonstrated both that the Convention would have a degree of indirect horizontal effect, and that it could exert a degree of transformative influence over the substance of causes of action at common law.[35] The Convention rights, it seemed, were to be accommodated within breach of confidence, rather than to supplant it.[36] Indeed, far from abandoning the established features of breach of a confidence in favour of the test explicitly driven by the Convention rights, the common law's traditional willingness to garner inspiration from other jurisdictions saw a test of offensiveness imported from the decision of the High Court of

---

[25] *Douglas and others* v. *Hello! Ltd* [2001] QB 967.   [26] *Ibid.*, para.88.   [27] *Ibid.*, para.166.
[28] *Ibid.*, 997–8.   [29] *Ibid.*
[30] *Coco* v. *AN Clark (Engineers) Ltd* [1968] FSR 415.
[31] *Ibid.*, 419.   [32] *Ibid.*, 420.   [33] *Ibid.*, 421.
[34] G. Phillipson, 'Judicial reasoning in breach of confidence cases under the Human Rights Act: not taking privacy seriously?' [2003] EHRLR (Special Issue: *Privacy*) 54.
[35] *Theakston* v. *Mirror Group Newspapers* [2002] EWHC 137 (QB); [2002] EMLR 22; *A* v. *B plc* [2002] EWCA Civ 337; [2003] QB 195.
[36] *Ibid.*, para.4 (Lord Woolf):

Australia in *Australian Broadcasting Corporation* v. *Lenah Game Meats* begin to exert an influence on the development of the breach of confidence action.[37] This horizontality was very much of the weak indirect model, allowing domestic judges a degree of discretion over the extent to which common law doctrines would be amended, so long as (broadly conceived) Convention-compatible results were the outcome.

The House of Lords decision in *Campbell* v. *Mirror Group Newspapers*, however, saw the test of offensiveness from *Lenah Game Meats* relegated in favour of giving much clearer effect to the directions of the Strasbourg jurisprudence through what one of the Law Lords regarded should be referred to as the tort of 'misuse of private information'.[38] *Campbell* shows that the three-stage test for breach of confidence in *Coco* v. *Clark* has been displaced by a test much more clearly driven by the Convention standards. Post-*Campbell*, a misuse of private information action will proceed on the basis of asking whether the relevant information is of a private nature – in other words, by asking whether it falls within the scope of private information as defined by Article 8 – and that, as a result, it can be said that there was a reasonable expectation of privacy on the part of the claimant.[39] If it can be established that the claimant was entitled to possess a reasonable expectation of privacy, then 'the court must balance the claimant's interest in keeping the information private against the countervailing interest of the recipient in publishing it'.[40] This balancing of Article 8 and Article 10 – parallel analysis as it has become known[41] – therefore

> The court's approach to the issues which the applications raise has been modified because under s 6 of the 1998 Act, the court, as a public authority, is required not to act 'in a way which is incompatible with a Convention right.' The court is able to achieve this by absorbing the rights which arts 8 and 10 protect into the long-established action for breach of confidence. This involves giving a new strength and breadth to the action so that it accommodates the requirements of those articles.

[37] *Australian Broadcasting Corporation* v. *Lenah Game Meats* [2001] HCA 63. Indeed, one commentator observed that, prior to *Campbell* v. *MGN*, the test from *Lenah Game Meats* 'had far more influence on the development of confidence as a privacy remedy than any principles derived from Article 8' (G. Phillipson, 'Transforming breach of confidence? Towards a common law right of privacy under the Human Rights Act' (2003) 66 MLR 726, 731).

[38] *Campbell* v. *Mirror Group Newspapers* [2004] UKHL 22; [2004] 2 AC 457, para.14 (Lord Nicholls).

[39] *Ibid.*, para.92 (Lord Hope). The test of offensiveness from *Lenah Game Meats* may be of residual relevance in those cases where it is not clear whether the relevant information is private or not (*ibid.*, paras.94–6 (Lord Hope)).

[40] *Ibid.*, para.137 (Baroness Hale).

[41] H. Rogers and H. Tomlinson, 'Privacy and expression: Convention rights and interim injunctions' [2003] EHRLR 37.

provides the avenue through which the Convention rights are given effect through the misuse of private information doctrine. The process of parallel analysis requires courts to look:

> first at the comparative importance of the actual rights being claimed in the individual case; then at the justifications for interfering with or restricting each of those rights; and applying the proportionality test to each.[42]

As a result of *Campbell*, the obligation of confidence (or more realistically, perhaps, of privacy) is, as a result, imposed solely on the basis of the information at issue, with the balance between freedom of expression and privacy to be gauged through a comparative analysis of the requirements of Articles 8 and 10. It is clear that cases such as *Douglas* and *Campbell* give life to a form of indirect horizontal effect. The specific nature of the judicial duty under s.6 of the HRA, throughout these cases, was not fully explained, leaving judges with a notable discretion over the degree to which the substance of the common law should be amended in response to the demands of the Convention.[43]

Towards directly effective rights to privacy and expression at common law?

Developments post-*Campbell*, however, have shown just how marked these amendments to the doctrine of breach of confidence have been. In *Campbell*, Lord Nicholls noted that, 'the time has come to recognise that the values enshrined in articles 8 and 10 *are now part* of the cause of action for breach of confidence'.[44] A series of lower-level decisions have made the implications of this statement clear. In the subsequent Court of Appeal decision in *McKennit* v. *Ash*, Buxton LJ – whose initial opposition to the horizontal impact of the HRA has already been discussed[45] – made

---

[42] *Campbell* v. *Mirror Group Newspapers*, above n.38, para.141 (Baroness Hale).

[43] See: G. Phillipson, 'Clarity postponed: horizontal effect after *Campbell*' in H. Fenwick, G. Phillipson and R. Masterman (eds), *Judicial Reasoning under the UK Human Rights Act* (Cambridge University Press, 2007). See also: *Kay* v. *Lambeth LBC; Leeds City Council* v. *Price* [2006] UKHL 10; [2006] 2 AC 465, para.61 (Lord Nicholls):

> The court of course is itself a public authority. Courts are bound to conduct their affairs in a way which is compatible with Convention rights. The court's own practice and procedures must be Convention-compliant. Whether, and in what circumstances, the court's section 6 obligation extends more widely than this, and affects the substantive law to be applied by the court when adjudicating upon disputes between private parties, still awaits authoritative decision.

[44] *Campbell* v. *Mirror Group Newspapers*, above n.38. para.17 (Lord Nicholls) (emphasis added).

[45] Buxton, 'The Human Rights Act and private law', above n. 9. See pp.183–5.

the striking assertion that, 'in order to find the rules of the English law of breach of confidence we now have to look in the jurisprudence of Articles 8 and 10', for those Articles form 'the *very content* of the domestic tort'.[46] Following *McKennit*, Eady J in *Mosley* v. *News Group Newspapers* spoke of 'the *direct application* of the Convention values and of Strasbourg juris-prudence as part of English law'.[47] As a result of these cases, the remodelled breach of confidence action – the tort of misuse of private information – stands on the cusp of being no more than a cipher through which Articles 8 and 10 can be given direct horizontal effect in English law. As Gavin Phillipson predicted in an article published in 2003:

> A thorough-going application of Article 8 in confidence cases would … have the effect of meaning that breach of confidence was treated sim-ply as an empty shell into which Article principles could, as it were, be poured.[48]

While the misuse of private information doctrine retains distinctive elements of the common law breach of confidence action, these elements can no longer be seen as the core components of the tort. For example, the question of whether the respondent is able to rely on a general defence of publication in the public interest[49] will now be effectively determined during the parallel analysis of Articles 8 and 10, while the contentious question of whether privacy rights might be waived as a result of prior conduct[50] has been 'marginalised' as a result of *Campbell*.[51] Instead, the engagement of Article 8 provides the basis of a prima facie claim, while parallel analysis will determine the balance to be struck between the claimant's right to privacy, and the respondent's right to freedom of expres-sion. As a result, Buxton LJ was right to state that the 'very content' of the tort is reliant on the substance of Articles 8 and 10 of the Convention.

It is undeniable, therefore, that the HRA has prompted a significant modification of the breach of confidence doctrine, to the point where it arguably exists only to give effect to the requirements of Articles 8 and 10 between private parties. While other common law causes of action have

---

[46] *McKennit* v. *Ash* [2006] EWCA Civ 1714; [2008] QB 73, para.11. Endorsed in *Mosley* v. *News Group Newspapers* [2008] EWHC 1777; [2008] EMLR 20, para.9 (Eady J).

[47] *Ibid.*, para.196 (Eady J). On which, see: K. Hughes, 'Horizontal privacy' (2009) 125 LQR 244.

[48] G. Phillipson, 'Transforming breach of confidence?', above n.37, 731.

[49] *Lion Laboratories Ltd.* v. *Evans* [1985] QB 526.

[50] *Woodward* v. *Hutchins* [1977] 1 WLR 760.

[51] See: H. Fenwick, *Civil Liberties and Human Rights* (4th edn) (Abingdon: Routledge-Cavendish, 2007), pp.918–20.

not been affected in such a radical manner,[52] the developments in relation to the protection of privacy at common law demonstrate that the potential for the Convention to transform the content of common law causes of action is huge. Indeed, it would seem that the potential for the common law to develop in a way which would exceed, or pre-empt, the requirements of the Convention, is also possible.[53] As Baroness Hale has recognised, just as it is open to Parliament to provide a statutory protection for rights which exceeds that provided for by the Convention, so too is it open to the courts to develop an extended protection by way of the common law:

> There is, of course, nothing to stop our Parliament from legislating to protect human rights to a greater extent than the Convention and its jurisprudence currently require; nor is there anything to prevent the courts from developing the common law in that direction.[54]

However, in those areas not governed by common law, the courts have not felt as able to assert their law-making role to extend the range of the Convention rights in the domestic context. Instead, domestic courts have largely been unwilling to exercise an overtly creative role, being more inclined instead to 'take their lead from Strasbourg'.[55]

The meaning and application of 'the Convention rights'

Under s.2(1) of the HRA, UK courts – in 'determining a question which has arisen in connection with a Convention right' – are directed to take

---

[52] For an early study, see: C. Gearty, 'Tort law and the Human Rights Act' in T. Campbell, K. D. Ewing and A. Tomkins (eds), *Sceptical Essays on Human Rights* (Oxford University Press, 2001). And for a more recent survey: Lady Justice Arden DBE, 'Human rights and civil wrongs: tort law under the spotlight' (Hailsham Lecture 2009, 12 May 2009) (available at: www.judiciary.gov.uk/publications_media/speeches/index.htm). For an example of the influence of the Convention on defamation, see: *Jameel* v. *Wall Street Journal Europe* [2006] UKHL 44; [2007] 1 AC 359.

[53] In *Campbell* v. *Mirror Group Newspapers*, above n. 38, the House of Lords did arguably pre-empt the findings of the European Court of Human Rights in *Von Hannover* v. *Germany* (2005) 40 EHRR 1, that the Convention imposed an obligation on the state to provide a remedy for breach of the Article 8 rights of private persons by other private persons or bodies. See pp.201–2.

[54] *R (on the application of Animal Defenders International)* v. *Secretary of State for Culture, Media and Sport* [2008] UKHL 15, para.53 (Baroness Hale).

[55] *Sheldrake* v. *Director of Public Prosecutions; Attorney-General's Reference (No. 4 of 2002)* [2004] UKHL 43; [2005] 1 AC 264, para.33 (Lord Bingham). See also: *Douglas* v. *Hello! Ltd* above n. 25, 989 (Brooke LJ).

account of 'relevant' decisions of the enforcement bodies of the ECHR.[56]
The approach of the courts to the domestic application of the Convention
standards has, perhaps unsurprisingly, seen a general tendency to place
quite heavy reliance on the findings of the Strasbourg institutions.
Domestic courts, subject to relatively narrow exceptions,[57] have read
the requirement that relevant decisions be 'taken into account' to mean
that clear authority should generally be followed, and have been hesitant to find meaning in the Convention which cannot be clearly traced
back to a Strasbourg decision or decisions.[58] The adoption by domestic
courts of this so-called 'mirror principle'[59] – under which the scope of the
Convention rights at both the domestic and Strasbourg levels should be
virtually identical – constrains their own ability to shape the meaning of
'the Convention rights' under the HRA, and, as such, clearly places limitations on the extent to which those rights can be applied creatively, or
perhaps even sensitively, to novel domestic circumstances.

'The Convention rights' in domestic law

The origins of the 'mirror principle' lie in the contested status of 'the
Convention rights' as legal standards in the domestic context. While the
HRA itself is obviously a creation of the UK Parliament, its terms cannot be
fully appreciated without making reference to the international treaty (and
its attendant case law) to which the Act was designed to give 'further effect'.

---

[56] Section 2(1) HRA provides:
   A court or tribunal determining a question which has arisen in connection with
   a Convention right must take into account any – judgment, decision, declaration
   or advisory opinion of the European Court of Human Rights, opinion of the
   Commission given in a report adopted under Article 31 of the Convention, decision
   of the Commission in connection with Article 26 or 27(2) of the Convention, or decision of the Committee of Ministers taken under Article 46 of the Convention, whenever made or given, so far as, in the opinion of the court or tribunal, it is relevant to
   the proceedings in which that question has arisen.

[57] For discussion, see: Leigh and Masterman, *Making Rights Real*, above n. 13, pp.62–6;
   J. Lewis, 'The European ceiling on rights' [2007] PL 720, 730–1; J. Lewis, '*In Re P and
   others*: an exception to the "no more, certainly no less" rule' [2009] PL 43.

[58] *R (on the application of Ullah)* v. *Special Adjudicator; Do* v. *Immigration Appeal Tribunal*
   [2004] UKHL 26; [2004] 2 AC 323, para.20 (Lord Bingham); *R (on the application of
   Animal Defenders International)* v. *Secretary of State for Culture, Media and Sport* [2008]
   UKHL 15; [2008] 2 WLR 781, para.37. For commentary, see: R. Masterman, 'Aspiration
   or foundation? The status of the Strasbourg jurisprudence and "Convention rights" in
   domestic law' in Fenwick, Phillipson and Masterman (eds), *Judicial Reasoning under the
   UK Human Rights Act*, above n. 43.

[59] Lewis, 'The European ceiling on rights', above n. 57.

As has been discussed, s.3(1) of the Act directs that courts interpret statutes, as far as it is possible for them to do so, compatibly with 'the Convention rights'. Similarly, s.6 makes it unlawful for public bodies to act in a way which would be incompatible with 'the Convention Rights'. While s.2(1) of the HRA directs courts to 'take into account' the decisions of the Strasbourg organs when 'determining a question which has arisen in connection with a Convention right', it offers little practical guidance on the question of how those Convention rights should be defined. On its face, the statutory obligation to 'take into account' the Convention jurisprudence may be open to a number of interpretations, each producing potentially varying effects; upon 'taking into account' Strasbourg case law, a court might attempt to apply the Strasbourg authority directly, might ultimately fail to apply it, or might come to a decision somewhere between the two extremes by either applying (or being influenced by) the Convention jurisprudence to a greater or lesser degree. As a result, Tierney has rightly observed both the flexibility, and uncertainty, inherent in this particular aspect of the HRA scheme.[60] In the courts, too, a degree of disagreement has been evident over the status of 'the Convention rights' in domestic law, and over how this should be translated and applied in judicial decision making.

The debate over the nature of the Convention rights revolves around their dual status as enforceable standards in domestic law under the HRA and standards of international law by which the conduct of the UK, as a state party to the Convention, can be assessed. The interpretational difficulty faced by the courts lies in the question of whether, by giving further effect to certain of those rights under the terms of a domestic statute, the nature of those rights as they apply in the domestic context differs in any way from those rights as enforced by the European Court of Human Rights. Do 'the Convention rights' as applied under the HRA possess exactly the same characteristics in domestic law as they would when applied by the Strasbourg court? Or has their transition into the domestic context – via the HRA – altered their characteristics in some way?

The opinion of Lord Hoffman in *In Re McKerr* is illustrative, for instance, of the latter perspective, treating the Convention rights under the HRA as *domestic* standards, to be applied and defined ultimately by domestic authorities:

> Although people sometimes speak of the Convention having been incorporated into domestic law, that is a misleading metaphor. What the Act

---

[60] S. Tierney, 'Devolution issues and s.2(1) of the Human Rights Act 1998' [2000] EHRLR 380, 392.

> has done is to create domestic rights in the same terms as those contained
> in the Convention. But they are domestic rights, not international rights.
> Their source is the statute, not the Convention … their meaning and
> application is a matter for domestic courts, not the court in Strasbourg.[61]

In the same case, Lord Nicholls appeared to agree, noting that the 'two sets
of rights now exist side by side', but also highlighting that there are 'significant differences between them'.[62] Such a reading discloses the ultimate
possibility that the meaning of 'the Convention rights' as applied in domestic courts might depart from the meaning of those rights as interpreted
by the Strasbourg court. In asserting that the 'meaning and application' of
the rights under the HRA is a 'matter for domestic courts' – and explicitly
denying this function to Strasbourg – Lord Hoffmann's stance envisages
the possibility of differing applications of the Convention standards at the
domestic and Strasbourg levels. In the more recent decision of the House
of Lords in *R (on the application of Animal Defenders International)* v.
Secretary of State for Culture, Media and Sport, the potential for a domestic court to legitimately differ from an interpretation of a Convention
right by the European Court of Human Rights was specifically noted by
Lord Scott, who recognised that 'the possibility of … a divergence is con-
templated, implicitly at least, by the 1998 Act'.[63]

The potential to depart from the readings of Convention rights adopted
by the Strasbourg court is often argued to go hand-in-hand with the
potential for a domestic court to adopt a more generous interpretation of
the right in question than endorsed at Strasbourg. The reasons for this are
twofold. First, the Convention is said to provide a 'floor of rights' protection rather than a 'ceiling'.[64] In other words, the Convention system lays
down minimum standards below which member states should not fall,
but upon which they should be free to expand. As Grosz, Beatson and
Duffy have argued:

> [T]here is no imperative that parties to the Convention should adopt
> a uniform approach, only that they should not fall below an irreducible
> minimum, which will be monitored by the Strasbourg institutions. It is

---

[61] *In Re McKerr* [2004] UKHL 12, para.65. Developing this theme more recently in a lengthy
(extra-judicial) criticism of the record of the European Court of Human Rights, Lord
Hoffmann has argued that 'human rights are universal in abstraction but national in
application.' ('The universality of human rights' (2009) 125 LQR 416, 422.)

[62] *In re McKerr*, above n. 61, para.25.

[63] *R (on the application of Animal Defenders International)* v. *Secretary of State for Culture,
Media and Sport* [2008] UKHL 15; [2008] 1 AC 1312, para.44 (Lord Scott of Foscote). Cf.
the views of Lord Bingham, para.37.

[64] HL Debs, vol.583, col.510, 18 November 1997 (Lord Irvine).

therefore open to national courts to develop a domestic jurisprudence under the Convention which may be more generous to applicants than that dispensed in Strasbourg, while remaining broadly consistent with it.[65]

Second, the direction to courts in s.2(1) of the HRA itself is a flexible one, allowing the judges a degree of discretion over how to give effect to the Strasbourg case law in the domestic context. However, due to the parallel responsibilities of courts themselves as public authorities under s.6, it is unlawful for them to provide for an inadequate protection – in other words, a protection which would fall below the minimum standard monitored by the European Court of Human Rights.[66] Courts would therefore seem to be prevented by law from providing a weaker protection than Strasbourg, but possess a discretion over whether to afford a more generous protection.

There are, of course, good reasons why the Convention rights as applied under the HRA *should* be treated differently when applied by domestic courts as opposed to the Strasbourg organs – for instance, when applied in the domestic context, the margin of appreciation afforded to states parties by the European Court of Human Rights should not factor.[67] However, separating the domesticated rights *in their entirety* from their Strasbourg-implemented relations would also be untenable; the HRA was, after all, specifically implemented for the purpose of allowing a domestic avenue for the realisation of individuals' rights which would save on the cost, delay and inconvenience of exhausting domestic remedies before mounting a legal challenge before the Strasbourg institutions. As a result, as Aileen Kavanagh has written, the Convention rights under s.1 of the HRA *cannot* be 'entirely autonomous from the Convention, from which they find their original legal source'.[68]

On balance, however, the tendency of domestic courts has been to downplay the potential for divergence between Strasbourg and domestic

[65] S. Grosz, J. Beatson and P. Duffy, *Human Rights: The 1998 Act and The European Convention* (London: Sweet and Maxwell, 2000), p.20. See also: HL Debs, vol.584, cols.1270–1, 19 January 1998 (Lord Irvine of Lairg); F. Klug, 'A bill of rights: do we need one, or do we already have one?' [2007] PL 701.

[66] Acknowledged by Lord Bingham in *R (on the application of Ullah)* v. *Special Adjudicator; Do* v. *Immigration Appeal Tribunal*, above n. 58, para.20.

[67] For an analysis of this, and further limitations of using the Strasbourg case law as a template for a domestic rights jurisprudence, see: R. Masterman, 'Taking the Strasbourg jurisprudence into account: developing a "municipal law of human rights" under the Human Rights Act' (2005) 54 ICLQ 907, 915–17.

[68] A. Kavanagh, *Constitutional Adjudication under the UK Human Rights Act* (Cambridge University Press, 2009), p.156.

interpretations of the Convention rights, and, as a result, has been towards
limiting the creative potential of national courts in applying those rights
in domestic law. The restrictive meaning given *in practice* to the application of s.2(1) of the Act further guards against compromising judicial
independence by 'making law': first by adopting a 'precedential' approach
to the Convention case law,[69] second by displaying a reluctance to find
meaning in the Convention which cannot be found in existing Strasbourg
case law. In the case of the latter, the denial of a creative role for domestic
courts in articulating and applying the Convention rights under the HRA
is best evidenced in the speech of Lord Bingham in *Ullah*:

> a national court subject to a duty such as that imposed by section 2 should
> not without strong reason dilute or weaken the effect of the Strasbourg
> case law. It is indeed unlawful under section 6 of the 1998 Act for a public
> authority, including a court, to act in a way which is incompatible with
> a Convention Right. It is of course open to member states to provide for
> rights more generous than those guaranteed by the Convention, but such
> provision should not be the product of interpretation of the Convention
> by national courts, since the meaning of the Convention should be uni-
> form throughout the states party to it. The duty of national courts is to
> keep pace with the Strasbourg jurisprudence as it evolves over time: no
> more, but certainly no less.[70]

This restrictive approach to domesticated readings of the Convention
rights themselves is founded in a view of the HRA itself as only designed
to make the rights and remedies available to applicants at the Strasbourg
level accessible in domestic courts:

> the purpose of the Human Rights Act 1998 was not to enlarge the rights or
> remedies of those in the United Kingdom whose Convention Rights had
> been violated but to enable those rights and remedies to be asserted and
> enforced by the domestic courts of this country and not only by recourse
> to Strasbourg.[71]

In general terms, the overriding judicial approach to the construction and
application of s.2(1) has been that 'clear and constant' jurisprudence of

---

[69] R. Masterman, 'Section 2(1) of the Human Rights Act 1998: binding domestic courts to
Strasbourg? [2004] PL 725.
[70] *R (on the application of Ullah)* v. *Special Adjudicator; Do* v. *Immigration Appeal Tribunal*,
above n. 58, para.20 (Lord Bingham).
[71] *R (on the application of Begum)* v. *Headteacher and Governors of Denbigh High School*
[2006] UKHL 15; [2007] 1 AC 100, para.29. See also *R* v. *Secretary of State for the Home
Department, ex parte Greenfield* [2005] UKHL 14; [2005] 1 WLR 673, para.19; *Huang* v.
Secretary of State for the Home Department [2007] UKHL 11; [2007] 2 AC 167, para.8.

the Strasbourg bodies should, in the absence of a small body of narrowly defined exceptions, be applied in a precedent-like manner.

The arguments in favour of this approach – given the nature of adjudication on questions of rights – can be easily appreciated. In one sense, following the 'mirror principle' can be argued to empower domestic courts. By tying the development of the Convention rights in national law very closely to those rights as defined at Strasbourg, domestic courts legitimate their actions when, for instance, adopting strained interpretations or reading in implied terms and additional words under s.3(1). Domestic courts are able to argue that utilising their powers to interpret legislation in such a way is *compelled* by the findings of unequivocal Strasbourg authority,[72] thus avoiding accusations that the content of the domestic human rights law is a product of overly imaginative judicial engineering, or less favourably, that it has simply been 'made up'.[73] A parallel can also be drawn with the precedential application of existing legal principles more broadly; a politically contentious judicial decision is much easier to defend as being legitimate when it is clearly shown that the case is a simple matter of applying established legal principles to the facts at issue.[74] The difficulty of progressive interpretation of the Convention rights themselves at the domestic level is that – in the absence of contrary parliamentary direction or subsequent clear restatement of the Strasbourg position – the courts' range of review would be extended yet further into the 'political' sphere.

However, a rigid adherence to the 'mirror principle' can also exercise a disempowering effect on the ability of courts to provide a remedy or adequate answer to the legal problem in front of them. In the absence of

---

[72] See, for instance, the comments of Baroness Hale in *Re P*: 'in all the cases in which either the interpretative duty in section 3 has been used, or a declaration of incompatibility made under section 4, it has been reasonably clear that the Strasbourg court would hold that United Kingdom law was incompatible with the Convention.' (*In Re P (Adoption: Unmarried Couples)* [2008] UKHL 38; [2009] 1 AC 173, para.116.)

[73] As suggested in: I. Loveland, 'Making it up as they go along? The Court of Appeal on same-sex spouses and succession rights to tenancies' [2003] PL 222.

[74] Take, for instance, the decision of Sullivan J in the 'Afghan hijackers' case (*R (on the application of S)* v. *Secretary of State for the Home Department* [2006] EWHC 1111). While the then Home Secretary, John Reid, was able to claim that Sullivan J's decision was 'bizarre and inexplicable' ('Ministers accused of fuelling myths on human rights', *The Guardian*, 14 November 2006), the Court of Appeal commented that 'we commend the judge for an impeccable judgment. This history of this case … has attracted a degree of opprobrium for those carrying out judicial functions. Judges and adjudicators have to apply the law as they find it, and not as they might wish it to be' (*R (on the application of S)* v. *Secretary of State for the Home Department* [2006] EWCA Civ 1157).

clear guiding authority at the Strasbourg level, the response of the courts
to the conundrum of how to proceed has been mixed. In the House of
Lords decision in *N v. Secretary of State for the Home Department*, for
example, the Law Lords' survey of the Strasbourg jurisprudence concluded that the relevant authority was 'not in an altogether satisfactory
state', lacked 'its customary clarity' and displayed evidence of reasoning
that was not 'entirely convincing'.[75] Yet, as Lord Hope argued:

> Our task, then, is to analyse the jurisprudence of the Strasbourg court
> and, having done so and identified its limits, to apply it to the facts of this
> case ... It is not for us to search for a solution ... which is not to be found
> in the Strasbourg case law. It is for the Strasbourg court, not for us, to
> decide whether its case law is out of touch with modern conditions and to
> determine what further extensions, if any, are needed to the rights guar-
> anteed by the Convention. We must take the case law as we find it, not as
> we would like it to be.[76]

When confronted with unclear authority, or jurisprudence which has
not been explained in adequate detail or on the basis of adequate factual
and legal grounds, then it is entirely arguable that a domestic court *should*
seek to fashion a clearer response, supported through detailed and transparent reasoning, which is broadly consistent with the principles inherent
in the Convention and what support can be gleaned from the relevant
authorities. Instead, Lord Hope's position presents a minimalist reading of the role of courts under the HRA which suggests that the courts
should do none of these things.[77] Lord Hope contended, in his opinion
given in the subsequent case of *Clift*, that in such circumstances – where
'the Strasbourg jurisprudence has not yet addressed [the] question' – 'a
measure of self-restraint is needed, lest we stretch our own jurisprudence
beyond that which is shared by all the States Parties to the Convention'.[78]
There are at least two objections to such a stance.

In the first instance, the adoption of a particular interpretation of a
Convention right by a *domestic* court will have no consequence whatsoever for the other States Parties to the Convention, unless and until a

---

[75] *N v. Secretary of State for the Home Department* [2005] UKHL 31; [2005] 2 AC 296, par-
as.11, 14 (Lord Nicholls) and para.91 (Lord Browne of Eaton-under-Heywood).

[76] *Ibid.*, para.25 (Lord Hope).

[77] Cf. *In Re P*, above n. 72, para.50 (Lord Hope).

[78] *R (on the application of Clift)* v. *Secretary of State for the Home Department; R (on the
application of Hindawi)* v. *Secretary of State for the Home Department* [2006] UKHL 54,
para.49 (Lord Hope); *R (on the application of Gentle and others)* v. *Prime Minister* [2008]
UKHL 20; [2008] 1 AC 1356, para.9 (Lord Bingham); *Brown v. Stott* [2003] 1 AC 681, 703
(Lord Bingham).

similar interpretation is adopted by the European Court of Human Rights itself.[79] Second, it should not be forgotten that in *Jackson* v. *Attorney-General*, one of the reasons given by the House of Lords for hearing and adjudicating over the dispute, was the uncertainty that would arise if they did not decide the issue and hand down a judgment.[80] A clear objection to treating areas in which clear Strasbourg authority is lacking as 'no go areas'[81] for the courts can be found in the potential injustice which might result for the applicants in question. It is one thing to hold at admissibility stage that no legal issue is raised on the facts of an individual claim, quite another to allow that claim to proceed as far as the highest court, and yet ultimately fail to give an answer to the legal issue raised on the basis of a lack of clear Strasbourg authority.

The scope for creative judicial interpretation of 'the Convention rights'

Before ruling out the possibility of a creative role in determining the scope of application of the Convention rights in domestic law on the basis of such authorities, it is important to distinguish between the different types of innovative exercise which may be proposed. In those instances where a court is being asked to extend the range of a Convention right in the domestic context into a completely new sphere, based on little or no relevant authority from Strasbourg, the court will rightly be legitimately hesitant to hold that the activity complained of falls within the scope of one of the Convention rights. By contrast, if the court is being asked to adjudicate on a purported infringement in an area of the law where the Convention jurisprudence is only partially applicable, or where it is being asked to build on the foundations – or clarify – an inadequately reasoned decision of the European Court of Human Rights, then this is arguably an entirely different, and more acceptable, judicial exercise.

---

[79] As recognised in *R (on the application of Gentle and others)* v. *Prime Minister*, above n. 78, para.56 (Baroness Hale).

[80] *Jackson and others* v. *Her Majesty's Attorney-General* [2005] UKHL 56; [2006] 1 AC 262, para.27 (Lord Bingham):

> The appellants have raised a question of law which cannot, as such, be resolved by Parliament. But it would not be satisfactory, or consistent with the rule of law, if it could not be resolved at all. So it seems to me necessary that the courts should resolve it, and that to do so involves no breach of constitutional propriety.

[81] Lewis, 'The European ceiling on rights', above n. 57, 732.

The possibility of the courts using their creative powers to engineer a 'reasonably foreseeable' development of the law in this regard was raised obliquely in the speech of Baroness Hale in *Gentle*:

> Parliament is free to go further than Strasbourg if it wishes, but we are not free to foist upon Parliament or upon public authorities an interpretation of a Convention right which goes way beyond anything which we can reasonably foresee that Strasbourg might do.[82]

While at pains to stress the institutional competence issues in such a proposed development, Baroness Hale's careful use of hyperbole does appear to suggest that it may well be open to courts to put forward an interpretation of a Convention right which incrementally develops, in a reasonably foreseeable way, pre-existing Strasbourg case law.[83]

The utility of this limited creative role was displayed in the House of Lords decision in *Limbuela*.[84] In that case, the 'only approximately relevant authority'[85] was the admissibility decision *O'Rourke* v. *United Kingdom*.[86] On the basis of that authority – which could hardly be described as 'clear and constant' – the House of Lords was not only able to fashion a remedy, but was arguably able to extend the scope of protection offered by Article 3 of the Convention in the domestic context in so doing.[87]

It is clear, then, that the courts' discretion to depart from the direction of the Strasbourg institutions is greater in those instances where the European Court of Human Rights has not formulated a position which could be described as 'clear and constant', or in those circumstances in which the margin of appreciation can be said to apply. As to the latter, the decision of the House of Lords in *Re P* has provided ample evidence as to the existence of an area of potential judicial creativity. As Lord Hoffmann noted in that decision, where the margin of appreciation applies at the Strasbourg level:

---

[82] *R (on the application of Gentle and others)* v. *Prime Minister*, above n. 78, para.56.

[83] Incidentally, the legitimacy of 'reasonably foreseeable' development of the law (engineered by the courts) would also appear to gain support from the European Court of Human Rights: *SW* v. *United Kingdom*; *CR* v. *United Kingdom* (1996) 21 EHRR 363.

[84] *R* v. *Secretary of State for the Home Department, ex parte Limbuela* [2005] UKHL 66; [2006] 1 AC 396.

[85] C. Warbrick, 'The European Convention on Human Rights and the Human Rights Act: the view from the outside' in Fenwick, Phillipson and Masterman, *Judicial Reasoning under the UK Human Rights Act*, above n. 43, p.48.

[86] *O'Rourke* v. *United Kingdom*, ECtHR No.39022/97 (2003).

[87] Lewis, 'The European ceiling on rights', above n. 57, 736.

> That means that the question is one for the national authorities to decide for themselves and it follows that different member states may well give different answers.[88]

As has been discussed, the margin of appreciation finds its justification in the acknowledgement that national authorities are better equipped to gauge 'what restrictions are necessary in the democratic societies they serve'.[89] Aside from those instances discussed above, as a general principle, the Strasbourg organs rarely prescribe which branch of government – if any – be responsible for shouldering the burden of realising the right(s) in question: the state is the responsible actor at the Strasbourg level; as a result, at the domestic level the legislature, executive and judiciary are collectively responsible:

> The margin of appreciation is there for division between the three branches of government according to our principles of the separation of powers. There is no principle by which it is automatically appropriated by the legislative branch.[90]

It is for reasons of institutional competence that the most striking development in this regard has been in the area of common law development. While *Campbell* v. *Mirror Group Newspapers* has already been noted for playing a central role in the metamorphosis of the breach of confidence action, *Campbell* is also notable for the reason that the House of Lords resolved the question of the Convention imposing an obligation on the state to provide the individual with a remedy for the breach of Article 8 rights by private parties, in advance of a conclusive decision on a point from the European Court of Human Rights.[91] While the decision of the European Court of Human Rights in *Peck* v. *United Kingdom*[92] had concerned the interference with Article 8 rights by the *state*, the only relevant decision on the particular *horizontal* application of Article 8 was in the form of the admissibility decision of *Spencer* v. *United Kingdom*.[93] At the time the case of *Campbell* came before the House of Lords, the duty on the state to provide a remedy for the breach of Article 8 by private parties was a 'difficult question' to which 'Strasbourg case law provide[d] no

---

[88] *In Re P*, above n. 72, para.31 (Lord Hoffmann).
[89] *Ibid*., para.118 (Baroness Hale of Richmond).
[90] *Ibid*., para.37 (Lord Hoffmann).
[91] Such a decision did not come from the European Court of Human Rights until *Von Hannover* v. *Germany*, above n. 53, handed down a month after the decision of the House of Lords in *Campbell* v. *MGN*.
[92] *Peck* v. *United Kingdom* (2003) 36 EHRR 41.
[93] *Earl Spencer* v. *United Kingdom* (1998) 25 EHRR CD105.

definitive answer'.[94] Yet in *Campbell* the majority in the House of Lords felt able to conclusively find that Article 8 imposed an obligation on the state to resolve breaches of that Article by private parties – in this case, the press.

Campbell marks an important step in creative reasoning under the HRA. While it is entirely arguable that *Campbell* is exactly the type of decision which Lord Irvine had in mind when he indicated that domestic courts should be able to 'give a lead' to Strasbourg, it also goes against the grain of the restrictive readings of s.2(1) of the HRA outlined above. It is worth recalling at this stage the words of Lord Hope in *N* v. *Secretary of State for the Home Department*: 'It is not for us to search for a solution … which is not to be found in the Strasbourg case law.'[95] *Campbell* shows the House of Lords finding a solution which – while not strictly mandated by clear and consistent authority – was nevertheless later shown to be consistent with Strasbourg's developing approach.[96] *Campbell* demonstrates that within the separation of powers on the HRA model, there is scope for both a creative development of common law standards and a creative interpretation of the requirements of the Convention rights in the domestic context. As a result, it is possible to argue that there are signs of an emerging – and progressive – rights jurisprudence which is not simply 'Strasbourg's shadow',[97] nor the sole preserve of Parliament.

Conclusion

Given the acknowledged creative abilities of courts in determining and developing the common law, it is no surprise that the most obvious attempts by the courts to loosen the grip of the 'mirror principle' are found in dicta and case law concerning that very body of judge-made law. Similarly, it is perhaps no surprise that the area of personal privacy has undergone significant legal development since the enactment of the HRA. The growing weight of judicial opinion that personal privacy should be afforded greater protection in domestic law prior to the coming into force of the Act[98] – and the failure of successive parliaments to legislate to give effect to such protections – no doubt spurred willingness

---

[94] Phillipson, 'Judicial reasoning in breach of confidence cases under the Human Rights Act', above n. 34, 57.

[95] *N* v. *Secretary of State for the Home Department*, above n. 75, para 25.

[96] As subsequently proven by *Von Hannover* v. *Germany*, above n. 91.

[97] Lewis, 'The European ceiling on rights', above n. 57, 730.

[98] See e.g. *Kaye* v. *Robertson* [1991] FSR 62.

to integrate the protections afforded by Article 8 into the common law. But while other areas of the common law have not undergone such a radical doctrinal reformulation, the transformative *potential* of the application of the Convention rights should not be underestimated. It is evidence of the judicial recognition of this potential – and the more regular and explicit forays into judicial law-making that its wholesale embrace would involve – that goes some way to explaining the comparative hesitancy of domestic courts to develop the meaning of the Convention rights themselves in the domestic context. The uncertainty surrounding the status of the Convention rights as tools of both domestic and international law means that any attempts to extend, or amend, the scope of application of a Convention right – by contrast with developments at common law – will be at the very fringes of judicial creativity. While *AF*[99] demonstrates that the precedential force of a decision of the Grand Chamber of the European Court of Human Rights will be considerable, *Re P* shows that the precedential approach to Strasbourg authority has its limits, and that when those limits are reached, the domestic courts may exercise a legitimate creative role to fashion domestic remedies which – while not driven by explicit authority from Strasbourg – take their influence from the Convention.[100]

[99] *Secretary of State for the Home Department* v. *AF* [2009] UKHL 28; [2009] 3 WLR 74.
[100] *In Re P*, above n. 72. On which, see: Lewis, '*In Re P and others*', above n. 57.

PART IV

The separation of the judicial branch

8

The independence of the judiciary

Introduction

It is the institutional and individual independence of the judiciary that underpins the ability of judges to adjudicate, impartially, between the parties that appear before them. In addition, it is this independence that grants legitimacy to the judicial role, for without it, claims to impartiality would rightly be regarded as a sham. Judicial independence, therefore – crucially – provides the foundations from which judicial analysis of politically contested issues can legitimately proceed. An independent judiciary – autonomous from the elected branches of government and impartial as between the parties to the case – is regarded as a fundamental requirement of the rule of law,[1] and has been argued to form the central pillar of separation of powers in the UK constitution.[2]

Judicial independence, however, is also an elusive concept that contains a number of distinctive and interrelated characteristics.[3] This chapter seeks to examine the status of judicial independence in its institutional and functional senses – that is, the structural independence of the judiciary from the elected branches of government, and the degree to which the judicial process can be regarded as being independent of executive and legislative influence. Judicial independence has what might be called *structural* and *individual* dynamics – the first concerning the separateness of the judges from the other branches of government, the latter ensuring the impartiality of individual proceedings. It is – for the most part – the former that concerns us in this chapter, though, as has already been seen in the context of the Strasbourg case law, these two aspects of judicial independence are difficult to separate in their entirety, for the reason that they are

---

[1] See e.g.: J. Raz, 'The rule of law and its virtue' (1977) 93 LQR 195; Lord Steyn, 'Democracy, the rule of law and the role of the judges' [2006] EHRLR 243, 248.

[2] See pp.26–30.

[3] See e.g.: D. Woodhouse, 'The constitutional and political implications of a United Kingdom Supreme Court' (2004) 24 LS 134, 136; R. Stevens, *The English Judges: Their Role in the Changing Constitution* (Oxford: Hart Publishing 2005), pp.96–7. Despite being difficult

mutually supportive.[4] How can a court be regarded as substantially structurally independent of the political branches of government – no matter what safeguards are in place for upholding the independence of *individual* decisions – if its membership is drawn from within the legislature?[5]

The functional independence of the courts is slightly more difficult to encapsulate. Of course, the independence of specific proceedings is protected by the *sub judice* rule, which – as described by the Joint Committee on Parliamentary Privilege – determines that the 'proper relationship between Parliament and the courts requires that the courts should be left to get on with their work' without parliamentary interference.[6] More difficult to articulate is the degree to which judicial processes can be regarded as being independent of legislative direction. As has already been seen, in the UK constitution, the function of the courts *vis-à-vis* the legislature is – at its most basic – to interpret and apply the law as determined by Parliament. While we have already seen that at the fringes of this relationship the courts have significant constitutional influence as authoritative interpreters of parliamentary language and its compatibility with the Convention rights, behind this lies the ultimate possibility that Parliament might overrule a specific judicial reading of the law, or – more routinely – may pass legislation directing a change in the law, or a new set of legal rules to be applied. In such cases, the judicial discretion to depart from a clear statutory direction may be severely curtailed.

The institutional independence of the judiciary

The distinction between institutional and individual independence

Various statutory, conventional and common law devices have traditionally been deployed in support of the notion of the independence of the

---

to define comprehensively, the House of Lords Select Committee on the Constitution has ruled out a number of potential interpretations of the meaning of judicial independence, arguing that it:

> does not and should not mean that the judiciary have to be isolated from the other branches of the State. Nor does it mean that the judiciary – individually and collectively – need to be insulated from scrutiny, general accountability for their role or properly made public criticisms of conduct inside or outside the courtroom.
>
> (House of Lords Select Committee on the Constitution, *Relations between the Executive, the Judiciary and Parliament* (HL 151), July 2007, para.27)

[4] See pp.79–80.

[5] See the discussion of *Procola* v. *Luxembourg* (1996) 22 EHRR 193 and *McGonnell* v. *United Kingdom* (2000) 30 EHRR 289 at pp.80–4.

[6] Joint Committee on Parliamentary Privilege, *First Report of 1998–1999* (HL 43-I; HC 214-I), para.192.

courts in the British constitution. The aim of each of these mechanisms is the same: to uphold the legitimacy of the judicial process by insulating courts from the controversies and party political pressures of the elected arms of government. The Magna Carta of 1215 endorses the independence of a trial process from the influence of prosecuting authority.[7] More saliently, the Act of Settlement 1701 provides that judges should hold office *quamdiu se bene gesserint*, that their salaries should be established by statute and immune from executive interference and that they might only be removed 'upon the address of both houses of Parliament'. It is testament to the enduring influence of these provisions that not only have they been reinforced in more recent times in the Appellate Jurisdiction Act 1876, the Supreme Court Act 1981 and most recently in the CRA 2005,[8] but that Parliament has not invoked the procedure to remove a serving judge from office during modern times.[9] The separation of judicial and legislative branches has also been – partially – ensured by the direction of the House of Commons Disqualification Act 1975 that judges are disqualified from membership of the lower House of Parliament,[10] while the establishment of a United Kingdom Supreme Court under the CRA 2005 has all but removed the institutional link between the highest court of appeal and the upper chamber of Parliament.[11]

Convention and common law have both also played a role in upholding the independence of the judiciary. By convention, judges should insulate themselves from party politics by resigning any membership of a political party upon appointment, and by the same means are shielded from direct and personal criticism by ministers in respect of judicial decisions made.[12] In addition to these guarantees of judicial independence, the common law has also developed its own protections for the

---

[7] For an outline, see: E. Wicks, *The Evolution of a Constitution: Eight Key Moments in British Constitutional History* (Oxford: Hart Publishing, 2006), pp.3–6.

[8] See also: Supreme Court Act 1981, s.11(3); Appellate Jurisdiction Act 1876, s.6; Constitutional Reform Act 2005, s.33.

[9] In fact, the procedure has only *ever* been successfully invoked once, when in 1830 Sir Jonah Barrington was removed from the Irish High Court of Admiralty, after he was found guilty of committing embezzlement.

[10] House of Commons Disqualification Act 1975, s.1 and sch.1.   [11] pp.225–7.

[12] Although it should be noted that the effectiveness of this latter convention has been doubted in recent times: see the response of David Blunkett MP to the decision of Mr Justice Collins in *R (on the application of Q)* v. *Secretary of State for the Home Department* [2003] EWCA Civ 364 (on which, see: A Bradley, 'Judicial independence under attack' [2003] PL 397). See now: s.3(1) CRA 2005.

independence and impartiality of the judicial process.[13] The common law on judicial bias makes clear that a judge should be independent of the parties to a case, and may be automatically disqualified from sitting in the event of being found to have a financial interest in the dispute,[14] or in the event of having a non-pecuniary interest in the outcome of the case (for example, after having promoted a cause with which one of the parties is associated).[15] The appearance of an independent and impartial judicial process is a maxim well established in the common law of England and Wales, reflected in the well-known dicta that 'justice should not only be done, but should manifestly and undoubtedly be seen to be done'.[16]

The cumulative effect of such devices has been to afford judicial independence a status within the constitution that has not been traditionally afforded to separation of powers theories more broadly.[17] Yet for all the endorsements of judicial independence as a constitutional fundamental, significant obstacles have largely prevented the judiciary from being seen as entirely *institutionally* independent of the executive and legislature. While protections for judicial independence at common law have emphasised that judges should be independent of the parties to the case at hand, domestic provision for the independence of the courts have not – by contrast with decisions of the European Court of Human Rights taken under Article 6(1) of the Convention – placed any consistent emphasis on the more abstract need for courts to be structurally independent of the other branches of government. As Robert Stevens has explained:

> Parliamentary sovereignty, the wide jurisdiction of the Lord Chancellor, together with the appointment of judges by a politician and the dual roles of the Law Lords, have thus made it difficult to have an institutional concept of judicial independence, based on a notion of separate branches of government. That, however, has never discouraged the English judges from believing that there is such a concept as the independence of the judiciary in some kind of ethereal collective sense.[18]

Such has been the emphasis placed by statute, common law and conventional devices on protections for the individual independence of judges

---

[13] T. R. S. Allan, *Constitutional Justice: A Liberal Theory of the Rule of Law* (Oxford University Press, 2001), pp.9–10.

[14] *Dimes* v. *Proprietors of the Grand Junction Canal* (1852) 3 HLC 759.

[15] *R* v. *Bow Street Magistrate, ex parte Pinochet Ugarte (No. 2)* [2000] 1 AC 199.

[16] *R* v. *Sussex Justices, ex parte McCarthy* [1924] 1 KB 256, 259.

[17] R. Stevens, *The Independence of the Judiciary: The View from the Lord Chancellor's Office* (Oxford: Clarendon Press, 1993), p.183. See also pp.26–30.

[18] Stevens, *The English Judges*, above n. 3, p.96.

that the notion of institutional judicial independence has largely been rejected by commentators.[19] For instance, Kate Malleson, in her book, *The New Judiciary*, argued in favour of a narrow conception of judicial independence which seeks only to preserve the ability of the judges to impartially determine the individual cases that come before them. Notions of structural, institutional or, 'collective' judicial independence, therefore, have no constitutional source or justification outside of their support for the individual impartiality of judicial decisions.[20] Malleson argued that as a result of:

> the broad overlap between the functions of the judiciary, the executive and Parliament ... a definition of judicial independence as a constitutional requirement based on the separation of powers cannot be sustained.[21]

And further suggested that:

> claims to collective judicial independence are generally weak since constitutional separation is neither a necessary nor sufficient condition for protecting party impartiality in individual cases.[22]

These views can be seen to have support from commentators and judges alike, a member of whom has stressed the lack of an 'institutional concept of judicial independence'[23] in the UK constitution, placing emphasis instead on the ability of the judge to exercise independent judgment in the individual case.[24] While Malleson's suggestion that the institutional separation of the judicial branch is not, of itself, an adequate guarantee of a fair and impartial judicial process which should be endorsed, it is questionable whether the parallel suggestion – that institutional separation is unnecessary as a safeguard of procedural fairness – can be sustained. In

---

[19] For perhaps the most well-known dismissal of the ideal of judicial independence amongst the English judges, see: J. A. G. Griffith, *The Politics of the Judiciary* (5th edn) (London: Fontana Press, 1997).

[20] K. Malleson, *The New Judiciary: The Effects of Expansion and Activism* (Dartmouth: Ashgate, 1999), p.63.

[21] *Ibid.*, p.62.

[22] *Ibid.*, p.69. Though, in a more recent work, Malleson has hinted at the emergence of a more tangible concept of institutional independence: K. E. Malleson, 'Modernizing the constitution: completing the unfinished business' in G. Canivet, M. Andenas and D. Fairgrieve, *Independence, Accountability and the Judiciary* (London: British Institute of International and Comparative Law, 2006).

[23] Stevens, *The English Judges*, above n. 3, p.96. See also: R. Stevens, 'A loss of innocence?: judicial independence and the separation of powers' (1999) 19 OJLS 366; D. Woodhouse, 'Judicial independence and accountability in the UK' in Canivet, Andenas and Fairgrieve, above n. 22, p.122.

[24] HL Debs, 5 June 1996, col.1308 (Lord Mackay of Clashfern).

the light of the requirements of Article 6(1) ECHR – that courts be independent of the executive branch, as well as being objectively structurally, and individually, impartial, to avoid perceptions of bias – it can be argued that institutional separation is anything but unnecessary for the purposes of safeguarding the impartiality of an individual court, and for guaranteeing the idea of judicial independence more broadly construed.

A broader construction of judicial independence therefore emphasises the value of 'maintaining public confidence in the system of justice' and more broadly still 'in the system of government' as a whole.[25] The importance of a broader understanding of judicial independence therefore goes hand-in-hand with the extension of judicial power into the political sphere; if judges are to be permitted to engage more closely with the merits of policy decisions, then faith in the judicial decision-making process as a tool of governance – as well as an avenue for obtaining individual redress – should be regarded as a constitutional imperative. If we are to accept the limited interventions made by courts into the realm of executive policy decisions and legislative direction, then – as we have seen – we must be able to accept the grounds on which those interventions are made, but also the objective independence of the courts that underpins their objective assessments of the necessity for intervention. The enhancement of judicial independence and avoidance of perceptions of bias at an institutional level, as collective ideals, should therefore be regarded as running in parallel with the increased susceptibility of political decisions to judicial review. This aspiration should be seen as being entirely consonant with the requirements of Article 6 of the Convention, which, as we have already seen, dictate that independence and impartiality is as much a question of perception as it is one of reality.

The enactment of the CRA 2005 has therefore seen a number of the obstacles to a meaningful conception of institutional judicial independence removed, such that it becomes reasonable to suggest that the judicial branch may finally be rightly regarded as being structurally separate of both legislature and executive and that this separation may be regarded as being underpinned by an institutional notion of judicial independence.

The pressure for increased institutional autonomy

The pressures exerted on domestic conceptions of judicial independence by the Strasbourg case law on Article 6(1) of the Convention have

---

[25] D. Woodhouse, 'The Constitutional Reform Act 2005 – defending judicial independence the English way' (2007) 5 *International Journal of Constitutional Law* 153, 157; Lady

already been introduced.[26] Following the enactment of the HRA, the influence of Article 6(1) on the position of the judicial branch was felt virtually immediately following a challenge lodged as a devolution issue under the Scotland Act 1998 to the appointment procedures for temporary sheriffs in Scotland. In the decision in *Starrs* v. *Ruxton*, Lord Reed's explanation of the influence of the Convention on the procedures for protecting the independence of the judiciary is worth repeating in full:

> Conceptions of constitutional principle such as the independence of the judiciary, and of how these principles should be given effect in practice, change over time. Although the principle of judicial independence has found expression in similar language in Scotland and England since at least the late seventeenth century, conceptions of what it requires in substance – of what is necessary, or desirable or feasible – have changed greatly since that time. What was regarded as acceptable even as recently as 1971 may no longer be regarded as acceptable. The effect given to the European Convention by the Scotland Act and the Human Rights Act in particular represents, to my mind, a very important shift in thinking about the constitution. It is fundamental to that shift that human rights are no longer solely dependent on conventions, by which I mean values, customs and practices of the constitution which are not legally enforceable. Although the Convention protects rights which reflect democratic values and underpin democratic institutions, the Convention guarantees the protection of those rights through legal processes, rather than political processes. It is for that reason that art 6 guarantees access to independent courts. It would be inconsistent with the whole approach of the Convention if the independence of the courts itself rested upon convention rather than law.[27]

The significant difficulty highlighted by this finding, and of course those of the European Court of Human Rights in *McGonnell* and *Procola*, among other cases, was that the notion of judicial independence at the apex of the domestic judicial structure was heavily reliant on both convention and understanding. The two most prominent structural infringements of the separation of judicial power from that of the executive and legislature – the office of Lord Chancellor and the position of the Lords of Appeal in Ordinary as a Committee of the House of Lords – relied on the operation of 'imprecise rules' rather than 'constitutional enactments'

Justice Arden, 'Judicial independence and parliaments' in K. S. Ziegler, D. Baranger and A. Bradley, *Constitutionalism and the Role of Parliaments* (Oxford: Hart Publishing, 2007), p.191.

[26] See Ch.3.   [27] *Starrs* v. *Ruxton* 2000 JC 208, 250 (Lord Reed).

to ensure that the judicial role was not compromised through its exposure to the day-to-day processes and pressures of executive and legislative politics.[28]

The office of Lord Chancellor

In pure separation of powers terms, the office of Lord Chancellor,[29] as it existed prior to the CRA 2005, was virtually indefensible; as Dawn Oliver commented in 2004, '[t]he office [was] extraordinary, breaching all the formal requirements of separation of powers doctrines'.[30] Of particular concern, to the concept of judicial independence at least, was the fact that the Lord Chancellor was both a member of the executive branch and head of the judiciary able to sit as a judge. The increasingly prominent role played by the Lord Chancellor in party politics had caused concern domestically as being potentially incompatible with the requirements of judicial independence. The external pressures of the Convention were even more pressing: as has been seen, the requirement of Article 6 that courts be independent of the executive is nothing other than clear.[31]

In spite of this, the last incumbent of the wholly unmodified office, Lord Irvine of Lairg, had resisted calls for wholesale reform of the position, and was reluctant to set down 'rigid rules' as to when he would, or would not, sit as a judge.[32] In the immediate aftermath of the decision in *McGonnell*, Irvine did undertake not to 'sit in any case concerning legislation in the passage of which he had been directly involved nor in the case where the interests of the executive were directly engaged'.[33] But subsequently, before the Joint Committee on Human Rights, Irvine seemed to perform something of a *volte face*, stating:

---

[28] D. Woodhouse, *The Office of Lord Chancellor* (Oxford: Hart Publishing, 2001), p.130.

[29] On which, see generally: *ibid*.

[30] D. Oliver, 'Constitutionalism and the abolition of the office of Lord Chancellor' (2004) 57 *Parliamentary Affairs* 754, 759.

[31] See e.g.: *Ringeisen* v. *Austria* (1979–80) 1 EHRR 455, para.95. See also: Draft Resolution of the Parliamentary Assembly of the Council of Europe, 'Office of Lord Chancellor in the Constitutional System of the United Kingdom' (Doc. 9798, 28 April 2003) (adopted in Resolution 1342 (2003)).

[32] See HL Debs, 20 October 1998, cols.WA137–8; HL Debs, 28 October 1998, cols.1984–5.

[33] HL Debs, 23 February 2000, col.WA33. These remarks were made in response to a question tabled by Lord Patten asking whether, following the decision in *McGonnell*, the Lord Chancellor would step down as head of the judiciary. Lord Irvine insisted that 'the position of the Lord Chancellor is unaffected by this case'.

> I have resolutely declined, and I do on this occasion decline, to define
> any category of cases which always and in all circumstances it would be
> inappropriate for a Lord Chancellor to sit.[34]

Irvine sat judicially on relatively few occasions in comparison to his pred-
ecessors as Lord Chancellor.[35] Nevertheless, his sitting in the cases of *DPP*
v. *Jones*[36] and *Boddington* v. *British Transport Police*[37] – cases which both
arguably involved an indirect governmental interest – caused a degree of
controversy. As the above examples make clear, the concrete limitations
on the ability of the Lord Chancellor to sit as a member of the Appellate
Committee of the House of Lords or Judicial Committee of the Privy
Council were few.

   However, the strongly-held view persisted that the Lord Chancellor –
far from posing a threat to judicial independence – facilitated effective
relations between the three branches of government. Lord Irvine, for
instance, defended the office in separation of powers terms as being
'the natural conduit for communications between the judiciary and the
executive, so that each fully understands the legitimate objectives of
the other'.[38] Lord Woolf, then Master of the Rolls, appeared to sympa-
thise with this view, stating in a lecture originally published in 1997
that:

> the Lord Chancellor of the day could ... act as a safety valve avoiding
> undue tension between the judiciary and the government and possibly
> between the judiciary and Parliament as well.[39]

Ultimately, however, this view could not be sustained, either in the face of
the pressures of the Strasbourg case law, or as a matter of constitutional
principle; as has already been seen, the idea of separation of powers as a
tool of institutional efficiency has never been fully embraced in the UK
constitution, so it would not have been usual in the least if such an argument had been allowed to displace that one aspect of separation of powers
that had been seen to be fundamental – judicial independence.

---

[34] Joint Committee on Human Rights, *Minutes of Evidence*, 19 March 2001 (HL 66-ii/HC
332-ii) para.64.

[35] T. Bingham, 'The old order changeth' (2006) 122 LQR 211, 216.

[36] *DPP* v. *Jones* [1999] 2 AC 240.

[37] *Boddington* v. *British Transport Police* [1999] 2 AC 143.

[38] HL Debs, 25 November 1997, col.934 (Lord Irvine of Lairg QC).

[39] Lord Woolf, 'Judicial review – the tensions between the executive and the judiciary', in
Lord Woolf, *The Pursuit of Justice* (Oxford University Press, 2008), p.135 (originally published at (1998) 114 LQR 579).

The Lords of Appeal in Ordinary

The potential for the Law Lords to compromise judicial independence – similarly to the unreformed office of Lord Chancellor – was to be found in the overlap of governmental functions inherent in the position of the Law Lords as both judges and as members of the legislature able to participate in the legislative business of the House of Lords.[40] Again, the conditions under which this latter role was exercised were governed by convention rather than statute. Lord Bingham, in response to a recommendation made by the Wakeham Commission,[41] outlined the general principles under which the Law Lords participated in parliamentary proceedings:

> First, the Lords of Appeal in Ordinary do not think it appropriate to engage in matters where there is a strong element of party political controversy; and secondly the Lords of Appeal in Ordinary bear in mind that they might render themselves ineligible to sit judicially if they were to express an opinion on a matter which might later be relevant to an appeal to the House.[42]

Prior to the clarification provided by Lord Bingham, recent examples of the potential problems associated with this dual role were not difficult to find. Woodhouse has recounted the confusion over the boundary between the Law Lords' legislative and judicial roles which became apparent during

---

[40] Appellate Jurisdiction Act 1876, s.6:
> Every Lord of Appeal in Ordinary … shall by virtue and according to the date of his appointment be entitled during his life to rank as a Baron by such style as Her Majesty may be pleased to appoint, and shall be entitled to a writ of summons to attend, and to sit and vote in the House of Lords …

See: G. Drewry and Sir L. Blom-Cooper, 'The appellate function' in P. Carmichael and B. Dickson (eds), *The House of Lords: Its Parliamentary and Judicial Roles* (Oxford: Hart Publishing, 1999), p.123; L. Blom-Cooper and G. Drewry, *Final Appeal* (Oxford: Clarendon Press, 1972), ch.10.

[41] Royal Commission on Reform of the House of Lords, *A House for the Future*, Cm. 4534 (2000). The full text of Recommendation 59 is as follows: 'The Lords of Appeal should set out in writing and publish a statement of the principles which they intend to observe when participating in debates and votes in the second chamber and when considering their eligibility to sit on related cases.'

[42] HL Debs, cols.419–20, 22 June 2000. It should also be noted that in June 2000 the Lord Chancellor's Department published a leaflet for the judiciary, entitled 'Guidance on Outside Activities and Interests' (available at: www.lcd.gov.uk/judicial/geninf/joutactfr. htm). This guidance relates – among other things – to financial interests, charitable and political activities, lecturing and participation in conferences and writing of books and articles. With regard to public speaking and extrajudicial writing, 'there is in principle no objection to members of the judiciary speaking on technical legal matters, which are unlikely to be controversial'.

the *Pepper* v. *Hart* appeal, as 'several of the Law Lords hearing the case ... had expressed strong feelings for or against the principle [that *Hansard* could be used as a tool of statutory interpretation where the intention of Parliament is unclear] in a debate in Parliament two years previously'.[43] In the *Fire Brigades Union* case,[44] Stevens has noted, constituting a bench for the purposes of hearing the appeal proved problematic, 'since so many law lords had already spoken out, legislatively, against the proposals'.[45] And following the *Pinochet* case, Lord Hoffmann was required to stand down from the libel proceedings involving Albert Reynolds,[46] the former Irish *Taoiseach*, and David Lange,[47] formerly Prime Minister of New Zealand, after counsel raised concerns about his prior involvement in the passing of the Defamation Act 1996.[48] The decision of the European Court of Human Rights in *McGonnell* only served to emphasise the potential for the dual role of the Law Lords to compromise the requirements of Article 6(1).[49] As a result, the contributions of the Lords of Appeal in Ordinary to the legislative process began to wither, and at least two senior judges had publicly declared that in order to preserve the independence of the judiciary, the links between the final court of appeal and the legislature be severed.[50]

Prior to the enactment of the CRA 2005, and since the passage of the House of Lords Act 1999, attempts to implement comprehensive reform of the Upper House of Parliament had produced mixed signals for the future of the Law Lords. In January 2000, the Wakeham Commission recommended that the Law Lords 'should continue to be *ex officio*

[43] D. Woodhouse, 'The office of Lord Chancellor: time to abandon the judicial role – the rest will follow' (2002) 22(1) LS 128, 138.

[44] *R* v. *Secretary of State for the Home Department, ex parte Fire Brigades Union* [1995] 2 AC 513.

[45] Stevens, 'A Loss of Innocence?', above n. 23, 398–9.

[46] *Reynolds* v. *Times Newspapers* [2001] 2 AC 127.

[47] *Lange* v. *Atkinson (No. 1)*, 28 October 1999, Privy Council (unreported). Judgment available at: www.privy-council.org.uk/.

[48] 'Pinochet law lord replaced again as judge', *The Guardian*, 8 July 1999. For discussion of the Law Lords' contributions to the legislative process, see: Lord Cooke of Thorndon, 'The Law Lords: an endangered heritage' (2003) 119 LQR 49, 61–2; Lord Hope, 'Voices from the past – the Law Lords' contribution to the legislative process' (2007) 123 LQR 547.

[49] R. Cornes, '*McGonnell* v. *United Kingdom*, The Lord Chancellor and the Law Lords' [2000] PL 166. See also: Joint Committee on Human Rights, *Minutes of Evidence* (2000–2001), HC 66, Q.103.

[50] Lord Bingham, *A New Supreme Court for the United Kingdom* (London: Constitution Unit, 2002); Lord Steyn, 'The case for a Supreme Court' (2002) 118 LQR 382.

members of the reformed second chamber and carry out its judicial functions'.[51] Again, the overlap between judicial and legislative competence was defended on the basis of efficiency and effectiveness; the Law Lords, it was said, took benefit from their direct exposure to the concerns of politicians and the practicalities of the legislative process, while Parliament derived benefit from the legal expertise of the Lords of Appeal in Ordinary. Thus, the Wakeham Report defended the ability of the Law Lords to contribute to the legislative business of the House of Lords on the grounds of their 'extensive judicial experience' which they might use to explain 'their understanding of how law works in practice'.[52] Further, Wakeham contended that 'the Law Lords can draw on their commitment to the rule of law and due process to identify proposed legislation or other developments which could threaten either of these concepts':[53] While, in evidence, the Commission heard – from a former Law Lord – that the Lords of Appeal in Ordinary derive benefit from 'a greater understanding of the problems of the legislator, of social trends, of the proper limits of judicial innovation'.[54] Again, ultimately, arguments in favour of potentially compromising judicial independence on the basis of efficiency and effectiveness could not be sustained. While the Government White Paper, which followed the Report of the Royal Commission, endorsed Wakeham's findings in this regard,[55] it was the House of Commons Public Administration Committee that proved to be prophetic, when, in 2002, it proposed a model for reform of the House of Lords which would see the Law Lords removed from Parliament and accommodated in a new Supreme Court.[56]

---

[51] Royal Commission on Reform of the House of Lords, *A House for the Future*, above n. 41, Recommendation 57. On which, see: M. Russell and R. Cornes, 'The Royal Commission on reform of the House of Lords: a House for the future?' (2001) 64 MLR 82.

[52] Royal Commission on Reform of the House of Lords, *A House for the Future*, above n. 41, ch.9, para.9.6. It is useful to note that the Royal Commission recognised that this role could be, and indeed is, also played by 'other members of the second chamber with legal expertise or experience' (para.9.7). For specific examples of serving Law Lords' contributions to the legislative process, see: Lord Cooke of Thorndon, 'The Law Lords', above n. 48, 61–2.

[53] *Ibid.*

[54] Royal Commission on Reform of the House of Lords, *A House for the Future*, above n. 41, evidence of Lord Wilberforce.

[55] Government White Paper, *The House of Lords – Completing the Reform*, Cmd. 5291 (2001), para.82.

[56] Public Administration Committee, *Fifth Report, The Second Chamber: Continuing the Reform*, HC 494-I, 14 February 2002, para.153.

Structural independence secured?
The Constitutional Reform Act 2005

The Labour government's response to the pressures of the Convention was to determine, in June 2003, that the office of Lord Chancellor would be abolished and replaced by a Secretary of State for Constitutional Affairs, a Judicial Appointments Committee established, and a Supreme Court for the United Kingdom created.[57] The clear aims of this project were to separate the judicial from the executive and legislative branches at an institutional level[58] and to 'redraw the relationship between the judiciary, the government and Parliament to preserve and increase our judges' independence'.[59] The original proposals were announced as an addendum to a cabinet re-shuffle, and initially thought – at least by their authors – to be a non-contentious change to the machinery of government. Yet, if the abrupt announcement of the reforms caused some consternation, that caused by the fact that the government had not consulted *at all* on either the merits or implications of the reforms was equally palpable.[60]

The enhancement of judicial independence – 'the traditional preoccupation of the English separation of powers'[61] – was central to the reform proposals that eventually became the CRA 2005.[62] Yet the irony of the 2005 reforms as they were first announced was that the proposed abolition of the office of Lord Chancellor was widely seen as being detrimental to the idea of the independence of the judiciary.[63] Much of the disquiet surrounding the proposed reforms centred not on the removal of the Law

[57] For the consultation papers which followed soon after the announcement of June 2003, see: Department for Constitutional Affairs, *A New Way of Appointing Judges* (CP 10/03, July 2003); Department for Constitutional Affairs, *A Supreme Court for the United Kingdom* (CP 11/03, July 2003); Department for Constitutional Affairs, *Reforming the Office of Lord Chancellor* (CP 13/03, September 2003).

[58] Department for Constitutional Affairs, *A Supreme Court for the United Kingdom*, above n. 57, para.34.

[59] *Ibid.*, para.7. See also: S. Prince, 'Law and politics: upsetting the judicial apple-cart' (2004) 57 *Parliamentary Affairs* 288, 293.

[60] See e.g.: Lord Windlesham, 'The Constitutional Reform Act 2005: ministers, judges and constitutional change: part 1' [2005] PL 806, 815–16; Lord Hope, 'A phoenix from the ashes? Accommodating a new Supreme Court' (2005) 121 LQR 253, 253–4.

[61] J. W. F. Allison, *The English Historical Constitution: Continuity, Change and European Effects* (Cambridge University Press, 2007), p.98.

[62] For a detailed account of the legislative history of the CRA 2005, see: Lord Windlesham, 'The Constitutional Reform Act 2005', above n. 60; Lord Windlesham, 'The Constitutional Reform Act 2005: the politics of constitutional reform: part II' [2006] PL 35.

[63] See: A. Le Sueur, 'New Labour's next (surprisingly quick) steps in constitutional reform' [2003] PL 368.

Lords from Parliament, nor the abolition of the Lord Chancellor's judicial role, but on the damage that would be sustained by the idea of judicial independence within this unique separation of powers. As Allison has commented, the paradox was that 'the ... separation of powers was being seen to be threatened at the same time as the Government was claiming to act as its champion'.[64] In spite of the failure of the office of Lord Chancellor to fit the institutional template prescribed by a pure separation of powers doctrine, in practice it was felt – especially amongst the judges – that judicial independence had generally been served well by having a defender at the heart of government. The potential loss of an influential ministerial voice in government caused significant concern among the serving judiciary, who felt that a Secretary of State for Constitutional Affairs, perhaps with no legal experience, might be in a much weaker position to defend the interests of impartial justice against party political objectives.[65]

The subsequent consultation period saw the agreement of a concordat – entitled 'The Lord Chancellor's judiciary-related functions'[66] – many of the provisions of which were subsequently adopted in the Constitutional Reform Act. The concordat represented an agreement between the then Lord Chief Justice, Lord Woolf, and the Secretary of State for Constitutional Affairs and Lord Chancellor, Lord Falconer, as to where responsibility for various matters relating to the administration of justice should lie. The concordat sought to delineate those areas which would continue to be within the responsibility of government – for instance, the allocation of adequate resources to the judiciary – and those areas which should fall within the responsibility of the Lord Chief Justice – such as the allocation of individual judges and the provision of education and training to the judiciary. The concordat also outlined a number of areas of shared responsibility – for example, judicial complaints and discipline – and areas in which consultation between the judiciary and government was necessary. Given the fact that the proposals of June 2003 had barely acknowledged the implications of structural reform for the practical mechanisms of the machinery of justice, the agreement of the concordat did much to enable the eventual passage of the 2005 Act.[67]

---

[64] Allison, *The English Historical Constitution*, above n. 61, p.97.

[65] R. Stevens, 'Reform in haste and repent at leisure: Iolanthe, the Lord High Executioner and Brave New World' (2004) 24 LS 1, 6.

[66] Department of Constitutional Affairs, 'The Lord Chancellor's Judiciary-Related Functions' (January 2004), available at: www.dca.gov.uk/consult/lcoffice/judiciary. htm#part5.

[67] See: Lord Woolf, 'The rule of law and a change in the constitution' (2004) 63 CLJ 317, 323–5.

Independence of the executive

As a result, the office of Lord Chancellor eventually survived, albeit shorn of the judicial roles that had made the position so dubious in separation of powers terms. Instead, the position of Head of the Judiciary in England and Wales would be taken by the Lord Chief Justice,[68] who would become responsible for the administration of justice, judicial training and discipline and for representing the views of the judiciary to Parliament and to the Lord Chancellor.[69] Nowhere is the centrality of judicial independence to the new settlement more evident than in the specific direction in s.3(1) of the CRA that '[t]he Lord Chancellor, other Ministers of the Crown and all with responsibility for matters relating to the judiciary or otherwise to the administration of justice must uphold the continued independence of the judiciary'.[70] This provision in favour of the institutional independence of courts is buttressed by a supplementary provision in support of the individual independence of the judicial process – section 3(5) provides: '[t]he Lord Chancellor and other Ministers of the Crown must not seek to influence *particular judicial decisions* through any special access to the judiciary'.[71] In discharging the functions of the office of Lord Chancellor, the holder is also given statutory directions to 'have regard to':

(a)   the need to defend [judicial] independence;
(b)   the need for the judiciary to have the support necessary to enable them to exercise their functions;
(c)   the need for the public interest in regard to matters relating to the judiciary or otherwise to the administration of justice to be properly represented in decisions affecting those matters.[72]

As the House of Lords Select Committee on the Constitution has recognised, the role of the Lord Chancellor in respect of the promotion of judicial independence is distinct from the obligations imposed by the Act on other ministers; while other ministers are obliged to 'uphold' judicial independence, the Lord Chancellor is also under the altogether stronger obligation to 'defend' judicial independence.[73] Additionally, prior to the CRA, this obligation was political only in nature: now the Lord Chancellor is not only *politically* accountable to Parliament for his actions

---

[68] Section 7 CRA 2005.   [69] Section 7(2) CRA 2005.
[70] Section 4 CRA 2005 makes similar provision in respect of Northern Ireland.
[71] Emphasis added. And see pp.223–4.   [72] Section 3(6) CRA 2005.
[73] House of Lords Select Committee on the Constitution, *Relations between the Executive, the Judiciary and Parliament*, above n. 3, para.39.

in defending the independence of the judicial branch, but is also placed under a *legal* obligation to uphold this particular aspect of the separation of powers dynamic.[74]

More broadly construed, the separation of powers is enhanced as a result of the CRA through the dilution of the (previously) considerable influence of the Lord Chancellor. While the Act and concordat delineate responsibilities relating to the administration of the courts between the Lord Chancellor and Lord Chief Justice, the holder of the former office is not only stripped of the ability to sit as a judge and to preside over the legislative business of the House of Lords,[75] but also now plays a much less significant role in the determination of judicial appointments. The establishment of a Judicial Appointments Commission has put in place a more transparent process than previously existed.[76] While the holder of the reformed office of Lord Chancellor retains the power to make recommendations for certain judicial appointments to the Queen, the recommendation is made on the basis of a shortlist drawn up by the Judicial Appointments Commission, which in turn is prepared with regard to criteria specified by the Act.[77] Parliamentary oversight of the processes of appointment is therefore both preserved – as the Lord Chancellor retains the formal power to make the recommendation for judicial appointment, and remains responsible to Parliament for so doing – and facilitated through an increased openness in the decision-making procedure. Power previously concentrated in the unreformed political office of Lord Chancellor is now effectively divided among the three branches, with one branch in particular benefiting from this division: '[t]he judges would not admit it, but they have emerged immensely stronger'.[78]

As far as responsibility for the administration of justice is concerned, the holder of the position of Lord Chief Justice has seen their specific constitutional responsibilities considerably expanded by the CRA and terms

---

[74] *Ibid.*, p.62 (evidence of Professor Kate Malleson). While these new statutory duties are clearly intended to add legislative weight to existing conventional protections for judicial independence, it is – as Andrew Le Sueur has observed – 'not clear how (if at all) the new duties may be effectively enforced' (A. Le Sueur, 'Judicial power in the changing constitution' in J. Jowell and D. Oliver (eds), *The Changing Constitution* (5th edn) (Oxford University Press, 2004), p.337.

[75] Section 18, and sch. 6, CRA 2005.

[76] On which, see: Woodhouse, *The Office of Lord Chancellor*, above n. 28, ch.6.

[77] CRA 2005, ss.63–6.

[78] R. Hazell, 'The continuing dynamism of constitutional reform' (2007) 60 *Parliamentary Affairs* 3, 17.

of the concordat; as Lord Phillips noted in 2007, while the Lord Chancellor and Lord Chief Justice hold joint responsibility for the administration of justice, 'as a matter of constitutional principle, the Lord Chief Justice is now the senior partner'.[79] The results of this change have been neatly summarised in separation of powers terms by Kate Malleson, who has suggested that '[w]hat has been created is an institutional relationship which envisages two *separate but equal branches* working together to manage the courts and judiciary'.[80] While the institutional separation of the judicial branch has undoubtedly been enhanced following the implementation of the 2005 Act, events have shown that structural division alone will not guarantee the continued independence of the judiciary.

The question over the ability of the existing relationships between the executive and the judiciary to withstand pressure exerted by government has led one commentator to suggest that recent experience has shown that the judges have been treated by government as 'part of the policymaking process to be cajoled and coerced into backing its positions'.[81] In so doing, the suggestion is also made that the courts have *allowed* themselves to be manipulated in this manner. While the resilience of conventional boundaries separating the executive and judicial processes has in recent years become open to question,[82] the weight of available evidence points to a significant judicial resistance to be influenced by executive pressure, and a profound awareness of the importance of preserving the institutional separation of the executive and judicial branches.[83] When, for example, the former Home Secretary, Charles Clark, suggested that judges and ministers might informally discuss the implementation and operation of the government's counter-terrorism policies, the response from the judges was terse: as Lord Steyn commented, 'Mr Clark apparently fails to understand that the Law Lords and Cabinet ministers are not on the same side.'[84] This view was echoed by the House of Lords Select Committee on the Constitution, which stated that Clark's suggestion

---

[79] Cited at House of Lords Select Committee on the Constitution, above n. 3, para.17.

[80] *Ibid.*, p.63 (evidence of Professor Kate Malleson) (emphasis added).

[81] M. Bevir, 'The Westminster model, governance and judicial reform' (2008) 61 *Parliamentary Affairs* 559, 573.

[82] A. W. Bradley, 'Judicial independence under attack' [2003] PL 397.

[83] See e.g.: *R* v. *Secretary of State for the Home Department, ex parte Anderson* [2003] 1 AC 837, 882 and 899.

[84] Lord Steyn, 'Democracy, the rule of law and the role of the judges', above n. 1, 248; A. W. Bradley, 'Relations between executive, judiciary and Parliament: an evolving saga?' [2008] PL 470, 476.

'risks an unacceptable breach of the principle of judicial independence'.[85] The independence of the judicial branch in this regard is now bolstered by both the general direction that ministers seek to uphold judicial independence, found in s.3(1), and the quite specific indication in s.3(5) that 'Ministers of the Crown must not seek to influence particular judicial decisions through any special access to the judiciary.'[86]

While the CRA and the concordat provide the relevant institutional framework from which relations between the executive and judiciary should proceed, it is also clear that the framework alone will not guarantee that judicial independence will be upheld. In June 2006, a row broke out over the sentence handed down to a convicted child abuser.[87] Craig Sweeney had been convicted of the sexual assault of a three-year-old girl, and sentenced to life imprisonment. The minimum tariff set by the trial judge was five years and 108 days. The apparent lack of congruity between the offence and the sentence prompted criticisms from the then Home Secretary, Dr John Reid MP, and from Vera Baird QC MP, then a Minister of State in the Department for Constitutional Affairs, both of whom 'inappropriately cast aspersions on the competence' of the judge in question.[88] The press was quick to join the debate, labelling the judiciary, among other things, 'deluded, out of touch and ... deranged'.[89] While such forthright and high-profile criticisms clearly contained the potential to upset confidence in the judicial process, Lord Falconer, the Lord Chancellor, was slow to respond publicly. Of this episode, the Constitution Committee remarked:

> The Sweeney case was the first big test of whether the new relationship between the Lord Chancellor and the judiciary was working properly, and it is clear that there was a systemic failure.[90]

To reinforce the provisions of the Act, the Constitution Committee recommended that the Ministerial Code be amended to contain 'strongly worded guidelines setting out the principles governing public comment by ministers on individual judges'.[91]

---

[85] House of Lords Select Committee on the Constitution, *Relations between the Executive, the Judiciary and Parliament*, above n. 3, para.97.

[86] Section 4 of the CRA provides a similar endorsement of the principle of judicial independence applicable to Northern Ireland.

[87] See: 'Paedophile case ignites sentences row', *The Guardian*, 13 June 2006.

[88] House of Lords Select Committee on the Constitution, *Relations between the Executive, the Judiciary and Parliament*, above n. 3, para.45.

[89] *Ibid.*, ch.2, Table 1.   [90] *Ibid.*, para.49.

[91] *Ibid.*, para.51. The government subsequently undertook to consider the recommendation when the Ministerial Code was next updated (Government's Response to the House of

Independence of the legislature

The establishment of a Supreme Court for the United Kingdom will finally see the emergence of – as Bagehot put it – 'a great conspicuous tribunal' from beneath 'the robes of a legislative assembly'.[92] The structural independence of the Supreme Court from the legislature offers obvious benefits for the insulation of the justices of the Supreme Court from the party political debates and controversies of the legislature. Separating the highest court from the legislature also removes the obstacle that had precluded devolution disputes from being handled by the Appellate Committee of the House of Lords. The handing of devolution disputes to the Judicial Committee of the Privy Council above the Appellate Committee was partly as a result of the 'impression that the Appellate Committee, as a part of the UK's Parliament, lacked the objective independence for dealing with division of powers disputes between Westminster and Belfast, Cardiff and Edinburgh'.[93]

In spite of the government's bold initial claim that the new Supreme Court 'will in no way be connected to the UK Parliament',[94] the fact that ten of the first twelve occupants of the new Supreme Court were all previously Lords of Appeal in Ordinary ensures that there will, at least in the immediate future, be a residual link to the UK legislature within the new Supreme Court.[95] Over time, however, this lingering institutional attachment will be extinguished, as future members of the Supreme Court are so appointed without having previously been members of Parliament. Beyond this, however, the CRA does not completely separate the Supreme Court from the House of Lords and envisages an ongoing link between court and legislature. In spite of the suggestion in the government's consultation paper that 'it would be better to sever completely any connection between the [new Supreme] Court and the House of Lords',[96] the CRA makes provision for a supplementary panel of judges who may be called upon to bolster the twelve justices of the Supreme Court.[97] Membership

---

Lords Select Committee on the Constitution's Report, *Relations between the Executive, the Judiciary and Parliament* (Cm. 7223), October 2007, para.6).

[92] W. Bagehot, *The English Constitution* (Oxford World's Classics edn) (Oxford University Press, 2001), p.96.

[93] A. Le Sueur, 'What is the future for the Judicial Committee of the Privy Council?' (London: Constitution Unit, 2001), p. 12.

[94] Department of Constitutional Affairs, *A Supreme Court for the United Kingdom*, above n. 57, para.20.

[95] Section 24 CRA 2005. See also: Department of Constitutional Affairs, *A Supreme Court for the United Kingdom*, above n. 57, para.29.

[96] *Ibid.*, para.36.   [97] Section 39 CRA.

of the supplementary panel is conditional on, *inter alia*, membership of the House of Lords.[98]

It is clear, then, that future members of the Supreme Court and members of the supplementary panel of judges may be members of the House of Lords prior to their appointment to the Supreme Court. The *complete* institutional separation of court from legislature is therefore not achieved by the provisions of the CRA. Consonant with the developments outlined above, the establishment of a Supreme Court was designed to enhance the structural independence of the judiciary from the elected branches of government, rather than to create an institutionally isolated judiciary.[99] Mechanisms for formal interaction between court and legislature remain,[100] but at the same time the likelihood for functional overlap between court and legislature – and for the potential challenges to judicial independence that may result – has been reduced, and will reduce yet further in time.

It may be, too, that over time, the structural independence of the Supreme Court prompts other developments of constitutional import. It may be plausible to speculate that the establishment of the Supreme Court – and the increased institutional separation from the legislature which will result – might coincide with an increased willingness on the part of the Court to assert itself against the executive, and possibly Parliament. The increased institutional separation between Supreme Court and legislature might – as Lord Woolf has suggested – 'act as a catalyst causing the new court to be more proactive than its predecessor'.[101] But at this stage – as the embryonic Supreme Court is delivering judgments in its first cases – it is equally plausible to suggest that creation of this separated judicial institution might not be accompanied by the Supreme Court's immediate assertion of its new-found independence. This is for the reason that the tensions between legitimate judicial intervention and democratic accountability, and between acceptable judicial creativity and unwarranted judicial law-making, have not simply evaporated upon the establishment of this new judicial institution. The Supreme Court is very much an institution designed – much like the HRA itself – to fit into the

---

[98] Section 29(2) CRA.
[99] House of Lords Select Committee on the Constitution, *Relations between the Executive, the Judiciary and Parliament*, above n. 3, para.27.
[100] Most obviously via the Lord Chief Justice's ability – under s.5 CRA – to make representations to Parliament. Section 5 also extends a similar privilege to the Lord President of the Scottish Court of Session and to the Lord Chief Justice of Northern Ireland.
[101] Lord Woolf, 'The rule of law and a change in the constitution', above n. 67, 326.

UK's unique constitutional template.[102] So while the institutional boundaries between courts, executive and legislature are being made more secure, the increased exposure of the judicial branch to policy choices in adjudication ensures that practical questions concerning the legitimacy of judicial method will continue to be as important in the long term as issues surrounding the structural independence of courts.

Independence, legitimacy and the separation of functions

It is the independence of the judicial branch of both executive and legislature that underpins the constitutional role of the courts. This detachment from the pressures of the political process and political debate provides judges with the legitimacy required to adjudicate over the legality of potentially divisive and contested political disputes. As Richard Bellamy has highlighted – though from a differing perspective than that advocated here – it is the legitimacy of process that is crucial to the effective resolution of conflict.[103] Independent judges are 'appropriately detached from both immediate administrative pressures and prevailing public opinion on any particular issue'.[104] Instead, decisions of the judiciary should be based on the objective requirements of the law. It is in this regard that the separation of executive, legislative and judicial decision making is required by the independent position of the judicial branch within the constitution: while the legislative and executive branches may take decisions based on the perceived needs of society at large, the demands of the economic climate, or many other diverse grounds, the judicial branch should make decisions based on the perceived requirements of the law and of constitutional principle. As a result, judicial decision making can be seen to be disconnected from the demands of political decision making that are the rightful concern of legislative and executive decisions.[105] This fundamental division in governmental decision-making power is a requirement of the independence of courts, and the basis of their legitimate intervention in political decisions.

---

[102] Indeed, a number of the more innovative proposals for inclusion within the jurisdiction of the Supreme Court were rejected for the reason that they would sit uneasily with the UK's 'constitutional' and 'judicial traditions' (Department of Constitutional Affairs, *A Supreme Court for the United Kingdom*, above n. 57, paras.23 and 24).

[103] See pp.139–41.

[104] Allan, *Constitutional Justice*, above n. 13, p.161.

[105] Sir J. Laws, 'Law and democracy' [1995] PL 72, 93.

The legitimacy – and independence – of judicial procedure is in a sense the crucial division of governmental power in the constitution and is evident in a number of characteristics of judicial decision making that are taken for granted. As David Feldman has written:

> the legitimacy of the judiciary arises from three ... different sources: *first*, the obligation to justify its decisions by means of rational arguments; *secondly*, the requirement that the reasons be formulated with reference to objective, publicly accessible standards with legal authority derived from a source other than the opinions of an individual judge; and *thirdly*, the independence of the judiciary from the political arms of government, guaranteeing an unbiased and objective assessment of the legality of the acts and decisions of the executive. This independence of political processes is a positive, not negative, characteristic, because of the distinctive role of judges.[106]

The two spheres of law and politics cannot be completely disconnected – as has already been discussed, techniques of judicial decision making serve the purpose of accommodating the differing considerations and aims of political and legal actors[107] – but the techniques of judicial decision making compared with those of the legislature and executive should rightly be regarded as a fundamental dividing line in the contemporary separation of powers.

Even within the unwritten constitution, there are arguments in favour of allocating certain decisions to officials for resolution, just as there are arguments in favour of trusting judges with the determination of particular disputes:

> The official is more experienced in this particular field, has a better understanding of the consequences of default (eg in respect of defective drains), and has a more rapid and cheaper procedure. On the other hand, the judge is independent, has no axe to grind, is more cautious in jumping to conclusions, has greater experience in the weighing of evidence, and usually pays more attention to the interest of the citizen.[108]

These institutional characteristics of judicial decision making, therefore, provide the core reasons for entrusting particular decisions to courts. It is not that courts will necessarily produce better outcomes, nor that certain decisions are necessarily more suited to exclusively political or legal

---

[106] D. Feldman, 'Human rights, terrorism and assessments of risk: the roles of judges and politicians' [2006] PL 364, 374–5.

[107] See Ch.5.

[108] I. Jennings, *The Queen's Government* (London: Penguin Books, 1961), p.150.

methods of resolution, more that certain decisions should be taken, or reviewed, through a procedure which is seen to be detached from political pressures and objectively fair.

The emergence of a separation of powers jurisprudence?

The views of the European Court of Human Rights on the interplay between judicial and executive roles in sentencing decisions have already been discussed, and have obviously acted as a catalyst for developments at the domestic level. At this juncture, however, it is the views of domestic courts that are of note, the degree to which sentencing decisions have been marked as an area of *judicial* authority, and the extent to which that authority might be regarded as being exclusive. Following on from the decision of the European Court of Human Rights in *Stafford*,[109] it might be thought that *Anderson*[110] – in which the House of Lords found an incompatibility on the basis of the Court's decision in that case – might be the appropriate authority in this area. However, the invocation of separation of powers in the earlier House of Lords decision in *Venables and Thompson*,[111] taken prior to both *Stafford* and to the HRA coming into force – is equally striking.

Domestic courts had – during a series of cases in the 1990s – begun to subject the exercise of ministerial discretion in sentencing cases to the demands of natural justice. In *Doody*, for instance, Lord Mustill had likened the ability of the Home Secretary to determine the tariff to be served by life prisoners to 'an orthodox sentencing exercise'.[112] Subsequently, in *Venables and Thompson*, a majority of the House of Lords endorsed this reasoning, imposing an obligation on the Home Secretary to 'act within the same constraints as a judge will act when exercising the same function'.[113] Lord Steyn went the furthest towards subjecting the executive power to the limits of constitutional principle, invoking the separation of powers doctrine in order to effectively declare the sentencing function as the exclusive domain of the courts. Lord Steyn argued, '[i]n fixing a tariff the Home Secretary is carrying

---

[109] *Stafford* v. *United Kingdom* (2002) 35 EHRR 32.

[110] *R* v. *Secretary of State for the Home Department, ex parte Anderson*, above n. 83.

[111] *R* v. *Secretary of State for the Home Department, ex parte Venables and Thompson* [1998] AC 407.

[112] *R* v. *Secretary of State for the Home Department, ex parte Doody* [1993] 1 AC 531, 557 (Lord Mustill).

[113] *ex parte Venables and Thompson*, above n. 111, 490 (Lord Goff) and 537 (Lord Hope).

out, contrary to the constitutional principle of separation of powers, a classic judicial function'.[114]

As we have already seen, when the case was subsequently heard by the European Court of Human Rights, it held that the Home Secretary, in fixing the tariff, had indeed carried out a sentencing exercise – a judicial function – and that in doing so had acted in breach of Article 6(1) EHCR as he, as a member of the executive, could not be described as an independent and impartial tribunal.[115] Yet the dicta of Lord Steyn in *Venables* is remarkable not only for the fact that it pre-dated *Stafford* and the coming into force of the HRA, but also for the reason that – contrary to the tenor of so many previous judicial invocations of this particular constitutional principle – it appears to suggest that separation of powers is a tool which might justify the imposition of restraints on executive power. Separation of powers in this sense is not accompanied by a plea for judicial caution; rather, it is a bold assertion that certain governmental functions lie exclusively within the constitutional domain of the courts.

When the House of Lords subsequently came to determine *Anderson*, Lord Steyn was under no doubt that the development of the Convention case law endorsed his earlier reasoning, stating that 'Article 6(1) requires effective separation of powers between the courts and the executive, and further requires that what can in shorthand be called judicial functions may only be exercised by the courts.'[116] Such was the emphasis placed on the importance of the separation of powers doctrine in *Anderson* that one commentator has speculated that the judgment may be 'a starting point for building a separation of powers jurisprudence which, although rooted in Article 6, extends beyond the existing objective and subjective tests for independence and impartiality'.[117] A stand-alone separation of powers jurisprudence – in which the invocation of constitutional principle will of itself provide a ground on which to legitimate judicial intervention – is yet to be realised in domestic law. But the influence of Article 6 of the Convention – running in parallel with the developing jurisprudence on procedural fairness – has had obvious repercussions for the division of governmental power in the UK, most obviously in the institutional reforms enacted in the CRA 2005. The difference in emphasis between cases such as *Venables and Thompson* and *Anderson*, and those judicial

---

[114] *R* v. *Secretary of State for the Home Department, ex parte Venables* [1998] AC 407, 526.

[115] *V and T* v. *United Kingdom* (2000) 30 EHRR 121.

[116] *R (Anderson)* v. *Secretary of State for the Home Department* [2003] 1 AC 837, para.40.

[117] M. Amos, '*R* v. *Secretary of State for the Home Department, ex p Anderson* – ending the Home Secretary's sentencing role' (2004) 67(1) MLR 108, 123.

invocations of separation of powers considered earlier in this work, is remarkable. Previously, separation of powers was frequently raised as an accompaniment to judicial caution, a reminder not to trespass on the respective territory of Parliament or the executive. Now, we are increasingly told, separation of powers is a 'fundamental'[118] and an 'essential part of a democracy'.[119] And, as Lord Steyn's dicta in *Anderson* perhaps demonstrates most forcefully, separation of powers is now as much presented as an accompaniment to robust judicial intervention as it is tabled as a precursor to judicial restraint.

Even critics of the applicability of separation of powers to the UK constitution have conceded that this line of cases seems to mark a turning point in the status of the domestic separation of powers.[120] As Adam Tomkins has noted:

> Before the Human Rights Act the separation of powers was a political ideal that could be variously used to describe or to criticise aspects of the British constitution, but it was not generally regarded as being a judicially enforceable rule. The sentencing context is one area where the courts have begun to talk of the separation of powers in more juridical terms.[121]

These assertions of the importance of judicial process in the area of sentencing have not, however, cemented the complete autonomy of the judicial role in the discharge of this particular constitutional function – something that Lord Bingham in *Anderson* was careful to acknowledge. Parliament remains competent to implement a sentencing framework within which courts must operate, which may specify that particular sentences be fixed to particular crimes. Parliament may not, however, influence the processing of particular offenders: 'the separation of powers ... seems to confirm that Parliament has considerable authority over sentencing policy, subject to the Human Rights Act and subject to the limitation that the legislature cannot prescribe a sentence for a particular offender'.[122] In the process of the individual case, therefore, the courts are substantially autonomous from both specific and individual legislative and executive interventions.[123]

---

[118] *R (Anderson)* v. *Secretary of State for the Home Department*, above n. 116, para.27.

[119] *Ibid.*, para.76.   [120] See Ch.1.

[121] A. Tomkins, 'The rule of law in Blair's Britain' (2007) 26 *University of Queensland Law Journal* 255, 260–1.

[122] A. Ashworth, *Sentencing and Criminal Justice* (4th edn) (Cambridge University Press, 2005), p.53.

[123] R. Brazier, *Constitutional Reform: Reshaping the British Political System* (3rd edn) (Oxford University Press, 2008), p.147.

Asserting the division between legislator and judge: procedural fairness at common law

While the most significant recent development regarding the structural separation of the judicial branch from the executive and legislative roles has come in the form of the CRA 2005, developments in the common law of procedural fairness – also driven by the perceived requirements of Article 6(1) of the Convention – have had the effect of engineering dividing lines between judicial functions and those of the other branches of government. Two cases are of particular note: *Davidson* v. *The Scottish Ministers*[124] and *R* v. *Secretary of State for the Home Department, ex parte Al-Hasan*.[125]

Endorsing the Convention's circumstantial approach

Davidson v. *The Scottish Ministers*[126] arose out of an appeal made by an inmate at HM Prison Barlinnie to secure his transfer to conditions which were in compliance with Article 3 of the ECHR. The question which arose in the course of these proceedings was whether, in the light of s.21 of the Crown Proceedings Act 1947, the prisoner could obtain an order for specific performance against the Crown, or simply a declaratory order. The appeal, heard by the Extra Division of the Court of Session – comprising Lords Marnoch, Hardie and Weir – was, by a majority, refused.[127] Davidson subsequently discovered that Lord Hardie, while holding the office of Lord Advocate, had taken part in the parliamentary passage of the Scotland Bill through the House of Lords. As a member of the government at that time, Lord Hardie had argued against the making of amendments to the Scotland Bill which would have had the effect of preventing courts in Scotland from making orders of specific performance against the Scottish ministers as a part of the Crown. Davidson challenged the decision of the Extra Division on the ground that Lord Hardie's involvement in the passage of the Scotland Act should have precluded him from adjudicating upon his appeal. The Second Division of the Court of Session upheld the challenge, finding that Lord Hardie's involvement in the passage of the Scotland Bill went beyond what could be called mere formality.[128] For the Lord Justice

---

[124] *Davidson* v. *The Scottish Ministers (No. 2)* [2004] UKHL 34.

[125] *R (on the application of Al-Hasan)* v. *Secretary of State for the Home Department; R (on the application of Carroll)* v. *Secretary of State for the Home Department* [2005] UKHL 13; [2005] 1 WLR 688.

[126] *Davidson* v. *The Scottish Ministers (No. 2)*, above n. 124.

[127] *Davidson* v. *The Scottish Ministers (No. 1)* 2002 SLT 420.

[128] *Davidson* v. *The Scottish Ministers (No. 2)* 2002 SLT 1231.

Clerk, Lord Gill, the level of involvement of Lord Hardie in the passage of the Bill was the decisive factor, amounting to a sufficiently proximate relationship between the legislative and adjudicative roles played to satisfy the common law[129] and Article 6(1) tests for independence and impartiality:

> The participation of Lord Hardie in the promotion of the legislation ... went far beyond formality. It involved the advocacy of an interpretation of those provisions that the petitioner was later to challenge ... In my opinion, active participation of that kind in the passage of the legislation in issue is a clear ground for disqualification.[130]

The court therefore endorsed the circumstantial approach to impartiality evident in the reasoning of the European Court of Human Rights; the direct link between the legislative and judicial activities undertaken was sufficient to give rise to an objectively assessed perception of partiality. The decision was appealed to the Appellate Committee of the House of Lords.

In the House of Lords the most substantial speeches were delivered by Lords Bingham and Hope, with both suggesting that the link between the legislative and adjudicative role played by Lord Hardie was the determinative factor as regards his partiality; the same question was at issue on each occasion. Each of the three remaining judges – Lords Nicholls, Woolf and Cullen – endorsed the findings of Lords Bingham and Hope, while leaving questions as to whether the decisive issue was the fact that Lord Hardie was acting as a government minister when the statements complained of were made. For Lords Woolf and Cullen, the *content* of what was said by Lord Hardie appeared not to be the definitive issue; it was the *context* in which it was said. This is not to say that Lords Bingham and Hope did not treat the issue of the link to the executive as going to the question of whether there could be said to be an objectively held view as to the risk of bias, more that – in line with *McGonnell* and the majorities in *Kleyn* and *Pabla KY* – they saw the decisive issue as being the fact that the statements made in Parliament were on the 'same question' or 'same issue' as the point which subsequently came before Lord Hardie in the Extra Division.

Lord Bingham noted that the correct test to be applied would be that found in *Porter* v. *Magill*, which would mean, in the context of this case, asking:

> whether the fair minded and informed observer, having considered [the statements] and the circumstances in which they were made, would conclude that there was a real possibility that he was biased in the sense that,

---

[129] As set down by the House of Lords in *Porter* v. *Magill* [2002] 1 All ER 465.

[130] *Davidson* v. *The Scottish Ministers (No. 2)*, above n. 128, 1236 (Lord Justice Clerk). See also 1239–40 (Lord Kirkwood).

having made these statements, he would be unable to bring an objective and undistorted judgment to bear on the issue raised by Mr Davidson in his reclaiming motion.[131]

Noting that in relation to this test, 'problems are liable to arise where the exercise of judicial functions is preceded by the exercise of legislative functions',[132] he added:

a risk of apparent bias is liable to arise where a judge is called upon to rule judicially on the effect of legislation which he or she has drafted or promoted during the parliamentary process.[133]

What Lord Bingham did not do, however, was to make specific the role played in this test by the fact that Lord Hardie held the position of Lord Advocate at the time these statements were made, only going so far as to say that the conclusion of the lower court 'was justified by the *nature and extent* of Lord Hardie's involvement in the Scotland Act'.[134]

Lord Hope raised the issue of Lord Hardie acting as a Law Officer – 'actively promoting the legislation on behalf of the Government in Parliament'[135] – when the relevant statements were made, but saw this as going to the question of whether a fair-minded and informed observer would appreciate a real risk of bias, rather than as actual evidence of partiality. In his summary of the effect of the European Court's judgment in *Pabla KY*, Lord Hope can be seen to fully endorse the proximity approach:

Applied to our own constitutional arrangements, *Pabla KY v. Finland* teaches us that there is no fundamental objection to members of either House of Parliament serving, while still members of the House, as members of a court. Arguments based on the theory of the separation of powers alone will not suffice. It all depends on what they say and do in Parliament and how that relates to the issue which they have to decide as members of that tribunal ... There must be a sufficiently close relationship between the previous words or conduct and the issue which was before the tribunal to justify the conclusion that when it came to decide that issue the tribunal was not impartial or, as the common law puts it, that there was a real possibility that it was biased.[136]

Lord Woolf's speech appears to indicate that the fact that the statements made by Lord Hardie were made in the House of Lords while he held the position of Lord Advocate – a Minister of the Crown – was decisive. His

---

[131] *Davidson* v. *The Scottish Ministers (No. 2)* above n. 124, para.8.
[132] *Ibid.*, para.9. [133] *Ibid.*, para.17. [134] *Ibid.*, (emphasis added).
[135] *Ibid.*, para.57. [136] *Ibid.*, para.53.

speech bears some of the hallmarks of the above-described strict separation approach – particularly as he makes an effort to distinguish the type of bias at issue here from that which may have been in question had Lord Hardie been an 'ordinary' member of the House of Lords. Lord Woolf stated:

> The apparent bias relied on in this case differs from that in other situations. This is because it depends not only on what Lord Hardie said in the House of Lords during the passage of the legislation but the capacity in which he made the remarks that were relied upon by Mr Davidson. He did so as a Government minister promoting the legislation on the very question which is at the heart of a fundamental issue in Mr Davidson's litigation as to the effect of the same litigation.[137]

Lord Woolf's next statement only serves to show how the ministerial role played by Lord Hardie was conclusive:

> If Lord Hardie was acting in a personal capacity in stating an opinion as to the desirability of the legislation and not as to its effect, the outcome could be different.[138]

Lord Cullen equally placed a degree of emphasis on the capacity in which Lord Hardie made the statements:

> The fact that Lord Hardie expressed an opinion as to the effect of section 21 is not in itself decisive. What he said cannot be considered in isolation: he said it in the context of his role as a Government Minister, and presumably in the light of considerations of policy, he was promoting the protection of the Scottish Ministers from judicial review. It was in the exercising of that role, rather than simply his expressing of an opinion about the effect of section 21, that persuades me that Lord Hardie was disqualified from sitting as a member of the Extra Division.[139]

Taken as a whole, *Davidson* can be seen to endorse the circumstantial approach evident in *McGonnell*; the mere ability to exercise both legislative and judicial roles will seemingly not automatically give rise to a real risk of bias. Hence, it would appear that the common law as influenced by Article 6(1) does not, of itself, require a strict separation of legislative and judicial power.

However, taking into account the executive role exercised by Lord Hardie, then it is at least arguable that the effect of the judgment is to require a *de facto* separation of executive and judicial roles. Lord Cullen, drawing a distinction between the issue of what was said and the role

---

[137] *Ibid.*, para.23.   [138] *Ibid.*, para.24.   [139] *Ibid.*, para.81.

played by the person saying it, indicated that Lord Hardie was a government minister and that it was the 'exercising of that role, rather than simply his expressing of an opinion about the effect of section 21, that persuades me that Lord Hardie was disqualified from sitting as a member of the Extra Division'.[140] Similarly, Lord Woolf placed reliance on the judgment of the European Court of Human Rights in *Procola*, noting that it was the 'capacity in which [Lord Hardie] made the remarks that are relied upon by Mr Davidson' caused the impartiality complained of 'to have the "structural" quality referred to in a different context in the judgment of *Procola v. Luxembourg*'.[141]

On the basis of *Davidson*, it is at least arguable that Article 6(1) does require – at least as interpreted by Lords Woolf and Cullen – a strict separation of judicial and executive power; when looking to the test of impartiality, the link between the two branches will be sufficient to amount to what the court in *Procola* called a 'structural impartiality', regardless of the circumstances. This is reinforced by the fact that, as noted above, the Strasbourg jurisprudence has consistently held that for a court or tribunal to satisfy the requirements of Article 6(1) it must be independent of the parties and of the executive.[142] However, remove the executive element from the equation and *Davidson* can be seen as an endorsement of the circumstantial approach evidenced in *McGonnell*, and by the majorities in *Kleyn* and *Pabla KY*. As such, in questions of the interplay between judicial and legislative power, there should be a degree of proximity between the judicial and legislative roles played sufficient to create an objectively gauged risk of impartiality.

Towards a 'strict' separation of functions at common law?

The circumstantial approach to gauging impartiality was again broadly endorsed by the House of Lords in *R v. Secretary of State for the Home Department, ex parte Al-Hasan*.[143] In *Al-Hasan* – concerning the procedural fairness of prison disciplinary proceedings – Lord Rodger of Earlsferry noted, 'the question will turn, not on theoretical administrative or other concepts as such, but on whether the tribunal can be regarded as impartial and independent in the particular circumstances'.[144] However, a closer analysis of that case reveals profound implications for the nature of the inquiry into the circumstances of a claim of bias.

---

[140] *Ibid.*   [141] *Ibid.*, para.44.   [142] *Ringeisen* v. *Austria* (1979–80) 1 EHRR 455, para.95.

[143] *R (on the application of Al-Hasan)* v. *Secretary of State for the Home Department; R (on the application of Carroll)* v. *Secretary of State for the Home Department*, above n. 125.

[144] *Ibid.*, para.4 (Lord Rodger of Earlsferry).

The case concerned the legality of an order made by the prison governor to strip search all prisoners in a number of cells in HMP Frankland – an order affecting some 184 inmates. The deputy prison governor had been present when the order was made, and was aware of the security reasons for initiating the searches. The deputy governor was subsequently called upon to conduct a disciplinary hearing following two prisoners' refusal to comply with the search order, with the prisoners concerned seeking to challenge the legality of the order to conduct blanket searches. The question for the House of Lords in the case was whether, through the mere fact that the deputy governor had been present when the order to search was made, he was prohibited from conducting the disciplinary hearing by reason of his involvement in the making of the order. The disciplinary proceedings took place before the HRA came into force, and so – as Lord Brown of Eaton-under-Heywood noted in giving the leading speech – their outcome rested entirely on 'well established principles of common law'.[145] The question for the Law Lords was: 'having been present when the general order for a squat search was approved by the governor, could he properly [decide on the adjudications]? Or might he reasonably be supposed to have pre-judged the issue?'[146]

In *Al-Hasan* the Appellate Committee found unanimously that the deputy governor could not have been impartial, as:

> by the very fact of his presence when the search order was confirmed [the deputy governor] gave it his tacit assent and endorsement. When thereafter the order was disobeyed and he had to rule upon its lawfulness, a fair-minded observer could all too easily think him predisposed to find it lawful.[147]

The court did take some assistance from the judgments of the European Court of Human Rights in *McGonnell*, *Procola* and *Pabla KY*, and while the making of the order and the adjudication on the legality of that order might – to use the phrases adopted in those decisions – be said to be in respect of 'the same case' or 'the same decision', *Al-Hasan* appears to leave little scope for argument as regards the degree of involvement in the decision-, or rule-making, process. The expression of a prior opinion on the order is not distinguished from the process of drafting the order, nor simply being present when the order is made. In fact, agreement, or otherwise, with the provision in question need not even be expressed: it may seemingly be deduced from the silence of the adjudicator in question.

---

[145] *Ibid.*, para.45. [146] *Ibid.* [147] *Ibid.*, para.39.

As such, *Al-Hasan* is a marked departure from the reasoning of the House of Lords in *Davidson* which, although stressing that the interaction between the legislative and adjudicative roles played must have been in respect of 'the same decision', equally indicated that involvement in the former must have been in some way *active*. Each of the Law Lords in *Davidson* called for analysis of both the statements made and the context in which they were made, suggesting that – links with the executive aside – as Lord Hope stated, the outcome will 'depend … on what they say and do in Parliament and how that relates to the issue which they have to decide as members of that tribunal'.[148] Looking back to *Davidson* in the Second Division of the Court of Session, the judgments of both Lord Kirkwood and Lord Gill can be read as suggesting that had Lord Hardie's involvement in the passage of the Scotland Bill been a mere 'formality', then the outcome of the case might have been different. Yet in *Al-Hasan*, the deputy governor made no statements which could be analysed, the focus of the Law Lords being only on his presence when the order was made and awareness of the security information used to justify the searches.

Regardless of the basis – or credibility – of the Law Lords' finding that the deputy governor had given 'his tacit assent and endorsement' to the order, the practical implications of this ruling are profound. A close adherence to *Al-Hasan* would suggest that at best *any* expression of a viewpoint on the provision in question might form the basis of a finding of partiality, similarly that *any* involvement whatsoever in the prior passage of legislation might be sufficient to infer a 'real risk of bias'; at worst, that awareness of the justifications for the making of a rule or provision be synonymous with giving assent to it.[149] As Paul Matthews has observed, this type of scenario is reminiscent of Conan Doyle's 'dog in the night-time', where the judge or adjudicator, without ever having expressed an opinion on the argument in question, is 'treated as a judicial imbecile, incapable of reaching an impartial and independent decision'.[150]

It can therefore be suggested that the cumulative effect of *Davidson* and *Al-Hasan* might be to impose a *de facto* separation of legislative, judicial and executive powers through use of the common law test for bias (as influenced to varying degrees by the Strasbourg jurisprudence on Article 6(1)). *Davidson* suggests that prior legislative involvement as a member

---

[148] *Davidson v. The Scottish Ministers (No. 2)*, above n. 124, para.59.
[149] The structural impartiality point in *Al-Hasan* may have been made more compelling by the fact that the deputy governor might have been reluctant to find the order to search illegal because it had been made by his direct superior in the prison hierarchy.
[150] P. Matthews, 'The Dog in the Night-Time' [2000] *Jersey Law Review* 164, 164:

of the executive in the passage of a provision will preclude future judicial involvement with that same provision; the test for impartiality will therefore be used to impose a separation of judicial and executive powers. Yet while *Davidson* also appears to allow for a degree of interaction between the legislative and judicial arms in certain circumstances – as the result is dependent on the nature and context of the statements made – *Al-Hasan* appears to reduce the scope of that interaction to the point of extinguishing it; even tacit acknowledgement of one side of an argument put forward might later be drawn upon as the foundation of an accusation of bias. Regardless of the structural reorganisation made by the CRA 2005, these two cases have each made a powerful endorsement of the place of the separation of powers doctrine in the UK's constitutional arrangements, albeit in markedly different ways: the result being that the 'circumstantial' approach is brought far closer to the 'strict' approach than the Appellate Committee in *Davidson* appeared to require.

While the scope for challenge to the judges of the new Supreme Court by reason of their past involvement with legislative activity will wither over time, the implications of *Al-Hasan* for institutional discipline and analogous hearings should not be understated. In *Davidson*, Lord Hope lamented the state of affairs where, after the event of an adverse judgment, barristers might bring evidence of a judge's partiality based on exhaustive trawling through 'previously undiscovered material ... that might be thought to undermine his objectivity'.[151] As regards the common law of bias more generally, if the effect of *Al-Hasan* is to allow challenges based on tenuous grounds, such as a judge's acceptance or 'tacit endorsement' of a viewpoint, then that decision only serves to increase the likelihood of that happening with more regularity.

The reach of separation by fair process

The cases examined above demonstrate that procedural fairness may require that a principled division should exist between legislator and judge. While a degree of interplay may be permissible, at the point at which that overlap raises an objectively gauged perception of bias, the courts will intervene. These cases therefore vividly illustrate the variable

'Is there any other point to which you would draw my attention?'
'To the curious incident of the dog in the night-time.'
'The dog did nothing in the night-time.'
'That was the curious incident,' remarked Sherlock Holmes.
(Sir Arthur Conan Doyle, *Silver Blaze*, from the *Memoirs of Sherlock Holmes*)
[151] *Davidson v. The Scottish Ministers (No. 2)* above n. 124, para.46 (Lord Hope).

nature of this aspect of the separation of judicial and rule-making power, with the permissible degree of interplay being substantially reduced where direct involvement in the rule-making process has been evident. The cases also illustrate why courts should not be excessively creative in their use of s.3(1) of the HRA, their development of the common law, or their potentially creative development of the meanings of the Convention rights. While creative deployment of judicial powers is permissible in all of these areas, each also contains the potential to undermine the objectively assessed impartiality of the judge if used excessively.

Consistent with the circumstantial approach to the interplay between adjudicative and rule-making functions, the reach of procedural fairness requirements is not such that all quasi-adjudicative, or administrative, functions should be fully Article 6(1) compliant and therefore carried out by an independent and impartial body.[152] As the House of Lords decision in *Alconbury* illustrates, the extent to which certain executive decisions are subject to the requirements of Article 6(1) will also be a matter of degree.[153] According to *Alconbury*, the reason for this lies in the necessary policy content of certain decisions. While sentencing decisions may take place within a statutory framework effectively shaped by political concerns, the necessity for individual sentencing decisions to be taken at a distance from party political pressures means that such decisions may rightly be regarded as being judicial in character. By contrast, decisions with a greater policy content – and in which individual need is in more even balance with the public interest – lend themselves less clearly to such a categorisation, and provide obvious opportunities for public bodies to assert justifications to which the courts may choose to defer.

Alconbury concerned a challenge – grounded in Article 6(1) of the Convention – to the ability of the Secretary of State for the Environment, Transport and the Regions to determine the outcome of certain applications for planning permission. The ability of the Secretary of State to determine such decisions violated Article 6(1), it was argued, on the basis that the relevant minister was so closely involved in the formulation and application of planning policy that it was impossible to approach the issue with an open mind and to determine the issue in the independent and impartial manner required by Article 6(1).[154] As we have already seen, in the case of administrative decisions that are 'directly decisive' of civil

---

[152] See e.g.: *Runa Begum v. Tower Hamlets London Borough Council* [2003] 2 AC 430.

[153] *Le Compte, Van Leuven and De Meyere v. Belgium* (1981) 4 EHRR 1, para.51.

[154] *R (on the application of Alconbury Developments Ltd) v. Secretary of State for the Environment, Transport and the Regions* [2001] UKHL 23; [2003] 2 AC 295, para.24.

rights and obligations, the European Court of Human Rights has held that Article 6 will apply. As we have also seen, notional Article 6 compatibility will suffice in respect of administrative decision-making processes, so long as the decision is subject to judicial review.[155] On the basis of *Bryan* v. *United Kingdom*, the Law Lords unanimously held that Article 6(1) applied, and that – as the determinations of the Secretary of State were susceptible to judicial review – Article 6(1) was not infringed. Thus, the ability of such policy-based decisions to be taken by an elected official was preserved.

The Law Lords felt that the ability of the Secretary of State effectively to determine a limited number of controversial or contested planning applications involved the application and determination of policy considerations unsuited to judicial determination. As one commentator has written:

> [t]heir Lordships appear to have been strongly influenced by the theory that in matters of state policy in an issue such as planning, the final word should rest with the democratically elected governors who were answerable through Parliament for the rights and wrongs of their policy.[156]

As much is undeniable; each of the Law Lords made reference to the desirability of policy decisions being taken by elected officials.[157] As Lord Slynn noted:

> The adoption of planning policy and its application to particular facts is quite different from the judicial function. It is for elected members of Parliament and Ministers to decide what are the objectives of planning policy, objectives which may be of national, environmental, social or political significance.[158]

And as Lord Hoffmann added: 'there are many decisions which have to be made every day ... in which the only fair method of decision is by some person or body accountable to the electorate'.[159] We have already seen that 'spatial metaphors' – such as those relied on by Lord Slynn – offer an inaccurate and inadequate explanation of the relationships between executive and judicial functions. The approach adopted by Lord Hutton,[160] emphasising the complementary nature of legal and political processes of

---

[155] *Bryan* v. *United Kingdom* (1995) 21 EHRR 342, para.47.

[156] S. S. Juss, 'Constitutionalising rights without a constitution: the British experience under Article 6 of the Human Rights Act 1998' (2006) 27 Stat LR 29, 34.

[157] *R (on the application of Alconbury Developments Ltd)* v. *Secretary of State for the Environment, Transport and the Regions*, above n. 154, paras.48, 61, 70, 139–40, 198.

[158] *Ibid.*, para.48.   [159] *Ibid.*, para.70.   [160] *Ibid.*, para.198.

accountability is therefore to be preferred, for the reason that it denies the exclusivity that tends to attach to such delineations of governmental power. Subsequent decisions have shown that suggestions that the greater the policy content of a decision, the greater the degree of deference due, will not carry weight.[161]

So while the imperatives of procedural fairness and the requirements of Article 6(1) of the Convention may impose a distinction between rule-maker and adjudicator in certain circumstances, they are not such as to require a wholesale subjection of governmental decision-making proc-esses to objectively assessed standards of independence and impartiality. As such, the separation between political and judicial decision making is preserved, and the ability of the elected branches to determine disputes in reliance on the basis of, *inter alia*, efficiency, the public interest or some other imperative is maintained, subject to a judicial supervision of the legality of the process.

Towards a constitutionally separate judicial branch?

Stevens has written that, in spite of the rhetorical support for the concept of judicial independence in the constitution, 'it is clear that – at least for the judges as a class – [judicial independence] is not a legal concept in England'.[162] Following the implementation of the CRA 2005, it is doubtful whether such an assertion can be fully sustained. The CRA amounts to a further break with the established order by placing the independence of the judiciary more firmly on a statutory footing. It reinforces the trad-itional understanding of the independence of the judges, but also recog-nises that the judiciary should be regarded as a branch of government, substantially structurally independent of the executive and the legisla-ture.[163] The impact of the 2005 Act in constitutional terms has been sum-marised by Bogdanor as follows:

> The Act recognises that the judiciary is a third branch of the constitution, separate from Parliament and the executive, and it acknowledges the vital importance of the separation of powers in buttressing the independence of the judiciary.[164]

---

[161] See Ch.5.   [162] Stevens, *The English Judges*, above n. 3, p.97.

[163] V. Bogdanor, *The New British Constitution* (Oxford: Hart Publishing, 2009), p.285; Lady Justice Arden, 'Judicial independence and parliaments', above n. 25, p.191; Bradley, 'Relations between executive, judiciary and Parliament', above n. 84, 487–8.

[164] Bogdanor, *The New British Constitution*, above n. 163, p.84. See also: Bradley, 'Relations between executive, judiciary and Parliament', above n. 84, 487–8; House of Lords Select

The House of Lords Select Committee on the Constitution has also endorsed this view of the developments precipitated by the government's announcements of July 2003, arguing that the CRA has increased the institutional independence of the judiciary.[165] Citing the evidence of Lord Woolf, the Committee indicated that the judges are 'patently free-standing' and that the division of power between courts and executive is now 'quite clear'.[166]

Taken together, the CRA and the concordat have been acknowledged to provide for a 'division of functions' between judiciary and executive,[167] the cumulative effect being that the institutional position of the judiciary within the constitution has been strengthened, with the consequence that the judicial branch should no longer necessarily be considered the 'weakest' branch of government: 'the new dispensation created by the Constitutional Reform Act and the Concordat requires the Government to treat the judiciary as partners, not merely as subjects of change'.[168] The responses of parliamentarians and of the judiciary in response to the proposals of June 2003 illustrated quite conclusively that what was thought by the government to be a routine amendment to the machinery of government was in fact a series of changes of immense constitutional significance.[169] This particular aspect of the separation of powers dynamic, thought by the government to be malleable and responsive to political pressures, in fact turned out to be more robust and resistant to change than had been anticipated. As a result, it seems hardly credible to continue to assert – as Sir Ivor Jennings once did – that the 'authority of Parliament is enough to destroy [judicial independence] at a blow'.[170]

Yet, enhanced institutional separation alone will not necessarily guarantee the continued independence of the judiciary. While the Craig Sweeney episode may be indicative of institutional uncertainty in the new arrangements, it also highlights the fact that personalities and the prevailing political climate will continue to be as relevant to perceptions of judicial independence as institutional relationships alone. While the implementation of the CRA undoubtedly gives weight to the suggestion that the judicial branch is a separate and distinct institution of government in the UK, it also highlights the relatively under-theorised nature

Committee on the Constitution, *Relations between the Executive, the Judiciary and Parliament*, above n. 3, p.68 (evidence of Professor Kate Malleson).
[165] *Ibid.*, para.31.   [166] *Ibid.* (citing the evidence of Lord Woolf).
[167] *Ibid.*, para.14 (citing the evidence of Lord Phillips of Worth Matravers).
[168] *Ibid.*, para.67.   [169] *Ibid.*, paras.12–18.
[170] Jennings, *The Queen's Government*, above n. 108, p.145.

of the ideas associated with judicial independence.[171] As the fluctuating divisions between executive, legislative and judicial powers examined in earlier chapters have demonstrated, and in spite of the increased structural independence of the judicial branch, it remains true to say that 'the role of the judiciary under the constitution is a matter of inference rather than express provision'.[172]

It is for this reason that the invocation of constitutional principle to draw a line between legislative, executive and judicial roles in the sentencing context has been so notable. Such developments show that the extent of separation of powers influence is no longer limited to being a tool of judicial rhetoric. Separation of powers, as Tomkins has observed, is being increasingly discussed in more 'juridical' terms as a result of, among other things, the HRA.[173] Rather than simply describing relationships between the branches of government, separation of powers is increasingly used as a tool of judicial reasoning capable of lending coercive support to limitations placed on the executive, and possibly Parliament. The application of Article 6 in the domestic context has undeniably resulted in the 'evolution of a more distinct approach to a British separation of powers'.[174] Yet separation of powers has not simply become a tool of judicial activism, nor has it become a concept which imposes rigid 'spatial' distinctions between judicial, executive and legislative functions across the range of governmental activities. Cases such as *Alconbury* emphasise the divisions of decision-making process that underpin the relationships among the three branches of government, and demonstrate that the variable requirements of the separation of powers may be sensitive to judicial restraint if the context of the case demands.

---

[171] Le Sueur, 'Judicial power in the changing constitution', above n. 74, p.341. Cf. 'United Nations Basic Principles on the Independence of the Judiciary' adopted by the UN Congress on the Prevention of Crime and Treatment of Offenders (1985).

[172] Lady Justice Arden, 'Judicial independence and parliaments', above n. 25, p.192.

[173] Tomkins, 'The rule of law in Blair's Britain', above n. 121, 260–1.

[174] Prince, 'Law and politics', above n. 59, 293.

9

Towards constitutional separation

Descriptive or substantive principles of separation?

The effects of the constitutional reforms that have been implemented since the first Blair administration came to power in May 1997 are nothing short of spectacular, given the generally incremental development of the UK constitution.[1] One commentator has gone so far as to suggest that the doctrine of sovereignty – for so long the closest thing to a fundamental principle in the constitution – has effectively been replaced by one of separation of powers.[2] The role of the judicial branch, as has been assessed in this work, is but one dimension of this broader conception of separation:

> The British constitution is now characterised not by the sovereignty of Parliament and a concentration of power at the centre, but by a separation of powers at the centre, and a quasi-federal territorial separation of powers between Parliament and the European Union, on the one hand, and the devolved bodies, on the other. Britain is in the process of becoming a constitutional state, one marked by checks and balances between the different organs of government, and a state in which the judiciary now has a crucial role to play in the determination of individual rights and in determining the scope of government action.[3]

The contemporary separation of powers as described in this extract is one in which human rights adjudication has caused many of the rigid spatial distinctions between supposed areas of judicial, executive and legislative authority to have become increasingly difficult to sustain. This is not to say that no such distinctions exist, but that those that do are concerned with institutional decision-making processes and institutional expertise

---

[1] For the exceptions to this organic development, see: E. Wicks, *The Evolution of a Constitution: Eight Key Moments in British Constitutional History* (Oxford: Hart Publishing, 2006).

[2] V. Bogdanor, *The New British Constitution* (Oxford: Hart Publishing, 2009), p.285. See also (for a slightly more hesitant prediction): D. Woodhouse, 'Constitutional and political implications of a United Kingdom Supreme Court' (2004) 24 LS 134, 153–4.

[3] Bogdanor, *The New British Constitution*, above n. 2, p.289.

rather than the straightforward authority of one constitutional actor or body to make decisions on a certain topic. *Primary* responsibility for a particular issue may lie with one branch of government, though this does not mean that its decisions should be insulated from scrutiny by another branch.

At the same time, however, the institutional independence of the courts has been secured as a result of the CRA 2005. The result of these changes is 'that while the Supreme Court is perceived as being more independent, in an institutional sense, than the Appellate Committee of the House of Lords, paradoxically, its members will be seen as more obviously part of the political process'.[4] It is for this reason that mechanisms which limit the nature of the judicial inquiry into political decisions and ensure that respect for the democratic underpinning of public body decisions, and the justificatory arguments advanced in support of those decisions, is a necessary facet of the increased range and intensity of judicial review if a separation of powers is to be achieved and judicial supremacy avoided. As such, arguments of non-justiciability have rightly given way to discussions over the appropriate degree of deference that courts should afford the elected branches. For the most part, the judicial branch has been able to defer to the elected branches without holding that significant areas of policy-making lie entirely outside the judicial remit. In checks and balances terms, the credentials of this contemporary separation of powers are far more compelling than when non-justiciability doctrines allowed executive activities to operate absent effective judicial scrutiny. As a result of this withering of non-justiciability doctrines, suggestions that the courts might review the legality – or constitutionality – of primary legislation do not seem so far removed from reality as they once might have done.

Proportionality and deference are therefore the tools with which the courts regulate their interventions in the political realm. Deference allows the courts to acknowledge the superior expertise or institutional legitimacy of decisions taken by the elected branches, while the structure of proportionality ensures that the judicial engagement with matters of political controversy should be regulated by a pre-determined and stable legal test that provides for a more exacting review than previously found under the *Wednesbury* standard. The concerns of the rights-sceptics – that rights adjudication prompts judges to rely on their own intuitive judgment as

---

[4] D. Woodhouse, 'Judicial independence and accountability in the UK' in G. Canivet, M. Andenas and D. Fairgrieve, *Independence, Accountability and the Judiciary* (London: British Institute of International and Comparative Law, 2006), p.128.

to where the public interest should lie – might be avoided if, as a part of a structured proportionality test, courts recognise the legitimate range of choices available to the public body decision maker, and afford respect to the grounds offered as justification for the choice in question.

While the parallel operation of deference and proportionality ensures that review of executive action and legislative provisions might show signs of both restraint and rigorous review, it is in the latter field that the creative powers of the courts are most evident. In their use of s.3(1) of the HRA the courts are able to modify the meaning, and effect, of primary legislation – so far as it is possible to do – without overtly amending the statute in question. The creative influence of the courts on legislation does not, however, end with the use of s.3 as, even in the event of a declaration of incompatibility being issued, the court's view of what is needed to achieve compatibility will be of relevance to the executive and legislative decisions of whether, and how, to amend the impugned provision(s). This realignment of the separation of powers has not, however, come at the expense of the coercive value of the judicial decision-making process. Judicial decisions have not, contrary to the suggestions of critics such as Nicol, been 'reconceptualised' as 'contestable' entities, easily overturned by the 'favoured interpretation' of the legislature.[5] So while the declaration of incompatibility was designed to ensure that parliamentary supremacy was preserved, practice has shown that the legislative annulment of a judicial use of s.3(1) or parliamentary failure to respond to a declaration of incompatibility will be rare indeed.

The ability of the courts to 'make law' can also be seen in the accelerated development of the common law that has been prompted by the HRA, and in the embryonic indications that the Convention rights in domestic law might differ in substance from their Strasbourg relations. Each of these creative possibilities is, however, limited, not only by the potential damage to legal certainty, predictability and stability that might result from an excessively activist ruling, but also by the potential to compromise one of the defining features of the separation of powers: the distinction between the theoretically unbridled legislative power of Parliament and the curtailed and limited legislative powers of the courts. So while courts may have a legitimate creative role in relation to statutory interpretation, the development of the common law and the meaning of the Convention rights in the domestic context, each of these distinct roles is, by definition, limited and relatively narrow in scope.

---

[5] D. Nicol, 'Law and politics after the Human Rights Act' [2006] PL 722, 743.

Underpinning all of this is the increased institutional autonomy of the judicial branch, and the emerging signs of areas of certain judicial functions which – subject ultimately to legislative direction – are to be regarded as being within the constitutional domain of the judges. Yet, consistent with the rejection of spatial metaphors to delineate areas of executive policy responsibility, while separation of powers is increasingly used as a tool of judicial reasoning which lends weight to the checking and balancing role of the courts, it is also invoked as justification for deference and in order to effect the legitimate policy role of the executive. The contemporary separation of powers both empowers and restrains the courts and is therefore best understood as a concept which explains the variable and dynamic interactions between courts, executive and legislature.

The litmus test of this contemporary separation of powers is, of course, the potential repeal of the HRA, perhaps the most obvious driving force behind this realignment of governmental – particularly judicial – power. The issue has been raised in the realm of administrative law by Tom Poole, who has asked whether the future of the HRA will ultimately determine the future directions of judicial review. Poole has written:

> The hypothetical [repeal of the HRA] is worth pausing over since … it would mean that the developments being touted here as fundamental are in fact fragile and quite possibly transient. If the Act facilitated the restructuring of judicial review, then does it not follow that this restructuring could be undone by the repeal of that Act? Not necessarily. Even if reformation does induce counter-reformation and Parliament reverses its position on the issue of judge-protected rights, this would not necessarily lead to a simple reversion to the status quo ante. For this particular genie is one that would be hard to force back into the bottle.[6]

Poole gives two specific reasons why these developments may be hard to reverse, even by legislative direction. First, greater judicial protection for individual rights at the domestic level runs in parallel with developments internationally.[7] Second, even if the HRA were to be repealed, the UK would (presumably) remain a party to the ECHR, whose enforcement bodies have found that even 'anxious scrutiny' fails to afford an effective remedy for the purposes of Article 13 the Convention.[8] We can add to this list the fact that, while the HRA has been the catalyst for developments in

---

[6] T. Poole, 'The reformation of English administrative law' (2009) 68 CLJ 142, 145.
[7] *Ibid.* And see: C. McCrudden, 'A common law of human rights? Transnational judicial conversations on constitutional rights' (2000) 20 OJLS 499.
[8] *Ibid.* And see: *Smith and Grady* v. *United Kingdom* (2000) 29 EHRR 493.

the arena of judicial review, the substance of that particular area remains largely governed by the common law. Removal of the statutory ground of public authority illegality under s.6 of the Act would not, in and of itself, prevent the continued use of proportionality through the existing heads of review. *Daly*[9] – the very case that ushered proportionality analysis into English administrative law – illustrates as much,[10] as its reasoning arguably owes far more to the existing domestic jurisprudence on access to a court and legal professional privilege[11] than to any of the Convention case law on prisoners' rights.[12] It is, of course, true that review under the HRA differs from judicial review as traditionally understood. But, as Paul Craig has written, we should be careful to treat the two jurisdictions as being entirely compartmentalised: '[t]he reality is that the court is concerned with substance and procedure in HRA cases and ordinary judicial review'.[13]

The potential role to be played by the common law, however, in the event of the repeal of the HRA, exceeds simply determining the standard of review. Just as judicial review remains largely a creation of the common law, it is equally true that the HRA has not entirely superseded the common law's own autonomous protections of human rights. In the HRA era, the two traditions have been seen to operate in tandem. Again, *Daly* provides a salient example. As Laws LJ has stated, 'the Human Rights Act 1998 now provides a democratic underpinning to the common law's acceptance of constitutional rights, and important new procedural measures for their protection'.[14] While the HRA may have spurred developments in the area of common law rights protection, those developments

---

[9] *R v. Secretary of State for the Home Department, ex parte Daly* [2001] 2 AC 532.

[10] *Ibid*. See esp. para.23 (Lord Bingham) and para.30 (Lord Cooke of Thorndon). See also: *R (on the application of Alconbury Developments Ltd) v. Secretary of State for the Environment* [2001] UKHL 23; [2003] 2 AC 295, 321 (Lord Slynn): 'even without reference to the Human Rights Act 1998 the time has come to recognise that this principle [of proportionality] is part of English administrative law, not only when judges are dealing with Community acts but also when they are dealing with acts subject to domestic law.'

[11] See e.g.: *Raymond v. Honey* [1983] 1 AC 1; *R v. Secretary of State for the Home Department, ex parte Anderson* [1984] QB 778; *R v. Secretary of State for the Home Department, ex parte Leech* [1994] QB 198.

[12] Of which *Campbell v. United Kingdom* (1992) 15 EHRR 137 is the only example cited by the House of Lords in *Daly* – although reference is made to *Smith and Grady*, above n. 8 and *Lustig Prean v. United Kingdom* (1999) 29 EHRR 548 to 'illuminate the distinctions between "traditional" … standards of judicial review and higher standards under the European Convention or the common law of human rights' (para. 32, *per* Lord Cooke).

[13] P. Craig, *Administrative Law* (6th edn) (London: Sweet and Maxwell, 2008), p.631.

[14] *International Transport Roth GmbH v. Secretary of State for the Home Department* [2003] QB 728, para.71; Lord Steyn, 'The new legal landscape' [2000] EHRLR 549, 552.

cannot be claimed to be wholly dependent on it. The same is arguably true of other developments at common law. It is unfeasible, for example, to suggest that the law of breach of confidence would suddenly revert to the days of *Coco* v. *Clark* in the event of the repeal of the HRA. The repeal of the HRA would not remove this existing and developing body of common law, nor would it preclude its future development.

Indeed, the common law might be argued to provide the foundation of a truly 'municipal law of human rights' in the event of the repeal of the HRA.[15] The rule, in *Simms*, that fundamental rights cannot legitimately be restricted through 'general or ambiguous words' is one of general application – it applies to 'fundamental rights beyond the four corners of the Convention'[16] – and may provide the bedrock for the courts to build a more comprehensive common law human rights jurisdiction in the absence of the HRA. Indeed, it has been argued that one way in which the domestic judiciary might legitimately provide for an enhanced protection of the Convention rights in domestic law, or to remedy deficiencies or lacunae in the Strasbourg jurisprudence, would be through the common law fundamental rights jurisdiction, rather than the domestic articulation of the 'Convention rights'. As Lord Mance argued in *Secretary of State for Work and Pensions* v. *M*:

> the … 'margin of appreciation' … is … to be understood in another sense, as referring to the freedom of national courts, or member states, to provide for rights more generous than those guaranteed by the Convention, though not as the product of interpretation of the Convention. In this connection, the United Kingdom already has, quite apart from the Convention, a developing body of common law authority underlining the importance attaching to fundamental rights …[17]

The common law rights jurisprudence is therefore autonomous of the HRA, and the developments precipitated by the Act, therefore, arguably possess a durability that may see them survive its potential repeal.

In the event of the repeal of the HRA, the powers of the courts to authoritatively determine the meaning of parliamentary legislation will also ultimately remain. While the balance between parliamentary government and judicial power is said to be preserved by the boundary between

---

[15] *Runa Begum* v. *Tower Hamlets London Borough Council* [2002] 2 All ER 668, para.17 (Laws LJ).

[16] *R (on the application of Anufrijeva)* v. *Secretary of State for the Home Department* [2004] 1 AC 604, para.27 (Lord Steyn).

[17] *Secretary of State for Work and Pensions* v. *M* [2006] UKHL 11, para.136, *per* Lord Mance; Lord Steyn, 'The new legal landscape', above n. 14, 551–2.

s.3 and s.4 of the HRA, it is becoming apparent that even in the event that the courts issue a declaration of incompatibility, the judicial reading of what the Convention demands is at the very least influential over the nature of the potential governmental or parliamentary response, or else otherwise taken as an authoritative reading of the legislative amendment necessary to achieve compatibility.

If we can accept that the courts possess the power to authoritatively determine the requirements of the law in a given set of circumstances – whether the dispute requires the interpretation of statute, application of the common law, or application, or balancing, of the Convention rights – and we can accept that it will be wholly unusual for the elected branches to seek to specifically overturn that decision, then we must accept that such judgments contain normative force, regardless of the form of the judicial decision taken. As the House of Lords asserted in *In re McFarland*:

> Just as the courts must apply Acts of Parliament whether they approve of them or not, and give effect to lawful official decisions whether they agree with them or not, so Parliament and the executive must respect judicial decisions whether they approve of them or not, unless and until they are set aside.[18]

The interpretative powers of the courts are so well established as to be 'politically entrenched'.[19] While the removal of s.3(1) from the statute books might reduce the frequency with which the courts deploy 'radical' powers of statutory interpretation, the potential for courts to alter the natural meaning of statutory language through interpretation should not be discounted; as Aileen Kavanagh has argued, s.3(1) merely prompted the courts to develop existing techniques of statutory interpretation.[20] The repeal of the HRA would therefore be unlikely to herald the immediate emergence of a new age of substantive legal formalism.[21] A mere assertion of the continuing sovereign power of Parliament is therefore an inadequate ground on which to entirely deny the coercive power which

---

[18] *In re McFarland* [2004] UKHL 17, para.7.

[19] T. Campbell, 'Incorporation through interpretation' in T. Campbell, K. D. Ewing and A. Tomkins (eds), *Sceptical Essays on Human Rights* (Oxford: Oxford University Press, 2001), p.87.

[20] A. Kavanagh, 'Choosing between sections 3 and 4 of the Human Rights Act 1998: judicial reasoning after *Ghaidan* v. *Mendoza*' in H. Fenwick, G. Phillipson and R. Masterman, *Judicial Reasoning under the UK Human Rights Act* (Cambridge University Press, 2007), pp. 137–42.

[21] R. Stevens, *Law and Politics: The House of Lords as a Judicial Body, 1800–1976* (London: Weidenfeld and Nicolson, 1979), chs.10 and 11.

the judiciary do wield over both of the elected branches of government. While it is true to say that, ultimately, Parliament may legislate to over-turn or reverse an individual judicial decision, it is also true to say that to do so would usually be regarded as an exceptional response. And even if Parliament does legislate to overturn a decision of the courts, it may be for reasons other than (re-)asserting its constitutional primacy.[22]

If elements of judicial reasoning in HRA adjudication contain the potential to withstand the repeal of the HRA itself, then it becomes pos-sible to discuss the contemporary separation of powers as not merely a series of descriptive dynamics, but as substantive features of the consti-tution. The dilution of the monolithic notion of the parliamentary sov-ereignty doctrine has, of course, been accompanied by the increased influence of the judicial branch.[23] Membership of the European Union and the devolution of power from Westminster – alongside the influence of the HRA – have given currency to the notion that constitutional con-siderations might temper the way in which parliamentary legislation is given effect, regardless of the clarity with which parliamentary intent is expressed.[24] In each of these spheres the courts act as the conduit between the theory of Parliament's unfettered legal power and its translation into practice. It is unsurprising that the idea of divided sovereignty has there-fore gained currency in recent debates over the nature of judicial power in the constitution,[25] with the case of *Jackson* showing a degree of sympathy towards the idea exists at the highest judicial levels.[26] However, far from envisaging exclusive subject areas of competence, the notion of divided

---

[22] See e.g.: *YL* v. *Birmingham City Council* [2007] UKHL 27; [2008] 1 AC 95 and the sub-sequently enacted s.145 of the Health and Social Care Act 2008. And, for an example outside the realm of human rights law, see: *Barker* v. *Corus* [2006] UKHL 20; [2006] 2 AC 572, subsequently overruled by s.3 Compensation Act 2006.

[23] House of Lords Select Committee on the Constitution, *Relations between the Executive, the Judiciary and Parliament* (HL 151), July 2007, p.68 (evidence of Professor Kate Malleson): 'What is clear is that the relationship between the courts and Parliament is in a state of transition between parliamentary sovereignty and constitutional supremacy.'

[24] See e.g.: *R* v. *Secretary of State for Transport, ex parte Factortame (No. 2)* [1991] 1 AC 603; *Robinson* v. *Secretary of State for Northern Ireland* [2002] UKHL 32.

[25] *X* v. *Morgan Grampian Ltd* [1991] AC 1, 48 (Lord Bridge of Harwich):
The maintenance of the rule of law is in every way as important in a free society as the democratic franchise. In our society the rule of law rests upon twin foundations: the sovereignty of the Queen in Parliament in making the law and the sovereignty of the Queen's courts in interpreting and applying the law.

[26] *Jackson and others* v. *Her Majesty's Attorney-General* [2005] UKHL 56; [2006] 1 AC 262. See pp.105–12. See also: Sedley LJ, 'Human rights: a twenty-first century agenda' [1995] PL 386, 389.

sovereignty is entirely compatible with the existence of complementary constitutional functions exercised by legislature and courts, indeed, '[t]he functional overlap between the roles of the courts and Parliament is the basis for the courts to fulfil their constitutional role as enforcement sovereign'.[27]

The increased institutional independence of the judicial branch is also, of course, a by-product of the coercive effects of the ECHR, though one which is likely to prove substantially immune from any amendment to, or repeal of, the HRA. We have already seen that the independence of judicial proceedings traditionally provided the central underpinning to the UK's separation of powers. This concept of individual independence has now been bolstered by a tangible sense of the emergence of the judicial branch as a distinct and fundamental arm of the UK government. While this increased independence affords the judiciary a legitimacy that underpins their engagement with politically contested issues, it does not – of itself – legitimate intervention. So though judicial independence may continue to form the hub of the contemporary separation of powers, the dynamic and fluid relationships between courts, executive and Parliament are just as fundamental to an understanding of the operation and nature of the constitution. The HRA has done much to drive and shape this contemporary separation of powers, but the realignment of judicial status and authority that has resulted may well prove to be of enduring influence.

---

[27] C. J. S. Knight, 'Bi-polar sovereignty restated' (2009) 68 CLJ 361, 387.

SELECT BIBLIOGRAPHY

Books

Allan, T. R. S., *Law, Liberty and Justice: The Legal Foundations of British Constitutionalism* (Oxford: Clarendon Press, 1993).

Constitutional Justice: A Liberal Theory of the Rule of Law (Oxford University Press, 2001).

Allison, J. W. F., *The English Historical Constitution: Continuity, Change and European Effects* (Cambridge University Press, 2007).

Ashworth, A., *Sentencing and Criminal Justice* (4th edn) (Cambridge University Press, 2005).

Bagehot, W., *The English Constitution* (Oxford University Press, 2001).

Bamforth, N. and P. Leyland (eds), *Public Law in a Multi-Layered Constitution* (Oxford: Hart Publishing, 2003).

Barendt, E., *An Introduction to Constitutional Law* (Oxford: Clarendon Press, 1998).

Beatson, S., S. Grosz, T. Hickman, R. Singh and S. Palmer, *Human Rights: Judicial Protection in the United Kingdom* (London: Sweet and Maxwell, 2008).

Bellamy, R., *Political Constitutionalism: A Republican Defence of the Constitutionality of Democracy* (Cambridge University Press, 2007).

Bickel, A. M., *The Least Dangerous Branch: The Supreme Court at the Bar of Politics* (Indianapolis: Bobbs-Merrill, 1962).

Bingham of Cornhill, Lord, *A New Supreme Court for the United Kingdom* (London: Constitution Unit, 2002).

Blom-Cooper L. and G. Drewry, *Final Appeal* (Oxford: Clarendon Press, 1972).

Bogdanor, V., *The New British Constitution* (Oxford: Hart Publishing, 2009).

Bradley, A. W. and K. D. Ewing, *Constitutional and Administrative Law* (14th edn) (Harlow: Pearson Longman, 2007).

Brazier, A., S. Kalitowski and G. Rosenblatt, *Law in the Making: Influence and Change in the Legislative Process* (London: Hansard Society, 2008).

Brazier, R., *Constitutional Reform: Reshaping the British Political System* (3rd edn) (Oxford University Press, 2008).

Cambridge Centre for Public Law, *Constitutional Reform in the United Kingdom: Practice and Principles* (Oxford: Hart Publishing, 1998).

Campbell, T., K. D. Ewing and A. Tomkins (eds), *Sceptical Essays on Human Rights* (Oxford University Press, 2001).

Campbell, T., J. Goldsworthy and A. Stone, *Protecting Human Rights: Instruments and Institutions* (Oxford University Press, 2003).

Canivet, G., M. Andenas and D. Fairgrieve, *Independence, Accountability and the Judiciary* (London: British Institute of International and Comparative Law, 2006).

Carmichael, P., and B. Dickson (eds), *The House of Lords: Its Parliamentary and Judicial Roles* (Oxford: Hart Publishing, 1999).

Clapham, A., *Human Rights in the Private Sphere* (Oxford: Clarendon Press, 1993).

Clayton, R., and H. Tomlinson, *The Law of Human Rights* (2nd edn) (Oxford University Press, 2009).

Craig, P., *Administrative Law* (6th edn) (London: Sweet and Maxwell, 2008).

Craig, P. and A. Tomkins (eds), *The Executive and Public Law* (Oxford University Press, 2006).

Denning, Lord, *From Precedent to Precedent* (Oxford: Clarendon Press, 1959).

De Smith, S. A., *Constitutional and Administrative Law* (3rd edn) (Harmondsworth: Penguin Books, 1977).

Dicey, A. V., *Introduction to the Study of the Law of the Constitution* (Indianapolis: Liberty Fund, 1982).

   Lectures on the Relationship between Law and Public Opinion in England during the Nineteenth Century (London: Macmillan, 1914).

Dworkin, R., *A Bill of Rights for Britain* (London: Chatto and Windus, 1990).

Dyzenhaus, D., M. Hunt and P. Rishworth, *A Simple Common Lawyer: Essays in Honour of Michael Taggart* (Oxford: Hart Publishing, 2009).

Elliott, M., *The Constitutional Foundations of Judicial Review* (Oxford: Hart Publishing, 2001).

Evans, C. and S. Evans, *Australian Bills of Rights: The Law of the Victorian Charter and the ACT Human Rights Act* (Chatswood, NSW: LexisNexis Butterworths, 2008).

Ewing, K. D. and C. A. Gearty *Freedom under Thatcher: Civil Liberties in Modern Britain* (Oxford: Clarendon Press, 1990).

Ewing, K. D., C. A. Gearty and B. A. Hepple, *Human Rights and Labour Law: Essays for Paul O'Higgins* (London: Mansell, 1994).

Fenwick, H., *Civil Liberties and Human Rights* (4th edn) (Abingdon: Routledge-Cavendish, 2007).

Fenwick, H. and G. Phillipson, *Media Freedom under the Human Rights Act* (Oxford University Press, 2006).

Fenwick, H., G. Phillipson and R. Masterman (eds), *Judicial Reasoning under the UK Human Rights Act* (Cambridge University Press, 2007).

Foley, M., *The Politics of the British Constitution* (Manchester University Press, 1999).

Forsyth C. and I. Hare, *The Golden Metwand and the Crooked Cord: Essays on Public Law in Honour of Sir William Wade QC* (Oxford: Clarendon Press, 1998).

Gearty, C. A., *Principles of Human Rights Adjudication* (Oxford University Press, 2004).

Can Human Rights Survive? (Cambridge University Press, 2006).

Greenberg D. (ed.), *Craies on Legislation* (8th edn) (London: Sweet and Maxwell, 2004).

Griffith, J. A. G., *The Politics of the Judiciary* (5th edn) (London: Fontana Press, 1997).

Grosz, S., J. Beatson and P. Duffy, *Human Rights: The 1998 Act and The European Convention* (London: Sweet and Maxwell, 2000).

Guest A. G. (ed.), *Oxford Essays in Jurisprudence* (Oxford: Clarendon Press, 1961).

Gwyn, W. B., *The Meaning of the Separation of Powers* (The Hague: Martinus Nijhoff, 1965).

Hailsham, Lord, *The Dilemma of Democracy: Diagnosis and Prescription* (London: Collins, 1978).

Harlow, C. and R. Rawlings, *Law and Administration* (3rd edn) (Cambridge University Press, 2009).

Harris, D. J., M. O'Boyle, E. P. Bates and C. M. Buckley, *Law of the European Convention on Human Rights* (Oxford University Press, 2009).

Hart, H. L. A., *The Concept of Law* (2nd edn) (Oxford: Clarendon Press, 1997).

Hartley, T. C. and J. A. G. Griffith, *Government and Law* (2nd edn) (London: Weidenfeld and Nicolson, 1981).

Hawkins K. (ed.), *The Human Face of Law: Essays in Honour of Donald Harris* (Oxford: Clarendon Press, 1997).

Hewart, Lord, *The New Despotism* (London: Ernest Benn Ltd, 1929).

Hogg, P., *Constitutional Law of Canada* (Scarborough, Ont: Thomson Canada, 2004).

Hunt, M., *Using Human Rights Law in English Courts* (Oxford: Hart Publishing, 1997).

Huscroft G. (ed.), *Expounding the Constitution: Essays in Constitutional Theory* (Cambridge University Press, 2008).

Huscroft G. and P. Rishworth (eds), *Litigating Rights: Perspectives from Domestic and International Law* (Oxford: Hart Publishing, 2002).

Irvine, Lord, *Human Rights, Constitutional Law and the Development of the English Legal System* (Oxford: Hart Publishing, 2003).

Jennings, I., *The Queen's Government* (London: Penguin Books, 1961).

The Law and the Constitution (5th edn) (University of London Press, 1967).

Jowell J. and D. Oliver (eds), *The Changing Constitution* (5th edn) (Oxford University Press, 2004).

Kavanagh, A., *Constitutional Review under the UK Human Rights Act* (Cambridge University Press, 2009).

King, A., *The British Constitution* (Oxford University Press, 2007).

Le Sueur, A., 'What is the Future for the Judicial Committee of the Privy Council?' (London: Constitution Unit, 2001).

Leigh, I. and R. Masterman, *Making Rights Real: The Human Rights Act in its First Decade* (Oxford: Hart Publishing, 2008).

Lester of Herne Hill, Lord and D. Pannick, *Human Rights Law and Practice* (London: Butterworths, 1999).

Leyland, P. and T. Woods, *Administrative Law Facing the Future: Old Constraints and New Horizons* (London: Blackstone Press, 1997).

Loughlin, M., *Sword and Scales: An Examination of the Relationship between Law and Politics* (Oxford: Hart Publishing, 2000).

The Idea of Public Law (Oxford University Press, 2003).

Loveland, I., *Constitutional Law, Administrative Law and Human Rights: A Critical Introduction* (4th edn) (Oxford University Press, 2006).

Lustgarten L. and I. Leigh, *In From the Cold: National Security and Parliamentary Democracy* (Oxford: Clarendon Press, 1994).

Madison, J., A. Hamilton and J. Jay, *The Federalist Papers* (London: Penguin Classics, 1987).

Malleson, K., *The New Judiciary: The Effects of Expansion and Activism* (Dartmouth: Ashgate, 1999).

Manfredi, C. P., *Judicial Power and the Charter: Canada and the Paradox of Liberal Constitutionalism* (2nd edn) (Ontario: Oxford University Press, 2001).

Marshall, G., *Constitutional Theory* (Oxford: Clarendon Press, 1971).

Constitutional Conventions (Oxford: Clarendon Press, 1984).

Munro, C., *Studies in Constitutional Law* (2nd edn) (London: Butterworths, 1999).

Nolan, M. P. and S. Sedley, *The Making and Remaking of the British Constitution* (London: Blackstone Press, 1997).

Richardson, G. and H. Genn, *Administrative Law and Government Action: The Courts and Alternative Mechanisms of Review* (Oxford: Clarendon Press, 1994).

Rishworth, P., G. Huscroft, S. Optican and R. Maloney, *The New Zealand Bill of Rights* (Oxford University Press, 2003).

Stevens, R., *Law and Politics: The House of Lords as a Judicial Body, 1800–1976* (London: Weidenfeld and Nicolson, 1979).

The Independence of the Judiciary: The View from the Lord Chancellor's Office (Oxford: Clarendon Press, 1993).

The English Judges: Their Role in the Changing Constitution (Oxford: Hart Publishing, 2005).

Tomkins, A., *Public Law* (Oxford: Clarendon Press, 2003).

Turpin, C. and A. Tomkins, *British Government and the Constitution* (6th edn) (Cambridge University Press, 2007).

Vile, M. J. C., *Constitutionalism and the Separation of Powers* (1st edn) (Clarendon Press, 1967); (2nd edn) (Indianapolis: Liberty Fund, 1998).

Wade, H. W. R. and C. F. Forsyth, *Administrative Law* (9th edn) (Oxford University Press, 2004).

Wade, H. W. R. and C. F. Forsyth, *Administrative Law* (10th edn) (Oxford University Press, 2009).

Waldron J. *Law and Disagreement* (Oxford: Clarendon Press,1999).

Waldron J. (ed.), *Theories of Rights* (Oxford University Press, 1984).

Wicks, E., *The Evolution of a Constitution: Eight Key Moments in British Constitutional History* (Oxford: Hart Publishing, 2006).

Woodhouse, D., *The Office of Lord Chancellor* (Oxford: Hart Publishing, 2001).

Woolf, Lord, J. Jowell and A. Le Sueur, *De Smith's Judicial Review* (London: Sweet and Maxwell, 2007).

Young, A. L., *Parliamentary Sovereignty and the Human Rights Act* (Oxford: Hart Publishing, 2009).

Zander, M., *The Law-Making Process* (Cambridge University Press, 2004).

Ziegler, K. S., D. Baranger and A. Bradley, *Constitutionalism and the Role of Parliaments* (Oxford: Hart Publishing, 2007).

Journal articles

Allan, J., 'Bills of rights and judicial power: a liberal's quandary' (1996) 16 OJLS 337.

'The Victorian Charter of Human Rights and Responsibilities: Exegesis and Criticism' (2006) 30 *Melbourne University Law Review* 906.

Allan, T. R. S., 'Human rights and judicial review: a critique of "due deference"' (2006) 65 CLJ 671.

Review of R. Bellamy, *Political Constitutionalism: A Republican Defence of the Constitutionality of Democracy* (Cambridge University Press, 2007) (2008) 67(2) CLJ 423.

Amos, M., '*R v. Secretary of State for the Home Department, ex p Anderson* – ending the Home Secretary's sentencing role' (2004) 67(1) MLR 108.

Barber, N. W., 'Prelude to the separation of powers' (2001) 60 CLJ 59.

Barendt, E., 'Separation of powers and constitutional government' [1995] PL 599.

'Is there a United Kingdom constitution?' (1997) 17 *Oxford Journal of Legal Studies* 138.

'Free speech and abortion' [2003] PL 580.

Bevir, M., 'The Westminster model, governance and judicial reform' (2008) 61 *Parliamentary Affairs* 559.

Bingham, Lord, 'The rule of law' (2007) 66 CLJ 67.

Bingham, T., 'The European Convention on Human Rights: time to incorporate' (1993) 109 LQR 390.

'The old order changeth' (2006) 122 LQR 211.

Blake, N., 'Importing proportionality: clarification or confusion' [2002] EHRLR 19.

Bogdanor, V., 'Devolution: decentralisation or disintegration?' (1999) 70 *Political Quarterly* 185.

Boyle, A., 'Administrative justice, judicial review and the right to a fair hearing under the European Convention on Human Rights' [1984] PL 89.

Bradley, A. W., 'Judicial independence under attack' [2003] PL 397.

'Relations between executive, judiciary and Parliament: an evolving saga?' [2008] PL 470.

Browne-Wilkinson, Lord, 'The infiltration of a bill of rights' [1992] PL 397.

Buxton, R., 'The Human Rights Act and private law' (2000) 116 LQR 48.

Clayton, R., 'Regaining a sense of proportion: the Human Rights Act and the proportionality principle' [2001] EHRLR 504.

'The limits of what's possible: statutory construction under the Human Rights Act' [2002] EHRLR 559.

'Judicial deference and "democratic dialogue": the legitimacy of judicial intervention under the HRA 1998' [2004] PL 23.

'Damage limitation: the courts and Human Rights Act damages' [2005] PL 429.

Cohn, M., 'Judicial review of non-statutory executive powers after *Bancoult*: a unified anxious model?' [2009] PL 260.

Cooke of Thorndon, Lord, 'The Law Lords: an endangered heritage' (2003) 119 LQR 49.

'The myth of sovereignty' (2007) 11 *Otago Law Review* 377.

Cornes, R., '*McGonnell* v. *United Kingdom*, the Lord Chancellor and the Law Lords' [2000] PL 166.

Craig, P., 'Competing models of judicial review' [1999] PL 428.

De Smith, S. A., 'The separation of powers in new dress' (1966) 12 *McGill Law Journal* 491.

Debeljak, J., 'Rights protection without judicial supremacy: a review of the Canadian and British models of bills of rights' (2002) 26 *Melbourne University Law Review* 285.

Devlin, Lord, 'Judges and law-makers' (1976) 39 MLR 1.

Edwards, R., 'Judicial deference under the Human Rights Act' (2002) 65(6) MLR 859.

Elliott, M., 'Parliamentary sovereignty and the new constitutional order: legislative freedom, political reality and convention' (2002) 22 LS 340.

'Parliamentary sovereignty under pressure' (2004) 2 *International Journal of Constitutional Law* 545.

'The sovereignty of Parliament, the hunting ban and the Parliament Acts' (2006) 65 CLJ 1.

Elliott, M. and A. Perreau-Saussine, 'Pyrrhic public law: *Bancoult* and the sources, status and content of common law limitations on prerogative power' [2009] PL 697.

Ewing, K. D., 'The Human Rights Act and parliamentary democracy' (1999) 62 MLR 79.

'A theory of democratic adjudication: towards a representative, accountable and independent judiciary' (2000) 38 *Alberta Law Review* 708.

'The futility of the Human Rights Act' [2004] PL 829.

Ewing, K. D. and C. A. Gearty, 'Rocky foundations for Labour's new rights' [1997] EHRLR 146.

Ewing, K. D. and J.-C. Tham, 'The continuing futility of the Human Rights Act' [2008] PL 668.

Feldman, D., 'Parliamentary scrutiny of legislation and human rights' [2002] PL 32.

'Human rights, terrorism and assessments of risk: the roles of judges and politicians' [2006] PL 364.

Fenwick, H., 'The Anti-Terrorism, Crime and Security Act 2001: a proportionate response to 11 September?' (2002) 65 MLR 724.

Fenwick, H. and G. Phillipson, 'confidence and privacy: a re-examination' (1996) 55 CLJ 447.

'Breach of confidence as a privacy remedy in the Human Rights Act era' (2000) 63 MLR 660.

Fenwick, H. and G. Phillipson, 'Direct action, Convention values and the Human Rights Act' (2001) 21 LS 535.

Fordham, M., 'Reparation for maladministration: public law's final frontier' [2003] *Judicial Review* 104.

'Common law illegality of ousting judicial review' [2004] JR 86.

'*Wednesbury*' [2007] JR 266.

Forsyth, C., 'Of fig leaves and fairy tales: the *ultra vires* doctrine, the sovereignty of Parliament and judicial review' (1996) 55 CLJ 122.

Fredman, S., 'From deference to democracy: the role of equality under the Human Rights Act 1998' (2006) 122 LQR 53.

Fuller, L., 'The forms and limits of adjudication' (1978–9) 92 *Harvard Law Review* 353.

Ganz, G., 'Allocation of decision-making functions' (part I) [1972] PL 215.

'Allocation of decision-making functions' (part II) [1972] PL 299.

Gearty, C., 'Reconciling parliamentary democracy and human rights' (2002) 118 LQR 248.

'Revisiting section 3 of the Human Rights Act' (2003) 119 LQR 551.

Greene, W., 'Law and progress' (1944) 94 *Law Journal* 349.

Griffith, J. A. G., 'The political constitution' (1979) 42 MLR 1.

'The brave new world of Sir John Laws' (2000) 63 MLR 159, 170.

Hazell, R., 'The continuing dynamism of constitutional reform' (2007) 60 *Parliamentary Affairs* 3.

Hickman, T., 'Constitutional dialogue, constitutional theories and the Human Rights Act' [2005] PL 306.

'The courts and politics after the Human Rights Act: a comment' [2008] PL 84.

'The substance and structure of proportionality' [2008] PL 194.

Hiebert, J., 'Interpreting a bill of rights: the importance of legislative rights review' (2005) 35 *British Journal of Political Science* 235.

'Parliamentary bills of rights: an alternative model?' (2006) 69 MLR 7.

Hoffmann, Lord, 'Human rights and the House of Lords' (1999) 62(2) MLR 159.

'The COMBAR Lecture 2001: Separation of Powers' [2002] JR 137.

'The universality of human rights' (2009) 125 LQR 416.

Hogg P. and A. Bushell, 'The Charter dialogue between courts and legislatures (or perhaps the Charter of Rights isn't such a bad thing after all)' (1997) 35 *Osgoode Hall Law Journal* 75.

Hood Phillips, O., 'A constitutional myth: separation of powers' (1977) 93 LQR 11.

Hope, Lord, 'A phoenix from the ashes? Accommodating a new Supreme Court' (2005) 121 LQR 253.

'Voices from the past – the Law Lords' contribution to the legislative process' (2007) 123 LQR 547.

Hughes, K., 'Horizontal privacy' (2009) 125 LQR 244.

Hunt, M., 'The "horizontal effect" of the Human Rights Act' [1998] PL 423.

Huscroft, G., 'The trouble with living tree interpretation' (2006) 25 *University of Queensland Law Journal* 3.

Jaconelli, J., 'Do constitutional conventions bind?' (2005) 64 CLJ 149.

Jenkins, D., 'Common law declarations of unconstitutionality' (2009) 7 *International Journal of Constitutional Law* 183.

Jowell, J., 'Beyond the rule of law: towards constitutional judicial review' [2000] PL 671.

'Judicial deference: servility, civility or institutional capacity?' [2003] PL 592.

'Parliamentary sovereignty under the new constitutional hypothesis' [2006] PL 562.

Juss, S. S., 'Constitutionalising rights without a constitution: the British experience under Article 6 of the Human Rights Act 1998' (2006) 27 Stat LR 29.

Kavanagh, A., 'Statutory interpretation and human rights after *Anderson*: a more contextual approach' [2004] PL 537.

'The elusive divide between interpretation and legislation under the Human Rights Act 1998' (2004) 24(2) OJLS 259.

'Unlocking the Human Rights Act: the "radical" approach to section 3(1) revisited' [2005] EHRLR 259.

'The role of parliamentary intention in adjudication under the Human Rights Act 1998' (2006) 26 OJLS 179.

King, J. A., 'The justiciability of resource allocation' (2007) 70 MLR 197.
  'Institutional approaches to judicial restraint' (2008) 28 OJLS 409.
  'The pervasiveness of polycentricity' [2008] PL 101.
Klug, F., 'The Human Rights Act – a "third way" or "third wave" bill of rights'
  [2001] EHRLR 361.
  'Judicial deference under the Human Rights Act' [2003] EHRLR 125.
  'A bill of rights: do we need one, or do we already have one?' [2007] PL 701.
Klug, F. and H. Wildbore, 'Breaking new ground: the Joint Committee on Human
  Rights and the role of Parliament in human rights compliance' [2007]
  EHRLR 231.
Knight, C. J. S., 'Monkeying around with free speech' (2008) 124 LQR 557.
  'Bi-polar sovereignty restated' (2009) 68 CLJ 361.
Laws, Sir J., 'Law and democracy' [1995] PL 72.
Le Sueur, A., 'The judicial review debate: from partnership to friction' (1996) 31
  Government and Opposition 8.
  'New Labour's next (surprisingly quick) steps in constitutional reform' [2003]
  PL 368.
  'Three strikes and it's out: The UK government's strategy to oust judicial review
  from immigration and asylum decision making' [2004] PL 225.
  'The rise and ruin of unreasonableness?' [2005] JR 32.
Leigh, I., 'Taking rights proportionately: judicial review, the Human Rights Act
  and Strasbourg' [2002] PL 265.
Lester, Lord, 'English judges as law makers' [1993] PL 269.
  'Parliamentary scrutiny of legislation under the Human Rights Act 1998' [2002]
  EHRLR 432.
  'Beyond the powers of Parliament' [2004] JR 95.
  'The utility of the Human Rights Act: a reply to Keith Ewing' [2005] PL 249.
Lewis, J., 'The European ceiling on rights' [2007] PL 720.
  '*In Re P and others*: an exception to the "no more, certainly no less" rule' [2009]
  PL 43.
Loveland, I., 'The war against the judges' (1997) 68 *Political Quarterly* 162.
  'Making it up as they go along? The Court of Appeal on same-sex spouses and
  succession rights to tenancies' [2003] PL 222.
Mackay, Lord, 'Can judges change the law?' Maccabaean Lecture (1987) LXXIII
  Proceedings of the British Academy 285.
Manfredi C. P. and J. B. Kelly, 'Six degrees of dialogue: a response to Hogg and
  Bushell' (1999) 37 *Osgoode Hall Law Journal* 513.
Martens, Judge S. K., 'Incorporating the European Convention: the role of the
  judiciary' [1998] EHRLR 5.
Mason, Sir A., 'Legislative and judicial law-making: can we locate an identifiable
  boundary?' [2004] *Adelaide Law Review* 15.
Masterman, R., 'Section 2(1) of the Human Rights Act 1998: binding domestic
  courts to Strasbourg?' [2004] PL 725.

'Taking the Strasbourg jurisprudence into account: developing a "municipal law of human rights" under the Human Rights Act' (2005) 54 ICLQ 907.

'Juridification, sovereignty and separation of powers' (2009) 62 *Parliamentary Affairs* 499.

Matthews, P., 'The dog in the night-time' [2000] *Jersey Law Review* 164.

McCrudden, C., 'A common law of human rights? Transnational judicial conversations on constitutional rights' (2000) 20 OJLS 499.

Mullen, T., 'Reflections on *Jackson* v. *Attorney-General*: questioning sovereignty' (2007) 27 LS 1.

Nicol, D., 'Are Convention rights a no-go zone for Parliament?' [2002] PL 438.

'The Human Rights Act and the politicians' (2004) 24 LS 451.

'Statutory interpretation and human rights after *Anderson*' [2004] PL 274.

'Law and politics after the Human Rights Act' [2006] PL 722.

O'Cinneide, C., 'Democracy and rights: new directions in the Human Rights era' [2004] 57 *Current Legal Problems* 175.

Oliver, D., 'Is the *ultra vires* rule the basis of judicial review?' [1987] PL 543.

'Constitutionalism and the abolition of the office of Lord Chancellor' (2004) 57 *Parliamentary Affairs* 754.

Pannick, D., 'Principles of interpretation of Convention rights under the Human Rights Act and the discretionary area of judgment' [1998] PL 545.

Phillipson, G., 'The Human Rights Act, "horizontal effect" and the common law: a bang or a whimper?' (1999) 62 MLR 824.

'Judicial reasoning in breach of confidence cases under the Human Rights Act: not taking privacy seriously?' [2003] EHRLR (Special issue: *Privacy*) 54.

'(Mis-)Reading section 3 of the Human Rights Act' (2003) 119 LQR 183.

'Deference, discretion and democracy in the Human Rights Act era' (2007) 60 *Current Legal Problems* 40.

Poole, T., 'Tilting at windmills? Truth and illusion in "the political constitution"' (2007) 70 MLR 250.

'The reformation of English administrative law' (2009) 68 CLJ 142.

Prince, S., 'Law and politics: upsetting the judicial apple-cart' (2004) 57 *Parliamentary Affairs* 288, 293.

Rawlings, R., 'Review, revenge and retreat' (2005) 68 MLR 378.

Raz, J., 'The rule of law and its virtue' (1977) 93 LQR 195.

Reid, Lord, 'The judge as law maker' (1972–3) 12 *Journal of the Society of the Public Teachers of Law* 22.

Rivers, J., 'Proportionality and variable intensity of review' (2006) 65 CLJ 174.

Roach, K., 'Constitutional and common law dialogues between the Supreme Court and Canadian legislatures' (2001) 80 *Canadian Bar Review* 481.

Rogers H., and H. Tomlinson, 'Privacy and expression: Convention rights and interim injunctions' [2003] EHRLR 37.

Russell M., and R. Cornes, 'The Royal Commission on Reform of the House of Lords: A House for the future?' (2001) 64(1) MLR 82.

Saunders, C., 'Separation of powers and the judicial branch' [2006] JR 337.

Sedley, Sir S., 'The sound of silence: constitutional law without a constitution' (1994) 110 LQR 270.

Sedley, LJ, 'Human rights: a twenty-first century agenda' [1995] PL 386.

Sedley, S., 'Above it all' 16 *London Review of Books* 7 (7 April 1994).

Sherlock, A., 'A new devolution settlement for Wales' (2008) 14 EPL 297.

Shute, S., 'Punishing murderers: release procedures and the "tariff", 1953–2004' (2004) Crim LR 873.

Smillie, J. A., '"Fundamental" rights, parliamentary supremacy and the New Zealand Court of Appeal' (1995) 111 LQR 209.

Stevens, R., 'A loss of innocence?: judicial independence and the separation of powers' (1999) 19(3) OJLS 366.

'The Act of Settlement and the questionable history of judicial independence' (2001) 1(2) *Oxford University Commonwealth Law Journal* 253.

'Reform in haste and repent at leisure: Iolanthe, the Lord High Executioner and Brave New World' (2004) 24 LS 1.

Steyn, J., 'Does legal formalism hold sway in England?' (1996) 49 *Current Legal Problems* 43.

Steyn, Lord, 'The weakest and least dangerous department of government' [1997] PL 84, 86.

'The new legal landscape' [2000] EHRLR 549.

'The case for a Supreme Court' (2002) 118 LQR 382.

'Democracy through law' [2002] EHRLR 725.

'Guantanamo Bay: the legal black hole' (2004) 53 ICLQ 1.

'Deference: a tangled story' [2005] PL 346.

'Democracy, the rule of law and the role of the judges' [2006] EHRLR 243.

Taggart, M., 'Proportionality, deference, *Wednesbury*' [2008] NZLR 423.

Tierney, S., 'Devolution issues and s.2(1) of the Human Rights Act 1998' [2000] EHRLR 380.

'Determining the state of exception: what role for Parliament and the courts?' (2005) 68 MLR 668.

Tomkins, A., 'In defence of the political constitution' (2002) 22 OJLS 157.

'Legislating against terror: The Anti-Terrorism, Crime and Security Act 2001' [2002] PL 205.

'Readings of *A* v. *Secretary of State for the Home Department*' [2005] PL 259.

'The rule of law in Blair's Britain' (2007) 26 *University of Queensland Law Journal* 255.

Tremblay, L. B., 'The legitimacy of judicial review: the limits of dialogue between courts and legislatures' (2005) 3 *International Journal of Constitutional Law* 617.

Trench, A., 'The Government of Wales Act 2006: the next steps on devolution for Wales' [2006] PL 687.

Wade, H. W. R., 'The basis of legal sovereignty' (1955) 13 CLJ 172.

'Horizons of horizontality' (2000) 116 LQR 217.

Waldron, J., 'A rights-based critique of constitutional rights' (1993) 13(1) OJLS 18.

'The core of the case against Judicial Review' (2006) 115 *Yale Law Journal* 1346.

Webber, J., 'Supreme courts, independence and democratic agency' (2004) 24 LS 55.

Windlesham, Lord, 'The Constitutional Reform Act 2005: ministers, judges and constitutional change: part I' [2005] PL 806.

'The Constitutional Reform Act 2005: the politics of constitutional reform: part II' [2006] PL 35.

Woodhouse, D., 'The office of Lord Chancellor: time to abandon the judicial role – the rest will follow' (2002) 22(1) LS 128.

'The constitutional and political implications of a United Kingdom Supreme Court' (2004) 24 LS 134.

'The Constitutional Reform Act 2005 – defending judicial independence the English way' (2007) 5 *International Journal of Constitutional Law* 153.

Woolf, Lord, 'Droit public – English style' [1995] PL 57.

'The rule of law and a change in the constitution' (2004) 63 CLJ 317.

Young, A., '*Ghaidan* v. *Godin-Mendoza*: avoiding the deference trap' [2005] PL 23.

'Hunting sovereignty: *Jackson* v. *Attorney-General*' [2006] PL 187.

'In defence of due deference' (2009) 72 MLR 554.

Reports and other publications

Department for Constitutional Affairs, *A New Way of Appointing Judges* (CP 10/03, July 2003).

A Supreme Court for the United Kingdom (CP 11/03, July 2003).

Reforming the Office of Lord Chancellor (CP 13/03, September 2003).

'The Lord Chancellor's Judiciary-Related Functions' (January 2004), available at: www.dca.gov.uk/consult/lcoffice/judiciary.htm#part5.

Review of the Implementation of the Human Rights Act (July 2006).

Voting Rights of Convicted Prisoners Detained within the United Kingdom (CP 29/06, December 2006).

Goold, B., L. Lazarus and G. Swiney, *Public Protection, Proportionality and the Search for Balance* (Ministry of Justice Research Series 10/07), September 2007.

Government's Response to the House of Lords Select Committee on the Constitution's Report, *Relations between the Executive, the Judiciary and Parliament* (Cm. 7223), October 2007.

Government White Paper, *The House of Lords – Completing the Reform* (Cmd. 5291), (2001).

House of Commons Constitutional Affairs Committee, *Constitutional Role of the Attorney General* (HC 306), 19 July 2007.

House of Lords Select Committee on the Constitution, *Legislative and Regulatory Reform Bill* (HL 194), 8 June 2006.

Relations between the Executive, the Judiciary and Parliament (HL 151), 26 July 2007.

Joint Committee on Human Rights, *Counter Terrorism Policy and Human Rights* (HL 50/HC 199), 7 February 2008.

Monitoring the Government's Response to Court Judgments finding Breaches of Human Rights (HL 128/HC 728), 2006–7.

Counter Terrorism Policy and Human Rights (HL 50/HC 199), 7 February 2008.

Joint Committee on Parliamentary Privilege, *First Report of 1998–1999* (HL 43-I; HC 214-I).

Labour Party, *Rights Brought Home: The Human Rights Bill* (Cm. 3782, 1997).

Ministry of Justice, *The Governance of Britain* (Cm. 7170), July 2007.

Voting Rights of Convicted Prisoners Detained within the United Kingdom (CP 6/09, April 2009).

Public Administration Committee, *Fifth Report, The Second Chamber: Continuing the Reform* (HC 494-I, 14 February 2002).

Taming the Prerogative: Strengthening Ministerial Accountability to Parliament (HC 422).

Royal Commission on Reform of the House of Lords, *A House for the Future* (Cm. 4534, 2000).

Select Committee on the Constitution, *Waging War: Parliament's Role and Responsibility* (HL 236-I, 2006).

INDEX

Note: Legislative measures are UK unless otherwise stated